Ancient Customs of Vietnam's Edé People

A translation of

Recueil
des Coutumes Rhadée du Darlac
(Hdruôm Hra Klei Duê Klei Bhian Dum)

Collected by Leopold Sabatier and
Translated into French and annotated by Dominique Antomarchi

Published in 1940 by
Ecole Francaise d'Extrême-Orient
Hanoi
Imprimerie d'Extrême-Orient

English Translation by Evelyn Desurmont
Edited by Kerry Heubeck

 www.trafford.com

North America & international
toll-free: 1 888 232 4444 (USA & Canada)
phone: 250 383 6864 ♦ fax: 812 355 4082

This translation
is dedicated to

H'Broih Nie,
the memory of Y-Blieng Hmok

and to their descendants

Ancient Customs of Vietnam's Edé People

A Translation of *Recueil des Coutumes Rhadée du Darlac*

Contents

Acknowledgments

Of course, this work would not have been possible without the efforts of Leopold Sabatier in collecting the Edé customs in the 1920's. Likewise, Dominique Antomarchi's translation into French in 1940 provided a base from which others might gain a more substantive understanding of the meanings behind the original words.

We are deeply indebted to Evelyn Desurmont who, under less than ideal conditions, translated Antomarchi's French into English from an extremely 'distressed' copy of the 1940 mimeographed publication. Our genuine appreciation goes to H'Cham Nie Heubeck for clarification of Edé words and phrases and her assistance in deciphering illegible type in the original.

To Jan Davidson we offer our sincere thanks for the excellent typing and proofing skills she brought to this project. We gratefully acknowledge Rita Trujillo for her assistance in organizing and editing the finished product, as well as Anne-Marie Emanuelli for her help with last minute translations.

And lastly, to the person who trusted me with his copy of the original book, I thank for his gift, with the hope that we have helped him preserve at least a portion of his culture.

Without any one of these individuals, this work would not have been as rewarding an experience. My heartfelt gratitude goes out to each of you.

Sincerely,

Kerry Heubeck

Notes on the Text and English Translation

In 1927, Leopold Sabatier published his collection of the oral traditions and laws of the Edé people of Viet Nam. Dominique Antomarchi translated Sabatier's Edé text into French with notations in 1940.[1] Our translation to English is derived from this later text.

The Edé people make up one of the largest of the Highland Montagnard tribes, centered around Banmethuot ("Buon Ma Thuot" in Edé), Dak Lac (formerly Darlac) Province, Viet Nam. They descend from Malay-Polynesian ethnic and linguistic roots.

This text and the earlier translations represent the Edé laws and customs that have been passed down orally through the generations. Until Sabatier's effort to preserve this orally transferred knowledge, the Edé "tribal memory" was an unwritten, stylized poetry traditionally learned by "those who remember."

As it was told to me: "In the old days, if a disagreement arose between two people, their families and respective elders would meet before the village chief and the elders of each side would alternately 'sing' the relevant old laws as they had been passed down orally over the years." The chief would then make his decision based upon such oratory.

Over how many centuries these "laws" have been passed down cannot even be guessed. The Edé that is recited is of such an archaic and poetic nature that many speaking the language today can make little of its meaning. The French translation done prior to 1940 is particularly important because the attempt to preserve the original meaning was transcribed at that time, when there were still "those who remembered."

The particular book from which this translation came is a mimeographed printing on age-yellowed newsprint-quality paper (obviously not archival) bound by large staples and black tape. The type is apparently that of a typewriter of that era. Typographic errors are not uncommon and the general quality is rather poor. Add to this the despoilment of time. Some pages are out of sequence or missing altogether. Some print is faded to such an extent as to be indecipherable.

---

1 SABATIER, L. (1927). *Ruôm Hrà Kley Duê*. Hanoi: Imprimerie d'Extrême-orient.
   (1940). *Recueil des coutumes Rhadées du Daclac. Traduites et annotés par D. Antomarchi.* Hanoi: Collection de Textes et Documents sur Indochine. IV.

This same volume was handed to me by an Edé friend on the 30th of April 1975, as North Vietnamese tanks were rolling into Saigon (the last day of the "American" war). He and a companion were going to attempt to escape Saigon on motorcycles to the town of Vung Tau on the coast, and there "take to the sea" and leave Viet Nam. He asked me to take care of the book, as he did not know how many still existed, and he was worried that the communists would confiscate and destroy it if they found it on him. "This may be the only thing left of my people."

That very day banners would be stretched across streets proclaiming in Vietnamese: "Viet Nam is one; the people of Viet Nam are one." Only later would I come to understand the full implications of this slogan when I asked a North Vietnamese Colonel how he thought the ethnic minorities would fare under the new regime (naiveté continues to be one of my strong points). He replied, "We have no ethnic minorities; we are all Vietnamese." I had just been awarded a hint of what some people have called the "cultural genocide" that was soon to take place in the highlands of the South, even though the bloodbath expected by some never occurred.

My friend and his comrade were not able to escape. They were stopped halfway to Vung Tau, their motorcycles 'confiscated' at gunpoint, and they were told to return to their homes. Fifteen months later my wife and I were able to take this book out of the country in our personal possessions. That day other Vietnamese publications would be confiscated, but the inspectors did not discover this one.

We recently learned that Antomarchi's French translation had been translated into Vietnamese by Nguyen Huu Thau shortly after the liberation of the South in 1975. In 1984 the translator revised these Vietnamese texts and they were published in 1992.[2]

In the year 2000, Ngo Duc Thinh of the Institute of Folklore in Hanoi published an anthropological study summarizing in English the Vietnamese translation of Nguyen Huu Thau.[3] This is the only reference to the text in English of which I am aware.

I doubt that many copies of the original text exist in this country. I do not know of any previous attempt to translate it into English. At least one member of the Edé tribe has expressed the opinion that the customs and manner of recital expressed in this publication probably could not be replicated today, as most of those, if not all, who "sang the words from memory" have died out.

Please note: page numbers listed alongside numbered topic headings refer to the pages in the original volume. The words Edé, Rhadé and Rhadée are interchangeable in the foregoing

2 DANG Nghiem Van, ed. (1992) *Tuyen tap van hoc cac dan toc it nguoi o Viet nam (Collection of literature of Vietnamese ethnic groups)*. Hanoi: Nha Xuat ban Khoa hoc Xa hoi.

3 NGO Duc Thinh, (2000)"Traditional Law of the Ede," *Asian Folklore Studies*, Volume 59, 2000:89-107

text. Not all "Judgments" have been included in the translation. The background of the cover depicts detail of a traditional Edé wedding blanket, hand-woven in the early 1970s.

You will undoubtedly find mistakes in this material. We welcome any help you can give us in making corrections or improving the wording. We offer these words to those generations of Edé growing up with a new culture and language.

Lac jak lu,
Ama H'Krih

English translation of
Recueil
des Coutumes Rhadée du Darlac
(Hdruôm Hra Klei Duê Klei Bhian Dum)

INTRODUCTION

Rhadé Customs is a very old oral document. Its origins, like those of the Rhadé Tribes, get lost in the night of time. Some texts (#5 & #197) mention the arrival of the Chams on the plateau, probably during the XV and XVI century.

The very many archaic terms confirm the antiquity of the "*Customs* " which is in reality a poem. The Rhadé judge tells the [appropriate] custom in verse. And the Rhadé poetry has a syntax and vocabulary which have almost nothing in common with the language that is currently spoken. Moreover, the use of elliptical forms has been pushed to its furthest limits (see examples of translation word by word). Of a long sentence containing three or four essential words, it is with those words that one can reconstruct the whole sentence.

This excessive elliptical use has been, all in all, only a mnemonic device, thanks to which the customs have been able to be passed on from mouth to ear for long centuries.

Another characteristic of the language of *Rhadé Customs* is in the abundance of metaphors, many of which would be enjoyed by our best poets, even without experiencing "does not yet distinguish the blue of the mountain from the blue of the sky"; a large house is "long like the resonant sound waves of the gong", etc.…

As it is presented, this work is not strictly speaking a book of customs. Each text is made up of several articles having to do with particular cases. This results in the same article being repeated in several different texts. It is, therefore, not possible to lean on a whole text to settle some matters. One must draw from different texts, articles or paragraphs regarding these matters; this way one will get new texts.

The layout of this [original] work, its structure and the lack of a table of contents make it difficult to consult. One will find in this work a table of contents in Rhadé and French [English, in this translation], an analytical table in alphabetical order, an index and a list of observations. A brief study of punishments expected in the old customs follows this introduction. The jurisprudence at the end of each text indicates the judgment by the court of Buôn Ma Thuôt from 1917 to 1938.

In spite of the shortcomings that one can find in its presentation, the "*Bi Duê*" stays one of the most beautiful monuments of the Rhadé oral literature. They can be grateful to M. Sabatier for having collected and written [it down] since he told them often "the words on paper [are better (original illegible)] than the words on the lips."

Buôn-Ma-Thuôt, 15 October 1939 [D. Antomarchi]

"I was a young man when my feet newly walked upon the land of Darlac, and it is in your country that the hair upon my head became white.

"During fourteen times twelve moons we drank the same water, ate the same rice, we were soaked by the same rains, burned by the same sun, bled by the same leeches."

L. Sabatier

(words of oath to Darlac 1926)

PENALTIES

All physical or moral harm caused to a person or someone's goods must be corrected (*mkra*); its author can or could be pursued (*bi kmhal*) for having violated the prescriptions of the custom.

The expected penalties as per the Rhadé custom are:

1•The sacrifice (kpih ou wat) whose aim is to pacify the gods (ya) that the culprit irritated. The sacrifice is said [to be] "wat" when it is done with a chicken, without emotion; it is said [to be] "kpih" when done with a pig, an ox or a buffalo or any other mammal and the feet are anointed with a mixture or rice wine and the blood of the animal.

To [pay] the cost of a sacrifice, the sentenced culprit must give the animal to be sacrificed.

2•The amending indemnity or fine (kdi) can be paid in kind or in money and can go from one piaster [1939 currency] (sa song) to twelve piasters (tlâo).

When the fine could not be paid, because of insolvency, the guilty committed for debts; he put his body as security (tuic asei) until his family has paid the fine that had been given to him. Following an extreme interpretation of the oral custom, the one engaged for debts was in fact slave for life. It is estimated that the work he put in hardly covered his keep and was of no profit for his master. It was the same for those who could not pay the ordinary debts they had acquired.

3•Replacing objects borrowed, lost or broken.

4•The reimbursement of theft. Stolen goods must be reimbursed three times their value (ngam tle sa kdrêch ba kdi tlå kdrêch).

5•The payment of the price of the body (tam ênua) to the family of the victim of homicide or assassination. The value of the person is assessed as a large flat gong (char) of one cubit and a span in diameter for a rich person and a large flat gong (char) of one cubit and one fist ...[illegible] for a poor person.

6•Slavery. The culprit who could not pay the price of the body was sold as a slave (hlun) in a country or a foreign country (Cambodia or a neighboring tribe).

7•The death penalty. The culprit is tied up then killed with blows of saber or spear or hung to a tree in the forest. His body was then left to the crows and vultures or ferocious animals.

D.A.

EXAMPLE: TRANSLATION WORD BY WORD
of a text from the Collection of Rhadé Customs

•individual have affair guilty him offer goods

•to chief so chief say give affair just his

•he woman look affair, man look trial, then he go find to chief powerful

•bracelet he come offer to banyan headwater, dishes offer, afraid chief stay this wayside strangers, follow side inhabitants, afraid chief follow behind non-parents

•afraid chief stay side chicken, accept side weasel, phrase fine, afraid follow other

•he want chief say give to approve, speak give to right, act give to just

•he not have legs he take legs rabbit, he not have strength, he take strength tiger, not have mouth take mouth chief powerful

•he not able walk come to climb elephant, not able come to climb horse

•he child feeble poor devoid alone hungry come to chief rich, so chief rich carry give like carry younger, make bathe give like bathe child, chief protect give so agreeable good

•for this goods he give to chief

•tree "kcik" all have roots, tree "êrang" all have roots, mother he come do with chief

•drew water he lean with mountain, obstruct river have stones [illegible] have [illegible] other he lean with rich chief

Chap. II, no. 8

page 14 Other examples of Translation

•buttocks wet, thighs damp, dead elephant young, broken gongs resonant, dead chief because him

Ch. II, no. 22

•he see he child, path not yet know understand, hole not yet know place, blue land with sky not yet know recognize

Ch. IX, no.7

•owl fascinate crab, woman takes off skirt seduce man, affair thought he seduce want eat goods others

Ch. IX, no. 9

•then goods he again add two, reimburse three, goods in front, behind he again give, so this way other accept

Ch. IX, no. 10

page 15 Glossary of Rhadé Terms

[note: "•" indicates additional diacritical mark not available on keyboard]

alê	small male bamboo
ao	vest, blouse
ba	name of certain pot, certain jar
be	old money valued at roughly one-half piaster
biê	name of pot
Bih	tribe of the Darlac of Cham language
blang	wild kapok
bô	name of jar
bung	name of pot
char	large flat gong
du	impose a fine, ask for an indemnity
cing	gong with a bulge in the middle
Êdê•	Rhadé; tribe of Darlac
Ênin	tribe of Darlac
ênôah-dôah	share of goods acquired in common going back to the family of the husband when he dies
epang	plant with very sweet smelling white flowers
hda	darts planted in the ground
Hrôe	Djarai tribe at the border of Phú Yên
kcik	tree with very hard wood
kdi•	matter, trial, disagreement; fine, indemnity
kdjar	tree with beehive, of which the owner of the ground keeps the honey
kêñ	fish of the river
kga•	Rhadé machete
khô	trap with spear
kir	inheritance, goods of the ancestors
klông	path, tree
knia	hirvingia olive tree
knôk	tree
nu'	debts
pla	to plant, put in the ground; darts
pô	owner
pô lan•	owner of the land

puic	herb whose fruit symbolizes a person without a family when he is young and a desirable young girl when she is older
am giêng	bind-weed, creeper
song	ancient money
knông	sign forbidding passage
ko	old money valued at 4 or 5 piasters; in the jurisprudence the indemnities or damage-interest paid by one party to the other are in ko; the amount in piasters are for fiscal fines
Ko'yông	Rhadé tribe of Darlac
kpang	tree
phal	slit bamboo used to dig the ground
kpang	tree
kpin	*pargne*, belt
pung	fish of the river
Kriêng	Rhadé tribe of Darlac
krôa•	fish of the river
kto'ng	tree containing a beehive whose honey is reserved for the *pô-lan•*
kung	sign prohibiting passage
lan•	land, ground, property
Mdhur	Rhadé tribe of Darlac and Phú Yên
mling-mlang	bird whose flight is interpreted as an omen
mnhai kpin ao	share of goods acquired in common that the family of the deceased wife must give to the widower when there is no replacement
Mnông	tribe of Khmer language
mnut	banyan; symbol of the chief
mo'ar	tree with large leaves
mo'ô	female bamboo, hollow
tiêt	sign indicating the presence of traps, or a forbidden house
tuh	to pour, spray, to water or irrigate
tuh-lan•	to make a sacrifice in order to purify the ground
tung	tree
wang kga•	(hoe, machete) goods that the family of the man gives him at the time of his wedding and which will be given back at his death

Index

[Note: Numbers refer to text numbers, not page numbers]

Chapter I

#1. Of penalties.

He whose voice resonates like the sound of the gong, who moves about constantly like the deer with a short tail, who has many affairs;

he who disobeys the tiger, who thinks he is more than the spirits, and is insolent towards the chief;

he who is like the bent handle of the hoe or the machete that cannot be straightened, he who does not listen to the given advice,

like the greedy dog that one corrects by making it swallow a hot eggplant, if he is bad, he will be punished; if he is insolent and does it again, he will be sentenced.

They will put the small pieces of meat in cones and the big pieces in baskets; also for a small matter, they will give him a small fine, for a serious matter, a large fine, all the cases of the inhabitants will this way be judged.

For a small affair, they will impose a fine of one piaster, for a big affair, they will impose a fine of four piasters, for a very serious matter over the price of the body, it is not possible to fix the amount of the fine.

The pig and the chicken are destined to be sacrificed, lose their bodies, the ox and the buffalo are destined to be sacrificed, lose their bodies. In the same way he who had a very serious matter will lose his body (his life or his freedom).

The hoe and the machete use a smooth stone or a rough stone on which to sharpen them, the guilty parties will be punished proportionally to the faults they committed.

Antomarchi's Notes: PAGE 24

Bi Kmhal: to punish, correct, inflict a sanction

Kdi: lawsuit, disagreement, business, amends, allowance

Sah mdrong (rich chief): poetic expression appointing the chief, that which [illegible] the authority, which orders .

Jih asei, tuic asei (to lose the blows) to become slave, prisoner, or to be [illegible] dead.

[pages 25-26 missing]

page 27

Antomarchi's Notes: **PAGE 27**

[Judgment(s) not translated]

NOTE: Cf. Code Hittite de Hrozny: "If an ox, a horse, a mule, an ass, somebody [?violates], its Master seizes it and takes it intact, and in addition to this one, is given two. (p. 61)

"If somebody finds objects and does not return them, if his Master finds them [the objects], three times restitution."

page 28# 2 Of those who strike until death follows.

Those who strike their heads like one strikes the turtle or catfish (to knock them out) without shame or self-control;

those who, like the hoe and the machete, and the stone on which one sharpens them, wear out simultaneously;

if they strike each other with equal violence,

if they both die at the same time, for this there is no problem.

page 29 #3 Of the amount of the theft must be reimbursed three times its value.

He who steals everything he finds, who uses his hand to steal that which belongs to someone else,

who steals while the owner is away, who walks without making noise and uses darkness of the night to steal,

he who has no meat to eat, no food, no tobacco to smoke, and does like the pig who finds his food everywhere, or the dog who catches anything he sees; he who steals without reason,

if they manage to catch him by his hair, to hold him solidly by the head, the objects he owns can be taken from him.

He will be taken in front of the original owner, the fig tree of the village, in front of the one who watches over all the inhabitants.

The original owner shall estimate the value of the theft, shall judge with a stick and definitely finish the affair.

The chief shall punish the culprit like one punishes a dog who steals, by making him swallow a hot eggplant; if he does it again, he will be punished more severely.

The culprit will have to reimburse also [in addition] twice the value, once in front, once in back (altogether three times the value);

if they have killed a pig or a chicken to find who stole, the culprit will have to reimburse the value of the animal killed.

ANTOMARCHI'S NOTES: **PAGE 29**

Judgment7/13/19193 times the value

Judgment 9/30/19233 months plus 3 times the value

Judgment6/6/261 yr & value of animal killed & 3 times the value

Judgment8/5/36same as 1923

Note—Cf. Code Hittite de Hrozny: "If an ox, a horse, a mule, an ass, somebody [?violates], its Master seizes it and takes it intact, and in addition to this one, is given two. (p. 61)

"If somebody finds objects and does not return them, if his Master finds them [the objects], three times restitution."

page 30 #4 Of proofs.

If of the woman, one knows well the body, if of the man, one knows well the master, if of the cows and buffalo, one knows well the keeper,

if (the culprit) has been caught by his feet, has been detained, has been caught by his arm and his face well recognized;

if he has been held like one holds a chicken by its legs or wings, if they have yelled for everyone to know,

if one has grabbed his headband or his vest, his saber or sword or any object (belonging to the culprit), if one has made a sign with his foot (at the place where he was caught), made a sign on trees, has broken a branch,

if the culprit denies, one would be able to indicate where he has been caught (if it was when he was doing it,)

And if there are 4 or 5 or 3 witnesses who have seen or heard,

There will be proof.

Antomarchi's Notes: Page 30

Judgment1/2/1919

[Illegible] Rhadée wants that any charge is supported [by] evidence and testimonies. The Judges autochtones [sic] of one Banmêthuôt always admitted this principle. Any charge not being able to be proven [?] considered unfounded and that which entest [sic] the object must be acquité [sic].

page 31 #5 Of appeal.

For a long time, the fire has been out, the tobacco (in the pipe) consumed, the forest has been entirely crossed.

The affair is in favor of the Chams and the defeat of the Annamites.

The cuts to the Tree '_tung_' and the Tree _blang_ (in order to climb them) are closed. The fine has been paid.

But today, he (the culprit) puts down what was high and high what was down.

However, the hole pipe (smoking) is well blocked, the pipe is full.

The affair was definitely finished, fingerprints gone, urine and feces had time to dry (and disappear).

But now the dry straw is getting green, alcohol that had become tasteless, becomes tasty again, the affair which was terminated, comes back to life.

The tiger that was asleep is awakened. The bear, half asleep is distracted. The nasty words are remembered.

And yet, the elephant had been well killed, the gongs well hung, the affair well judged.

Now the ball of rice (in the mouth) is turned around (by the tongue); the words (of the judge) are changed. The decision (by the parties) that had been accepted, is reopened.

He (the culprit) is like the loud gong, like the deer with a short tail, he always has stories.

If he talks to poor people, he is rude, if he talks to rich people, he is disrespectful.

This one is guilty, it is between him and the others.

Antomarchi's Notes: PAGE 31

[Judgment(s) not translated]

This habit is also applicable to the disagreements which were not presented to the Court within a normal time.

Judgment7/10/186 months & 30 $ 00

11/7/246 months & fine & animal

6/18/255 years

9/25/251 month & fine & animal

page 32 #6 Of the violation of contracts.

He who speaks one way at night and another way during the day, who changes his mind as soon as he turns around;

he who goes to the forest without taking water, who goes to the field without bringing his garden tools, who says he will do this and that and does not do it or does it badly;

he who speaks easily and a lot but speaks nonsense;

he who goes even though it [the path] is closed, he who walks into the forbidden area, disobeys the chief's order, who does not do what he said he would;

he who is like the eggplant, which looks different when crushed, like the bamboo _ele_ (from far, it looks straight while it is broken), who does not do what he said he would;

he who in the morning is like the male red bird, in the evening like the female red bird who, once in the forest, looks for new trouble;

he whose voice sounds like breaking bamboo or the voice of the calao (hornbill);

he who is like the grass which wants to be taller than the bamboo, like the wild animals who want to jump over the trees in the forest;

he who is like a strong horse but is not agile, he who knows nothing but talks a lot;

he who does not obey signs of entrapment is caught by them, he who does not obey orders he received will be condemned;

he who is like the loud gong, the deer with the short tail, who always gets in trouble,

he who interrupts the chief, opens his mouth , splitting his lips like an open bracelet;

He is guilty and will have to deal with others and himself.

page 33 #7 Of employees who leave their employers without notice.

He who had asked to be employed as a man who carries water, she who had asked as a woman to clean the house;

he who is in bad health but has agreed to work,

and who, now, cannot work from morning to evening, does not want to stay home until morning, who is quickly tired of working the garden, who cannot do any work,

he who goes secretly, alone without opening his mouth, without telling anybody, without showing himself, without letting known his intentions, without letting his employer know he wanted to leave.

That one is a culprit.   [Judgment(s) not translated]

page 34 #8 Of accomplices.

Those who carry one [the culprit] who cannot walk, who chew the food for those who cannot eat, who teach those who know nothing;

Those who give vegetables or rice to someone who had none, who advise someone illiterate;

Those who give a horse (to the culprit) and a whip, who help someone who knows nothing;

Those who follow (the culprit), who adopt his way, who take his side;

Those are culprits.

Judgments—

1/2/173 years extortion4/20/23$100(killing)

7/16/18$12 & restitution6/9/33$30 (homicide by prudence?)

7/16/181 yr (theft)9/9/3315 yrs & 10 yrs (murder)

7/16/1820 years (extortion)

10/19/263 mo. & $100 (killing)

6/11/273 mo. (theft)

5/31/2915 days & $75 (murder)

page 35 #9 Of accomplices.

Those who accept the stick [ideas] (of the witch) or the word of the healer, get involved in the problems of others and as the ghosts and witches listen to everything;

those who wish to eat mushrooms or eggplants, those who try always to open their mouths for no reason;

those who want to carry [others (culprits)] who cannot walk, who want to chew the food for one who cannot eat, who want to instruct one who knows nothing,

those are guilty and will have to deal between others and themselves.

page 36 #10 Of those who are accomplices of the guilty.

Those who accept the ruling of the stick [ideas] (of the witch) or the healer, who believe everything they are told such as witches and ghosts;

those who always want to eat mushrooms and eggplants, who cannot stay without opening their mouth;

those who fill their abscess that was healed, who reheat the cold rice, who excite people who were calm and quiet;

those who carry people who cannot walk, who chew the food for the women who cannot eat, who create problems for those who don't have any;

those who cut with a sword or a knife a piece of bamboo which is not sharp, who create problems where there are none;

those are guilty and will have to deal between others and themselves.

page 37 #11 Of those who hide a very serious crime from the chief.

He who gives food and drink (to the guilty) while hiding, who hides his doing;

he who feeds him in his bedroom, who brings him chickens outside, who hides arms underground, who hears bad words and lets no one know, who learns there has been mischief and does not tell the chief;

he who stays with the strangers, who does not stay with those of his village, who follows some strangers;

he who feeds them, gives them drinks, puts himself in bad way.

He who hears the noise of the wind around the village, the clap of thunder behind the gate, who hears the shouts of the inhabitants from East and West, who knows there is a guilty one and does not tell (the chief),

he who meets faces of strangers, who has seen them by his own eyes, who recognized their voices, their odor, who heard them talk and understood what they were saying, who looked at them for a long time, who heard through their own ears what they were saying and did not run to tell the chief;

He whose body is in the village and his ass is outside the gate, he who pulls out his sword or knife, who wants what belongs to someone else, who fools with the drum (to stop the alarm),

[several lines illegible]

He is guilty and must deal with the chief.

page 38 #12 Of being an accomplice.

He who carries those who cannot walk, who chews the food for those who cannot eat, who instructs those who do not know anything;

he who offers vegetables and rice to those who lack them, who indicates the place to those who do not know it;

he who gives a horse and the whip to hurt it, who tells those who know nothing;

he who follows the culprit and agrees with him,

That one is guilty.

page 39 #13 Of selling strangers, slaves or prisoners.

He who is the banyan tree of the spring [chief], the fig tree of the village, who watches over the inhabitants,

Before giving food (to the culprit), he must tie him up before feeding him,

under no circumstances must he hide the spoon [hide the activities],

he must not keep the word to himself;

he must not hide strangers, slaves or prisoners who escaped, those who came from far away, who have rice (home), several days and nights of walking [whose home is far away].

Each owns his field, his river for water.

The chief who allows strangers to stay a day in his village, to rest for one night, who invites strangers without interrogating them,

while they come to see the country,

in the village they try to have relations with the rich people, selling tobacco or salt, exchanging rice or iron,

at the same time they try to avoid the one who raises pigs, the slave who raises chickens for the owner [who might recognize their motives].

The rich must avoid the strangers who might steal.

page 40

The chief who does not take away the plate, who does not check the man, who does not open the vest or the belt (to see and be informed);

he who feeds strangers, prisoners in the fields, who gives them to drink behind the bush, who gives them a basket of food,

he who gives them, in hiding, rice and vegetables, who lets them stay in his village because he wants to steal the rich man's slave, the servant of others,

he is guilty and must deal with others and himself .

[Judgment(s) not translated]

page 41 #14 Of those who harbor a guilty person without asking who he is, where he comes from, where he is going.

Those who, seeing a pig or a dog, want to feed him; seeing a human being, let him in and keep him under their roof,

those are guilty because they did not question the man or the woman, the young man or the young girl who enters their house.

If they see a horse or a buffalo, they capture it, if they see someone's slave or a prisoner running away, they let them in and feed them without thinking of what they are doing.

Because of this, they are guilty since they give them vegetables, they cooked rice in hiding, they allow them to stay;

they are guilty because they keep them to work the rice and are happy to have a young man and young girl;

because they eat raw meat and raw fish without chewing, because they keep, without thinking, the rich man's slave,

because of all this, they are guilty and have to deal with others and themselves. [Judgment(s) not translated]

page 42 #15 Of punishments inflicted before judgment.

He whose trial is like a blanket or a rug still useful, like a sickness that the healer has not yet diagnosed,

he who, before the judges have judged the matter, rumbles like thunder, jumps (on his prey) like the tiger, gets close like a coffin or a boat (becomes demanding).

He whose face cannot be met, whose features cannot be distinguished, who never clears the field to its end (who does not wait until the matter is settled).

He who considers the accused as an idiot, who makes him crazy as one makes one sick,

when the matter has not yet been settled, the stick has not yet been measured, when the talks have not ended,

He who, before the judge's verdict, shows a rope to the accused, attaches him with a rope, seizes his horses and his elephants

because he covets someone else's beautiful horse, the large elephant who trumpets nicely;

He who acts in this manner without the advice of a woman, without being pushed by a man, who wants to settle the matter by himself.

He sows the discord and that is a very serious fault.

He will give a castrated pig and a jar to the accused (his victim) and will pay him a fine of six ko.

page 43 #16 Of illegal arrests.

He who tries to shackle, arrest, tie up or put in bondage without legal motive;

he who covets the gong and who chases the one who carries it; he who, in order to own the elephant or the goods of the rich, stops the people;

he who throws himself (on passers-by) to rob them,

he who grows poisonous plants to scare the villagers, who stops and ties up the inhabitants who live quietly, if there is an old matter (to settle), an old matter like a tube of bamboo already hollow [not important], who consults the banyan of the spring, the fig tree of the village, he who watches over nephews and the inhabitants.

If he has a debt to demand, let him demand it, if he has a case to settle, let him consult the chief of the village.

But if he is like the grass of the swamp which wants to grow as high as the reeds, like the straw which wants to grow higher than the bamboo, if he is like the wild animals which want to jump higher than the top of the trees;

if he refuses to enter into the high house, and jumps over the low house; if he scorns the house (of the chief) where they often eat beef or buffalo,

for this he will have to deal with others and himself. [Judgment(s) not translated]

page 44 #17 Of slanderous accusations.

He who slanders the rich or the poor without motive;

he who maintains that the trunk of the kapok tree is hollow, the mortar [for grinding rice] is broken, when he does not know anything;

he who accuses the innocent man or woman, the innocent "Bih" or the "Mnong" ,

by telling that he has seen them eating buffalo or beef, seen them walking on the path hidden in the bush;

he who climbs the ginger tree or camellia [bush] to falsely accuse the rich without motive;

he whose voice sounds like the voice of the roe deer, his mouth like the mouth of the snake, who always talks a lot of rubbish,

he who says that the horses and the buffalo have eaten the rice (in the field) without having seen them, without anybody knowing about it,

when the rice had not been husked, the squash has not been picked, and when the sun has never been touched,

that one is like the tiger having missed his prey, like the roe deer unable to run away, like the rich having lost a legal argument.

His parents advise him, but he does not listen to them, he would rather play the flute until he dies.

The water and the smoke swirl between his legs, the problems he has, he created himself.

Because of this, he must deal with others and himself.

The pig and the buffalo, destined to be sacrificed, are killed, he who creates problems for himself will lose his body,

nobody will care for him, nobody will defend him. [Judgment(s) not translated]

page 45 #18 Of slanderous accusations.

He who slanders the rich and the powerful, who says that they ate buffalo while they ate beef, that one walked on the road to the cemetery (when they did not);

he whose mouth lies, whose words are guilty, who tells that one is warped (nasty) like the handle of the axe or the machete;

he who says that someone has harrowed or cleared, that one has picked up the dead wood (when it is not true),

he who throws the basket far away and then accuses someone else [in order] to harm him,

that one is guilty and must deal with others and himself.

If later he claims that someone has driven stakes into the cotton tree or the kapok tree without making cuts, that someone caused him a problem without reason,

he will be told that the reason is for someone else.

If he'd have acted rather by ignorance, because no one advised him, because he has not been instructed,

there will be a problem with himself (and the chief) because he ignored the forbidding signs, because he did not obey the chief's advice.

Antomarchi's Notes: Page 45

See with No. 18 new page.

page 46 #19 Of lies.

He who says one thing at night and another at day, who acts in a different way as soon as he turns his back;

he who is (a gossiper) like a loud gong, like the deer with a short tail, who tells a lot of stories;

he (who turns around) like the eggplant and the green chili (in the pot), who is sometimes on his back, sometimes on his stomach;

he who, hiding, spreads his hand as a thief,

that one is guilty and must deal with himself. [Judgment(s) not translated]

page 47 # 20 Of deception.

He who says that the sap of the banyan is the sap of the fig tree, that the male elephant is a female elephant, that this one is another;

whose voice sounds like the creaking of the breaking bamboo, the cry of the black hornbill who wants everyone to be as he says,

who owns only one basket of cooking pots in the West (in his home) and one basket of bowls in the East, who lives alone with his wife (and wants to make believe that he is rich),

who has a house where one can see the stars up above, and the pig's excrement below, has to huddle up to sleep with his wife,

because he is lazy to build his house, to work his field, too lazy to clear his field.

He who speaks wildly, who says about anything and therefore creates trouble for the others,

he is guilty and must deal between the others and himself. [Judgment(s) not translated]

page 48 #21 Of insults.

He who has a mouth like the one of a roe deer or the one of a snake, and who insults others without cause,

he who screams insults, who scratches and hurts the rich or the strong ones without cause, who always itches on his chin as if he ate some "taro";

he who screams like the black hornbill, or like the creaking bamboo, who speaks and insults (the people) without thinking;

he who insults the mother or father (of his enemy) who hopes that the hands will be cut, who screams obscene insults to others without cause,

he is guilty and must deal with others and himself.

If he insulted a poor person, he will sacrifice for that person a pig valued one *song* If he insulted a rich person, he will sacrifice a white pig. [Judgment(s) not translated]

page 49 #22 Of abuses and insults.

He who abuses the mother, insults the father (they are antagonists), who wishes that the hands be cut, who screams obscenities,

why is he screaming so? Is it because the hoe is broken or the flint is broken? For what matter is he angry and why does he scream insults? Why is his heart bad, why does he look so?

If he insults too much, beyond all measures, his case will be serious.

If asked where is his wound, where he hurts (what makes him suffer), if asked what makes him angry, he insults and abuses.

If he has abused the mother of a poor [person], he will sacrifice a pig. If he has abused the mother of a rich [person], he will sacrifice a buffalo;

If he has abused the parents of the king or the queen, he will give slaves or elephants. [Judgments illegible]

page 50 #23 Of violation of customs.

Each year after the cold season, once the harvest is ended, the custom is that the Big Chief celebrates the new year by offering drink and food, in sacrificing pigs and buffalo.

For this event, each gets his baskets ready, all friends and parents get together;

Every brother, people of the village, the nephews and nieces, all the inhabitants come near the big chief.

All those who have children and grandchildren will teach them since the big chief wants everyone to know this custom.

As for those whose feet are not light, whose heels are not hard, those who are not in a hurry to come, those are guilty and will deal with the village and themselves.

Antomarchi's Notes: Page 50

Note--"Feast of the Snake", January 1st since 1926 in Darlac. It acts gives [illegible] of a news which it is necessary to know fairly with the inhabitants and the chiefs.

[Judgment(s) not translated]

Chapter II

page 51 #24 Of disobedience to the chief's orders.

He who is instructed and does not listen, he who is ordered and does not obey, he who believes he is stronger than the tiger, smarter than the genius, who opens his mouth insolently;

he who does not listen to what he is told, who does not accept the rules given to him, who acts like a fool or an idiot;

he who would rather live among bamboo, in the bush like wild animals,

he will be punished like one punishes a greedy dog by making him swallow a hot eggplant, like one punishes bad subjects, like one punishes those who are rude (towards the chief). [Judgment(s) not translated]

page 52 #25 Of disobedience to the chief.

He who does not remember the chief's suggestions, who does not obey his orders, who does not listen to those who speak in singing,

like the pig or the cow destined to be sacrificed, if he creates stories, he may lose his body (his life or his liberty).

If his parents are rich, they might be able to pay the fine (that has been imposed);

but if they have nothing (he will be left) like old tools and if his problem is serious, he will have to give his body (in lieu of paying the fine or indemnity).

The woman who will not obey, the man who does not listen to what he is told, or will not obey the chief's orders, those who do not want to follow their parents' suggestions,

Those are guilty and must deal with themselves [assume responsibility]. [Judgment(s) not translated]

page 53 #26 Of disobedience to the chief.

He who does not speak to the banyan when there is a banyan, who does not consult the fig tree when there is a fig tree ; who does not ask the mother or the father when there is a mother and a father;

he who behaves like the fire that clears the valley, like the flood that passes over the dam, who ignores the words of the chief;

he who is like the deer with beautiful antlers jumping in the fields (when it feels alone, away from danger),

he who holds a gray cat in his hand and a black cat under his clothes and excites one against the other;

he who strides over the puddle of water, who jumps over the brook, who scorns the chief's authority,

he who does not respect the signal of the forbidden, or the chief's orders;

he who moves continually like the horse wounded on the back, like the deer with the short tail, he who always has problems;

he who is like the overflowing brook, like the nasty spirits causing death, who looks for problems for everyone, he will lose his body.

Like the pig or the buffalo destined to be sacrificed, he will lose his body.

ANTOMARCHI'S NOTES: PAGE 53

(1) The banyan and the fig tree symbolize the chief.

(2) It creates incidents between chiefs in addressing themselves and another chief and [illegible] that of one's village which is one's immediate senior in rank.

(3) He will lose his body: he will be condemned, killed or be put into slavery, or today go to the prison.

[Judgment(s) not translated]

page 54 #27 Of respect for the chief and parents.

He who does not ask the banyan tree when there is a banyan tree, who does not consult the fig tree when there is a fig tree, who does not tell the father and the mother when there is a father and mother;

he who is like a knife or sword whose blade is heavier than the [unreadable], like a child believing he is bigger than an adult and who never asks his parents' advice;

he who never consults the banyan tree of the spring, the fig tree of the village, the man who watches over his nephews and nieces and all the inhabitants;

he who goes to get wood without asking his father, goes to the spring without asking his mother, buys and sells without asking his grandparents (the old ones),

That one is guilty.

page 55 #28 Of the choice of a chief.

Let someone stir up the fire and assemble everyone, call all the sparrow hawk brothers, the spirits of the village, the nephews and nieces, the mothers of these, the fathers of those, the grandfather and grandmothers, the widows, the sons-in-law and daughters-in-law, all those whose parents are dead, let us assemble all in the center of the village.

Let everyone debate at the bottom, debate at the top (rich and poor), let the sisters debate their brothers, let everyone be consulted.

Let everyone indicate whom they prefer, choose the one who will be the banyan of the spring, the fig tree standing up high in the village, who will watch over the nephews and nieces, all the inhabitants,

Let everyone express an opinion, not hide his spoon, let no one hide their thoughts.

Antomarchi's Notes: Page 55

At the death of the chief, it was his son-in-law, or the substitute to his widow [see further laws on substitutes] or his brother-in-law (husband of his wife's sister) who succeeded him.

When the substitute was too young, the eldest of the house had to help him in his duties as chief.

The choice of a new chief happened only when there was no successor. Today the chief of the village is selected by the provincial administration from among its functionaries.

page 56 #29 Of those who want to settle the disagreement of others.

He who wants to eat mushrooms or fruit, who always itches in the mouth as though he ate green taro.

he who refuses to admit that each mountain has its summit, that each village has its chief;

he who tries to make others accept his decision as though it is the decision of the judge or the decision of the healer;

he who claims that his words are the words of the good spirits, the words of the bad spirits or ghosts, who tries to judge the disagreements of others,

he is guilty and must deal with himself.

Antomarchi's Notes: Page 56

This text is concerned with the usurpation of functions. [Judgment(s) not translated]

page 57 #30 Of those who disobey the orders of the chief.

He who acts against the orders of the chief, who leaves when told to stay, who acts as though he were angry;

He who behaves like the grass which wants to grow higher than the weeds, like the straw which wants to climb higher than the bamboo, like the wild animals which want to jump over the tops of the trees;

He who shouts louder than the tiger, stronger than the spirits, he who opens his mouth with insults, who does not obey the chief's orders,

like the dog who steals and who is punished by making him eat a hot eggplant, like all bad subjects, he will be punished. [Judgment(s) not translated]

page 58 #31 Of the guilty who offer gifts to the chief so that he will agree with them.

He who is in trouble, she who has a disagreement, come to the chief. They give the bracelet to the banyan, offer goods to the fig tree, in fear that he will take sides with the strangers or the unknown, he will take sides with the non-relatives.

In fear that the chief be with the chicken against the weasel, that his words defend the case of others,

he who wants the chief to say that his case is good, that his case is just, who wants the judge to be nice;

he who has no legs and asks for the legs of the hare, who has no strength and asks for the strength of the tiger, he who has no mouth and asks for the mouth of the rich and powerful chief (to defend him);

he who cannot walk and asks to ride an elephant, who cannot run and asks to ride a horse;

he who says he is weak like a poor child, an abandoned orphan and who comes to the chief,

so that the chief will carry him (with care) like one carries the younger son, to bathe him like one bathes a child, to protect him, that everything be beautiful and pleasant;

he who, for these reasons, offers goods to the chief,

because like the trees he needs roots (to be held up),

because he wants the chief to be like a father and mother,

because when coming back from the mountain spring (being tired) one leans upon the embankment, when building a dam one needs flat stones, when in trouble one looks to the chief's help.

He (who acts this way) is guilty.

page 59 #32 Of slandering accusations against the chief to make him look guilty.

The chief carries (the inhabitants) as one carries a little brother, he bathes them as one bathes a child, he protects them so that it is agreeable;

he looks after them as one looks after the beds, the stairs, the benches and the ladders, he takes care of them as he takes care of his wife and children.

He who is like the sharp hoe or machete, who is insolent with his mother and father, he who takes out the gongs 'cing' and 'char' enclosed in the pits, because he is evil and envious of the goods of others without reason;

he, like the bamboo of which the wind always moves the top, like the small family being moved everywhere, to the East or West;

he who does not have venom goes and gets the venom of the python or the snake to take to the rich and powerful chief;

he who offers to the chief a morsel of tongue or piece of shoulder meat to make him accept as true (the lies he tells),

he who acts like the tiger grabbing its prey by the ear, like the weasel catching its prey by the coat, who accuses people (by slander) without reason;

he who makes the green bamboo dry up, who makes the strong bamboo break, who tries to make problems for the rich and powerful chief,

that one is guilty and there are grave problems with him.

Like the ox or the buffalo destined to be sacrificed, if he has problems, he will lose his body. [Judgment(s) not translated]

page 60 #33 Of those who leave their village without informing the chief.

He who goes to live in the village in the West, the village in the East, without telling the banyan of the spring, the fig tree of the village, to the one who takes care of the nephews and nieces, of all the inhabitants;

he who takes no notice of forbidding signs, who disobeys the chief's orders;

he who has no esteem for the chief, who despises him like a dog, who does not acknowledge his authority,

even though the chief never did anything bad to him, never bothered him,

even though the chief never reproached him, never did him any injustices,

he is guilty and there is a case between the chief and himself. [Judgment(s) not translated]

page 61 #34 Of those who carry away the inhabitants without telling the chief.

He who blows the whistle when the forge is out of air (fire out), who searches in the hole with a stick to make the mouse come out, who finds and scares the boar or the deer who grazes peacefully;

he who seizes with his beak, takes in his mouth, takes on his back, who takes away the inhabitants of the village;

he who carries those who cannot walk, who chews the food for those who cannot eat, who teaches those who do not know;

he who steps over the puddle of water, who crosses over the river, who disregards the chief's orders,

that one is guilty and must deal with the chief and himself. [Judgment(s) not translated]

page 62 #35 Of those who mistreat the chief because he takes care of the inhabitants and settles their differences.

He whose chest inflates with anger, whose throat tightens with vexation, he who gets mad easily,

he whose patience is short, who is no longer master of his acts, who does not know the difference between good and bad,

he who, seeing the banyan, cuts the banyan, seeing the fig tree, cuts the fig tree, seeing that the father and the mother or the chief wants to educate and give him advice, beats them badly;

he who is dangerous like the sharp hoe, as a machete well sharpened, who can no longer be ordered;

> he who, like the dry straw hut, like the too dry joint (in bamboo) (breaking easily), he who gets angry easily, with whom one cannot reason,

he who does not want to listen to what he is told, who does not obey orders given him, who does not accept the chief's decisions;

like the greedy dog being punished by making him swallow a hot eggplant, as the bad person being punished, if he is impertinent, he will be punished. [Judgment(s) not translated]

page 63 #36 Of the help that all inhabitants owe their chief.

All sparrow hawk brothers, the spirits of the village, the nephews and nieces, all those of here or there,

They must assist the chief when in the labor of building his house, working his field, repairing his home,

being afraid that the chief gets a headache, a stomachache, afraid he will not have enough to eat.

All must help him carry the firewood for heating, to carry the water in the basket on the back, to hoe and rake his field;

all must repair his hut (of the field) if it is about to fall, repair his house and reinforce it if it leans, all must give thread if the skirt of the woman is torn, never must they desert him;

this way, there will be much rice wine (to offer) as long as he will be alive, much rice (to offer) when there is a death in his house, and the brothers and sisters will stay always united,

because all will listen to him as one ear when he talks, all will talk as one mouth (when speaking to him), all will be happy to help the chief.

As to those who want to believe themselves stronger than the tiger, more powerful than the spirits, those who would open their mouth with arrogance,

those are guilty and must deal with the chief and themselves;

for a light fault, they will pay a small fine, for a serious fault, they will pay a larger fine.

page 64 #37 Of trouble makers.

He who places the stick in the hole of the python, in the hole of the snake, who tries to speak in the name of the chief;

he who has no meat to eat, no food to cut up, no tobacco to smoke,

and who tries to steal the chief's goods, the goods of the rich, the goods of the brothers (the inhabitants);

he who plays with the salt container, lines up the seeds of corn, who tries to deceive the rich (to obtain what he wants);

he who carries the machete on his shoulder, who holds the ax in his hand, who shakes the skin of a tiger to scare the inhabitants;

he who, with his mouth, imitates the sound of the flute played by nobody, who imitates with his fingernails the sound of the guitar, who starts problems with those who don't have any;

[he who catches the fish "pat" with many hands (works with many people)] like the hoe loose in the handle and needing lots of lacquer to be fixed, he who starts disorder in the quiet village;

he who carries poisonous plants in his hand to scare the people, who disturbs the calm and quiet people,

he who wants meat and fresh fish, who tries to eat the goods of the rich;

like the bananas that nobody picks up, like the older sister that nobody touches, like the used knife that nobody fixes,

like the pig and the buffalo destined to be sacrificed (killed), he who looks for problems, will lose his body. [Judgment(s) not translated]

page 65 #38 Of those who spread disorder by talking in the name of the chief.

He who goes to exchange tobacco, get salt, sell yeast or iron;

he that no one has been able to employ to cut wood, to draw water, who is always alone, anywhere;

he who has no meat to eat, no food to cut, no tobacco to smoke;

he who pretends to polish the salt container, to put away the grains of corn to deceive others;

he who pretends that he has been ordered to clear the field, who pretends that he speaks in the name of the chief;

he who wishes for the pretty cloth like a child, who wishes for the turban like a young man, who covets the goods of others;

he who tries to pick up a clump of bamboo, who tries to take what is in the spoon, who tries to grab the goods of others,

he who says that the stained stick is a snake, that the flecked ears are those of the tiger, that his words are the words of the chief;

he who wants to make believe that he can produce water, stones, rain, man or woman, who goes everywhere trying to get his words accepted (as though he was sent by the chief),

he is guilty and must deal with the others and himself.

[Judgment(s) not translated]

[Illegible] paragraphs of this text concern the business of sorcery (par. 9 and 10)

page 66 #39 Of those who incite the inhabitants to not obey the orders of the chief.

He who tears out the handle of the hoe, who breaks the handle of the machete, he who says that the orders given by the chief are bad,

he who makes the burst abscess to fill up again, that the cold rice is reheated [stirring up old problems], that the peaceful heart of the inhabitants becomes nasty;

he who measures (the length) of the handle of his machete, who compares his strength to the strength of the chief;

he who measures the beams (of the chief's house) by the arm length, the rafters [length and width of the house], who compares the number of jars and gongs of the chief to his own,

that one is guilty and has to deal with the chief and himself. . [Judgment(s) not translated]

page 67 #40 Of those who scare the inhabitants with lies.

He who say that in the past there was nothing, that one could not see anything, that one did not obey, did not submit to anyone;

that all this has been invented lately, since only now, that he only knows of things of the past,

he who ignores signs indicating traps and finds himself trapped, he who violates the elders' customs, creates problems for himself.

He who is like the blade of the knife which wants to be thicker than the handle, like a child who believes he is bigger than the adult and does not obey his parents;

he who does not consult the banyan when there is a banyan, who does not ask the fig tree when there is a fig tree, who does not consult the big chief when there is a big chief,

he who cuts the bamboo beyond the length allowed, who ignores the chief's orders,

he who does not inform the chief so that he would know, who does not show for him to see, who never says anything;

he who hides what he knows under a leaf, who does not tell anything to his brothers,

he who holds a grey cat in his hands and a black cat in his clothes (and excites one against the other), he who is always looking for new problems,

he who is like the weeds which want to be higher than the rush, the straw wanting to be higher than the reeds, like the animals wanting to jump over the tree tops;

he is guilty and it is very serious for him.. [Judgment(s) not translated]

page 68 #41 Of those who preach revolt in the villages in order to cause the inhabitants to abandon their chief.

He who tries to pull out the handle of the hoe, or the handle of the machete, he who tries to create problems for the inhabitants of the neighboring villages;

he who goes after a piece of filet, a piece of leg (meat), he who tries to excite the inhabitants by telling them that his cause is good;

he who pricks like the point of the rhizome of bamboo, like the stick (used to dig to find tubers); whose words aim to excite the people.

He who cuts with a knife or a saber the stick which is not sharp, who renders spiteful the heart of inhabitants which was good, who excites problems to the brothers who live peacefully;

he who carries one that cannot walk, who chews the food for those who cannot eat, who creates problems to those who don't have any;

he who always has problems, she who has lots of debts, those who like the fish and frogs, have many dens to take refuge,

he who inserts a stick in the hole of the python to make it come out, who inserts a small stick in the hole of the snake to make it come out, he who tries to spread the bad words in the villages;

he who makes the burst abscess fill up again, who heats the cold rice, who causes the peaceful heart to become bad, the calm chief to become worried;

this one is guilty and has to deal with others and himself. . [Judgment(s) not translated]

page 69 #42 Of blows and wounds to the chief and assassination of the chief.

He who covets the very straight tree, or the sharp machete, who is jealous of the working (and rich) man,

and, for that reason, trades a bracelet (with others) to have friends (accomplices);

he who gets together, up in the valley or down in the ravine, with two or three individuals so that they will help him harm the chief;

he who gets together with others in order to get poison, several spears to kill the chief,

he who covets the chief's elephant tied up in front of the house, the gongs hanging from the bar, and who, for that reason, polishes his saber, sharpens his knife because he is jealous of the chief and intends to hit him or knock him out.

he who cuts the top of the budding plant, who hits the one who has been made chief to kill him,

he who tries to harm people without reason, to hit them without motive because he is jealous of the rich (or similar ones),

he is guilty and there is a serious matter against him.

The pig and the buffalo destined to be sacrificed lose their body, he who creates problems will lose his body.

If there are three or four accomplices, they will be pursued, as well as his parents and sisters if in hiding they gave him food and drink, if they gave him baskets, they will all be arrested. . [Judgment(s) not translated]

page 70 #43 Of those who hurt the chief by having accomplices.

Those who take rice in the field (for the pirates); those who take them water in the bush, who give them baskets outside the village;

those whose bodies are in the village, but whose feet are outside, those who pull the knife or the saber out (of the sheath) to help the chief's enemies;

those who cut dozens of bracelets, who bring baskets full of rice (to the enemy), agree (with them) to hurt the chief;

those who conspire up in the valley, by the side of the river, those who get together, four or five, two or three;

those who hold up the elephant, who hang up the gongs, who seal the contract, who give their word, who become accomplices (of the enemy);

those who touch the stick, those (women) who agree with the words (of the enemy), who agree (with them) afraid that the next day or another day the water will be spilled, the pile of wood demolished, the fault of all be thrown on only one;

those who go in groups, who get up all together (in the morning), who tighten or protect (the string of the crossbow) at the same time;

those who help (the enemy) to poison, who help (them) by loaning their lances or their spears;

page 71

those who want to pierce the bamboo which is not (pierced), who want to dig dens for turtles and gibbons, who do not have [dens], those who want to harm the chief without motive;

if of the woman, one knows the body, of the man, one knows the face, as one can know the owner of oxen and buffalo in seeing their keeper, if they are four, they will be chased and arrested, if they are three, they will be followed, tied up, their brothers and sisters will be also arrested, if they behaved like the turtledove looking for the warmth of the sun, like the parakeet looking for the blowing of the wind, if they have helped the culprits, if they have become their accomplices;

like the pig or the buffalo destined to be sacrificed (to the gods), those who make themselves guilty (of such crimes) will lose their bodies. . [Judgment(s) not translated]

page 72 #44 Of rebellious ones.

Those who do not carry the basket (on their heads), who do not pay taxes, who do not do the works as ordered by the elders;

those who do not give rice, who do not take care of the roads, who do not do the works as ordered by the elders;

those who are rude, lose their temper, reckless, who beat with the saber those who come near and pierce them with their spears;

those who, like the straw, the dry bamboo (which breaks easily), easily get mad;

those who lick the dew till full, who bite the iron till it breaks,

those who help others by bringing rice and vegetables;

those will be pursued;

those who hide in the huts, in the attics,

sleeping on the straw, trying to kill those passing by;

those who hit who enters, who kills who comes to see them, who do not know which is good and which is bad,

those who force everybody to lie before them, to obey.

In the past, they were hung on a tree and their bodies given to wild beasts.

page 73

They no longer got rice and good vegetables to eat,

they were traded for oxen with people of Laos, for buffalo with 'Mdhurs' [tribe living in Mdrak near Kanh Duong], for goods with people of Cambodia or Vietnam;

they were sold to foreigners, they were exchanged with the 'Mdhurs', they were sold as slaves to the 'Bihs' [Buon Mblot] and the 'Mnongs' [Dak Lak].

The rough stone is worn down by the hoe it sharpens, the machete is worn down by the smooth stone which sharpens it, the rebellious are severely punished by those they have ill-treated. [Judgment(s) not translated]

page 74 #45 Of trouble-makers of disorders.

Those who make the thigh wet, the buttocks damp, the gongs broken, the elephants dead, the chief killed;

those who lean against the tree 'klong' or the tree 'kpang' like the elephant of the god crocodile, those who try to move in the house of the rich;

those who estimate the strength of the tiger, who estimate the strength of the bear and try to see if the claws are sharp or dull, who taste the soup to know if it is bland, seasoned or spicy, those who pester the chief to know if his is weak or vigorous;

those who destroy the forest where they settle down, who destroy the bush where they settle down, who spread disorder where they live;

those who run after one who carries a gong to grab it, who run after the elephant to seize it, those who, to become rich, hurt everybody;

those who cut down the trunks where they settle, cut the roots where they settle, who make the chief die where they live;

those who hit with the saber, who whip with the rattan, who kill without reason,

inciting the anger of the husband, the hatred of the wife, the anger of the chiefs,

those are guilty and there is a very serious affair between the others and themselves. [Judgment(s) not translated]

page 75 #46 Of the traitors who give information to the enemy on the affairs of their village.

He who puts the stick in the hole of the python, or in the hole of the snake, who goes and repeats outside what he has heard in the village;

he who carries a small gong in his hand, and big gong at arm's length, who carries the words of the chief in the villages of the West and the East, who acts like a mad man and an idiot;

he who feels like he wants to eat mushrooms, who wants to eat fruit , who itches in his mouth as though he ate green taro [wants to gossip (itchy mouth)];

he who has heard, who knows and pretends he does not know anything, he who tries to inform the foreigners of what is happening in his village;

he who has heard some words and tries to distort and exaggerate them, who has seen one footprint and says he saw a lot, he who listens the chief and goes and repeats his words (to the enemy);

he who eats and cannot stop, he who drinks but cannot restrain himself, he who goes in the bush to tell what he heard in his village,

that one is guilty and must deal between the chief and himself.   [Judgment(s) not translated]

page 76 #47 Of those who help the enemy fight the village.

He who does not stay on the side of the chicken, who adopts the side of the weasel; who obeys the words of others;

he who has his body in the village and his behind outside of it, who pulls out the knife and the sword, who hates the inhabitants of the village;

he who throws a stone in the beehive, who listens to the village and takes in the words of the enemy, who has his lips here and his tongue there, who feed himself of the air and becomes accomplice of the enemy,

she who has many problems, he who always has problems, who always sides with strangers;

he who is sharp like the hoe or the machete and is arrogant towards his mother or father, he, young man or young girl, who is arrogant towards the chief, the inhabitants of his village;

he, man or woman, who always has problems, or debts; he who is like the fish or the frogs who have many dens [in which] to hide;

he who walks at the same pace (as the pirates), who goes forward at the same speed, who follows others by following their footprints,

he is guilty and must deal with the others and himself.   [Judgment(s) not translated]

page 77# 48 Of those who become accomplice of the pirates.

He who carries those who cannot walk, who chews the food for those who cannot eat, who teach those who do not know;

he who guides them in the forest, who shows them the forks, who shows them the way in the dark of the night;

he who agrees with them near the spring, who leads them along the river, who shows them the way (to the village);

he who holds up the elephant, who hangs up the gong, seals a pact of friendship,

he who knows well the toughness of the fence, of the big door, the weak spots of the wall, who tells them the weak spots of the fence or the door; the pits where the jars and the gongs are hidden, the posts where the horses and elephants are tied up;

who points out (to the pirates) the strong spots of the fence or the door, the rich houses,

who helps pull out the lancets [stakes] (protecting the village), who leads a hundred or a thousand individuals, and who is the cause of a hundred or a thousand killed or taken away (as slaves), houses and rice granaries burned, that the hindrances are given to the inhabitants, that they tie those up to become slaves or prisoners,

that the male elephants and the female elephants are taken away, that the big or small jars are taken, that all the inhabitants are taken away,

if of the woman one knows the body, of the man one knows the person, if of the oxen and buffalo one knows the keeper,

with the big saber he will be beheaded, with the sharp knife, he will have his throat cut and his body will be thrown to the vultures and crows.

page 78 #49 Of traitors who come to terms with the pirates and inform them of the actions of their chief .

He who, at dawn, goes (towards the pirates) hiding, or in the middle of the night while everyone sleeps;

he who goes to warn (the pirates) without the chief and the inhabitants knowing, who, hiding, goes to find them to let them know that his chief will go fight them in their village,

that he (his chief) as already given an armful of bracelets to his allies, sent them rice, has already summoned other rich and powerful chiefs, (has told everyone):

"You men keep a good watch, you women will be very careful, all will be very cautious, nobody will leave (the village) alone,"

"You will reinforce the fence, strengthen the big door, you will be cautious and attentive."

He who did so that the warned enemy drive their oxen out of the village, push their buffalo into the forest, send their wives and children into the mountains,

hide their very valuable jars, their jewels and their crockery, in boxes all their objects and all their goods;

if of the woman, one knows the body, if of the man (guilty) one knows the person, if of the oxen and buffalo one knows the keeper;

with the big saber he will be beheaded, with the sharp knife he will have his throat cut and his body will be thrown as food for the vultures and crows of he will be taken into the big forest, he will be hung from a tree and left to the wild animals,

because he does not know where to go or not to go.

Like the pig or the buffalo destined to be sacrificed, he who is guilty (of treason) will lose his body.   [Judgment(s) not translated]

page 79 #50 Of escape of prisoners.

He who has given his word to stay quiet, not to move, to work hard for the chief,

and who thinks one thing at night and another during the day, who acts very differently as soon as he turns his back;

he who leaves behind his chains to run away, who leaves his pillory to run away;

he who hides in the forest of bamboo, in the forest of reeds, who scorns the chief's orders;

he who makes himself free like the top of the bamboo waving in the wind, like the movable home (not attached to the floor), he who goes West or East;

he who being (hidden) on a small mountain is looking for a higher one, being on a small river is looking for a bigger one;

he who splits the mouth (of the chief), who cuts the lips, who opens (gives up) the bracelet he had accepted;

he who runs away forever, who hides without making any noise, who stays quiet but refuses to work still for the chief;

he who thinks one thing during the day and another thing during the night, who acts differently as soon as his back is turned,

that one is guilty and must deal with the chief and himself. [Judgment(s) not translated]

page 80 #51 Of those who do not rush to take to its destination the bracelet entrusted to them by the chief, and who linger on the way.

He who (has received order by the chief) to go up or go down, who has been put in charge to take the bracelet, he to whom has been (given the stick on which) a pepper and a piece of coal has been attached so that he will go quickly;

he who in spite of this has a thinking head, a heavy stomach, who goes slowly, who delays the transmission of the bracelet or necklace, who arises only in the morning, or in the middle of the night, or late in the evening when everyone is asleep, he who acts as though he as lost (the bracelet) in the bush or the river, as though he threw it to the ants or termites, as though he fell asleep in the middle of the path and therefore the bracelet could not arrive in (in time).

That one is guilty and must deal with the chief and himself.

page 81 #52 Of not registering births with the chief.

When the kidneys (of the woman) become hollow, the body leans backwards, the stomach goes forward,

and comes the season when the mango trees are in bloom, when the trees lose their leaves, when the pregnant woman must give birth;

when the boy or the girl is born with pretty hands, when the birth has been easy,

in the morning, at dawn, what has been promised (to the spirits) will be given so that the [mother] recovers, that she gets well fast, that everything be well;

after a man or a woman will remove the bark, open his vest and loincloth in front of the banyan of the spring, in front of the fig tree of the village, in front of the one who watches over the sparrow hawk brothers, the spirits of the village, in front of the one who watches over the nephews and nieces in order for him to know.

He who will hide (the birth) under a leaf, who will conceal the birth, who will not go tell the chief,

he will be guilty and will have to deal with the chief and himself.

page 82 #53 Of not registering deaths with the chief of the village.

When someone is sick or has a fever, when she stays always by the fire, one calls the healer to take care of her.

If the sick one does not get better, his health deteriorates; he always stays under the blanket;

if they sacrifice pigs and buffalo without the sick one getting better, if the will of the spirits is that the body should die;

if the sick one dies and becomes like the rotten grain of rice in the earth, the rotting grass, if his body is taken away by devils and ghosts;

and if no man or woman of his family goes to tell the banyan of the spring, the fig tree of the village, he who cares for the nephews and nieces and the inhabitants,

because they are afraid that the dead has debts to pay, business to take care of, borrowed oxen from the king, buffalo from the rich, goods or money from the neighbors,

if the dead is a newborn or a child who died from a child sickness, or a child who is still held on someone's knees and of someone does not go to take out the bark, open the best and the loincloth in front of the chief,

if the dead is a child and someone is afraid he will not be able to cry (while telling the chief), if the dead is an adult and one is afraid of his unfinished business and therefore does not go and tell (the chief of the death),

for this: one is guilty and will deal with the chief, will pay a fine of one "ko" and will sacrifice a pig of one "song" [castrated pig if word is bong].

page 83 #54 Of those who use the chief's objects or tools without authorization.

He who takes the hoe, hanging from the rod, the machete to cut, he who uses without authorization objects that others keep carefully,

he who uses parakeets and parrots to catch others with bird lime [or glue] , who uses the hunting elephant (of others) to catch others with a lasso, who borrows without authorization the objects of the rich to use them;

he who does not ask to cut down the palm tree, to use the piece of iron, who takes the chief's objects without asking him;

he who is like the heat of the fire warming the legs (of the one squatting in front of the fire), like the water of the river swirling around the legs, he who creates problems at high noon (needlessly),

that one is guilty and must deal with the chief and himself.

page 84 #55 Of the inheritance of the goods of the chief (or a person) when his children have left him to live separately.

The children, the grand children are like the corn, the cucumbers that one cultivates; the parents have created them, have carried them, have worked hard to keep them clean, to see they are not cold and do not have bad nights.

If, when big and strong, they (the children) leave the home, go and cultivate another field, eat meat and vegetables away from home;

if they do not know their parents any more, do not want to see them, do not show any love towards their parents;

if the parents adopt a child from the tribe of the Darlac, bring him up, feed him, make him their real child to have someone to work for them, work the field, grow corn, cucumbers and vegetables, being afraid to have no one to care for them when old or sick;

afraid of having nobody to go get wood, to get water, to cook the rice and the vegetables, to weave blankets, skirts and vests, they adopt a child of a bee or a hornet, a child who owns nothing, no bracelet, no crockery,

ANTOMARCHI'S NOTES: PAGE 84

(1) Bih, Mnông, Kriêng, Ky'yông: Tribes of Darlac.

page 85

In case that they have a headache, if their arms and legs are tired, the adopted children care and help them.

And if later, when they will be rotten like the grain of paddy, when they will be dead, their own children do not come to see and help them, if they abandon and forget them, if during their sickness, they have not come to keep a vigil and help them if they have not offered alcohol to care for them when they have some, if after their death, they did not come to help roll them (in a mat), if they did not come to give their last respects,

then, all their good left over after paying the man or female healer, will go, not to their real children, but to their adopted children who stayed with them, everything they possess will go to them in full.

page 86 #56 Of those who scorn the chief's authority by hiding where they come from or where they go.

He who hides his word, who conceals what must be said, who does not let the chief know everything;

he who thinks about his head (the chief's) as a stump, his feet as a log, he who does not know the (power of) the chief;

he who thinks about him with contempt, who treats him like a dog, who does not want to recognize the chief's authority;

he who meets the chief in the middle of the high road, at the foot of a tree, on the path, where many inhabitants walk and who, when the chief asks or questions him, does not remove the bark, does not open his vest and loin cloth,

This one is guilty and will deal with the chief and himself.

Chapter III

page 87 #57 Of concealment of individuals.

He (the chief) who hides the spoon, who keeps silent (when he must tell), who conceals (guilty) individuals,

when one must burn (until the earth) clears, one must cut (the wood until one sees) clearly (inside), one must talk to let know;

of a woman or a man refuse to obey (the chief) if they do not carry out his orders,

he (the chief) must go peel the wood, strip the bark, open the vest and the loin cloth (in front of the chief).

The stakes and the nails are well driven in, the horses and the elephants are well tied up (instructions have been given);

the rod has been secured, the straw hut fastened, the rattan securely attached and having taken the stick of bamboo, the finger, the tip of the nail (sold to him, he has promised to execute the orders).

For this, he is guilty. [Judgment(s) not translated]

page 88 #58 Of the chief who hides some inhabitants (subject to taxes).

The banyan of the spring, the fig tree of the village, he who watches over the inhabitants,

if he has said that not one man or one woman had not been (registered).

whereas some are found living in the forest or in the huts (in the field), living alone, men and women;

if he did not talk, if he did not say what he should have said,

he is guilty because he lied, because he did not say what should have been said, because he meant to deceive.

By hiding so (the inhabitants) he has robbed (the tax department);

(he has acted) like one who runs to steal the gong (from the one who carries it), to grab the elephant or the money of the rich.

For this, he will reimburse twice over and above, altogether three times, once in front, once behind (the amount of the theft), he will give.

After this, he will not be able to say that the tree has been cut without wounds, that he has been given a fine without reason;

he will have to acknowledge that the cut to the tree has hurt it, that the fine given is reasonable.

<u>ANTOMARCHI'S NOTES</u>: PAGE 89

[Judgment(s) not translated]

The inflicted fine is sometimes proportional to the number of personal taxable dissimulated. The chief can also be held as the person in charge of the liquidation of the taxes which should have been had by those which he did not register at the village.

page 89 #59 Of the chief who hides the problems of the inhabitants.

He who, the spider weaving its web, like the hare running away, hides the disagreements between the inhabitants;

he who did not talk, did not say what he should have said, who does not tell of the disagreements of the inhabitants because he does not want to settle them;

who does not go burn in order to see the earth, who does not explain clearly, who does not go (to the big chief) to let hem know;

That one is guilty and must deal with the big chief and himself. [Judgment(s) not translated]

page 90 #60 Of the chief who takes away inhabitants of neighboring villages.

He who takes away the inhabitants of the rich village, of the prosperous village, to set them up in his own village;

he who does not move apart (the weeds) to help see, who does not inform to let know when people (of another village) come settle in his own village,

he is guilty and must deal with himself.

page 91 #61 Of the chief who oppresses the inhabitants.

He who is the banyan of the spring, the fig tree of the village, who watches over all the inhabitants,

if he does not protect well the inhabitants and oppresses them, if he crushes the sparrow hawk brothers;

if he acts like the man or the woman having many problems, if he acts like the man or the woman having many problems, if as soon as he turns his back, he acts differently;

if he turns around every which way like the eggplants and the pepper (in the pot), if he cuts once in the length once crosswise;

if of those who bring him filets or shoulders (of beef) he accepts the reasons

he is guilty and must deal with himself. [Judgment(s) not translated]

page 92 #62 Of the chief of the village who does not take good care of the inhabitants.

When the plant of pumpkin is dry, it must be watered, when it spreads too much, the last bud must be cut, when it grows too much, it must be brought back towards the ground.

If (the chief) does not off the bark (to chew), if he does not protect well the inhabitants, if he does not take good care of them;

if he does not carry (them) like one carries the little brother, if he does not bathe them like one bathes the children, if he does not watch well over them;

if he does not bite well the bracelet and does not take good care of the inhabitants so that they will live quietly;

if he bites those who become guilty and devours those who fall, if he breaks their arms and legs (instead of helping them);

if (because of him) the pig that one raises, does not fatten up, if the buffalo does not become a beautiful male, if one can never drink the alcohol of the jars 'tuk' and 'bô' (because one does not live quietly),

because he knocks out with the hammer or the joist, because he oppresses the poor and the unhappy;

because he is a mother or a father bringing up badly his children, because (of his fault) nothing is left in the bottom of the baskets (cupboards).

page 93

He is a mother like a weasel-mother, a father like a tiger-father, instead of protecting (the inhabitants), he scratches them with his claws.

(because of him) Those who bathe cannot find coolness, those who live in the swamp cannot find tranquility, those who take refuge between the paws of rhinoceros or elephants do not feel warmed up.

those who make a mistake, he oppresses them, those who make a slight mistake in drinking or eating, he gives them a fine.

If someone speaks badly, he listens, if another one makes a mistake, he acts ruthlessly, even those of his clan are not spared.

For these the chief is guilty. [Judgment(s) not translated]

page 94 #63 Of arbitrary arrests.

If (the chief) tries to hold up, arrest people, to tie them up, or shackle them without motive;

if he chases to get the gong or the elephant, of to become richer he arrests people;

if he pounces on those persons and arrests them (to rob them);

if he grows poisonous plants to scare the inhabitants, he disturbs those who live peacefully,

those who, when they have a matter as old as the hollow tuber, a matter of the past, always go find the banyan of the spring, the fig tree of the village who watches over the inhabitants, those who having a debt to collect, ask for it (as is the custom), who have a disagreement to settle, usually consult the chief;

if he behaves like the grass of the swamp which wants to grow higher than the reeds, like the straw hut wanting to be higher than the bamboo, like the wild animals wanting to jump higher than the top of the trees;

if he refuses to go under the big house (of the big chief), would rather step over (suppress) the little house (of the poor), if he scorns the house where often people eat beef or buffalo (the authority of the big chief).

For these he is guilty and must deal with himself. [Judgment(s) not translated]

page 95 #64 Of arresting someone in somebody else's house.

He who arrest people without motive, who enters in the house without reason to arrest the rich or the poor arbitrarily;

he who takes as with a net or a hook, jumping on his prey like a sparrow hawk or a weasel;

he who carries away the beams and rafters by tying up the persons (guilty) in the home of the rich or the poor,

That one is guilty and must deal with himself and another (the master of the house, (because)

he scorns the long house (of the rich), he jumps over the short house (of the poor), the house where they often eat beef or buffalo he does not respect.

He looks at people with contempt, he looks upon them as dogs, he does not respect the persons.

He irritates the thunder and the gods and debases the home or others.

If he arrests someone who happen to be in a rich house, he will pay a fine of one "ko" and will sacrifice one buffalo to the owner of the house.

If he arrests someone who happens to be in a poor house, he will pay a fine of three "ko" and will sacrifice a pig of two "song" (to the owner of the house).

page 96 #65 Of the chief who wants to judge an affair which is not in his jurisdiction.

(an important affair like) making a fire from a small flame of bamboo, he wants to judge it alone, with all his heart and spleen, hiding, without getting together with his assistants, or his family;

The set apart (elephant's) tusks, he wants to bring them nearer with a ring of rattan, the front paws [feet], he wants to shackle, he wants to tie up all four paws.

He does not get the inhabitants together, he does not fix up the damaged basket, both sides, he does not hear them.

He set the amount of the fine, he breaks the judge's baton, without consulting anyone, he settles the affair alone.

Because of these, he is guilty and must deal with the big chief and himself. [Judgment(s) not translated]

page 97 #66 Of the chief who refuses to judge an affair in his jurisdiction.

If the banyan of the spring, the fig tree of the village, the one who watches over the nephews, the brothers and the inhabitants,

if when there is an affair for this or that, he does not set the amount of the fine, if he does not break the judge's baton (justice), if he does not end the disagreement;

if, when the inhabitants have between them an insignificant disagreement, like the bulge of the ford or the neck of the bottle, a slight disagreement, he refuses to settle it,

(because of this) the hoes are always chipped, the lighters are broken, there are always troubles between the inhabitants.

(this because) The damaged baskets are not repaired, the screens are not mended, because he who became chief does not settle the disagreements of the little sparrow hawks, the spirits of the village,

because the straw hut which dangerously, he does not fix it, because the house which threatens to fall, he does not reinforce it with supports, because he does not want the torn skirt.

For this he is guilty because he wipes out all the inhabitants.

For the sow about to give birth, he dies not prepare the bedding, for the hen about to lay an egg, he does not fix a nest, to the inhabitants divided by all sorts of disagreements, he does not dispense justice. [Judgment(s) not translated]

page 98 #67 Of the chief who accepts goods from a culprit to prove him right.

He (the chief) who claims to see and hear, like the crabs and the snails, people laugh and talk;

while they sing (to blame him) while land clearing, eating while laughing (being critical) at those, men or women who have problems or the chief who is unjust;

while the inhabitants are like the birds "mling" and "mlang" singing in the evening during the dry season, the young men and young girls keep singing (complaining against the chief);

while he has heard the murmur of the wind outside the village, the rumbling of thunder on the other side of the fence,

while one hears people repairing their hoes and their machetes, talk among themselves of the disagreement to settle;

If he is certain that the man or the woman (accused) is guilty and, like the tiger and the rhinoceros afraid of traps, afraid of being punished and offers him goods (to be proven right); if in spite of their guilt, he admits that coming back from the fountain one needs to lean against the embankment (to rest), that to build a dam on a river, one needs flat stones, that one must support those who give the most;

page 98

 If he holds the fat tree like the thigh or the calf, if he does not punish the one who entered someone else's home, if he does not say what must be said, if he fixes the hoe (of the guilty), if he does not say who is wrong and who is right, if the culprit is not bothered,

that his legs will be wet again, his thighs rubbed with ginger, his hair combed again when all tangled;

if the chief fails to settle a disagreement and finds normal the behavior of the culprit because the latter gave him goods;

if he blames the one who is right,

for this he is guilty. [Judgment(s) not translated]

Chapter IV

page 99 #68 Of the wanderers who do not want to stay in their villages.

He who wanders, eats all the gourds, catches his chin everywhere, when he no longer likes a village he goes to another.

He acts like one pricks the buttocks with a needle, his body is in the village but his behind is outside, he pulls out the saber or the knife from the sheath and does not put them back in.

When he is alive, he is like the wild buffalo (he can be met); when he dies he is like the spirit of the buffalo (that no one can see); when he will have become a sparrow hawk (after death), there will be nobody to miss him.

He will be thrown in the grave in the bottom of the ravine, his limbs will break and no one will cry;

because he has a big mouth like the opening of a big basket, lips like a bigger basket, and that nobody can correct him; because nobody can repair the basket, repair the screen, neither the powerful chief, nor the brothers, nor the inhabitants, nobody can give him advice.

If he is like the mosquito who tries to bite, like the man or woman who creates problems, nobody will take care of him, nobody will stand up for him; he will be left to his fate and he will be carried away by the current of the river.

Like the pig or the buffalo destined to be sacrificed, he has problems, he will lose his body. [Judgment(s) not translated]

page 100 #69 Of wanderers without a permanent home.

He who is like a bent knife, like a used machete, and always has problems,

he who is like an abandoned horse or buffalo, who does not remember to which family he belongs, who has neither father nor mother;

he who is like the ignorant not instructed by anyone, like the mute with whom nobody talks;

he who takes his legs towards the East and his head towards the West like the wild ox in the swamps,

he who not having meat to eat, food to cut, tobacco to smoke, cannot stay put and looks for nasty problems in all the villages he goes through.

He who holds a hairy caterpillar or a fat green caterpillar in his hands to scare the inhabitants of the villages of the East or West, and who always acts like a fool or an idiot,

that one is guilty and must deal with himself.

Like the pig or the buffalo destined to be sacrificed, if he looks for problems, he will lose his body. [Judgment(s) not translated]

page 101 #70 Of those who settle in the hut in the field.

Those who live in the fields, in the middle of clumps of bamboo, who live anywhere, in the clumps of bamboo male or female, like wild animals;

those who let the fence or the large gate (of their village) fall into ruins, who look in the gongs and gars pit, in the fields where there are horses and elephants;

those whose behind is on the ladder and the face is turned towards the door because they think of escaping to the high mountain;

those whose body is in the village and their behind outside and who pull the saber or the knife out of the sheath because they are jealous of the rich;

those who live in the swamps, hide in the deserted huts, who live alone,

those are guilty and must deal with themselves. [Judgment(s) not translated]

page 102 #71 Of bad curses [spells].

He who leaves the village taking the mats and the blankets, the baskets and the trays, the cooking pots and the bowls, the jars and the dishes, the pigs and the chickens,

if because of this someone gets sick in the village, they will send a man or a woman to let him know so that he comes to see the slightly or badly sick one since it is because of him that the spirits became angry, the healer said so by measuring the stick, it is because he walked in front of the fountain, the field, the places where they often go fishing.

If for the person slightly or badly sick, pigs and chickens have been sacrificed, they will be shown to him so that he will see them by his own eyes.

If the sick gets well, can leave the mat and the blanket, everything spent to heal him, he will have to reimburse.

If the sick does not get well, if he cannot leave the mat and the blanket, if he dies, he will have to pay the price of the body since he died because the dead ones and the spirits are angry, because he left taking his mats and his blankets, without offering a little bit of rice or corn (while passing in front of each house).

Acting like he did, the dead took revenge, the spirits became angry and this is why the sick died.

For this he is guilty. [Judgment(s) not translated]

page 103 #72 Of those who being sick transmit their sickness to others.

In the fateful years, when it is very hot, when the spirits of the sky spread evil,

if the sick that the gods have stricken, the sky made him sick,

cannot stay home like when one is in mourning, if he cannot keep quiet;

if like the elephant of the spirit-crocodile, he tries to rub himself against the tree "keik" or "kpang", if he tries to rub against the rich and healthy inhabitants,

being so the cause of the death of people young and strong, rich or poor, people well built (still able to work like sharp hoes and machetes, people fit and strong,

for this there is a problem between others and himself. [Judgment(s) not translated]

page 104 #73 Of those who spread infectious sickness.

He who transmits scourge and scurf, who spreads them in the villages of the East or West, who infects the rich inhabitants;

he who transmits smallpox or spreads disease forcing the others to care for themselves with acrid or bitter medicines;

he who does that [so that] women will no longer be able to have children, no girls no boys, that they will not be able to have large families like the germs of evil, large as though they had a hundred or a thousand stomachs because he has given them smallpox or yaws,

he who does that the family will not multiply, that the tobacco plant will not bud, the human race will not proliferate;

he who cut the top of the budding bamboo "alê" or "mo'ô", who extinguishes the race of the rich inhabitants who were able to have many children,

that one is guilty and has a very serious problem between others and himself.

Antomarchi's Notes: Page 104

[Judgment(s) not translated]

(Adulterous husband having contaminated his wife.)

page 105 #74 Of non-revelation of infectious diseases.

At the dry season, when it is very hot, many people are sick; some have smallpox, others, the yaws, for others their legs hurt; in spite of all the care given, they cannot get better.

People become sick while asleep, others die after eating, men and women. Many have a cold, a cough, a stomach ache, vomit or have diarrhea, they die.

All these sicknesses can spread out and reach the inhabitants of other villages if nobody, man or woman, goes to tell the banyan of the spring, the fig tree of the village, the one who watches over the nephews and nieces, all the inhabitants,

it is as though one tried to let in the house a python* or a water snake, one was jealous of the inhabitants in good health.

For all those matters, especially those which are bad, one must always go and tell the chief;

if one conceals what must be told, if one has too long teeth, of in the village there is some matter and no one goes to tell the chief,

> For that one is guilty and will deal with the chief.

Antomarchi's Notes: Page 74

A python in the house is regarded as a desecration, as a warning from the spirits; therefore the house is always abandoned.

page 106 #75 Of the necessity to confine the lepers by building a hut in the forest.

He who has smallpox, leprosy or yaws, he must not be kept in the village,

in the fear that he transmits leprosy, smallpox or yaws, to the other inhabitants.

To avoid this, his parents or his family will build him a hut in the forest, a shelter in the bush and he will have to live there alone.

They will build him a small house, a shelter in the bush, and will be forbidden to come back to the village, to enter in the house, to drink at the same spring as the inhabitants, to bathe in the same river, afraid that he will transmit (his sickness) to the inhabitants of here or there.

In the fear that he gives smallpox, leprosy or the yaws, to others, they will turn against the mother who gave him birth, the father who brought him up, if they don't know how to care for him, they don't know how to keep the child that the spirits have stricken, the sky cursed by making his body suffer;

for this, there will be a problem between others and them (the parents). [Judgments & notes not translated]

page 107 #76 Of those who accuse without proof someone of suffering a contagious disease.

He who slanders with the mouth, whose teeth are long, who makes up stories;

he who shortens the bamboo rising very high, who acts the same way with others without cause;

he who puts a creeper around the neck of healthy people or gives them a rope in order to create problems;

he who tries to create bad problems, problems of an idiot, in accusing unfairly the others of being sick.

He who claims that the kapok tree is hollow, that the mortar is broken, that he has seen some inhabitants suffering from smallpox or yaws;

He who slanders esteemed persons, persons rich without proof,

that one is guilty and must deal with others and himself. [Judgment(s) not translated, Notes illegible]

page 108 #77 Of those who, discovering a corpse, do not tell the chief or do not recognize [identify?] the body.

He who hides what he eats, what he drinks, who hides everything,

if he sees someone stretched out in the middle of the road or across the path either because he is drunk, because he died following an epidemic, during the hot weather, when the sky spreads the evil,

he must be afraid that the horses do not crush him, that the elephants do not step on him, that the tiger does not carry him into the bush.

If he does not go close to see, of he does not go recognize the body, of he does not go see if death has already claimed him, he is guilty.

If he sees someone (stretched out) in front of him and he runs away,

it is as though he had killed him himself with a club or a stick, as though he killed him in the bush while hiding,

it is as though he had pierced him with a spear, strangled him with a rope, or hit him with a saber.

For this, he must deal with himself.

page 109 #78 Of those who hide the epizootics and do not inform the chief.

During the disastrous years, during the hot season, the Master of the Sky spreads on earth the waters which kill the oxen and the buffalo;

the oxen with weak shins, the buffalo with feeble legs can no longer eat or drink.

Having drunk and eaten (at the yearly feast), the chief gave advice, all the inhabitants of here or there he instructed;

he prescribed (that in case of epizootics) the animals must be fed and given water under the house, he said that each village must take measures of protection,

by reinforcing the fence, blocking the large gate and the path giving access, by hanging the skulls of oxen and buffalo outside the village.

He who is the banyan growing at the spring, the fig tree growing over the village, he who watches over the brothers and nephews, over all the inhabitants;

[break?] and who does not listen to the advice given by the chief, who does not obey his orders;

he who disobeys the tiger, who thinks he is more powerful than the gods, who ignores the words of the chief;

he who does not keep the fire going, who does not gather the inhabitants to instruct them;

he who does not brush aside the grass in order to see, he, when there are sick buffalo and oxen, does not inform the chief;

that one is guilty and there is a very problem with him. [Judgments & notes not translated]

page 110 #79 Of those who do not know how to care for their livestock in periods of epizootic.

During the disastrous years, when it is very hot, the Master of the Sky spreads evil.

During the disastrous years, during the dry season, when it is very hot, the sicknesses spread to all the inhabitants, in all the villages, in all the regions, in all the countries, by all the roads.

Villages must protect themselves, signs "kung" and "knông" ["prohibited"] will be put along all roads coming in, oxen and buffalo (of other villages) will be forbidden to enter (the village).

Of this, all the children and grandchildren (all the inhabitants) will be instructed; all the oxen and buffalo will be watched (isolated).

He who disobeys the tiger, because he believes himself more powerful than the spirits, who ignores the words (of the chief) by leaving his buffalo and oxen free, in letting them go in the herds of others, of the oxen and buffalo of others die, he will be guilty and there will be a problem with him.

Like the pig or the chicken destined to be sacrificed, if he creates problems he will lose his body.   [Judgment(s) not translated]

page 111 #80 Of forest fires.

Those men or women who light a fire without thinking, without paying attention, like the blind or the dead;

those men or women who start a fire anywhere, without the utmost care, like fools or idiots;

those who cut the top of the budding bamboo, who stop, by holding them by their feet or hands, the spirits who give wealth;

those whose fault it is that the bamboo "alé" and "mo'ê" [smaller and larger varieties, respectively] are destroyed, that the home of the hares and civets are burned,

those will have a very grave problem with others (the society).

Each must teach his children and his grandchildren,

afraid that if they go to the fountain or the woods where they should not go,

afraid that they light a fire with a torch

afraid that they go to work in the field where they should not go,

that if they carry a torch, they will set fire to the bushes or the brushwood by throwing it in the undergrowth,

and so the fire starts, consumes the forest, the bushes, the reeds, the straw hut and everything growing and living (in the forest);

page 112

afraid that the fires consume the houses and the villages, the huts in the forest, the huts in the fields if around it has not yet been cleared.

If someone recognizes the (guilty) man or woman, there will be a very serious problem with them.

If they have goods (to pay the indemnity), they will be sentenced (to the maximum), even to the loss of their body.   [Judgment(s) not translated]

page 113 #81 Of those who, not putting out their fire, caused the village to burn.

He who falls deeply asleep because he is tired, he drank too much, without putting out the fire, without taking out the torch, might cause a fire consuming houses and goods.

Before drinking and eating (the day of the yearly feast), everybody has been warned, everybody has been instructed (by the chief); the same thing has been said and said again many times.

He is therefore guilty, the one who is like the spinning wheel or the corn sheller operating badly, like the ox or the buffalo who does not accept the advice (of the chief);

because he does not listen to the one who talks to him, he does not follow the advice given to him, he acts like a fool or an idiot, his children and grandchildren he dies not educate them, he acts as though he wants to harm others.

For this, there is a matter between others and himself.   [Judgment(s) not translated]

page 114 #82 Of fires in villages.

The fire ate everything, the water took everything away, the big baskets (the earth's surface) are wiped out.

The columns of the houses, the pillars of the attics, the rice in the barns, everything is destroyed.

The pots to dye in, the baskets of potash, the stones to sharpen, the pots for vegetables, everything has been destroyed.

The cots and the big benches, the ladders and the stairs, the drums leaning against the columns, everything has been wiped out.

The big red jars, the beautiful "mnong" jars, the jewels and the dishes enclosed in the big baskets;

The pretty "Jarai" baskets, the baskets with covers, the bags and the satchels, the large and the small packages, all that has been destroyed.

The black and red vests, the vests with gold brocade or with broaches, the precious objects, the invaluable goods, all the wealth, everything has been wiped out.

The long joists, the big beams the rice and the paddy, everything burned.

Afraid of this, before drinking and eating (at the yearly party), the nephews have been warned, the inhabitants educated, everyone has been advised.

The ignorant have been educated, the mute taught (by gesture), the mouth (of the chief) did not stay closed, his lips did not stay motionless, he did not miss instructing or advising.

If one ignores the signs of traps, does not listen to the words of the chief, does not follow the advice he gave, disobeys the one who educates, does not remember customs as being sung;

if one disobeys the tiger, wants to believe himself more powerful than the spirits, does not listen to the mouth who educates,

for this, there is a very serious matter.

page 115 #83 Of those who force their way into the banned village.

Poke the fire and gather all the nephews and nieces, all the inhabitants (to hear this):

At certain times, in the disastrous years, when it is very hot (and there are epidemics), the village is banned so that the inhabitants feel well and their minds put at rest.

Someone puts signs "kung" and "knông" on the roads to prevent strangers from entering the village and upsetting the peacefulness of the inhabitants.

On all the roads, someone fastens ropes on which circles of rattan are hung, or someone piles up thorny branches.

If a stranger goes through the barrier, someone will seize all he carries on himself, he will be held and kept in the village as long as the prohibition lasts, either prohibited for traps or prohibition to eat meat of ox or buffalo, this cannot last more than three days and three nights.

As soon as the thorny branches and the circles of rattan are taken away, as soon as the roads are reopened, his liberty and goods will be returned to him.

But because he was ignorant, he forced (the entrance) without thinking, without asking himself if what he was doing was allowed or forbidden, he will pay a fine; for a small prohibition, he will pay a small fine, for a larger prohibition he will pay a bigger fine.

page 116 #84 Of those who force their way into a banned village because of epidemic.

When the year is disastrous, the season dry and torrid, the sky spreads evil;

when everybody is in mourning (because of an epidemic), in order that the year be good, the season better, all the inhabitants ask that the village be banned.

He who enters the village when the sighs of prohibition are on the roads, he is guilty.

If the spirits get angry, the sky annoyed, if again they spread the deadly sickness, he will be held responsible.

The pigs and chickens sacrificed and the jars offered (to the gods), he will have to reimburse.

If the sick do not heal, cannot leave their mats and blankets, he will be entirely responsible.

If death follows, he will have to pay the price of the body, if there are only wounds (after-effects), he will have to pay an indemnity.

page 117 #85 Of those who do not treat properly the sick.

Those who do not take care of the sick, who do not watch over them, who, having rice and alcohol, do not treat them;

those who do not call the midwife or the healer (in time) who do not dream of having the sick cared for;

those who do not give him the necessary care, so not keep him clean, who, owning pigs and chickens, forgets to sacrifice them (to the gods to obtain his recovery),

and make it so that the sick stay a long time on the mat, under the blanket, until he is weak and cannot even speak;

those having oxen and buffalo do not keep them to offer them to the souls of the dead;

those who do not give water (to the sick when he is thirsty), cook rice, force him to eat,

if the banyan of the spring, the fig tree of the village, he who watches over the inhabitants,

does not educate the ignorant, does not teach the mute, he does not go see (the sick) once in the day, once in the night, he never takes care of the sparrow hawk brothers, the spirits of the village, the nephews and nieces,

if he always stays home, quietly, as though he was hiding, if he does not go see those who are sick, if he does not take interest in them and does not ask news from the inhabitants who pass by his house,

For that he is guilty and must deal with himself. [Judgment(s) not translated]

page 118 #86 Of those who hide or run when called for help or assistance.

Those, men or women, who do not listen to the advice given, who disobey the chief's orders;

those who believe they are stronger than the higher, more powerful than the spirits, who are arrogant with the chief and ignore the advice given;

those who do not listen with a big ear, who do not speak with the same mouth, do not have the same heart (than all the inhabitants and the chief),

those who do not run when called for help, to chase the pirates or the elephants, who do not go to aid the families [who are] victims of the sorcerers and ghosts, who do not help bury the dead;

those who always stay home, remain silent as though they were hiding, without worrying about anything,

those who do not help to chase the rhinoceros and the elephants, to kill the tiger when called for help, who do not help the chief or the inhabitants when there is important work to be done,

those are guilty and must deal with the chief and themselves.

page 119 #87 Of the obligation for all the inhabitants to help each other for all work.

The heavy bundle of wood, one must help to carry, as well as the heavy load of water; one must help finish the house being built, see to those who are sick.

When a living person (gives a party) many must go drink his alcohol, when someone dies, all must go to the burial, when someone has forgotten what he had learned, he must be helped to learn again.

All must listen with the same ear, talk with one mouth, wanting with the same heart.

All, servants and inhabitants, nephews and nieces, all those of here or there must always help each other.

Those, man or woman, who do not accept advice, who reject those words, do not like to take these into account, those will be guilty and there will be an affair with the chief and them, they will sacrifice for the chief a pig of one "song" ["bong"?].

page 120 #88 Of arbitrary arrests in the house of a third party.

Those who arrest someone without orders, who enters someone else's house without permission to seize the rich or the plain inhabitant;

those who catch like with a net or a hook, who seize like a sparrow hawk or a weasel;

those who covet the big joist or the long beam and who for that reason, arrest a person when that person is in the house of the rich or of the inhabitant,

those are guilty and there is a matter with them.

page 121 #89 Of the lazy ones who do not want to work in the field.

Those who are lazy to dig the earth, to work the field, to cultivate corn and cucumbers,

those who, after a good meal, do nothing, go to bed after drinking without thinking about poverty and misery;

those who do not follow their mother's advice, who do not listen to the words of the chief, who do not remember the customs being sung,

those who have no rice, no vegetable to eat, no food to eat like everybody else;

they have no hut (in the field), their house is empty, the rich despise them.

In the evening they eat in this house and in the morning in that house, where they happen to be they sleep, but never do anything.

The greedy dog is being punished by having to swallow a (hot) eggplant, the bad man is punished, he who is lazy to work the field will be punished also. [Judgment(s) not translated]

page 122 #90 Of wandering women who do not work the field, the house and do not have a known home.

She who is like a fly or a mosquito without family, like a child without father or mother;

she who is like the hen looking (for a nest to lay an egg), who not liking this village, goes to another, finding this house bad, goes to another;

she who like the wanderers has many bowls, eats vegetables in one house and rice in another, who goes to bed and sleeps wherever she happens to be;

she who cannot stay quietly, does not behave well, who does not work the field, does not go get wood or to the fountain or the hut in the field (to keep an eye);

she who does not get the cotton or the thread ready, who does not handle the pestle or mortar, who behaves badly;

she whose legs go to the East, her head in the West, (who drifts) like the wild ox in the bush, she who does not listen to the given advice, who does not obey those who give orders, acting always like a fool or idiot;

she whose mouth is as big as the spinning of a net or a basket and who incorrigible,

like the greedy dog cured with a hot eggplant, like the bad man being punished, she who acts badly will also be punished. [Judgment(s) not translated]

page 123 #91 Of those who do not help put our the fires in the villages.

When there are rhinoceros and elephants (in the field) one must help chase them, when the sorcerers and the ghosts give sickness or death, one must assist (the affected families), when there is a hardship, one must always help.

He who stays quietly at home, who stays put as though hiding, he who sees the fire burning the houses and attics does not go help fight the fire;

he who acts like he is not from the village, like he was a stranger and remains unconcerned (in front of the disaster);

he who does not hurry to fight the pirates with saber or spear, who never helps (others) when there is something pressing to do in the morning or evening,

that one is guilty and there is a matter between the chief and him. [Judgment(s) not translated]

page 124 #92 Of arson on houses and rice granaries.

He who is jealous of his neighbor, wicked like the spirits and tries to start a fire at the straw hut to destroy the house of the rich, the house of the brothers, without knowing why,

if of the (guilty) woman, one recognizes the body, if of the man, one recognizes the person, if of the oxen and the buffalo one recognizes the keeper, if one can catch him by the hair on the arm, if he is recognized by his face, he will be tied up with a rope, will be tied down and will be kept as a slave or prisoner.

If it is a man, his head will be cut, if it is a woman, she will be sold for oxen to the king, for buffalo to the rich, for goods to the brothers (inhabitants).

This so the pig no longer knows, the dog loses its habits, the bowls and pans are no longer broken (the guilty ones can no longer do it again). [Judgment(s) not translated]

page 125 #93 Of burying cold rice in someone else's field.

He (who buries cold rice) desecrates the earth, the waters and the woods of others, and because of this the rice no longer grows the millet does not sprout, the forest no longer grows, the clan can not thrive, the human race becomes extinguished, all that because someone has committed a very grace sin.

Because of these, the earth will no longer grow green, water will no longer flow (from the springs), the banana trees and the sugar cane planted will not grow, rice and millet will not give ears or grain, they will not grow (like before).

If one recognizes the culprit, like one can recognize the owner of oxen and buffalo by seeing their keeper, if one knows the one who buried the cold rice in the field, let him be caught by the basket, held by the arm, let one look at his face and take him to the banyan of the spring, the fig tree of the village, the one who watches over the nephews and nieces, all the inhabitants.

The banyan of the spring will investigate the matter, will judge and will try to settle it once and for all.

But if the man or the woman does not accept his decision, the banyan of the spring will lead him to the chief of the hamlet. The chief of the hamlet will bring him to court which will question him again.

If he (the guilty) admits to his error, confesses his crime, admits he acted badly, acted rashly like the deaf or the blind, he will be declared guilty because he has been harmful like the spirits of the dead.

And there will be a matter between others (the owner of the field and the owner of the ground) and hem.

He will give a pig worth two "song" to the owner of the rice field

and one pig worth one "ko" (to the owner of the property) to purify the earth. [Judgment(s) not translated]

page 126 #94 Of building a small grave on someone else's field.

He who desecrates the earth, the waters and the forests of others and so doing the millet does not come up, the rice does not grow; no more ears nor grains, the earth produces nothing, the forest no longer grows, the clan cannot thrive because he committed a very grave sin;

if he had built a small grave in someone else's field, made a burial mound and put in funeral posts, while doing this, he jokes excessively, he has fun without moderation, he creates for himself very serious problems.

He will have to reimburse the value of the harvest, pay an indemnity (to the owner of the rice field and the owner of the property), to wipe out the effects of his sin, to erase the evil he did, so that the millet and the rice grow well again, that everyone be in good health.

For this, there is a matter.

To purify the earth, he will gibe a white buffalo to the owner of the ground.

to the owner of the field, he will give a white pig for the sacrifice.   [Judgment(s) not translated]

Chapter V

page 127 #95 Of engagements (and breaking off engagements).

If they want each other, if they are in love, the young girl and the young man, if this is their only worry,

let them gather the brothers and sisters, the uncles and aunts, let them introduce their witnesses to the pipe [a musical instrument ?] in the mouth, the bracelet on the wrist.

The necklaces and the bracelets will be exchanged, his bracelet given to her, her bracelet to hem, the bracelet of the woman to the man, the bracelet of the man to the woman.

The rope will not be put by force around their necks, like done to the oxen and buffalo, they will not be forced to get married; if they love and want each other, the bracelets will be placed on a mat, they will pick them up alone, freely, nobody will present them, nobody will put them in their hand.

But if in the morning of the next day, at sunrise, the man having spoken a certain way at night, speaks another way during the day, if as soon as he turns his back he acts differently, if he does not become the husband of the one he had chosen,

in acting so he scorned her, he will have to sacrifice a castrated pig to her.

page 128 #96 Of nonpayment of the dowry.

What has been promised must be given, the set dowry, it must be paid (to the family of the husband),

on the day set in the contract, without delay, without postponing.

But if one is like the blanket rods (which sway), if one prevaricates, postpones year after year lets the months and the years go by and each time waits until the cicadas sing;

if one shows the mangoes and the leeches and does not give them, if one does not give willingly what had been promised and one gives nevertheless a son-in-law;

if one offers with regrets meat or fish, if one promises to the chief to pay and each time changes the spots on the coat of oxen and buffalo (promised);

if one speaks one way in the daytime and another way at night, act differently when someone turns his back;

if one is like the tree "knia" (olive tree) whose trunk is knotty, like the banyan tree "mnut" whose trunk is twisted;

if (the family of the wife) has been hurt in their hearts, if the spots on the oxen and buffalo have been changed, if one refuses to drink (from the jar) and the bracelet has been rejected;

if there is a matter to settle, let it be said, if the river overflows or is dry, if bad words have been said, let it be known.

If it is an old matter, of the past, it will be settled.

But if one does not give what has been promised, if one does not pay on the set day, if one breaks the contract after having accepted it;

page 129

if one makes them wait months and years, time to make ten new fields, cultivate five old fields;

if one acts like those who buy gongs and elephants unable to pay for them, if one buys a scented flower and deeps it for his own pleasure;

that very night, that very day, he must pay (the dowry) since it is not because the son-in-law works badly the field or the garden (of his parents-in-law), it is not because he stays in his father's house in the morning, in his mother's house in the evening (that the dowry is not paid).

If (the parents-in-law) do not pay that very night, the husband will go back to his family;

and because of all this, the parents-in-law will be guilty.

page 130 #97 Of replacing a dead spouse.

When the strut breaks, it is replaced, when the floor breaks, it is repaired, when someone dies, he is replaced by another,

This is to keep the seed of the straw hut, the cluster of the "knôk", to keep the seed of the human race handed down from the past.

It must be kept like one keeps the old field, the old log of wood, the seed of the elders, uncles, aunts; it must be kept carefully like one keeps the seed of the early rice or the late rice.

It is the custom to put up the rafters on the beam, the whole country, from East to West; it is the custom to re-tie, to give a substitute (to the deceased spouse), this since before, since [time of] the elders of the past.

This has not been recently invented, it cannot have been known before the elders [it is ancient].

Afraid that the home crumbles, the house falls in ruins, the fence breaks up, the words do not tell of the despair;

the custom repairs what is broken, strengthens what is weak;

afraid that the family scatters in the fields like the clump of rice, afraid that it will be wiped out, that the human race dry up like the water in the dry mountain, afraid that there will be no more children and grand-children;

because of this the custom says to always retie, always replace (the dead spouse).

Antomarchi's Notes: PAGE 130

The law known as "bi cuê brei nuê" (to join again by giving a substitute) [Illegible] the death of one of the husbands of the family of late replaces it [illegible]. The marriage binds, not only the man has the woman, but the clan of the man [has that] of the woman. Once it was further sealed nothing should be able to break the links, even by death.

The law of the replacement consolidates, gives the marriage and ensures some perenniality. Its violation involves the disintegration of the hearth, divides the inheritance and sows discord in the families.

page 131 #98 Of obligation of always replacing (the dead spouse) by a brother, a sister or a nephew, or if need be by a child of a woman belonging to the same clan.

When the joists are weak, they must be strengthened, when the floor is in bad shape, it must be replaced, when this one dies, he must be replaced by that one.

What is broken must be repaired, what is weak must be strengthened; it is a very old custom to always replace.

When the uncle dies, the nephew replaces him, when the grandmother dies, the grand-daughter replaces her, when someone dies he is replaced by someone else in order that there is always someone (to carry on the family, the clan).

One cleans the shallow parts to plant some cabbage palm, one cuts the reeds to plant sugar-cane, if one has no child, even very small, in his family (to replace the dead), one will look for one in his sister's families, if there are none in the village, one will look in another providing he belongs in the same clan [of the same family name] (as the dead must be replaced).

The child of the older sister will be paid, the younger sister will be bought, the rich (parent) will exchange for goods;

afraid that the family will crumble, the house fall into ruins, the mouths not tell of their desperation

the custom is to always keep the family   [last part illegible]

page 132

If it is the family of the (deceased) man who does not want to give a substitute, only a small part of the inheritance will come to the nieces of the dead one.

If it is the family of the (deceased) woman who refuses to give a substitute (to the widower), a big part acquired in common will go to the nieces (belonging to the clan) of the widower, and the children from his marriage (with the deceased woman) will have only a small part.

Antomarchi's Notes: PAGE 132

#25 of 4/2/1925 - the chief of the clan of the deceased has been condemned to jail until a substitute has been given to the widower.

(Note of an inhabitant) I bring to the attention of Mr. Superior Inhabitant on this important judgment and the very interesting law which caused the sentencing of Y-Dju. It ensures the continuation of the founders and the increase of the family's patrimony. Its non-observance and its infringement since about twenty-five years have been one of the main causes of the social decline of the Malayo-Polynesian tribes of Darlac; the large families have been enormously diminished or have disappeared, and the wealth squandered.

Y-Dju stayed in jail only twenty-four hours; the substitute who was wavering has been found in the shortest time possible.

#21 of 2/8/1926 - Restitution of goods taken under the excuse that a substitute had not been found and a dowry not paid.

page 133 #99 Of replacing the deceased wife by a too young girl.

When the struts or the floor are in bad shape, they must be changed, when a person dies he must always be replaced.

That which is broken must be repaired, which is weak must be strengthened, always (the deceased) must be replaced by grand-children,

(this) so that the home does not crumble, the house does not fall in ruins, the spoken word not be desperation,

to still have someone to work the earth, do the field, cultivate the corn and cucumbers in the morning.

If the young girl (given as a substitute) is still a child, sleeping on a mat, wrapping herself in the blanket, not able to be away from her parents;

if she is too young, she will have to be protected and the adult man (to whom she is given) must know to wait,

if she is timid, she must be reassured by giving her some bracelets, if she is shy, she must

be soothed by giving her necklaces.

page 134

And if (the man) has his feet in the path, his hands in the bush, he fornicates with a woman, it does not matter, there will be no problem; but he may not forget to well work the earth, do the field, cultivate the corn and the cucumbers;

he must well clear around (the field), pull the weeds, yell at the female parrots and the [male] parrots (to chase them out of the field.

He must well keep the bracelet (of the wedding) and take care of the young girl (substitute) to make everything beautiful and agreeable;

he must well keep the hoses and the buffalo (of the young substitute), the pigs under (the house), the chickens under (the overhang), the jewels and the dishes in the baskets, he must keep them.

But if he cannot wait, sees the yellow flower in the bush, the red flower among the ferns, if he sees another woman and wants her (as his wife), he will be guilty and all his goods will belong to the substitute, he will also have to pay her a fine and he will leave (the house of his parents-in-law) naked, without taking anything, not even a chew of betel.

page 135 #100 Of the old woman who must take a young substitute; she must give him a concubine, afraid that the human race dies down, the house falls in ruins.

When the beams or the rafters are weak, they must be strengthened, when the woman is old, can no longer cook, cannot see to cook the rice (can no longer have children) she must strengthen (the home) by giving her own grand-daughter, by giving a concubine to the substitute (of her deceased husband).

Thus afraid that the seed be lost, afraid there will be no more children, because the head is getting old, the leaf of tobacco withers.

If she can no longer have children, if she does not want the home to crumble, the house to fall in ruins, the posts of the fence pulled up;

for the human race not to die out, she will again re-tie, for the root not to weaken, she will strengthen it, she will see to it that she is replaced by her grand-daughter because she wants the field worked, the family well protected, well taken care of, well fed, as beautiful and good as always, she wants the human race to carry on, buds like the tree "mo'ar", multiplies always.

In this case, a concubine must be given.

page 136 #101 Of old woman must give a concubine to her substitute.

When the head of the spouse gets old, when her face is wrinkled, her hair white and falling out, her lips sagging, she can no longer cook rice, make soup, she cannot see to weave belts and vests for her young substitute;

when the beam is rotten, it must be replaced, when the rafter weak it must be strengthened, when the woman is old, she must give (choose) one of her granddaughters and offer her as a concubine to the substitute of her husband.

Because the substitute is young and strong, his face is fresh, he is still agile, he is solid and can still work the field, he wants someone to follow him to carry the water, to bring him rice, he wants someone to weave his belt and vest (he wants a young woman).

He wants a large family like in the old days, a family of a thousand bellies, he wants children like before afraid that the dyke breaks, the path no longer visible because his wife is old, her eyes do not see, her face is wrinkled like a dry leaf of tobacco, she can no longer have children.

When the woman or man is old, it is done so. It has always been the custom, since the time of the elders; this has not been invented lately, since today, it has always been the custom.

page 137 #102 Of marriage of an adult man with a too young woman, if the man is unfaithful to his wife, it is not a big deal.

If the wife is still a little girl with her breasts not yet developed, not yet knowing to want a man;

if she still has small breasts, the vulva is narrow, if she still acts like a young girl;

if her hair is not cut, her teeth not yet filled, if she does not know how to do anything,

if she is still a child playing on the ground, if she still has to hold on to climb the steps, if she still cannot be away from her parents,

if she still sleeps on the mattress, if she still wraps herself up in the blanket, still looks for her father and mother;

her husband will have to wait until she grows up, since she still does not know how to prepare the soup, cook the rice, offer the tobacco and the betel, want the husband.

If her husband has his legs on the road and the hands in the woods, if he has some relations with another woman (married or not) there in no matter against him. [Judgment illegible]

page 138 #103 Of the too young husband who does not yet want a woman; his wife can have a lover without it being a big deal.

What disappeared, must be replaced, what is weak, must be strengthened, it is the custom to always replace.

If the struts are broken, they must be replaced, if the floor is broken, it must be repaired, if this one dies, he must be replaced by that one, if one wants nephews who follow in front and behind, one must always take (the substitute) in the family of the dead, even if he is a little boy as high as one's knee or hips.

Afraid that the home crumbles, the house falls in ruins, the words do not tell of the sadness.

If (the substitute) does not yet know how to clean around the field, cut the bunches of weeds, scream at the parrots, it does not matter; if he is ignorant, he will be taught, if he is dumb/mute, he will be taught by gesture, if he is lazy to work the field, he will be taught to work hard.

She, the woman, knows the problem, she is the trained elephant, she is already a mother, she can watch over all the work.

If she meets a man and lures him into the forest to play, she can do it without committing a fault, but she must well prepare the rice and the vegetables, weave well the belt and vest for the substitute.

Her eyes must not be heavy (sad), her head not tired, she must not hate talking or laughing with her substitute. There is no problem since he is still young.

page 139 #104 Of replacing the deceased to have another chief.

When the joints are weak, they must be replaced, when the floor is broken, it must be repaired, when the chief of the village dies, one must summon the wild banana trees, the sisters, to renew, to give a substitute, to put somebody on the chief's bed, to hold the cover of the basket of goods, to have someone to keep the dishes and the gongs, to have someone who commands the inhabitants like the deceased did.

Someone must be given to stay on the chief's bed, to sit on his ladder, to keep the wife and the children of the deceased.

This by fear that the home crumbles, the house fall into ruins, the words not tell of sadness.

Afraid that the sparrow hawk brothers, the spirits of the village, the brothers and the nephews be scattered in the fields, scattered among the rice, afraid that they spread everywhere.

In the old field, they plant banana trees, in the new field, they plant pineapple; to the substitute, a dowry no matter how small will be given, they will sacrifice a pig for the father (of the substitute), a sow for the mother, in order that the substitute, works well the earth, cultivates well the field, plants cucumbers and corn.

The elephants will again be shackled, the gongs hung, the talk of marriage renewed.

page 140 #105 Of too young substitute who becomes chief, the chief's son must help him.

He who cannot walk, they carry him, he who cannot eat, they chew his food, he who does not know the business, they teach him.

He who cannot climb the mountain, they help him in pulling, he who does not know how to come down the slope, they help him by holding him back, he who knows nothing, they will instruct him so that he knows.

If (the substitute) is still a young child, he is like a young girl, if the print of his foot is not yet equal to an adult's,

if he has not yet traveled, if he has not been everywhere, if he has seen nothing nor heard anything;

if he is only a child, he must be taught, if he is only a young man, he must be advised, if he is like the young male or female elephant, he must be trained.

He must be helped from behind and in front, he must be taught to speak and to debate.

For this, the son of the chief helps him to take care of the affairs of the village because he is like the horsefly which does not yet know it way, the bee which does not yet know her nest, he does not yet know how to watch over the inhabitants of the village.

page 141 #106 Of the woman who, having no children, adopts a girl of her clan; at her death, all her goods go to the child she had adopted.

She who is infertile and cannot have children, no daughter (to keep) the seed of the seed of the paddy [family name], no child high up to her knee or hip, she looks to adopt the child of her older or younger sister; if she does not find one there, she will go to others, in families of the same clan.

This because she has no one to go get wood or draw water, to do the field and work for her;

because she is afraid that if she has a stomach ache or a head ache if she has no appetite, she will have nobody to tend the fire, to bring her water, to cook the rice and the vegetables, to weave her skirts and vests;

because she is afraid that if she becomes sick, she will not have anybody to keep and care for her, if she dies, nobody to close her eyes and tie up her feet, to put up the funeral posts and make her coffin, afraid to have nobody to wrap her (in a mat or blanket);

because she is afraid of not having anyone to kill the oxen and the buffalo which she owns, nobody to dig her grave and bury her.

For this, all the good she owns, she will leave to the child she adopted and [she] will receive the full inheritance.

page 142

But if the adopted child does not work well for her (her adoptive mother), if she does not do well in the field, if when (her mother) is sick, she does not take care of her and does not nurse her, if she does not do well the ritual sacrifices, if she abandons the field and the hut, if she eats somewhere else, if when her adoptive mother dies, she does not wrap and bury well the body, does not put up the funeral posts and does not have a beautiful coffin made, she did not give her the nursing when she was sick,

she will not be able to inherit all the goods that the adoptive parents have, she will leave naked, without taking anything, she will not be allowed one piece of her parents, she will have to leave the house with nothing.

But if she took slight care of her adoptive mother, helped her a little, she will be able to inherit a little.

page 143 #107 Of the infertile woman who adopts a girl of sisters or family.

She to whom the gods have given no daughter, no son, who cannot have children,

She can take the child of her older or younger sister, if she cannot find one, she will have nothing but to look elsewhere, and the child she will adopt will become her own as though she had given birth.

This because she is afraid that having a headache or a stomachache, being sick and unable to feed herself, there will be no one to cook the rice, to bring her water and tend the fire, nobody to talk with;

because she wants someone to guide her steps, to hold her up by the arm, because she wants a child who would be for her as though a child from her bell;

because she is afraid of not having someone to cook the rice, to prepare the vegetables, to weave the skirts and the vests;

because she wants someone to close her eyes (at her death), to tie up her feet, bury her body, put up funeral posts and have a coffin made, to wrap her (in a shroud).

For this, all bowls in the shape of a nest of a sparrow hawk, the basins in the shape of a vulture's nest, everything that her ancestors left her, will go to (her adopted daughter), the little saucers, the little copper bowls, all the small objects, the cracked pots, the rice bowls, the jars in the pits, the cauldrons from the country "Hrue" [today?], the pots from the country "Enin" , all the goods in the house will go to her adopted daughter (at her death).

page 143

For this, she adopts a girl to keep the seed of the rice, to have a child who reaches her knee or hip, because she is afraid that her family will disappear, her family die out. [no girl - no family because tribe is matrilineal].

page 144 #108 Of not replacing the deceased spouse: the family of the deceased loses her share of the inheritance.

Everywhere they put the rafters on the beams, everywhere from West to East, when someone dies, the custom says he must be replaced, to give a substitute; it is always the custom to replace what has disappeared, to always fill in the emptiness.

But if instead they do not replace the deceased, if they do not give a substitute, if they do not want to renew with the nephews of the deceased;

if they do not repair the broken joists, redo the damaged floor, replace by another the one who died;

if they do not repair the chipped hoe, the broken flints, come and co needlessly,

whereas the pigs have been killed, the buffalo sacrificed (for the deceased funeral), the children's mistakes absolved by a sacrifice,

whereas the sick had been well nursed, well watched over, had not lacked of alcohol and rice,

whereas they have not been greedy with oxen and buffalo the sacrificed what was needed to heal the sick,

whereas (the funeral mound) of the grave is not cracked, the coffin did not raise, the widow grieved properly and respected all things banned,

why then is there nobody to re-tie- why do not they give the widow a substitute?

But if they (the deceased's family) have no pity for the abandoned field (the widow), for the old founder, if they have no pity for the widow,

page 145

the family of the deceased will have no claim to any share of the inheritance, it will be allowed only a small hoe, a small machete, an ordinary crossbow with a bow , one sandal only, a small knife to cut and that will be all. [Judgment(s) not translated]

page 146 #109 Of the indissolubility of the union.

They love and want each other, the man and the woman, they have agreed to live together.

They have exchanged the pearl necklace, exchanged the bracelet of this one to that one, the woman's bracelet to the man, the man's bracelet to the woman, they exchanged it on their own, freely.

The horse is not forced to wear the harness; the buffalo to accept the rope, the man and the woman, nobody forced them to accept the bracelet and the necklace.

They have asked the chief to hold u the elephant, to hang the gongs, to sign the contract, (now) they are like the bow and the shaft of the crossbow, they are husband and wife.

Afraid that later they do like the male bird in the morning, the female bird in the evening , that entering in the woods, they look for an affair.

One must stay with his wife till death, one must drink the alcohol until it becomes tasteless, strike the gong (without stopping) until another takes the drumstick.

Afraid at night the man speaks one way and in the day another way, in turning his back, he thinks differently.

page 147

He has been well advised, afraid he does not search the earth looking for ginger, pull up at night what he planted in the morning.

It is not the storms or the Spirits of the Sky, it is not sickness which separates them, all of a sudden, without motive, they want to leave each other.

They ignore the sign "kung" [prohibited] and the sign "Knong" [boundary], they ignore the words of the chief (who had educated them).

Like the fire jumping the chasm, the flood over the dam, they ignore the talk and the words of the chief.

If they try to create problems, they will be punished as is punished the greedy dog with a (hot) eggplant, as is punished one who is arrogant towards the chief because the husband must always follow the wife, always he must go with her to the field.

If they act like this, it is not a very serious matter.

But if they have the teeth filed, if the bracelet which was sealed, is open, if they ignore the sign "tiet" [tall grass] and are hurt by some darts, if they ignore the sign "pla" [warning] and are hurt by lancets [of traps], if they ignore the words of the chief and the talk of marriage, then there is a problem between the chief and them. [Judgment(s) not translated]

page 148 #110 Of non-consummation of marriage.

The man and the woman, the young man and the young girl have been advised.

One forces the horse to carry the pack saddle, the buffalo to accept the rope in his muzzle, but no one forces the man and the woman to get married,

afraid that they talk one way at night and another way during the day, afraid that having turned their backs, they act differently.

Today they agree freely, one accepts the bracelet of the other, without dreaming that later they might be lazy to hoe, tired to clear the land, without thinking that another day or another month, they would no longer want to live together.

Now they have exchanged the necklace, they have exchanged the bracelet, the man's bracelet to the woman, the woman's bracelet to the man.

The dowry has been given, the pig eaten, the alcohol drunk.

The goods have been given, the dowry, the money, everything has been given,

The bracelet is on the ground, the necklace on the floor, the parents and witnesses were present, if you want the woman, take her freely, the bracelet is on the ground, we are your witnesses, we do not force you to take [her] afraid that later you criticize us for having forced you to accept.

But if you accept freely and later you decline to live together, then you will be guilty and there will be a problem between the others (family of the wife or husband) and you.

Antomarchi's Notes: Page 148

Cf. Code Hittite: "If a man the girl does not take yet refuses, then the purchase price of the woman that gave it."

page 149 #111 Of he who leaves his wife as soon as she has a child and no longer takes care of them.

He who has no home, no field, who goes one way and leaves his wife the other way;

he who eats the vegetables in one house and the rice in another, goes home, takes a step back, goes back to his family;

he who does not build the straw hut , does not work the field, does not even think of putting up traps, who does not take care of his wife and children, that one is guilty.

page 150 #112 Of the lazy ones who do not take care of their wives and children, and only wander.

He who is lazy to build the straw hut, to work the field, to cut down the trees and prepare the ground;

he who does not build the straw hut, does not work the field, who never thinks of working;

he who eats vegetables in this house, rice in another, who lies down where he goes, spends the night wherever he happens to be;

he who spends the night where he eats, sleeps where he drinks, who spends months and years everywhere he happens to go;

he who wanders and has no gourds to eat, who wanders and has no house to live in, has nowhere to sleep;

he who wanders like Y-Tria, who is fond of food like Y-Run, who is like the one who has no feet, no head;

he who does not take care of his wife and children, who only tries to be the young man with other women;

he who falls asleep and does not wake up, who lies down and does not get up, does not listen to his parents who give him advise, that nobody can correct;

he who does not think of starvation, whose ears remember nothing, who does not try to get out of his poverty and misery,

that one is guilty and must deal with others and himself.

page 151 #113 Of obstacles to marriage.

If the joints are broken, they repair them, if the floor is broken, they repair it, if someone dies, they re-tie, that which is weak, they strengthen, they must always replace.

She (the widow) wants the bones (a substitute), she prefers the meat, she wants with all her belly and all her heart, afraid that the home crumbles, the house falls into ruins, the words do not tell of the sadness, afraid of not having someone to carry on the hips, afraid of having nobody to take care of the children of the widow, the children of the deceased.

For this, the broken tie must be re-tied, what is about to break must be strengthened, the brothers-in-law must give (the substitute) and accept the bracelet to have someone to look after the children, to look after the good like before, the straw hut does not fall, the fence is not pulled out.

The mother gives birth (to the child), the father carries it, however they (the brothers-in-law) act like the male bird in the morning, the female bird in the evening, when they enter the forest, they act differently.

In the morning they plant, in the evening they pull up; at night they give (the substitute), in the morning they take him back.

At night they speak one way, in the day time they speak another way, as soon as they turn their backs they act differently.

They turn around without stopping like the eggplant and the pepper (in the pot), they cut everything inside out (in the wrong way).

They draw beautiful figures (make beautiful promises) but the sacred words they deny, they look for new troubles while singing.

page 152

Before they hid the spoon, the words, the day they forget to take the vest (they don't think), they ignore the words of the chief, the words of the brothers, the bracelet on the wrist, the witness, the flute in the mouth, they ignore all this.

For this there is a problem between the others (widow, witness, chief) and them (the brothers-in- law).

page 153 #114 Of adultery.

He who goes into the chambers, enters into the bedroom, brushes against the wife of the rich, the wife of the brother, who takes her in hiding;

he who looks for a favorable corner, who lures the woman to talk to her in a low voice;

he who holds up the elephant or hangs the gongs in hiding, who has a secret talk, who gets along with someone else's wife;

he who thinks he is powerful, thinks he is strong and daring, who gets over the steep mountain, who tries to have the wife of the rich.

He who wants someone else's wife to be his, who wants her to fall into his power;

he who grabs the horn of the rhinoceros, the tusk of the elephant, who grabs the wife of the rich;

he who cuts the tail of the elephant, who breaks the bowl for the taxes, who touches the wife of the rich,

he is guilty and must deal with others and himself.

ANTOMARCHI'S NOTES: PAGE 153

[Judgment(s) not translated]

Note: Cf. Code Hittite: "If a man, in the mountains, grabs a wife, it is a crime by the man and he dies. But if he grabs her in the house, the wife has also sinned, the wife dies. If the man (husband) finds them, he can kill them and there will be no punishment for him." (p. 149)

page 154 #115 Of adultery between a man and a woman already married.

It is not necessary to talk a lot, to go further because the rhinoceros and the elephant drank at the same place.

It is not necessary to speak loudly, to debate in a high voice;

because the matter is clear, the bush has spread.

To eat, one does not need to crush, to chew, one does not need to move his tongue, to settle this matter one does not need to yell loudly.

The man and the woman have confessed the turban, the vest, the saber, the machete; all kinds of objects have been seized (as proof).

They are certain that they went to hide in the forest.

The man has accepted the judges decision (has confessed), the woman has confessed to adultery, the elephant and the rhinoceros have been seized by the tails, also they have been caught in the place, in the act.

Their heads are like that of the porcupine, their ears like those of the mouse (ignorant), they have looked for evil, for a fault,

this one already has a wife, that one already has a husband, each one has his or her own straw hut and basket.

She who has cheated on her husband will pay him a fine, he who has cheated on his wife will pay her a fine.

Because they were hiding between a blanket in front, and a bundle of sticks in the back, she has a husband and cheated on him, he has a wife and cheated on her.

Their parents gave them advice but they did not listen, they love playing the flute until their death.

For this they are guilty.   [Judgment(s) not translated]

page 155 #116 Of the widow guilty of adultery when the grave of her husband is not yet deserted.

The grave is not yet covered, the burial mound not finished, they still attend to the soul of the body.

And the tomb opens and the coffin goes up because the widow does not mourn well,

because she does not let her hair fall in a mess, because she does not put her chin in her hands, because she does not mourn well her deceased husband, rotten like a grain of paddy.

She sleeps with everybody, with two or three, with a hundred or a thousand lovers.

The bag of tobacco, she divides in two (one for the dead, one for her lover), the pack of salt she divides in three, in hundreds, in thousands because she wants two, three, a hundred, a thousand lovers.

She seduces the men, she sleeps with the husbands, she takes them into the forest.

When the tomb is hardly covered, when the burial mound is still kept, when they are not finished taking care of the dead, when the banana tree and the potato have not yet been planted (on the burial mound), when the chick has not yet been let go (in the ditch), when the dead is not yet forgotten, when the tomb is not yet deserted.

For this she is guilty and must deal with the family of the dead and herself (the unfaithful widow).

If the family of the dead is poor, she will sacrifice a pig worth two piasters and pay a fine of twelve piasters.

If the family of the dead is rich, she will sacrifice one buffalo and pay a fine of twenty piasters.

page 156 #117 Of the widow who wants to remarry before the tomb is deserted, if the family of the dead cannot give her a substitute, it can authorize her to take one somewhere else.

The rice is rotten, the body in putrefaction, all is well ended, little brother (of the dead) there is none, nephew (son of the sister of the dead) there is none (to replace the dead).

The older sisters (of the dead) have been consulted, the younger sisters have been heard, the matter of the substitute has been viewed and settled.

To replace the dead, the give a substitute, to the widow, there is nobody, (and the family of the dead says to the widow):

If the cucumber and the corn can reproduce alone (man cannot), if you see the man of the village in the West or East and you like him, you can get married.

Afraid that your home crumbles, your house falls in ruins, the words not tell of desperation,

afraid that you will have no one to clean around the field, to cut the invading clumps [of weeds], to scream at the female parrots and the parrots (who come to eat the rice);

afraid that your child cries, your field invaded with weeds, that you have no more straw hut, baskets,

afraid that you have nobody to feed your pigs, to take care of your hens, nobody to talk to the inhabitants;

page 117

afraid that you have nobody to take care of the elephants, to order your slaves, to make rice wine in jars, you can look yourself for the husband you want.

We will not oppose by force, by words, we will not stop you from choosing a husband.

We will not look for a matter [over which to argue], we will not ask for compensation, but you will sacrifice a pig on the grave, sacrifice a chicken on the tomb of the dead, you will drink rice wine during the sacrifice so the spirits know, the soul of the dead know.

So there will be no problem, and we will exchange the bracelet to seal our agreement.

page 158 #118 Of taking away the husband or wife of somebody else.

He who believes himself fearsome and climbs the steep mountain;

he who grabs the horn of the rhinoceros or the tusk of the elephant, who takes away the wife of the rich or his brother;

he who does not take into account the advice of his mother or father, who does not listen when they discuss matter while singing;

he who measures the handle of the hoe or the handle of the machete, who compares his strength (to the strength of the husband),

he who measures the length of the beam in feet, the length of the rod in cubits, who counts the jars and the gongs,

that one is guilty and there is a very serious problem between the others and himself.

For a poor (husband) he pays an indemnity of six "ko" and one pig of one "ko" for the sacrifice; if the husband is rich, he will pay him an equal indemnity of the value of one gong "char" and of great width , and a buffalo for sacrifice.

And if (the woman taken away) prefers the flower "tông-mông", if she prefers the multicolored feathers, if she prefers her abductor (to her husband),

page 159

all the goods, the cups, the little copper bowls, all the little objects, the Jarai baskets, the trays, the bags, the satchels, the little packages, the big and small jars,

the horses, the oxen and the buffalo, the pigs under the house, the chickens on the overhang, the bracelets and the necklaces, the dishes, everything will stay with the one who carries the crossbow and the quiver (the husband).

They will appraise the house, measure the fields in length and width,

they will wrap the little pieces of meat in a paper cone, they will string the big pieces on a skewer, they will count the number of heads of deer and boars (killed by the deserted husband).

If he has killed a small amount of game, the indemnity will be small, if he killed many, it will be many (this if he is poor), if he is rich they will assess [his value and consequent payment].   [Judgment(s) not translated]

page 160 #119 Of the woman who seduces the husband of her sister.

She who grabs the red thread or the black thread, the pot for vegetables or the pot of rice, the husband of her older or younger sister;

she who grabs the husband of her older or younger sister, to make hem hers, who acts like she was a stranger (of the clan), if the older sister commits this fault, she covers herself with shame in the eyes of everyone.

Because she is born of the same back, the same root, the same mother who carried them in her belly, they cannot impose a fine on what is evil, it is the husband will stay with both women, but she will be only a concubine; then a pig will be sacrificed for all three, they will offer it to the and to the dead so that they know; so that they still can work their fields, grow corn and cucumbers, the millet will come up, the rice grows well and gives beautiful grains.

As for the husband, he will pay a fine to his wife (because he cheated on her).

page 161 #120 Of those who sleep with their slave, that one will be emancipated.

The gray cat, the black cat which usually stays on the cover of the basket, comes down to eat the food of the pigs and the dogs.

He, the man, goes into the forest with his water carrier slave, with the one who works the field, who does the cooking for him.

If she is unhappy, he soothes her with tobacco, with bark and betel, if she resists, he tempts her with a bracelet, with a necklace so she will give in; not giving in she is afraid that the knife will be taken out of its scabbard, the saber comes out, she is afraid of the one who bought her (she cannot refuse).

After this, if the wife sees her husband crushing the dead leaves, if she sees the slave with bark on her head, if she sees them in the bushes, the slave and the man, she will seize them by the hair, by the head, she will seize the turban, the vest and will show them to her brothers-in-law.

If she confesses, if the man confesses, there will be no need to discuss the time and the mistress slave will be free like the cricket or the grasshopper, like the rice outside, her body will be free and she will go back to her family.

As for the husband, he will pay a fine to his wife; if he is poor, he will sacrifice to her a pig of one "song" and pay her a fine of three "ko". If he is rich, he will sacrifice a buffalo and pay her a fine of six "ko".

page 162 #121 Of the woman who leaves her husband to remarry with his slave.

Her parents looked for a husband for her, her brothers had a hard time finding one, the husband agreed, the woman accepted him, the gongs were hung, the shellac and the resin glued to the tree, all the brothers warned ,with the blood of the buffalo and the ox they have been joined, the dowry has been paid (to the parents of the husband), the pig eaten, the rice wine drunk; the maternal aunts, the cousins, her own took part in the sacrifices.

She did not even stay with her husband until evening, not even morning and already she looks for another husband; she prefers the white flower, the multicolored flower, she prefers the slave of her parents who is in the house; for this she leave her husband in the valley, in the gully, she leaves without motive.

She will pay him a fine and like the little one of the ox or the buffalo who comes back to its mother, like the little one of the pig or the chicken who comes back to its mother, the husband will go back to his parents.

She takes the basket in the West and puts it in the East, she takes the cushion in the common room and takes it into her bedroom, she takes the slave who is in the house and makes him her husband.

Her parents give her advice and she does not follow it, they instruct her and she does not listen, she acts like a fool and an idiot.

She has a mouth as large as the opening of the hoop, big like the round basket; she is a girl who can no longer be put right.

page 163

Her new husband is lazy to build the straw hut, to work the field, lazy to hoe and clear the ground, he eats the goods of his parents-in-law that he obtained easily.

When he has had enough to eat, he goes to bed, when he has had too much to drink he falls asleep, he tries only to eat the goods of his parents-in-law.

If he lacks vegetables or rice, he buys some with his wife's money, but he never thinks to work the field; the oxen and the buffalo, the flat gongs and the blown-up gongs , the jars, all the goods, all the inheritance from his parents-in-law, he sells everything, he eats all;

because of this they are both guilty.

page 164 #122 Of suspicion.

He who hits with the arrow, who hits with the broom, who suspects others without motive;

the man who talks a lot of rubbish, the woman who talks without knowing what she says, those who talk like the blind (who do not see anything), the deaf (who do not hear), who get angry without motive;

those who suspect everyone, who throw the sparrow hawk into dirty water, who insults the child of the rich (child of the chief) without motive (who suspects) the innocent man or woman,

if they are sure that the man is making love in the forest, why did they not catch him by his hood, why did they not seize him solidly by the arm in order to recognize his face; if he dropped his knife or his turban, why did they not pick them up?

But they hear the wind growling around, they hear the thunder rumbling behind the fence, and they believe everything told on the road to the forest or the spring.

Those who hold the stick in hand and look to hit right and left, who try to whisper bad words,

those are guilty; they are like the sorcerer who accepts everything he is told, like the bad spirits who grant all the curses; they are wrong to believe everything they hear.

For this, there is a problem between others and themselves.

If they have suspected a poor person, they will sacrifice a pig of 1$00, if the person is rich, a pig of 4$00 [sic].

page 165 #123 Of slanderous accusations of adultery.

Those who hit with the arrow, who hit with the broom, who are jealous without motive;

The jealous man who speaks without knowing anything, the jealous woman who talks without thinking, those who speak like the blind and deaf,

if they see a man and a woman in the woods, that they seize them by the hand, like one seizes the tail of the elephant or the rhinoceros who wants to run away, they catch them at the place, on the fact.

Those who are jealous and insult the mother or the father without motive, who abuse people rudely and accuse them without motive, those are guilty because they did not try to see over the house, over the trees, across the partition, because they have not watched, they have not spied in the night without anyone knowing.

Because they act like those with the oxen and the buffalo who hit them on the backs (to see if they are nasty).

The paddy in the granary, one must look to see if there is any, the bowl of bamboo, one must slit it open to see if there are insects inside (to be guilty, they must be caught in the act).

If they accuse those who are innocent like the white rice, innocent like the fruit "êpang", like a ray of the sun; if they accuse the innocent man and woman like the Bih and Mnong strangers,

the man will be free, the woman will be released, the Bih or Mnong will be innocent.

If they accuse the poor because of jealousy, they will sacrifice for him a pig of 1$00, the rich, a pig of 4$00 [sic].

page 166 #124 Of one of the spouses who catches in the act of adultery the other without witnesses.

If one has caught (the guilty one) all alone, when nobody has seen or heard anything;

if one did not bring friends, did not call a friend, did not warn two, three, four, or five persons;

if one tries to whip (the lover) with the arrow, tries to his with the broom, is jealous without motive, unable to show proof;

if one has caught the culprits as in a net, has caught them as on a line, has laid a hand on them, caught like the sparrow hawk and the weasel catch their prey;

if one offers the filet or the shoulder (of beef) to the chief to try to bribe him and to be probed right;

if one caught the culprits without proof, without witness, if one accuses the brothers without reason,

because one wants a straight tree, a sharp machete, a nimble and strong man (wants to get reparation)

there is no matter (of adultery).

page 167 #125 Of slanderous accusations of adultery.

He who tries to pronounce guilty the innocents, who disturbs the healer, accuses others without proof;

he who pulls the straw from the straw hut, the others, who is beautiful , who introduces trouble into the peaceful house, who drags the snakes onto the mat and blanket of quiet people.

He who slanders very quiet people, the rich people without reason.

He who has nobody to go up into his house and to advise him, nobody to come down from his house to instruct him, nobody to trample the rice field with the elephant or the rhinoceros .

He who always wants mushrooms, eggplants, always feels like doing something bad.

He who catches the others in the act, the man in the thicket, the woman in the bush, he should seize them by the hood, forcibly by the arm, recognize their faces without mistake.

If the woman runs away, let him grab her scarf or her vest, if the man runs away, let him grab his saber, his machete or any other objects, this way there will be certainty.

And to eat, it will not be necessary to chew, to swallow, it will not be necessary to chew, if one has proof there will not be much discussion.

If one grabs only objects belonging to the man or the woman, there will be no affair (not enough proof).

page 168

 But if one has seized objects of both sides, objects of the woman, objects of the man, one will stay on the tree of beehives or the tree with resin, everyone will be informed, then they will go inform the chief.

And if one person has been informed, three persons have been told, if a hundred, a thousand persons have heard, they will have sure proof and there will be an affair.

Otherwise, like the tiger, one will have kicked in the emptiness, like the deer who gave a thrust in the emptiness and the chief will not be able to judge (for lack of proof). [Judgment(s) not translated]

page 169 #126 Of accusations of adultery without proof.

He who accuses innocent persons without reason, who accuses the rich without motive, if he is certain that the man and the woman went into the forest to make love, that they went in the bushes to hide, why did he not seize the turban, the vest, the saber, the machete or the objects belonging to them?

If they ray away, why did he not grab the pig, the vest or the scarf?

Why did he not grab the man and the woman by the hand, remember where they were lying, the place where they rolled out the mat and the blanket, let those near by see and touch, in that case he would have had real proof.

If the man had crushed leaves on the ground, if the woman had twigs in her hair, it would be proof that they went into the forest, that they lay down in the bushes, in the thicket and they would be sure that the man and the woman were joined.

If one sees frogs mating, toads mating, if one catches the culprits in the act, grabs them by the hand, one is sure (of their guilt).

Of the man one will seize the turban, of the woman the skirt and they will be introduced to the banyan of the spring, the fig tree of the village, to the one who watches over the nephews and the brothers, the inhabitants of the village.

But if instead he accepts the decision of the stick, the words of the sorcerer, the stories that people tell, if like the sorcerers and the devils, he believes everything he is told,

then he is guilty and there is a problem between the others and himself. [Judgment(s) not translated]

page 170 #127 Of spouses who leave each other when there is a contract.

If the husband and the wife are already joined, if the flat gongs and the larger gongs are already hung, if the marriage contract is already sealed;

If they leave each other without reason, if they make the fault when there has been no problem, if the husband of the sister and the wife of the brother leave each other without motive;

if the elephants have already been shackled, if the gongs are already hung, if the contract has joined them like the bow on the shaft of the crossbow, the husband to the wife (if one leaves the other), he will have to pay back (the dowry).

To those who have kept the flute in their mouth, those who accepted the bracelet of guarantee, to those who spoke and organized the union (the witnesses) they must ask the conditions in the contract.

If the elephant has been well shackled, if the gongs have been well hung, if the talks have been well sealed it [the dowry] must be reimbursed as agreed.

If the bracelet which was closed is open, if the welded bracelet is broken, if the horses and the elephants go in different pastures, if the necklaces have been exchanged, the man's bracelet will be given back to the woman, the woman's to the man, and in that way there will be no more matters; the husband will be able to look for a [new] wife, the wife for another husband.   [Judgment(s) not translated]

page 171 #128 Of the one who breaks the contract by leaving his wife to take another.

She goes up the steps to the bedroom, crosses the common room, looks for her husband, because she has nobody to clear around the field, to cut the bamboo, she no longer has nobody to help her.

She sends her brothers to ask her husband (why he left).

Yet he had been willing, he had accepted the bracelet, his mouth had said yes.

The brothers and the uncles (of the wife) had brought the rice and the chicken (to the family of the husband), they had bothered to get him, to take him to the house.

The pig had been killed, the rice wine prepared, all the village had been invited,

the feet had been joined, the feet of the husband and those of the wife had been united, like the bow and the [shaft of the] crossbow.

A boar had been sacrificed for the father-in-law, a sow for the mother-in-law, the dowry paid, the pig eaten, the rice wine drunk by the whole family, the sisters, the aunts, the uncles, the brothers, all reunited for this [affair].

Then given eight bracelets, a blanket, a belt, a copper bowl, to pay back the mother who brought him up (the man).

In this way, the elephant had been well shackled, the gongs well hung, the contract sealed, afraid that he gets bored hitting the gongs and [they], looking at the other.

page 172

The sacrifice of the pig and the rice wine have been offered to the parents, the witnesses paid.

But now, he (the husband) speaks one way in the morning, another way at night, he turns his back and acts differently.

He wants the yellow flower in the forest, the red flower in the bushes, he sees another woman and wants her.

He leaves his wife because he is bored, he leaves because he does not love her anymore and he goes to live in another village.

He ignores the signs "kung" and "knông", he ignores the words of the chief, he breaks the contract, he slits the mouth of those who advise him; the bracelet he had accepted is open.

For this he is guilty and there is an affair between others and himself. [Judgment(s) not translated]

page 173 #129 Of those who get married without telling the chief.

Those who get married alone, without telling, without warning anybody,

without telling the banyan of the spring, the fig tree of the village, the one who watches over the brothers, the nephews, all the inhabitants;

those, husband and wife, who live together (cohabit), who get married without telling anyone,

without the elephant being shackled, the gongs hung, the contract sealed.

Those who do not say anything for others to know, who do not tell that they got married;

those who go by the high house, step over the low house, who look down on the house (of the chief) where they eat beef and buffalo;

those who jump over the puddle, who step over the torrent, who ignore the chief's orders,

(those are guilty and) must deal with the chief and themselves. [Judgment(s) not translated]

page 174 #130 Of he who emigrates to another country and abandon his wife to take a foreign wife.

He who takes his legs in the East, his head in the West, his legs in the North, his head in the South, who goes anywhere;

he who abandons his wife in the common room, leaves her in a corner, without thinking about her, without any regrets;

he who wants the yellow flower in the thicket, the red flower in the field, who, seeing another woman, wants to live with her;

he who is similar to the horse or the buffalo which break their bonds and that one follows by their tracks, if he leaves, his wife will follow and look for him.

He who acts as though he had a porcupine's head, a mouse's ears, who has many problems;

he who settles somewhere else forever, who builds his own straw hut and works the field in another country, in the country of strangers;

he who eats the fruit of the [illegible-check Edé] without opening it the nut of without spitting anything , who leaves for the country of strangers without telling the chief of the village;

he who eats a cucumber without telling his sister, the watermelon without telling his brother, who has an affair and does not tell his parents,

that one is guilty and there is a very serious problem between the others and him.

The pig and the buffalo to be sacrificed lose their body; he who looks for problems also risks his body (his life or liberty). [Judgment(s) not translated]

page 175 #131 Of he, who being married, has a child with a young girl.

The man already has the bow and the stock [of the crossbow], he is already married.

She (the young girl) is like the machete without a handle, like the crossbow without string; she is single, does not yet have a husband.

He wants her like one wants a green fruit, sweet vegetables; he wants her since yesterday, the day before yesterday.

If he wants her, he can have relations with her, but he must be careful, at the new moon the bracelet must be open, taken off and given back, the horse and the elephant must go in different pastures.

But if he stays with her until the tuber gives shoots, the potato bursts out of the ground, until the nipples darken, the chest is thrown out, the belly sticks out,

because of this, he will have to give the blanket to the midwife, the mat for the newborn baby, the knife to cut the bamboo (to cut the umbilical cord).

And to the young girl who will be alone to carry the child, he will have to pay for help, he will give her goods for the value of one "ko" and will sacrifice for her a pig and a jar of rice wine.

page 176 #132 Of he who is married with a woman and leaves her as soon as she has a child.

Those who get married alone, with no witness, no contract;

those who seeing a pig, feel like eating meat, seeing a jar, feel like drinking rice wine, who, meeting someone, feel like living together,

and never think of shackling the elephant, hanging the gongs, sealing the contract (of marriage);

he who stays with a woman until the tuber gives shoots, until the potato bursts upon the ground, until the nipples darken, until a child comes,

and then abandons her in the precipitous ravine, in the dry valley, abandon without reason;

since nobody forced the horse to carry the tether of the elephant, the buffalo to carry the rope around its neck, nobody forced him (the man) to exchange the necklace and the bracelet (with the woman),

he who has never asked his parents or his brothers to go and inform the parents of the young girl,

and who later does not want his wife anymore, does not want her in the morning or the evening, who is tired of his wife and does not want to live with her,

that one is guilty, he will pay his wife a fine in order that she can bring up her child, as if there was a breaking of contract.   [Judgment(s) not translated]

page 177 #133 Of the young man and the young girl who have relations until they have a child.

It is not a new thing; it does not date from today that everywhere the rafters are put upon the beams, from west to east, since always the young men and young girls look for each other.

But one must be careful, one must not go too far and when the new moon shows up, one must discontinue.

If they make love in the immediate surroundings of the village, they must hide from the father and the mother and since it is the custom that young men and young girls, men and women, look for each other, one must watch that the straw hut is in its place, the field well marked, the banana trees and sugar cane be well lined up (they must avoid incest).

But if they make love without modesty, love each other with no moderation, if when the new moon shows up, they do not put away the bracelet (they have exchanged), if they do not go each in his direction like the horses and the elephants;

if they see each other until the back (of the woman) becomes hollow, her belly shows, until the manioc has shoots, the tuber bursts upon the ground, until the nipples become brown, until there is a child,

for this the man is guilty, if he marries his mistress there is no problem.

But if he does not marry her, he will have to give her enough to buy a blanket for the midwife, a mat for the newborn, a knife to cut the blade of bamboo (for cutting the umbilical cord), a blanket, a belt (a skirt), all that is necessary to sew the placenta.

page 177

All this having a value of one "ko" and he will also give her a pig of one "song" for the sacrifice.

page 178 #134 Of the husband taken prisoner or slave; his wife does not have to wait for him and can remarry.

If the pigeon pecks on his eggs, if the kingfisher flies on top of the water, if the hair on the leg or the thigh sting, if the man has an affair he had looked for.

If the skewer pricks the meat, if the three-pronged fork pierces it, it is not the spirits doing it, if he made himself guilty it is because he wanted to.

If the wife waits too long, she loses weight, she becomes old and there will be no one to chase the female parrots and the parrots (from the field). The children will cry, the field [will be] full of weeds, the sack, the basket, the rice and the vegetables will be lacking.

There will be nobody to build the straw hut, work the field, chase the male and female parrots.

She has waited for him more than a year, several dry seasons; now one year has gone by, a new dry season has arrived; she cannot any longer, she wants a new husband.

What one person knows, three people see, a hundred, a thousand people hear well,

afraid that the others (the family of the husband) say that she abandoned her husband in the precipitous ravine, in the arid valley, that she abandoned him without motive.

Then she informs her brothers, her nephews, her brothers-in-law, her children, her grandchildren so that everyone knows and has heard.

page 179 #135 Of a woman whose husband has been gone for several years can remarry.

She cannot wait another year, another season, her body is getting old, she does not have a husband anymore.

She will have a headache and a bellyache, will have no appetite and there will be nobody to poke up the fire, to cover her, she will be alone and that is not good.

She will be hungry and there will be no one to get the tubers and the potatoes, nobody to dig (the ground) with the "knih" or the "kphal" (bamboo to dig).

There will be nobody to clear around the field, to cut the clumps of small shrubs, to chase the male and female parrots.

She can no longer wait, she had said nothing until now, but now she cannot stay without a husband.

She has waited long winters, long summers, she has waited until the cabbage palm has leaves, she has waited for the husband her parents had selected until now.

But he left his head in the East and his legs in the West, like the wild ox, since several years, several months; maybe he got lost, maybe he died; she can no longer be in mourning.

Then she will ask her brothers to find her another husband, to find someone who can work.

She will inform her family, her sisters, she will tell of the matter, she will tell her nephews, her brothers to keep them informed, she will give back the bracelet (to her husband's parents) since she will have waited during several years, several dry seasons, several rainy seasons, and she is able to look for a new husband .

Therefore, there will be no problems.

page 180 #136 Of he who leaves the village to look for another wife without getting a divorce from the first.

He already has a wife and a child, his feet have been joined [to hers].

The boar has been sacrificed to the father, the sow to the mother.

The goods have been given to his family, the dowry paid to his mother, the meat of the pig eaten, the rice wine drunk.

They have made the sacrifice to the aunts, to the sisters, to the mother (of the husband), the sacrifice of the chicken for everybody.

The elephant has been shackled, the gongs hung, the contract of marriage sealed.

The ignorant has been instructed, the mute told, the chief informed.

How he wants to leave to the South or the North; in the morning he stays in his father's house, in the evening in his mother's house, he does not build the straw hut, does not work in the field, does not think of what needs to be done, he does not set the traps, does not take care of his wife and his children.

He is like the bamboo swaying in the wind, like the portable stove, always moved, he wanders always in the East and West.

He eats the vegetables in one house, the rice in another, where he eats he goes to bed, where he drinks he falls asleep, where he goes he stays.

He sees the yellow flower in the field, the red flower among the ferns, he sees a woman and wants her.

He wants the flower "tômg-mông", he wants the polychrome plumes, he wants the woman he sees.

He loves her, hiding, in the woods, he loves her until they are like husband and wife, until they have children.

He no longer takes care of his first wife, he does not think about her.

page 181

He leaves her in the common room, in a corner, he forgets her and does not regret [leaving] her.

He leaves her in the ravine, the valley, the desert, he leaves her without roots and branches (without help).

He is afraid that like the tiger they know his strength, like the rabbit they discover its cunning, the boar and the deer, they know their hideout.

So he goes back, goes back to the watering place, goes back to the village to give back the dowry of his wife.

he opens the sealed bracelet and like the horse and the elephant who go in different pastures (they leave each other).

He is like the river before it overflows, the straw hut tied up in bundles, he loves his new wife and she loves him also, from before (his marriage).

For this he is guilty and has a very serious problem with others and himself.

The sacrificed pig dies, the sacrificed buffalo dies, if he looks for problems, he will incur grief. [Judgment(s) not translated]

page 182 #137 Of those who hit their wives until they are wounded.

He who debates with his wife, if he hits her with all his strength, beyond all moderation, if he hits her until blood spurts out, the flesh torn open, the bones are broken, the teeth broken in her mouth;

if he hits properly, with moderation, there is no problem.

But if he hits until the blood spurts out, the bile spreads through the body, the soul escapes definitely [illegible].

For this there will be a problem.

And if the wife dies, he will have to pay the value of the body, if she is only wounded, he will pay an indemnity. [Judgment(s) not translated]

page 183 #138 Of abortions.

(One reproduces) like the seeds of tobacco being spread, like plants with large leaves who grow to multiply and make the race survive.

But the woman who hides to empty her belly, to tear up her womb, to kill a child,

That one is guilty and must deal with herself.   [Judgment(s) not translated]

page 184 #139 Of slanderous accusations of abortions.

He who slanders with the mouth, who has long teeth, who thinks only of slandering;

he who slanders the poor or the rich without reason;

he who rubs others with the fruit of the creeper "sam-niêng" to give them the scabies (when they don't have them), who pricks them with an awl to give them pimples, who creates problems to those who don't have any;

he who accuses a woman of hiding to empty her belly, to massage her womb in order to kill her child, of her own initiative (without consulting her husband);

if it is true that this woman has emptied her belly, has crushed her womb to kill her child, there must be at least one person who knows, three people who have seen, a hundred and thousand who have heard talk;

but here nobody knows, no three who have seen, [nor] a hundred or a thousand who have heard talk;

he slanders the poor without reason, the rich without motive;

for this, there is a very serious problem between others and himself.

ANTOMARCHI'S NOTES: PAGE 184

Cf. [Judgment(s) not translated]: The culprit was condemned [to] one year of prison, and has to pay has the woman on whom it had calumny a reparation fine of 20$00[sic] and the price of the body (a large gong called char).

According to a principle of the Rhadée habit [,] the sanction pronounced against the slanderer must be equivalent to that which one would pronounce against the woman if it had fallen through.

page 185 #140 Of the woman who always gives birth to still-born babies; she can have an abortion without problems.

She who the spirits do not allow to have girls or boys, the gods do not give a numerous lineage like the germs, like the women with a hundred bellies, a thousand bellies;

she who usually gives birth to still-born boys or girls, who the spirits always make the seed disappear, like the man and the woman agreeing (to love each other), the husband and wife will agree to empty the belly, free the womb, make the fetus disappear when the wife is pregnant during a short time, a month or two.

And because of this, there will be no problem.

page 186 #141 Of the woman who aborts without her husband and her family knowing.

She who starts eating without telling, without warning, without even asking two or three persons;

who hides to empty her belly, to massage her womb, to kill her child by her own wish, not letting anybody know;

if she did not empty her belly and did not massage her womb, if she did not kill her child, that child could have been a girl and the spirits could have made her a midwife or a healer, it could have been a boy knowing how to hold the saber and the shield, to wage war and fight the enemies, knowing to look for jewels and dishes for his wife and his children, the spirits might have made him rich and powerful.

Everywhere, from East to West, people put rods on rafters on the beams; everywhere, in every country, people want the family to grow like the buds of the

"moar" tree, that girls and boys become many.

The rich who own oxen and buffalo offer them as sacrifice to have children, the poor sacrifice pigs and chickens.

She who dares stick in the stake, who has the guts (to abort), who climbs up the sharp mountain, who kills the child that the spirits gave her to increase the family.

She is guilty, and must deal with her husband and herself.

page 187 #142 Of the husband must entrust his wife with everything he owns.

They look for meat and fish to put in the pot; they work the rice field or the field for one's wife and children.

If the husband owns gongs, jars, horses, buffalo, copper trays, washbowls, small bowls, small cups, has any other goods, he must give them to his wife, for her to look after.

But if the wife does not prepare well the food, weave the cloth, carry the wood for heating, if she does not go get the water, if she does not roll down the mat, work well the field, the husband will be able to entrust his goods to his parents or his sisters.

But if she prepares well the meals, weaves well the cloth, clears well the field, works well the rice field, carries the wood and the water, rolls down the mat (to receive her husband), if she sweeps the house, prepares the cotton, if she weaves and spins well, if she takes good care of the mortar and pestle, takes care of all her work, the husband will not be able to give what he owns to his parents or his sisters.

If he gives his goods to his family, he will be guilty and there will be a matter between his wife and him.

Chapter VI

Page 188 #143 Of the parent's responsibility towards their children.

Those who cultivate the cucumbers and the corn, the parents who have children (must take care of them).

If the children do this or that, if they wander, are like the idiots, they eat too much, drink too much and vomit at the feet of the jars, near the gongs, if they go stealing, they rob and hide, if they stretch their hand to take whatever they can reach, everything bad a child can do,

the parents are responsible.

page 189 #144 Of girls who disobey their parents.

She who does not listen to the advice of her mother, does not obey the orders of her father, who clears the ground instead of hoeing, who ignores what is good.

She who does not accept what she is told, who refuses to obey, who plays the flute until losing her body, who never listens to the given advice;

she who accepts no advice, refuses the good words, who acts like a fool, who always wanders;

she who refuses to bring in the wood for heating, to work the field, never thinks of work;

she who does not want to pick the cotton, does not want to spin it, does not want to use the rice pestle, who refuses to work;

if she is like the rush which wants to go higher than the reeds, like the straw hut wanting to go higher than the bamboo, like the wild animals wanting to jump higher than the bushes;

if she wants to be stronger than the tiger, higher than the spirits, she opens her mouth insolently, like the pig destined to be sacrificed, it will lose its body, like the buffalo destined to be sacrificed, it will lose its body, if she has problems, she will lose her body.

Her parents will no longer be able to take care of her, they will no longer be able to defend her.

There will be no one to pick up the banana, no older sisters to receive her, no one to put back the handle onto the knife.

page 190 #145 Of girls who abandon their parents to go live in another village.

She who wishes for the "Mnong" buffalo, who covets the vest and the skirt, who abandons those who gave her birth to go live in another village;

she who acts like the mosquito without a family, like the fly without a mother, like those who have no parents;

she who leaves, her legs in the East, her feet in the West, like the wild ox;

she who wants the flower that no one must cut, who in order to have jewels prefers strangers to her parents;

she who abandons her parents forever, who leaves without hope of return like what is taken away by the river, abandons those who brought her up,

those who always kept her clean, nicely warm, spent bad nights, and who now will have no one to go get wood, to draw the water, to watch over the oxen and buffalo, to keep guard on their goods;

she who goes into an unknown forest, on the sharp mountain, in the country of the "Bih" or "Mnong" (where one never goes);

she ho acts like those who always have problems, if her parents have goods, they will pay for her fines or indemnities, but if they have nothing, they will only be able to give her an old used pestle or an old broken mortar,

and then like the pig or the buffalo destined to be sacrificed, because she creates problems, she will lose her body.

[Judgment(s) not translated]: The guilty girl is disinherited; if she wants to enjoy the goods left by her mother she can go to live with that which looked after [her mother's] days and who inherited [the goods].

page 191 #146 Of children or grand-children who do not take care of their parents or grand-parents; they will not be able to inherit, and the inheritance will go to the woman who took care of them in their old age and whom they have adopted.

Those who planted corn and the cucumber, the parents who brought them up, they abandon them, leave them alone, without ever thinking about them.

Because of this, the parents (or grandparents) will adopt a girl of their older or younger sister, they will make her their adopted daughter to keep the seed of rice, they will think of her as their own daughter, to have some one to get the wood or the water, work the field, assist and nurse them when they will be sick, prepare the rice and the rice wine when they are old.

And if, when sick or disabled, their adopted daughter takes them in her home in her arms or in a palanquin and her [mother or grandmother] own children come back in the house to take away in their bags or with a curse, all the goods they own.

Because of this the adopted daughter inherits nothing since their children took everything, those who before abandoned them.

For this they are guilty and must deal with the adopted daughter and must give back the inheritance from their parents to her. [Judgment(s) not translated]

page 192 #147 Of sons-in-law, children and servants who are impertinent towards their parents or their masters.

The mother gives birth, the father begets, they bring up the children, they toil to keep them clean, keep them warm; they have struggled whole nights, had the healer come to nurse them (when they were sick). And when they (the children) became big, when the girl begins to have breasts, when they are old enough to get married, they abandon the home, they do a different field, they eat separately sweet or sour vegetables;

if they make it so that their parents have nobody to get the wood, draw the water;

if they no longer go see their parents, if they do not go help those who have so much toiled for them, who carried them until they had worn shoulders and who now have no one;

if on top they feel their legs strong, their thighs so big as to hit their parents, if they are like the sharp hoe or the machete and turn against them (to insult or hit them) those are guilty and there is trouble between their parents and them. [Judgment(s) not translated]

page 193 #148 Of parents who encourage their children to steal.

The parents whose child is like the pig rummaging everywhere, the stealing dif, like those who look to steal someone's goods;

those whose child takes a bowl in someone else's house, the washbowl in the big room, those whose child tries to go alone into someone else' s room when everyone is away and is working in the field;

those whose child opens the baskets of cloth, the baskets of dishes, to steal the goods of others;

those whose child wanders everywhere, taking advantage of the darkness of night to steal everything he comes across;

those who have an ignorant child and do not instruct him;

those who are like the turtle dove looking for a ray of sun, like the female parrot letting herself be taken up by the wind, those who approve of their child and help hem to steal and pilfer;

those whose child is lazy to work at home or in the field and thinks only to rob someone's goods;

those who approve so all the acts of their sons or daughters and become their accomplices,

those are guilty and must deal with the others and themselves.

page 194 #149 Of those who render themselves guilty of fornication in someone else's home.

He, the man, who is ignorant and does not hide in the bush to fornicate,

she, the woman, who brings dirt (into the house) up to the knees, mud to the hips, who fill with dirt someone else's home;

those who dirty someone else's pillow, the cabinet , the corner where the tobacco and betel are kept;

those who mate in the bushes (near the house) without hiding from their parents, who do not behave like the Cambodians and the Vietnamese; who do not prepare the cotton following the custom, who do not know how to fornicate according to customs of the past;

those who are ignorant and enter private rooms where they desecrate the red vest, enter the large room and dirty the back-plate of a cuirass [leather armor ?] hanging from the beams, the packsaddle set down on the overhang , who dirty the tethers and the shackles, the objects in gold or silver, the corner where the rich keep their goods,

those are guilty and must deal between others and themselves. [Judgment(s) not translated]

page 195 #150 Of the head of the family sleeping with his slave; the slave will have to be set free.

He is like the black cat who stays on top of the basket, he only comes down to eat the food of the pigs and the dogs.

The woman looks to give herself, the man looks for his pleasure; if the husband enters a hut (to steal), his mistake will fall back on his wife and children, if he verbally abuses, his mistake will fall back on his nephews and sisters who will have to repair [the situation] by giving goods to his wife and children.

If the nephews and sisters cannot reimburse (the price of the slave) later, when he will be dead, the machete and the hoe will go to the bottom or the water and his nephews and sisters will not inherit his share (because the slave, having to be set free, the dead man's family will have to either pat the value of the slave, or give up the inheritance).

(1)The family (clan) of the spouse is only responsible for certain actions of the spouse. If the actions of the spouse elicit any benefit for his wife, it's she or her family who are responsible. If the actions of the spouse don't elicit any benefit for his wife or his parents in-law, it's his family who are responsible.

(2)Wang Kga (cut-cut and "binette"). These two words represent the belongings (items) that the man receives from his family when he gets married. These items are mostly work equipment.

(3) Kir-duah ênuah-hrui (Ênuah-duah). Share of items owned together go to the family of the married man at his death.

Note—Cf. Hittie Code of Hrozny, p. 147: "If a free man with female slaves, sleeps with these or those, there is no punishment."

page 196 #151 Of the young man who fornicates with someone else's slave.

(He who is like) the hen or the rooster entering in the henhouse (of others), he who is incorrigible and looks to fornicate with somebody else's slave.

Like the horse eating grass and keeping it (in his stomach), like the elephant drinking water and swallowing it, he who fornicates with the slave of the rich, will become slave of the rich, if his parents have goods, they will reimburse the price of the slave (to the rich) and will pay a fine for him.

And if his parents own nothing but their persons, his brothers-in-law can only deliver him (as a slave) to someone (the master of the woman-slave).

[Illegible] Code Hittite of F, Hrozny (Oriental Library of Paris, 1922) "If a female has a free son, the purchase cost (marriage gift) given and as the spouse he takes it, then no one makes him leave (his social status) (p.25)

page 197 #152 Of rape.

He who seeing salt, wants to taste it, seeing horse or buffalo wants to ride, seeing the daughter or the wife of the rich, the daughter or the wife of an inhabitant, wants to rape her without reason;

he who seizes, like the tiger snatching, like the animals who mate like the pigs and dogs without feeling any shame;

he who looks for the white face, the clear face, who wants them with all his heart since yesterday or the day before yesterday,

if he has raped a poor woman, a pig of three "song" and an indemnity of three "ko" he will give;

if he had raped the wife or the daughter of the rich, he will give a buffalo for the sacrifice and an indemnity of six "ko".

ANTOMARCHI'S NOTES: PAGE 197

Note: Cf. Hittite Code of Hrozny: "If a woman takes a man, it's the man's crime and he dies (is killed). But if he takes her in the house[,] similarly the woman has sinned; the woman dies. If the man of the woman finds them, he can kill them, punishment won't be his. (p. 149)

page 198 #153 Of rape during sleep.

He who tries to eat the tender vegetables in the evening, in the darkness;

he who, seeing a pig, wants to eat meat, seeing a jar, wants to drink rice wine, seeing a sleeping woman, wants to rape her;

he who cannot stay quiet, who cannot control himself, who seeing a woman asleep or intoxicated by alcohol and whose ears do not hear, tries to rape her;

he who wanders at dawn or in the middle of the night, who removes the skirt and takes off the vest, who acts like he was drunk and enters (in the rooms) to rape the wife of someone else in her alcove, taking advantage of the darkness of the night,

this one is guilty and must deal with others and himself.

[Judgment(s) not translated]

page 199 #154 Of seductions.

If the woman removes the skirt to seduce the man like the chuan cat teases the crab (to grab it);

if the eggplants are cooked in a small pot and the mushrooms in a big one, if the woman rubs herself against the man who does not want to follow her;

if she pulls him by the finger, if she takes him by the end of his nails, if she calls and invites him for this, there is no problem,

because she is like the fruit "puic [v over c]" opening, like the ripe fruit "êpang" because she wants the man and tries to seduce him.

page 200 #155 Of those who rape pre-pubescent girls who do not yet know the desires of the body.

He who goes out at dawn, in the middle of the night, at the hour when everybody sleeps;

he who goes (with the intention of) raping, who cannot hold back, who acts like he was angry;

he who takes advantage of the darkness to go eat the tender vegetables, the mashed vegetables,

he who gives the smallpox or the yaws and does such that the sour water or the acid water will be necessary to care (for the sick);

he who does such that the girl will be sick for a long time under the blanket, tired on the mat, that the healers don't know her sickness, will not be able to nurse her,

she who is only a child, still playing on the ground, still clings to the steps, still sitting on her parent's knees;

he who forces the horse to accept the bridle, the buffalo to accept the lead, he who forces a girl to accept the bracelet or the necklace,

who opens a large mouth, who presses his chest (against the young girl), who stops her from calling for help;

he who acts like the tiger (with his prey), who comes near like the wild animals, who mates like the pigs and the dogs without feeling shame,

while she (the young girl) is still pre-pubescent, she does not yet want a lover;

page 201

he who tries to rape (the young girls), who cannot control himself, who cannot tell between good or bad;

he whose mouth is as large as the opening of a fish trap, like a big basket, he whom nobody can correct;

he who does not listen to his mother's advice, does not obey his father's orders, who plays the flute until his body dies,

like the pig or the buffalo destined to be sacrificed, if he becomes guilty (of rape) he will lose his body.

page 202 #156 Of those who seduce children to strip them.

He who, having no meat to eat, food to cut up, tobacco to smoke,

offers rice in a gourd to coax (the child), offers rice in a pot to seduce him, small birds to fascinate him;

he who seduces a child in offering bananas or sugar cane, who tries to instruct him when he is ignorant;

he who makes beautiful boxes in bamboo, who aligns (harmoniously) seeds of corn to trick a young child,

that one is guilty.

page 203 #157 Of incest between related parents.

Those who do not fear incest, who come near parents, love each other being brothers and sisters, while the same back carried them, they came from the same belly, the same mother gave them birth;

those who make themselves guilty of incest, who want each other being father and daughter, mother and son, while the mother gave birth (to her child), the father carried him, they conceived him, cared for him, brought him up, fed him, supported him;

those who take (their child) in the forest, who hide to rape, who drag in the bushes the child they kept on their knees, have carried on their backs,

and who acts so the watercress dries in the water, the taro withers in the pond, because they play between brothers and sisters, daughter and father, mother and son;

those who desecrate the basket (the earth), who desecrate the backs of the elders (I) [see note, page 204],

and so the mango tree will no longer flower because boys and girls do not behave well, because when eating they behave badly,

those will (give) a pig to purify the forest, a jar of rice wine to purify the earth; the jewels, the skirt and the vest (worn by the woman) will be given to the owner of the ground;

the necklaces they (the guilty ones) were wearing around their necks, the earrings, the hats on their heads, the turbans around their heads, the hoe to find the ginger, the machete to cut the bark, the bowl to pour (the rice wine), the bracelet to close (around the wrist), the spear to drive into the ground, the dish for the meat, all those they will give;

page 204

the earth will be sprayed, water will be poured, the back of the elders will be repaired (purified by the owner),

in order that the earth becomes green again, that the water (of the spring) runs again; that the inhabitants feel secure,

in order that the rain falls suitably, the millet grows well, the gongs stay well hung, the shellac and the resin come well from the trees .

They will make the blood spurt out from the finger (of the guilty) and they will offer to the spirits bolides [exploding meteors] and wasps, to the spirits garbage and dirt (to erase the blemish of the incest).

And if (the guilty parties) do not want to leave each other (want to stay united) like the hanging gongs, like the shellac and the resin glued (to the trees), they will be forced to eat the rice in a trough like the pigs and the dogs because like the pigs and the dogs they do not recognize the ties of parents which join them.

If the guilty woman and man are found, a pig to purify the forest, a jar of rice wine to purify the earth, they will give the woman to the owner of the ground, the man to the chief. (II)

[Refes to page 203, #157] (I) The van, the back of ancestors symbolizes the earth.

(2) The chief has the responsibility to enforce village customs. He is responsible for errors made by the inhabitants. It is normal, therefore, for those who violate the custom to pay a fine. In this case, they will be judged by the caretaker of the earth (pôlan) because the earth has been profaned by the incestuous person, and the person must also answer to the village chief because the custom was violated (broken law).

[Judgment(s) not translated]

NOTE: Cf. Hittite Code de Hrozny: "If a man rapes his own mother, there will be punishment. If a man violates [a daughter], there will be punishment. If a man violates a son, there will be punishment. "Into the kings chamber she is taken and the king either kills her or lets her live." (p. 145 and 145)

page 205 #158 Of incest between distant relatives.

Those who have an incestuous relationship, who love each other between parents, between sisters and brothers (of the same clan/family);

Who cause the watercress to dry in the water the taro to wither in the pond, because they play between parents (of the same clan/family),

those who desecrate the big basket, who soil the back of the elders,

a pig to purify the forest, ajar of rice wine to purify the earth, and goods they well give to her, the guardian of the earth,

the black bracelets , the necklaces they wore on their necks, the loops they had in their ears, the hats on their heads, the turbans around their heads,

the skirt (that the woman had spread) on the ground, the blanket (of the man) she admired, the hoe to find ginger, the machete to cut the bark, the bowl to hold the rice wine, the bracelet to put on the wrist, the spear to drive into the ground, the dish for the meat, they will give to the owner of the ground.

The earth will be sprayed, water will be poured to purify the back of the elders,

so that the earth becomes green again, the water runs again, the inhabitants feel secure, the rain be beneficial, the millet grows well, the rice grows well and has beautiful grains.

They will make the blood of the finger burst out (of the guilty), they will offer to the spirits some bolides, to the spirits to erase the soiling of the incest.

If they know the guilty woman and man, a pig and a jar of rice wine to purify the earth the woman will give to the owner of the ground

the man, to the chief of the village

Antomarchi's Notes: **Page 205**

[Judgment(s) not translated] (I) See note 2, page 204.

page 206 #159 Of act of fornication with domestic animals.

He who talks insanely, who laughs with excess, who makes up unlikely stories which happened only to him;

he who is not afraid to commit acts disapproved by everybody, does not see where there is sin or where there is none;

he who makes the watercress dry up in the water,

the taro, in the marsh, while playing with the mares, the female buffalo and with cows;

he who desecrates the big basket, who soils the back of the elders,

that one is guilty and he must deal with the guardian of the ground.

Antomarchi's Notes: **Page 206**

Note: Hittite Code of Hrozny: If a man rapes a cow, there is punishment: he dies. He is taken to the kings chamber, and the king decides to kill him or let him live." (p143)

If someone rapes a pig or a dog , he dies." (p. 149)

If a bull is covered by a man, the bull dies (is put to death), but the man does not die. The sheep replaces the man so one [illegible] [kills it][?]

If a pig is covered by a man, there is no punishment.

If a man rapes a horse or mule, there is no punishment.

Chapter VIII

Page 207 #160 Of voluntary murders.

He who loses control easily, has a short patience, who stands with his head down and his feet up;

he who is frail like a blade of grass or a dried creeper, who loses control and kills without reason,

because he is jealous like the souls of the dead, wicked like the bad spirits;

because he covets the very straight tree, the sharp machete, because he is jealous of the healthy man;

he who strangles with a cloth or hangs with a rope, who hits with a spear or a saber,

because he made the blood run, he will give a "bung" pot, because he disturbed the inhabitants, he will give a "biê" pot; the saber which pierced the belly and the cloth to catch the soul (of the dead) he will give (to the family of the victim).

A jar (to put at the foot) and another (to put at the head of the coffin) and goods he will give.

To pay the mourners, he will give a "ba" or "bung" and to have disturbed the village, he will kill an ox or a buffalo,

because this affair is very serious.

If he has killed a poor person, he will pat the belly of the body with a gong of one cubit and one span (in diameter); if he has killed a rich person, he will pay a gong of two cubits (in diameter).

[Judgment(s) not translated]

page 208 #161 Of child killings.

She who dares (crush with) her foot, kills with her hand, smothers the new-born when he comes out of her womb,

the new-born who, growing up, if a girl, could have been a midwife or a healer, if a boy, would have handled the shield and the machete, gone to war against strangers, and would have become rich and powerful, gone to war against the "Mnông" and would have amassed goods and jewels;

She who kills her son, who makes her daughter disappear, who removes her lineage.

She is guilty and there is a very grave affair against her.

page 209 #162 Of poisoning by water, alcohol, or food.

He who makes someone swallow a black spider, a slug, who kills by mixing poison to alcohol and drinking water, rice and vegetables (to eat);

he who pours poison while hiding, who cultivates poisonous plants in secret, prepares sour or hot liquids like coal or pepper, who gathers the poisonous sap of trees to sicken, who is wicked like the sorcerers, scary like the spirits without motive,

if he has poisoned a child, he will reimburse (the price of the body) with a female elephant, if he poisoned an adult, he will reimburse with a male elephant, if he has poisoned the chief or one of his children with ten sets of large gongs and ten flat gongs.

Because he had no reason, even very old, no old affair to settle with him .

For this he is guilty. [Judgment(s) not translated, illegible]

page 210 #163 Of those who bring death to all the inhabitants by poisoning the spring.

He who gathers poison, who cultivates poisonous plants, who touches the spouts at the spring [developed for drinking water], because he is wicked like the sorcerers, jealous like the gods without reason;

he who pours poison in the waterfalls, who dilutes it in the rivers, puts it in the water of the ponds, who disturbs the tranquility of the inhabitants without motive;

he who tries to destroy the rich village, the thriving village, who tries to devastate the village of his brothers without motive, without reason,

if someone owes him, let him ask for it, if he has a lawsuit or a matter, let him settle it.

But if he tries to give poison, to make someone eat poisonous plants, to kill young men and young girls, adults and the elders without reason,

for this he is guilty and there is a very serious matter with him. [Judgment(s) not translated]

page 211 #164 Of murder of someone accused of witchcraft.

He who murders brutally, who kills without reason, who causes death in the forest,

if he (the victim) is a sorcerer, he (the murderer) prepares a pot, heats the resin in it, gets heating wood and calls a few or many people;

those like the bent knife, the warped machete, let him call few or many people (to see the result of the ordeal),

but if instead he hits with the saber or the knife, he gives for food to the crows and vultures (the body of the one he accused),

if he does not inform (the family of the sorcerer), if he does not say anything to the parents, does not exchange the bracelet;

if he does not let known his intentions;

if before this, he ties up (the sorcerer) with a creeper, if he strangles him with a turban and throws (his body) in the bushes;

if he ties him up with a creeper, strangles him with a rope, hits him with a spear or a saber,

because he is jealous of the straight tree, wants the sharp machete, jealous of the man with good legs to walk and run,

if he accuses the ugly man to be a sorcerer, the ugly woman to want the husband of someone else,

if he kills, he will reimburse the price of the body, if he injures him, he will pay a fine.

If he kills a child, he will give a female elephant, if he kills an adult, (he will give) a male elephant, if he kills a chief, he will give ten large gongs and ten flat gongs;

page 212

if blood spurts out, he will give a big pot, if the blood has run, he will give a medium size pot;

the saber which has pierced the bowels, the cloth to wrap up the soul (of the dead),

a jar to put at the feet (of the dead), a jar to put at the head, and other objects he will give (for the funeral);

he will also give a jar "ba" and a pot "bung" to the mourners and he will kill oxen and buffalo for having bothered the inhabitants. [Judgment(s) not translated]

page 213 #165 Of those who become guilty by listening to bad advice.

He who accepts the decisions of the stick, who follows the words of the healer, who obeys the bad advice of those pushing him to do evil;

he who does not consult the banyan when there is a banyan, does not consult the fig tree when there is a fig tree, who does not ask the father and the mother when there are a father and a mother;

he who is like a pool of water that one can empty, like a stream that can easily be rerouted, like a dog pushed when it does not want to enter in a trap, like the vultures and the crows being thrown blades of saber or spear when they do not want to eat, like those who do a bad act when ordered;

he who wants the ceremonial machete, the basket of salt, the shoulder of beef or buffalo;

he who is guilty because he agrees to walk an any road, to run on any path, because he is like the deaf who hear nothing, because he does not know the difference between good and bad;

He is being manipulated like the leg of a spider that can be articulated, like the little dog that one can make bark by pinching him; he call mother or father all those who call themselves his mother or his father.

For this he is guilty.

page 214 #166 Of unintentional murders.

He who did not want to pierce with the spit, to prick with the spear, and who the gods made him act;

if he did not want to hit with the rattan, batter to death with a club, it is unintentionally that he killed his brother (his fellow);

if it is the sky or his fate, of it is the spirits who wanted him to kill;

if he had not wanted to try his machete, see if his ax was sharpened, if he had not planned (his act) since the morning or since the day before;

if he had no bad intention, if he did not plan (the murder), if he never had any intention to kill, he will pay an indemnity,

he will be judged considering that he killed without intention.

But if since the morning he had planned (the murder), if he thought about it since the day before, if he nurtured it for a long time, he will pay the price of the body.

[Judgment(s) not translated]

page 215 #167 Of those guilty by constraint.

He who is all alone like the wild ox, like a piece of potato end no longer having any parents;

they catch him like with a net or a hood, they seize him like the weasel or the sparrow hawk (seizes his prey),

they make him sell all that they want, hurt anybody, throw in the bushes,

they lead him like a monkey having lost its female, like a female monkey having lost its male, like somebody having no one to guide him;

they crush him like one crushes the grass, they stamp like one stamps the stubble, they make him do what they want.

He does not know neither what is bad nor what is good, if he has a problem he does not let anybody know.

For this, there is a problem with others. [Judgment(s) not translated]

page 216 #168 Of blows given without reason.

He who has a matter as old as the hollow tubercle, a matter that goes way back, let him speak.

If it is a matter of large gongs or flat gongs, let him say it, if it is a matter of elephant, let him tell.

Why does he start by getting angry, by insulting the mother and the father?

Why does he speak loudly, loses control, stir up the torch?

If the vulture does not turn his back, if the crow does not come back, if the rich does not show himself (respectable).

For this, he can insult the mother, manhandle the father (he has a reason).

Why is he bad like a chipped hoe, like a broken flint, why does he have a bad temper,

since before they (the two antagonists) ate together the rice and the vegetables, they ate beef liver or buffalo liver on the same plate, they drank the dame strong or weak rice wine?

Why then does he hit, kill, insult the mother and the father?

If he hits the head, let him tell the reason, if he hits the body, let him give the motive, if he hits the chief, let him say why.

But if he hits without reason, insults without motive, there will be a matter.

[Judgment(s) not translated]

page 217 #169 Of rapes.

He who is wicked like the tiger, who takes in his jaws like the animals, who mates like the pigs and the dogs without any shame;

he who wants the fruit or the flower, who seeing a young girl, pretty and all alone, tries to rape her;

he who seeing a pig wants to eat meat, seeing a jar wants to drink rice wine, seeing a woman go to the forest or the garden alone tries to rape her, seeing somebody else's wife or daughter tries to rape her by any means, she being asleep or not;

he who tears the skirt, takes out the vest, he who sees a woman alone in the house or the field and tries to rape her,

that one is guilty and there is a very serious affair between the others and himself.

page 218 #170 Of the master who hits a pregnant servant until she aborts.

He who hits as hard as he can, without moderation, until the bones of the knee or the hip show;

he who hits until the blood spurts out, the flesh is torn, the blood and the bile spurt out and rise up to the sky;

he who seeing (his servant) same as a tubercle raising from the ground, the potato coming out of the earth, seeing her nipples darken, her belly swollen,

hits her until the little child (that she carries) dies, the fetus stops living, this child who if a girl could have become a midwife or a healer, if a boy, would have handled the shield and the machete, fight the enemy, look for wealth.

If he cuts the top of the budding bamboo, if he kills the child of a rich person to wipe out the race,

it is as though he had strangled (the child of his servant) with a turban, hung him by a rope, hit him with the spear or the saber, hung him on a leaning tree, abandoned him to wild beasts.

For this there is an affair between others and him.

ANTOMARCHI'S NOTES: PAGE 218

Note: Cf. Hittite Code, p. 15 "If someone delivers the child of a slave, if it's the 10th month, 5 coins of silver are paid [given]."

page 219 #171 Of buying slaves.

He who buys men or women without thinking,

by giving many copper bowls, many washbowls, many goods,

stirs up the anger of the husbands, the disapproval of the wives, the indignation of the rich.

If he does not go to the banyan or the fig tree to ask for advice, if he does not consult his parents;

if he buys all by himself, saying nothing, without anybody knowing;

if he does not tell the chief, says nothing to the children, if he does not talk to four or five people;

if he goes to the forest without warning the father, to the spring without telling the mother, if he buys and sells people without consulting the grandparents;

if he ignores the signal "kung" and the signal "knông", if he disobeys the mouth who teaches;

For this, there is an affair.

[Judgment(s) not translated]

page 220 #172 Of selling slaves.

He who sells (a person) like one sells the bags of salt, or bags of tobacco, (who takes advantage) of the darkness of night to go sell (persons);

he who covets the rounded shield, the bag embroidered in gold, the goods of the rich and tries to sell someone else's person without motive;

he who sees a horse alone or an abandoned buffalo, sees an individual without family, without father or mother, catches and sells him;

he who brings (the captive) on the roads of Cambodia or Laos, in the forest of the "Kung" or the "Bahma" to sell him;

he who sells (a person) to have salt to eat, iron to forge, turbans to wear, blankets to wrap himself in, jars "tuk" and jars "ba" to prepare the rice wine,

This one is guilty and has a very serious matter.

[Judgment(s) not translated]

page 221 #173 Of servants or workers who hurt or kill themselves.

He who takes a job of carrying the water, getting wood, going to the spring, working the field;

he who eats the rice and vegetables (with his master), if he has a headache, does not feel well, one must take care of hem, nurse him, give him the medicines to cure him, and if one has pigs or chickens, make the ritual sacrifice to obtain his recovery;

if he dies, one will wrap up his body, will bury him, make a coffin and (funeral) posts will be planted, he who had wanted himself to take a job, who had gone over the steep mountain, asked to eat, to be boy or girl to carry water, to clean (without consulting his parents) if he dies, there will be no indemnity to pay (his family);

but his parents will have a matter to settle with others (with his master) because they are guilty, because their child having run away in the morning, they did not look for him in the evening, having run away at night, they did not look for him during the day, having run away today, they did not look tomorrow,

because they abandoned him like the horse or the buffalo that one lets out (after the harvest), because they have abandoned the child who disobeyed, because they abandoned him in the current of the river that took him away, they did not worry about what he became;

because they abandoned him like the rattan that one throws in the mud, like the tribute that one pays to the "cams" [v over c] [chams ?], they let him go without regrets, no longer thinking about him.

For this, there is an affair between the others (the master) and them (the parents), since because of them, the pillars, the struts have been desecrated, the house (of the master) has been desecrated as well as the blanket (hanging) up high,

the packsaddle put on the overhang, the elephant's shackles, the horses bridle;

page 221

 bis the yellow vest , the red vest, the vest embroidered in gold, the vest decorated with flowers, the vest one puts on for the yearly feasts.

page 222 #174 Of accidents caused by indicated traps.

When one finds a swarm of bees, big or small, one puts a signal, when one finds a fruit tree or a tree from which dye is drawn, one notches it;

when one sets a trap with a spear or darts, one drives [in the ground] a signal and informs the uncles and the aunts (everybody).

One sets traps to have the meat of a boar to put on a skewer, the meat of a deer to put to dry (on top of the fire), rabbits and civets to feed his wife and children.

He who goes to the river without saying anything, to the forest without telling anyone, who does not say anything to those who have set up traps, he is guilty and if he went by the path were traps with spear or traps to kill, if he has been hit in the knee or the thigh, if he has been wounded;

he will sacrifice a pig of one "ko" for one who set up the traps.

ANTOMARCHI'S NOTES: PAGE 222

Note:He who set up the traps is not responsible for accidents that can happen, if he had signaled their presence in accordance with the local customs and if he respected all the stated directions.

The one who is wounded by an indicated trap must repair the harm done to the owner of the trap; if he dies, his family well be responsible for him.

All deaths, all wounds with effusion of blood, desecrate the earth. The wounded one or his family of the dead, must do a sacrifice (tuh lăn) to purify the dirtied earth.

page 223 #175 Of accidents caused by non-indicated traps.

When one finds a big or small swarm of bees, a fruit tree or tree from which dye is drawn, and does not mark them (to let it be known that they are reserved).

He who puts up traps with spear or traps to kill without indicating them, without saying anything to the children, to the young men or the young girls, without telling that he had set up (traps) in the brush;

he who does not say anything, who does not open his mouth, who does not even tell four or five people;

he who sets traps with a spear or darts without telling the uncles (the inhabitants);

if (the victim) dies, he will pay the price of the body, if he is only wounded he will pay an indemnity;

if he get better, is cured, stops groaning, can leave the mat and the blanket,

he will pay an indemnity of six "ko" and will do for him the sacrifice "kpih" with a pig of one "ko".

But if the victim does not get well, his state gets worse, he does not stop groaning, cannot leave the mat and the blanket (if he dies);

he will have to pay the price of the body with a big flat gong and make the sacrifice "kpih" of a buffalo to the family of the dead.

[Judgment(s) not translated]

page 224 #176 Of accidents caused by non-disarmed traps during the day.

He who sets traps with spear or traps to kill and is too lay to go see them,

If someone is caught in his traps, there is a problem.

If the victim dies, he will pay the price of the body (to the family), if he is only wounded, he will pay an indemnity.

VARIATION ADDED BY THE TRANSLATOR [Antomarchi]

He who sets traps with spear or darts without informing the uncles, he who sets traps to kill or traps to topple without telling the inhabitants,

he who sets traps with spear or darts around his field, is guilty if he does not go see them (the daytime to disarm them).

If someone is caught in his traps, there is a problem.

If a man dies, he will pay the price of the body with a big flat gong, a buffalo for the sacrifice he will give the family of the dead, a pig of two "song" he will give to the owner of the ground to purify the earth and goods of one "ko".

If there is only a wound, he will pay an indemnity of three "ko", he will give a pig of one "song" to the wounded for the sacrifice.

[Judgment(s) not translated]

ANTOMARCHI'S NOTES: PAGE 224

NOTE: Fields are always looked after during the day, but at night, it is not possible to protect them effectively against the wild animals. Traps are then set around the field, on the paths usually taken by the beasts.

The custom says to disarm the traps during the day to avoid accidents, but those rules are not always observed.

All accidents which happen during the day, must therefore bring proceedings against the one who set the traps, that those be designated or brought to the attention of the passer-by.

The price of the body is equal to a flat gong of one cubit for the poor, of one cubit and one span for someone rich.

All violent death desecrates the earth and a sacrifice must be made by the one who is on watch to purify the earth. It is always the culprit who pays the cost of the sacrifice.

page 225 #177 Of crimes committed by the insane.

He who the spirits have hit, the sky has cursed, who can no longer recognize East and West, creates problems for his parents.

But the indemnity (they would have to pay) will be reduced, their responsibility will be lightened, they will pronounce a light sentence not to ever be more than the price of the body, they will always remember the mitigating circumstances,

because one cannot look at the faults of an insane person as the faults of a normal one, cannot kill one with a saber who is suffering from skin disease, one cannot hit with the machete one who is sick, one has been hit by the spirits with a curse, one cannot prosecute him.

Those who hit badly the gongs bother the one who hits the drum, the parents who abandon their child like one abandons the horses (after the harvest), who abandon their child who had become crazy or an idiot and does not tie him up or shackle him, those are guilty.

Antomarchi's Notes: PAGE 225

NOTE: The insane are not responsible for their acts. Their parents are entirely responsible, if they do not take care of them, do not watch well over them. If, in spite or their watching, the insane ones manage to commit faults or crimes, their responsibility will be lightened. [Judgment(s) not translated]

page 226 #178 Of crimes and offences committed in a state of intoxication.

He who eats but does not know how to eat, who drinks but does not know how to drink, who drinks until he is sick, who breaks someone else's gongs and jars, who strikes people brutally;

he who after eating tries to strike, after drinking, tries to shove, he who acts like a deaf person, who easily loses his temper, who insults and scratches;

he who eats and is not able to stop, who drinks without moderation, who when he has drunk and eaten, strikes his wife and children with the ladle for vegetables, strikes his brothers and sisters;

he who insults someone else's mother, strikes the father, insults others crudely;

that one is guilty because he does not know how to eat with moderation, to drink moderately.

For this, there is an affair between others and him.

If he strikes someone until death follows, if he cuts (with the saber), he will pay the price

of the body (to the family of the victim); if he only wounds he will pay a fine.

[Judgment(s) not translated]

page 227 #179 Of sons-in-law who strike their parents-in-law until death follows.

He who is like the hoe or sharp machete and who rebels against his mother or his father, who rises up against his parents-in-law and strikes them;

he who hits until he causes pain, until death follows;

like the pig or the buffalo destined to be sacrificed, if he creates problems, he will lose his body.

If he is like the woman who creates problems for herself, if he makes himself guilty by enter someone else's hut or granary, his fault will fall back onto his wife and children; if he makes himself guilty by being impertinent or rude, his fault will fall back on his brothers and nephews who will have to pay the fine or indemnity for him .

If they (the dead) cry because of him, if the field is overrun by grass, if the trays and baskets are missing because of him,

if there is nobody to clean around the field, to cut the invading weeds, to chase the male and female parrots (from the field),

then, (his share) of bananas and potatoes he will give up, he will give money to the widow and the children of the dead; if there are four parts, he will give one part;

and when he will have repaid the price of the body , paid the indemnity, bury him (the dead) decently, then the affair will be definitely settled, will leave no trace, the droppings and the urine will be dry.

Antomarchi's Notes: Page 227

[Judgment(s) not translated]

(1) V. note p 195

(2) Note: Cf. Code Hittite de Hrozny, 133: ""If among men who [illegible] themselves and a certain person dies, the guilty one must give someone."

page 228 #180. Of those who mistreat their mother or father.

The rhizomes (of bamboo) grow because they are bamboo, the geckos can live because there are trees, men grow and become a hundred or a thousand because there is a mother and a father.

He who is ignorant, they instruct him, he who is deaf is instructed by yelling loudly, children who are lazy to work in the field or at the hose , their parents give them advice,

Because if the girl has problems, the boy has a legal case, if they become guilty by wandering, not walking well, have problems with others, the responsibility will fall back on their parents.

But if they (the children) are like the hoe or the machete wounding the one who handles them, if they show themselves impertinent with their parents when they instruct or advise them, they become angry and strike them;

for this they are guilty.

[Judgment(s) not translated]

Chapter IX

page 229 #181. Of the keeping of property.

The bowls in the shape of the nest of the sparrow hawk, the copper washbowls in the shape of the nest of the vulture, the goods of the ancestors.

the ancient goods, the old jewels, goods of the past, the jewels of the ancestors,

they must use them all together.

They must help to cover (the pit for jars), to close it with the help of [illegible] must help to watch over it, to guard it all together.

the little earthenware cups, little copper bowls, the tiny objects, they cannot sell them [in order] to eat,

they must always keep them.

The djarai baskets, the trays, the bags, the satchels, the smallest objects, it is the older sister, who like the mother, must keep them.

The reeds [frame?] of the loom, the   that one holds on one's thigh, the [illegible] to card, the embroidery frame, the bars to stretch the thread, the brush to wet the fabric, it is the older sister who must keep all these.

The reeds, the rods, the silk brushes from boars, it is to the older sister that they are entrusted.

The copper pots hidden in the forest or in the pond, all the goods carefully hidden, it is always the older sister who must watch over them.

The red jars, the precious "Mnong" jars, the bracelets, the new dishes, the silver, the vests with flowers, the objects used for the feasts, the goods of the rich ancestors, it is the older sister who must keep them.

page 230

The black vests, the red vests, the vests embroidered in gold, the vests with flowers, the objects used for the feasts at the end of the year,

The large gongs and the flat gongs, the elephants, and the slaves, the gigs and the chickens, the oxen and the buffalo, it is the older sister who must guard them.

The saddled horses, the hammocks in which one climbs to sleep, the pans to fan oneself, it is the older sister who must keep them.

The washbowls in enameled iron, the trays for place settings, the spittoons, the fire boxes, the candle holders, have been entrusted to the older sister.

The jars in which to ferment the rice, the cauldrons to hold water, the flat gongs to hit, the axes to cut wood, the servants, the slaves, have been entrusted to the older sister.

The bananas and the tubercles in pieces , the silver coins that they share, the pancreas of oxen or buffalo to be shared, all that must be shared has been left to the older sister to share with her younger sisters.

All the broken pots, the chipped gourds, the coins of money, she does the sharing.

One must never fight, never be divided (between the sisters), never refuse the big or small objects, valuable or not, the pots or bowls (given to each by the older sister).

[Judgment(s) not translated]

page 231 #182. Of one part of the goods of the deceased husband, must be given back to his mother or his older sister.

At the death (of the husband) the hoes and machetes must be given back (to his mother) or to the one who had succeeded her, as well as the bracelets, necklaces, bowls for rice, vegetable plates, the awl to pierce, the axes, knives, hammers, sandals, the small hoes and small machetes, the crossbows and the quivers, all that must be given;

the hoes and machetes must go back to (the family of the deceased); this nobody knew before the ancestors, it is now the custom.

(if the deceased) has picked the vegetables, carried wood for himself, killed game and kept the jaws, if he has worked in the house or the field, if he had buried the jars in the earth, if his feet have crushed the straw (if he has traveled), if he had legal cases pending, one will try to find out.

If the pieces of meat are small they will be put in a corner, if they are big, on a skewer, if he had killed boars or deer, one will count the tusks or the bones;

if the deceased was poor, the inheritance will be small, if he was rich, it will be large, but it is not the custom to keep (the share due his family).

page 231

The part of his goods called "ênuah-duah" must go back to the one (his mother or older sister) or the one who succeeded her, in no case can the brothers-in-law allocate it for themselves to give to their wives or children.

Antomarchi's Notes: Page 231 bis

Note: At the death of the husband, part of the goods which he had must be returned to his family. It is understood which goods his family gave him when he married, and those assets he owned jointly. Primarily, especially including tools and weapons must be returned to his family. This one equal died right has a small share on the seconds. It is this small share that is indicated by the expression, "ngăn kir-dua [illegible] hrui" or simply, "ênuah-duah".

[Judgment(s) not translated]

page 232 #183. Of the single young man who has goods must entrust them to his mother or sisters.

He who is still single, who carries the water, who stays with his parents, if he owns copper bowls, plates, big enamel bowls, small copper bowls, objects of large or small value, he must give them to his parents or his sisters to be watched over or kept;

afraid that if he has a headache, a stomachache, he does not have enough to eat, if he does not feel well, he would have nothing to pay the healer.

If in time of plenty, one has goods, when there will be a food shortage, one will be able to get rice, when sick, able to buy pigs and chickens to cure himself.

The young man who has many copper bowls should not spend them needlessly, if he has many washbowls, he must not give them away, if he has lots of goods, he must not give them to non-parents.

If he owns some goods: a silver coin, a necklace, a bracelet, he will give them to his father and mother, his sisters.

If he does not give , he is guilty.

[Judgment(s) not translated]

page 233 #184. Of the brothers-in-law who squander the goods their sisters-in-law inherited.

(Those who appropriate) the bowls in the shape of the nest of a sparrow hawk, the big washbowls like the nest of vultures, the goods left by the ancestors,

because they see that the heir is still a child sleeping on the mattress, wrapping herself in the blanket, because she has not yet come past the age of childhood's sicknesses, the age when she stays on her mother's knees, because she is still very small;

those who operate like the leg of the spider, like the small dog, who make her, at their will, go from right to left;

those (whose mouth) is a beak of a blackbird or a beak of a dove, those who know how to talk well (to cheat);

those who, hiding, take, who , crawling, move forward, who try to take the goods of their nieces to give them to his wife and children;

knowing well that the bowls in the shape of the nest of a sparrow hawk, the washbowls as big as the nests of the vultures, that the goods left by the ancestors,

they do not have the right to eat them nor sell them, that they must always be kept.

page 233

bisThose who, in spite of all this, despise (the heir), who deprive her, who seeing her still pre-pubescent or hardly nubile and not yet wanting a husband, take her goods to eat or sell them,

those are guilty and there is a very serious affair with them.

[Judgment(s) not translated]

page 234 #185. Of the impossibility for the husband to give the goods of his wife or daughters to his nieces and nephews.

The goods of the past, the bowls and the washbowls in the shape of sparrow hawk's nest, the objects left by the ancestors; the husband cannot give them to his nephews and nieces, nor to those of is family (sisters and aunts); if he gives them cucumbers, if he offers them corn ,

he will have to reimburse the value or replace them by goods of the same price.

But if for an urgent affair, an important affair, his sisters are in debt, if they borrowed copper bowls or plates, a hundred or a thousand measures of rice, he will be able to give (goods belonging to his wife), he will always have to reimburse or replace the borrowed goods, never can he abandon them (to his sisters).

If the goods have been spent for food, if the husband ate with his wife and children, with his sisters and sisters-in-law, there is no matter.

But at his death his nephews and nieces (children of his sisters) will not be able to claim a large part of his hoes and machetes; they will only have a right to small hoes and small machetes.

And if the husband has had problems (lawsuits) and the sisters and nieces did not pay the fine he was given, if they did not repair the wrongs he had done, the share of hoes and machetes, their right to the inheritance will go to their brother or uncle.

Antomarchi's Notes: **Page 234**

[Judgment(s) not translated]

Note: The man, even married, is still a member of his family. If the family doesn't fulfill it's responsibility to the man, when he dies, his family may [illegible] to the share of "kip-duah ônuah hrui."

page 235 #186. Of purchases made rashly.

He, man or woman, who buys without thinking, buys anything,

he who gives many bowls, distributes large quantities of wash bowls, who gives many goods in order to buy,

and in this way causes the anger of the husband, the disapproval of the wives, the reproaches of the rich;

he who dies not ask (the advice) of the banyan or the fig tree, the father and the mother;

he who buys all alone, without consulting anybody, without anybody seeing or knowing (what he buys);

he who does not ask (advice) neither to the adults not the children, who never speaks (of the purchases he planned);

he who goes to the woods without warning the father, goes to the well without telling the mother, who buys or sells without consulting the grandparents,

he who ignores the signs indicating tarps, ignores the mouth instructing and advising,

that one is guilty and has a problem with others (his family and him).

Antomarchi's Notes: PAGE 235

Note: This text concerns the purchase of stolen items.

[Judgment(s) not translated]

page 236 #187. Of those who buy goods from minors.

He who searches the earth with his foot, who digs with the pointed bamboo, who pickaxes with the hoe;

he who covets (the goods of a child) like one wants the acid fruit, the sweet vegetables, who covets since yesterday or the day before (for a long time) the goods of the rich;

(he who covets) the bowls in the shape of the nest of the sparrow hawk, the washbowls as big as the vulture's nest, the goods left in the past by the ancestors;

he who pretends to take the handle of the hoe or the machete to deceive (the child) and take over his goods;

he who makes a case for , or aligns the seeds of corn to deceive the rich child, the seduce him and take his goods;

he who sees a child who dies not yet know his way, does not know where there are holes, does not know the difference between the far away blue of the mountain and the blue of the sky,

and who, like the screech owl bewitching the crab (to seize it), like the woman taking off her skirt to seduce the man, tries to seduce the young child;

he who is like the dove looking for the hot ray of the sun, like the female parrots letting themselves go with the wind, he who always thinks like the child (he wants to seduce);

he who digs the earth to sink into it up to his knees or hips,

who tries to bring a lot of soil (of goods to him),

this one is guilty and there is a problem with others and him.

page 237 #188. Of those who refuse and depreciate the merchandise.

Those who enter without taking anything, who go (into a shop) and turn down (everything shown to them),

because the price of the bracelet, the quality of the goods, they cannot appreciate,

(let them remember that) the Vietnamese offers his goods, fixes the price, the Rhadé is free to accept it or turn it down;

Before eating, one calls everyone (for the meal), (for this, for the matter of purchase) all the inhabitants have been informed,

those who refuse to pay for the goods or refuses on the pretext of bad quality;

those who will act like the blade of the knife wanting to be bigger than the handle, like the child wanting to believe he is taller than the adult, like one wanting to know more than his parents,

those are guilty and there will be a problem with them.

page 238 #189. Of goods sold too expensively.

He who speaks too much, laughs with exaggeration, who makes up constantly new stories, trades without moderation;

(he who acts like) the fire crossing the valley, the flood over the dam, who ignores the given instructions;

(he who acts like) the grass wanting to climb higher than the reeds, like the straw wanting to raise higher than the bushes,

he who wants to eat lard or fat (to get fat), who covets the goods of others to get richer;

he who takes the goods of others,

who demands the objects of others to take them;

he who says that in a cubit of cloth there is six feet, in the basket of salt there is a stick, in the bracelet there is a roll of copper thread;

(he who acts like) the screech owl bewitching the crab, like the woman taking off her skirt to seduce the man, who deceives (the customers) to eat their goods.

that one is guilty and there is a matter between others and him.

page 239 #190. Of those who borrow goods and never return them.

He who borrows the king's oxen, the rich man's buffalo, any objects of others, and does not give them back or replace them or does not reimburse their value;

(he who acts like) the screech owl bewitching the crab, like the woman taking off her skirt to seduce the man, he who deceives others by borrowing goods (with no intention of returning them);

he who having no meat to eat, no food to cut, no tobacco to smoke,

tries to borrow copper bowls or plates;

he who has nothing to eat and tries to borrow the goods or objects of others to buy food and does not return them;

he who borrows constantly food to eat, rice, goods from the brothers (the inhabitants);

without ever dreaming of returning, or replacing, or reimbursing the value of things he borrowed;

if he does not give back on the agreed day, if the fixed time limit has expired, he will have to give back more than what he had borrowed (he will have to pay interest).

He will have in addition double (what he borrowed), or three times: one in front, one in back (the borrowed object).

And if at the expiration of the fixed time, he refuses point-blank to give back (what he borrowed), one is allowed to seize the gongs hanging, the jars tied to the posts for liberation and if he is away or asleep, one will wake him up, in front of him, one is allowed to seize that he does not want to return without being afraid of being guilty (of breaking into the house).

[Judgment(s) not translated]

page 240 #191. Of those who damage the objects they borrow.

He who takes the big copper pot to use it, the clay pit to use it, the blat gongs and the large gongs to strike them, the jars to prepare rice wine,

if he does not take care, does not hang well (the gongs), does not know how to watch over them and keep them, if he breaks them, he will have to reimburse the value or replace them.

If he had broken a pot, he will have to make another, if he has broken the cotton thread, he will have to spin another, if he has broken objects belonging to brothers (to inhabitants) he will have to replace them or reimburse their value;

if he breaks a sacred jar, irritating the spirit who lived in it, there will be a problem and he will have to pay a fine.

But no additional charge, no profit can be asked above the value (of the broken object).

page 241 #192. Of healers who try to eat the goods of others.

He who having been instructed and warned ignores the mouth who advises him;

he who want to eat lard and grease to become fat, who tries to get rich,

and who, as soon as he had received bowls or plates does not feel like (continuing to take care);

he who is like the leech sucking (the blood) by its two mouths, who walks the path invaded by the brush or grass,

he who claims that the colorful stalk is a snake, the streaked   are those of a tiger, he who calls himself the envoy of the chief;

he who bends down to make believe he hoes, who sways to make believe he is preparing the ground, who tries to catch the stump and the log (he who makes believe he is taking care in order to get as much money as possible from the sick person,

this one is guilty and must deal with himself. [Judgment(s) not translated]

page 242 #193. Of healers guilty of swindles and trickeries.

He who is renowned in all houses, in all the villages to know how to consult the stick of the sorcerer, how to read in the water to be able to detect all the points where sicknesses develop;

he who, when someone is sick under the blanket, tired on the mat or hurts in the back of the legs, makes believe he knows how to consult the stick, knows why the gods are irritated;

he who prescribes the parents or the family (of the sick) to sacrifice oxen and buffalo without the sick getting cured, not recovering his health, not able to leave the mat and the blanket;

he who acts like the screech owl bewitching the crab (to devour it), like the woman taking off her skirt to seduce the man, who looks for a way to trick the inhabitants of the village;

because he has no meat to eat, no food to prepare, no tobacco to smoke;

the pigs that have been sacrificed needlessly, he will have to replace them, the chicken sacrificed without result he will have to give back, the oxen and buffalo sacrificed in vain, he will have to reimburse or replace,

because he is like the bent knife, the used machete because he has many problems;

because he is a bone without flesh, like a paralyzed jaw, because he owns nothing and tries to create problems (to swindle others).

The oxen and buffalo destined to be sacrificed are killed, he who provokes problems, will lose his body (his life or his liberty).

[Judgment(s) not translated]

page 243 #194. Of those who make a big affair from a small one in order to make a profit.

He who wants sour fruit or sweet fruit, who covets other's goods since yesterday or the day before yesterday;

he who seeing a person alone like the wild ox, like the peelings of potato, without aunts or grandparents, without family, without sisters or brothers,

tries to create problems by encouraging her to put up traps on the paths to his field or hut, traps with spear or darts on his road, to accuse her later to have wanted to pierce him, of having tried to kill him;

he who covets the high tree or the straight beam to build his house;

he who tries to pierce the intact bamboo, who tries to rub against another (to rob him);

he who takes like one takes with the net or the hook, who seizes like the sparrow hawk seizes the weasel;

he who rubs with the fruit of the stinging creeper those who do not have itches (to give them), who stabs with an awl, who has no pimple, who provokes problems to those who don't have any .

because he sees that those are like children still playing on the ground, holding onto the steps (to climb), still staying on the knees of their parents, still learning to put traps with spears or darts, thinking only of playing in the fields (where graze) the oxen and buffalo;

he who is wicked like the spirits of the dead and the [evil] spirits;

page 244

he who asks for a fine without motive, tries to have sentenced without reason a person he sees alone like an abandoned horse, an abandoned buffalo, because he sees her without family, without father or mother;

he who cuts the straw and the bushes (around himself), who weeds around his feet,

he who wants another to become his slave,

that one is guilty, and there is a problem between another and him.

[Judgment(s) not translated]

page 245 #195. Of those who pay themselves on the third party's debts owed him.

He who cuts bamboo to weave a basket, he who abandons to the rich the bracelet of his debtor to ask for the fine someone else owes him,

because in his family they are used to taking from the rich his beautiful horses and his fat elephants, to rob him without reason of his objects and his goods;

he who wants sour fruit or sweet vegetables, who covet without reason other's goods;

he who tries to rob without motive, to kill without reason, to take the horses and the elephants of the rich;

he who hits with strength the head of the fish "krua" or the fish "kêñ" without feeling any shame (who asks with insistence),

if one sees gongs hung on the beams (of his house), one will take them, if one sees jars fixed to the libation posts, one will take them, if he is away or asleep, it matters little, one can take them without witnesses and there will be no crime (breaking into a home), because he gave the bracelet of the debtor in order to steal horses and elephants.

All that one sees in his home, objects, food, oxen, buffalo, horses, one will take to recover what he stole (by taking from another what a third party owed him).

page 246 #196. Of those who inflict unwarranted fines to deprive another.

He who eats uncooked meat or fish, who like the fish "kruah" and "êpung" swallow greedily anything, not knowing what is good or bad;

he who, for a matter of one piaster, harasses someone;

he who goes into the forest without telling, who eliminates the small calf and female buffalo,

because he has wanted sour fruit or sweet vegetables for a long time,

because he wants the very straight tree, the very sharp machete, the man strong and agile;

he who cuts the straw and bushes around him, who hoes and weeds around his feet, within hand's reach;

he who braces a rope (across the path), who puts the cangue [a wooden collar three or four feet square used in Oriental countries for confining the neck and sometimes also the hands for punishment] (around the neck of another). who wants others to become his slaves, prompting the hatred of husbands, the resentment of the wives, the anger of the chiefs,

that one is guilty and there is a matter against him.

[Judgment(s) not translated]

page 247 #197. Of those who enter alone into the home of another.

Those who enter alone into the house of another without four or five persons, or two or three, entering first or following them;

those who enter the common room or the private rooms to touch the baskets for cloth or the baskets for jewels;

those who went up into the house of another at the time the Chams entered the village, when the bar (of the door) fell, or the horses bite their feet (to scratch), at noon, without anybody seeing them,

if at the same time, one realizes the disappearance of goods,

if one has cut a piece of bamboo, has bent the rattan (to remember),

if one has been able to hold them by the basket, seize them by the arm, well recognize their faces;

the jar they broke, they will knead again, the thread they broke, they will spin again, the food they ate, they will replace or reimburse its value,

because they make themselves guilty of entering alone in someone else's house,

for this, there is a matter with others and him.

[Judgment(s) not translated]

page 248 #198. Of those who enter at night into another's house when everybody sleeps.

He who enters (into another's house) in the evening because there is tobacco or betel, who enters in the early morning or in the middle of the night to take everything he wants;

he who goes all alone trying to lie down at the feet or the head (of the master of the house), to pierce the mat or the blanket (to steal);

he who, like a thief or an idiot, wanders in the early morning, or in the night, trying to go through the fence, force the big door, to steal yeast in other's jars [for making rice wine], pigs under (the house), the chickens (on the roost), the goods, the jewels, the dishes in the baskets;

he who tries to know what is in the pits of gongs or the pits for jars, who lifts the cover of the jars "tuk" or "bô" (to see what is inside);

he who notices the openings in the fence, the state of the big door, the posts to tie up the horses and the elephants, the paths to the fields.

this one has a problem with others.

[Judgment(s) not translated]

page 249 #199. Of armed robberies.

He who devours big mouthfuls, who follows in the forest, who refuses the calf or young buffalo (offered to him),

if someone owes him, let him ask for it; if he has a problem, let him pursue (in front of a judge),

but if he steals, he takes everything within hand reach,

if he goes alone (to steal) without anybody seeing him,

without four or five persons or two or three able to see him;

if he takes by stretching his hand, if he moves forward rummaging, he steals in the dark of the night, thinking that the awl driven into the tree will leave no (trace) of wounds, that the fault he is doing will not make him guilty, that he could not be accused of wandering like an idiot,

for this, there is an affair.

[Judgment(s) not translated]

page 250 #200. Of thefts.

He who goes prowling, who, hiding, steals, who takes what is within reach;

he who steals rice or millet, tries to steal the goods of the richer the goods of brothers (inhabitants);

he who takes in stretching his hand, who goes forward rummaging, who takes advantage of the dark of the night to go steal;

he who steals without motive, prowls without reason, who robs the brothers needlessly,

because he has no meat to eat, food to cut up, tobacco to smile,

like the dog who steals, made to swallow an eggplant (hot, to punish him), the bad man will be punished, if he does it again, he will be punished more severely.

[Judgment(s) not translated]

page 251 #201. Of servants who rob their masters.

He who finds his food everywhere like the pigs, who steals like the dogs, who tries to steal goods of the rich;

he who is afraid of nothing, who exaggerates in everything, who tries to take or steal the goods of the rich or the goods of the brothers without reason;

like the greedy dog punished by having to swallow a (hot) eggplant, if he is bad he will be punished, if he does it again, he will be punished more severely.

[Judgment(s) not translated]

page 252 #202. Of those who steal goods that cannot be watched.

The pearl necklaces, the metallic bracelets, the objects left by the ancestors a long time ago;

he who tries to steal them, call them his own, wears them,

knowing well that the female parrots cannot be kept, that the parrots cannot be watched over, that the objects buried under ground during the dry season cannot always be watched;

if the banyan of the spring did not repair the basket, did not sharpen the awl,

if he had not poked up the fire, pull the string of the kite (to bring it back), if he did not call all the inhabitants to instruct them and advise them

for this there is a matter with all the nephews, all the inhabitants.

[Judgment(s) not translated]

page 253 #203. Of stealing cereal (grain).

He who grabs the turban or the shoulder bag of those who wear them, he who pursues like the spirits of the dead or the gods, those who work the field;

he who steals handfuls or full baskets of millet or paddy, who steals the rice of the rich or the rice of the brothers,

he who steals paddy is as guilty as the one who kills ,

and because of this, there is a very serious matter.

Antomarchi's Notes: Page 253

Note: Cf. Hittite Code of Hrozny, "If a slave steals in a grain attic, and he takes grain from the attic, he fills the grain attic; likewise he gives [pays] 6 coins of silver, is obligations are satisfied." (par. 97)

[Judgment(s) not translated]

Note: Cf. Hittite Code of Hrozny, p. 75 "If a slave steals in a grain attic, and he takes grain from the attic, he fills the grain attic; likewise he gives [pays] 12 silver coins, his obligations (of the past) are satisfied." (p 96)

page 254 #204. Of the violation of a grave to steal.

He who lifts the corpse, takes out the coffin,

he who takes out the flesh and the bones and leaves them for the ants and the termites;

who steals the necklaces in the coffin, the bracelets in the tomb, the soiled objects (?).

he who, hiding, steals, takes everything he sees, seizes all that is within reach,

because he has no meat to eat, no food to cut, no tobacco to smoke;

he who acts like the (wicked) spirits, like the sky (in wrath), who tries to split the cut down tree, crushes the cut bamboo, who always acts like the wicked dogs,

like the mosquito who always tries to bite, like those who always have problems,

that one is guilty.

The pig or the buffalo destined to be sacrificed are killed. He who creates matters (violation of a grave) will lose his body.

[Judgment(s) not translated]

page 255 #205. Of theft of objects hidden in the ponds.

(He who steals) the big or small pots entrusted to him for hiding,

because they think of him as their own grandson:

he who later goes back to steal them, to take them back in hiding, searching with his hands;

he who goes this way to take back the big pots into the forest, the small pots in the pond, the objects that had been hidden to be kept;

he who is like a hoe or a sharp machete, who is impertinent towards his parents, who goes back to the pond to steal the goods he had been entrusted to hide;

he is guilty and there is a very serious matter with him.

Like the pig and the buffalo destined to be sacrificed, he will lose his body if he creates problems for himself.

page 256 #206. Of stealing honey on the trees "ktong" and "kdjar".

He who drives stakes in the trunk of trees "ktong" and "kdjar" "Hopea perrei" to climb them to steal the honey (of the beehives situated there);

he who climbs at night the trees that one indicated by driving a signal at the foot or in clearing the weeds;

if one catches him by the basket or his arm and knows his face,

if one catches his machete or his saber, catches him when he is climbing the tree,

one will get a rope, will tie him up, will keep him as a slave or prisoner,

because he is not afraid to climb the trees "ktong" and "kdjar" that everyone knows well, to steal the beehive of the owner of the ground, the honey of the rich;

because the one who watches over the earth, who protects the forest, who had the monopoly (of the honey) of the trees "ktong" and "kdjar" of his domain,

(he is not afraid) because he dares drive in stakes (in the trunk of the reserved trees), because he does what is forbidden, because he got over the high mountain;

for this there is matter with another (the owner) and him.

page 256

A pig and a jar, he will give (to the p™ lan), for sacrifice to the earth and the forest, in order that the bees come back, the earth grows green again, the springs flow always, the plants grow.

Moreover he will give back the wax and the honey to the owner of the ground and the trees "ktong"and "kdjar"; as for the theft, if he stole little, he will pay a small fine, if he stole a lot, he will pay him a large fine.

ANTOMARCHI'S NOTES: PAGE 256

Note: "If someone steals a bee hive, and there are no bees inside, he pays three silver coins." (p. 73)

page 257 #207. Of theft of game killed or trapped by another.

He who takes the game he finds to eat in hiding, while other worked hard to cut the trees (to make traps), to go (put up traps) where there are tracks;

he who always tries to steal other's goods, to grab everything within reach of his hands;

knowing well that the game killed by a tiger has many wounds, the game bitten by a snake is swollen where he was bitten, the game caught in a trap with a spear or killed by someone bleeds fresh blood (by the wounds he received);

(if it has to do with the theft of game) whose paws have been tied, ears cut off, the body covered with leaves.

for this, there is a matter with other and him,

because one worked hard to go get poison, to hunt with a crossbow,

because one worked hard to look for game, follow it to have meat or fish for his wife and children,

if he is jealous of the Rhadé, wicked like the spirits, tries to steal, to call his own everything he finds in the dark of the night,

he will have to reimburse the value of the theft and pay a fine,

a hundred buffalo, a hundred oxen, a hundred pigs he will have to give.

page 258 #208. Of stealing fish in someone else's nets.

He who walks along side the bank looking for nets and steals the fish and crabs inside,

when one had set up the nets to catch the fish of the river, the crocodile of the deep waters, to have food;

he who is jealous like the soul of the dead, wicked like the [evil] spirits,

and tries to steal everything he sees, to put his hand in someone else's net to take the fish;

if one had been able to seize him by his basket or his arm, if he knew his face,

if he had been held by his hair, by his head, if one had been able to seize objects (he had with him at the time of the theft) and took them to the chief,

if one had nicked a tree to recognize the place (where he stole), if one broke a branch to indicate the spot,

if he denies, one will be able to point out the spot, the place where he had been caught.

This way he will not be able to say that he had not been caught in the act, was mistreated without reason, that one added unfairly a fine (to reimburse).

If a chicken has been sacrificed (so that the spirits help find the thief), he will reimburse the chicken, if a pig has been sacrificed, he will reimburse the pig, since there is a matter with him.

page 259 #209. Of stealing domestic animals to eat them.

He who steals everything he finds, picks up all that one lets fall,

without anybody seeing him, without three persons knowing, without a hundred or a thousand persons hearing about it;

he who wanders everywhere and takes advantage of the dark of the night to steal everything he finds;

he who dares drive in (a post) , who disobeys his consciousness, who climbs the high mountain, who maintains that the domestic animals (he killed) were wild animals,

for each head (of stolen animal) he will give a jar "ba". for each ear he will give goods of a value of four "ko".

If he claims that he found the animal in the middle of the big forest or the main road, or in the woods where everybody walks,

he is guilty because having climbed on the stump, he did not let anybody know, having been in the woods, he did not tell anyone.

For this, there is a matter with himself.

A̲N̲T̲O̲M̲A̲R̲C̲H̲I̲'̲S̲ N̲O̲T̲E̲S̲: PAGE 259

[Judgment(s) not translated]

NOTE: Cf. Code Hittite, p.59: "If a cow someone steals, in the past , twelve oxen he had to give, mow he gives six oxen: two oxen, two years old, two, one year old , two, six months old (par. 6)."

"If someone steals a pregnant sow, six coins of silver he will give, and for the piglets, for 2 piglets, one basket of grain he will give. (par. 83)."

page 260 #210. Of stealing domestic animals.

He who steals the chief's buffalo, the oxen of the rich, the animals of others without reason,

he who is afraid of nothing, who fears nobody, who climbs the high mountain because he wants to own the buffalo of others,

(the buffalo whose) length of tail has been measured, the chest exactly measured, the buffalo the owner knows perfectly well.

He who seeing some oxen outside the village, buffalo in the pastures, tries to steal them because he is jealous of others;

he who during the day goes around the pond for buffalo and at night finds out where the oxen and buffalo of others lie down and spend the night, and who, as soon as the inhabitants are home, steals them and takes them to his village;

he who is insolent and bold and is not afraid of stealing the oxen and buffalo of his brothers and sisters to make them his own,

he who wants sour fruit and sweet vegetables, who covets the oxen and buffalo of others since yesterday and the day before yesterday (since a long time),

if he has stolen an animal and later ate or sold it, he will reimburse the double, or in fact three times, once in front, once in back, he will give extra.

page 260

 bis And if he has not yet sold it, not yet killed and eaten it, he will pay an indemnity of one "ko" to the owner, he will offer a sacrifice "kpih" and will give back the ox and the buffalo he had stolen.

ANTOMARCHI'S NOTES: PAGE 260

[Judgment(s) not translated]

Note: Cf. Code Hittite, P. 51: "If someone steals a beef cow, a horse, a big mule, a donkey, the owner takes it back whole, so he must give two times and his obligations are satisfied."

page 261 #211. Of those who, finding a canoe swept by the current, hide it and do not tell the owner.

Those who, finding a pirogue swept by the wind, by the current, hiding it to steal it,

if they don't tell, do not show it, if knowing that they are looking for it, do not let them know, if they do not say anything to the one asking morning and evening, day or night;

(if they to not tell that they have found) a pirogue covered with moss, already clogged up (by hand) or already soiled by dirt (of the feet), because they want the straight tree, the very sharp machete, because they covet the goods of others since yesterday or the day before yesterday,

a saucer or a plate, they will give to pay for the tiredness (of the one who did the searching) and the owner will take back his pirogue.

Those are guilty who hide (what they found) under the leaves hiding the pirogue of somebody else.

For this there is an affair with him.

page 262 #212. Of the reward to give to those who, having found a pirogue, tell the owner.

The pirogue swept by the wind, by the current, if one finds it in the bushes, he must take it to the village.

He who tells people to go see, recognize it because he heard that they were looking for it, they ask everywhere if it has been seen;

he who takes out the bark so that they can see the wood,

who informs the owner of the pirogue;

he who does not hide the spoon, does not conceal what he knows, who speaks morning or evening when they question him in the morning or evening, who tells the owner, during the day or the night,

(that one will be rewarded) in giving him a saucer or a plate because he took the trouble to look (for the pirogue) in the bushes and to bring it back to the village, for these they will give him something.

Like one measures the house or the field, they will measure the pirogue in length and width, if the pirogue is small the reward will be small, if it is big, the reward will be big.

page 263 #213 Of the hiding of found objects belonging to someone else.

He who hides (what he has found) in order to make it his own;

he who says nothing so that they do not see, remains silent so that they do not know, who does not inform the inhabitants when there is a matter (of lost objects);

he who hides under the leaves (what he has found), conceals (what he finds) to make it his own;

he who does not climb a tree to let (everybody) know (what he had found), does not go to the chief to inform him;

he who hides the spoon, conceals his words (what he knows), who hides the gourd with grain,

that one is guilty.

If one loses his oxen or his buffalo, one goes looking for them, if one loses this or that, one asks everywhere if anybody has seen or found them,

and if the next morning, at sunrise, or the day after, or the following day one finds them

(he who hides what he finds) will have a matter with him.

he will reimburse double on top of the value (of the object) or three times its value, once in front and once in back (the object) as if he was guilty of the theft,

as if he had stolen in hiding, taking advantage of the night to enter the house of someone else.

A_NTOMARCHI'S N_OTES_: P_AGE_ 263

Note: Cf Code Hittite of Hrozny, p. 95 "But if it is not attested to by witnesses (his discovery) and then his master finds the lost object, then he will be held guilty: 3 times it restores.

but if it does not make attest by witnesses (his discovery) and that then its Master finds it the lost object, then it becomes held guilty: 3 time it restores

page 264 #214. Of found object given back to their owner.

He who finds (an object) in the middle of the main road, on the street, on the path where the inhabitants go;

he who finds the king's oxen, the buffalo of the rich, the objects of the inhabitants in the bushes,

and who shows them so people can see them, who speaks so they know, who lets it be known that he found oxen or buffalo, whose owner he does not know, some objects or goods and ignores who the owner is;

he who does not hide (what he finds) under the leaves, who does not try to conceal it;

he who, having found an ox, asks about its owner, having found an object tries to find its owner, having found some game tries to find the hunter who killed it, after a month or a year,

of the rich, he will be allowed to eat the ox or the buffalo or dry the meat in the drying shed.

If (nobody) neither man nor woman asks for the found objects, does not try to see them, declares the loss,

at the end of three years, the objects or the animals will become the property of the one who found them.

But if one ends up knowing the owner, one will give them back but the owner will have to give a reward: for an old find a large reward, for a recent find, a small reward, to pay for the effort (of keeping his objects or animals).

Antomarchi's Notes: **Page 264**

NOTE: Cf. Code Hittite de Hrozny, p.94: "If someone finds utensils or an ox, a sheep, a horse, a donkey, to his master he will give back. If he cannot find his master he has to get witnesses; and if later he finds his master what his master had lost, he will take from him intact." (parag, XXXV).

page 265 #215. Of those who receive stolen objects.

He who, like the dove looking for a hot ray of sun, like the female parrot letting itself go with the wind, become accomplice (of the thieves);

he who helps the pig to find his food, the dog to steal, who encourages theft;

he who helps to hide the spoon, to conceal the faults (of others), it is like he was an accomplice;

he, man or woman, who approves of the acts (of the thief) and incites him to steal,

he who helps hide under the leaves, to hide the objects or the goods stolen (by another),

that one is guilty and there is a matter between others and him.

[Judgment(s) not translated]

page 266 #216. Of the breaking of fences to obtain firewood.

One fences the fields and the gardens so that the animals cannot enter.

He who is lazy to lift his foot, to move his legs and who, to have firewood, demolishes the fence of the pens of oxen and buffalo;

he who destroys the fences made to protect the house, to enclose the field and stop the domestic animals from entering;

he who is afraid of nothing, who because he is lazy, finds it easier to break down the fence of the field or the house of someone else,

that one is guilty and there is a matter between the others and him.

page 267 #217. Of the enticing away of slaves and servants.

He who tears off the handle of the hose or the machete, who pushes those in the house to leave and go to his house;

he who smokes out the termites nest and makes another's slave leave, who sets fire to the weeds and becomes friend with the servant of someone else;

he who prepares the rice in the field and goes offering water at the edge, he who pulls the basket and the trays out of the field, because he is jealous of the rich or the inhabitants who have slaves and servants;

he who tears off the turban from those wearing one, who tears off the satchel from one who carries it on his shoulder, who is jealous of those who work the field regularly;

he who turns around legs like the smoke of the fire or the water of the river to start problems, this one is guilty and there is a matter between others and him.

ANTOMARCHI'S NOTES: PAGE 267

[Judgment(s) not translated]

Note: Cf Code Hittite of Hrozny, p : "If a person, man or woman, from the town of Itattusas, has something stolen by a man from Lûjja and he takes iit to Arzavva, his master seizes it, so his house iif given [to him].

"If in Huttasas a man from Huttasas steals something and takes it to Lûjja, in the past twelve people were given, but now six people are given and his obligations are satisfied."

page 268 #218. Of those who, having found a jar, are accused by the owner of having stolen it.

If someone finds a necklace in the middle of the path, a bracelet at the foot of a pillar, or a jar in the forest,

and if, back in the village, he climbs on his balcony to call the inhabitants or stays in the middle of the [village] common (to show the found object), if he, in this way, tells everyone including the chief,

in order that the owner (of the object) recognizes his goods, if that one, recognizes his jar, accuses the person who had found it of having stolen it,

if he accuses him of having stolen (his jar) in the evening, in the dark of the night,

without being very sure that this jar is his, not able to recognize the odor and the taste [of the yeast or wine inside], without anybody able to bear witness that it really is his,

for a matter like this, there is no need for a long trial, it is not necessary to go far to water the elephants and the rhinoceros, the jar will be sold, vest and skirts (from the sale) will be shared, each will have a big or small share and that way the affair will be settled.

Chapter X

Page 269 #219. Of those who covet the goods of others.

He who covets the sour fruit, the sweet vegetables, who covets them since yesterday or the day before yesterday (since a long time),

he who gives (to eat) spiders, who puts slugs (in the food), who prepares poison to kill the horses or the elephants of others,

because he is jealous and wicked like the [evil] spirits,

that one is guilty and there is a matter between the others and him.

page 270 #220. Of bad treatment inflicted upon domestic animals.

He who is rough, who loses his temper and mistreats the domestic animal without shame or regret;

he who is violent, loses his temper easily, who has a too big mouth;

he who mistreats the animals of someone else without feeling shame or regret;

he who is cruel, cannot control himself, who is afraid of nothing or nobody, who does not listen to the given advice;

he who holds in his hand a torch of one cubit or six feet (to scare the inhabitants), who often has his liver and his spleen swollen by anger and mistreats the domestic animals without remorse;

he who has a large mouth like the opening of a net or a basket and who nobody can correct,

he will be abandoned like one abandons a piece of bamboo in the mud, like one throws away the fermented rice when drunk, and nobody, boys or girls, will miss him.

Like the pig or the buffalo sacrificed to obtain the recovery of a sick person, he who creates problems for himself will risk his body;

his parents will no longer care for him and will abandon him (to his fate).

page 271 #221. Of those who mistreat domestic animals until they are wounded or they die.

He who hits the animals of the rich, knocks out the animals of the brothers without reason because he is jealous and wicked like the [evil] spirits and the souls of the dead,

if he has killed an animal of the size (value) of a pig, he will reimburse its price, for the head he will give a copper pot, for two ears, iron bars, for four legs, goods equal to four "ko" he will give the owner of the animal.

If it is a bigger animal, a horse, an ox, a buffalo, if he only wounded it, he will pay for the medicine and the necessary care and if the animal gets well, he will give a pig and a jar of rice wine to offer a sacrifice to the spirits;

but if the animal dies, he will have to reimburse its value, he will give a copper pot for the head, two iron bars for the two ears and for the four legs, four slaves (or the value of four slaves).

He will always have to reimburse double extra, or triple (the value of the animal), once on top, once under,

because he is insolent and rough, he is incorrigible and climbs the high mountain.

For this, there is a matter between the others and him.

page 272 #222. Of those who work the animals of others until they are wounded or they die.

He who carries (pulls) whole or split bamboo, male or female bamboo with an elephant belonging to someone else),

if the elephant becomes sick, if he hurts his legs, if he strikes a stump,

he will have to take care of it, to bandage it, to say the prayer that stops the bleeding, give the bracelet and the hoe to obtain the recovery, apply the medicine to heal the wounds.

If the bleeding does not stop, the wound does not dry, the wound does not heal (if the elephant dies),

he will have to reimburse its value or replace it by an elephant of the same size.

If the bleeding stops, the wound dries, if the elephant recovers, why would there be an affair?

But if one cannot put a packsaddle on the elephant, if one can no longer put the rug of bark on its back, if he no longer eats grass and drinks the water, the one who used it will be responsible;

he will have to reimburse the cost or replace it by another elephant of the same value (same size).

page 273 #223. Of oxen and buffalo who fight until wounding or killing one another.

(After the harvest) when the rice is beaten, the sesame is harvested, at the dry season, one lets the oxen and buffalo go free;

the oxen go where they want, the buffalo wander freely;

If they fight, get involved in a battle and get killed, it is not important, there will be not affair, only to burn (the killed animal) and eat it.

If at the time when one must keep (the animals), the herders get together so that the oxen and the buffalo fight, if an animal dies, has a broken leg or becomes blind, there is no affair;

But if one did not close well the pen, build a solid fence or not watch well over (the animals),

if the oxen and the buffalo fight with nobody knowing and kill the oxen and buffalo of somebody else, or break their legs or puncture their eyes,

for this there will be an affair with others and the owner of the animals (who wounded or killed the others).

He will have to reimburse the price of the animals killed (or wounded) or replace them in giving animals of the same value (same size) and the wounded or killed animals will stay with the owner of those who killed or wounded.

[Judgment(s) not translated]

page 274 #224. Of domestic animals who injure or kill human beings.

If nasty oxen or buffalo attack a rich person or any inhabitant,

if they kill, their owner will have to pay the price of the body and the animal will be put down and offered as sacrifice (to the gods) for the dead.

For the price of the body, a big gong "char" of one cubit [+ 18 inches] and one span [+ 9inches] in diameter (or goods of equal value) will be given.

If the person only is injured, he will be paid an indemnity, but the house will be appraised, the field measured in length and width (the severity of the wound will be judged).

If the wound is light, the indemnity will be small, if the wound is serious, the indemnity will be big.

page 275 #225. Of abandoning animals before the usual time.

He who abandons his oxen or his buffalo and lets their feet go to the East and head to the West like wild oxen;

he who does not watch well over his animals, who never goes to see them or who is lazy to build a pen or a fence or take care of his animals;

he who sets loose his animals in the morning and does not bring them back in the evening, who does not gather them to put them in the pen when night comes,

he who owns buffalo and does not watch over them in the morning, does not look for them in the evening lets them wander in the brush like wild animals,

if his buffalo go eat and devastate someone else's crops,

because the horses or the buffalo he raises, the jewels and the utensils he acquired, he does not guard well and does not watch over them,

this one is guilty and there is a matter between others and him.

page 276 #226. Of the devastation of harvests by domestic animals.

If some domestic animals eat some plants, one will have to compensate, if they eat (only) the leaves, one will make a sacrifice, if they eat everything, one will have to replace:

If all the millet or all the paddy is devastated, if the cucumbers and the corn are plundered;

if almost nothing remains, if the damage is important he will have it verified.

For having disturbed the soul (of the plants) and having put out their breath (of life), to the talisman of good harvests, the soul of the rice, one will offer a sacrifice, because he is guilty, the one who does not take care of his animals and does not watch well over them,

and for this, there is a matter with himself.

[Judgment(s) not translated]

page 277#227. Of domestic animals caught in traps set up around a planted field.

He is guilty who does not guard well (his animals), who does not take care of them well, because the animals he raises go everywhere, in the forest, in the gardens, the rice fields or someone else's field, if they are caught in traps with spear or clubs, he will have raised it needlessly, they will be lost and there is no problem.

One sets traps with spear or darts (around the field) for the boars or the deer, afraid that they enter the gardens, the rice fields or the field to eat the plants.

And when one sets up traps with spear or darts, one the uncles and the aunts (the inhabitants) know,

this is why the animals (caught in traps) are lost (for the owner).

page 278 #228. Of those who kill the domestic animalswho enter their fields or gardens.

He who dares drive in (posts), acts against his conscience, and climbs the peaked mountain;

he who is violent, loses his temper easily, does not know how to control himself, this one risks his body.

If some domestic animals have eaten a little or a lot (in his field), let him record it and let him send a man or a woman to inform the owner of the animals.

But if instead he hits wildly, follows (the animals) as far as the brush to kill them;

if he is wicked and jealous like the souls of the dead and the [evil] spirits,

if he has killed animals of others, he will reimburse the cost or will replace them with animals of equal value;

if he had only wounded them, he will pay an indemnity.

As for the amount of the damage done to his harvest, it will be a loss for him, and there will be no case.

Antomarchi's Notes: **PAGE 278**

Note: Cf. Code Hittite, p. 69: "If a meadow pig goes to a field or garden, and if the master of the meadow, field or garden injures the pig badly and it dies, then he must give the pig back to its owner; but if he doesn't give it back, he himself is detained."

Chapter XI

page 279 #229. Of keeping the land.

The daughters are like the seeds of paddy, they are the ones who carry the vest and the blanket, who keep the baskets and the sieves, the back of the ancestors (the land).

The older sister must be looked upon as a mother, the older brother-in-law like a father;

they are the ones who must keep the land (the property), watch over the groves and if the mango trees and the bamboo do not flower well, the young men and the young women act badly (incest), they must be punished.

If the herbs [watercress] dry up in the streams, if the taro withers in the marsh, if some fornicate between parents of the same clan, the owner of the ground will ask for an indemnity.

The rolls of copper wire, the loads of pumpkins, the man cannot take them;

If the aunt dies, the niece will inherit, if the grandmother dies, her grand-daughter will inherit, if that one dies another will inherit (the land and the goods).

If only one man or woman is left, they keep the baskets and sieves, they keep the back of the ancestors;

they will always keep the land, they will always watch over the groves and always watch over the land they own.

When their children are grown, they will instruct them when their grandchildren will be big enough, they will instruct them, because the (tie) which is broken must be tied again, that which is weak must be reinforced.

page 280 #230. Of the obligation to always keep the land.

If the aunt dies, the niece will succeed.

If the grandmother dies, the granddaughter will succeed.

If that one dies, another will succeed.

That way no one will dare take (the land),

nobody will be able to divide it to call it his own.

page 281 #231. Of the rights and duties of the owners of land.

The earth, the water, the groves, the flat baskets, the deep baskets, the back of the ancestors,

it is to the owner to keep them, to keep the "hole" , the forests, the trees with beehives, afraid that the mango trees and the bamboo do not flower well, afraid the young men and young women do not become guilty (of incest) by behaving badly.

If he does not know, he should ask the chief of the village;

if there is a lot of wilted watercress in the streams, many wilted taro in the marsh, it means that the young men and young women have played between parents, between brothers and sisters;

the chief of the village will sentence the guilty to pay an indemnity by giving a pig or a chicken.

If they behaved badly, the chief of the village will impose a fine.

A pig or a jar of rice wine to purify the ground and the forest, they will give;

If of the woman the body is known, if of the man, the person is known, a pig they will give;

the woman will give to the owner, the man to the chief of the village.

But if the chief of the village accuses them unfairly, two male elephants, three female elephants, he will give because he slandered them, and there will be a case between them and him and not between them and not the owner of the ground;

and it will be too bad for him.

It is the hole called "Adrêñ Bâng" or left Rhadés according to caption. The guard of the turn has always been entrusted to the members of [?island] Hdre which left the first hole.

page 282 #232. Of the rights of the owners of the ground (Pô Lan).

All those (owners) who have children or grandchildren must instruct them and tell them this:

One cannot climb trees with beehives "ktong" and "kdjar" because one would be as guilty as if one cut the tail of an elephant, broke the bowl for taxes or if one slept with the wife of the rich or his brother; for this there is a case.

One must not climb the trees "ktong" and "kdjar", this is forbidden, it is a transgression.

On the other hand, one can burn here or there, can fish in the river, this, one can do.

Everyone can harvest the honey on the small shrubs and bushes.

The reeds, the straw, the bamboo to build the houses, everybody can take them without paying (the owner).

One can burn (the bush) to encircle the game, fish the river, for these there is no fault.

But if the owner cannot carry his wood, he must be helped, cannot carry the water, he must be helped, cannot build his house, he must be helped, if he is sick, he must be visited.

If he is alive he must be offered something to drink, if he dies, one must help to bury him, never must he be abandoned.

All must listen to this with the same ears, talk with the same mouth, everybody must agree to this (recognize the rights of the owner);

All the little sparrow hawk brothers, the spirits of the village, all the nephews and nieces, all the inhabitants of here or there, all must well remember this.

[Judgment(s) not translated]

page 283 #233. Of the duty to visit one's land.

The big round basket, the oval basket, the back of the ancestors, the owner must visit.

He must visit them so that the earth always grows green again, the waters run clear, the banana trees and the sugar cane always grows well.

It cannot be that the earth (the property) be like a horse without a master, like oxen without a keeper.

The custom since the grandmothers and grandfathers, the ancestors, since a long time ago,

the custom is that every seven years the owner must visit his land at least once.

page 284 #234. Of attacks on the ownership of the land.

The earth, the waters, the woods, nobody can take them, call them his own.

The earth, the waters, the woods are the property of the owner who cannot part with them.

ADDED TEXT BY THE TRANSLATOR [Antomarchi].

If one tries to take your land, you will only have to tell its limits.

And at this time sacrifice a buffalo so that you will be recognized as the natural owners.

And later, to affirm your rights of ownership, you will do each year the following sacrifices:

A male buffalo and five jars of rice wine for the earth and for you, five jars of rice wine and a castrated pig.

If you do not have a buffalo, you will sacrifice a bull and three jars "tuk" for the earth, a vérat and three jars of rice wine for you.

If you do not have a bull, you will sacrifice for the earth one castrated pig and five jars of rice wine, and for you one vérat and three jars of rice wine.

That way, the earth will always grow green, the waters will run clear, the banana trees and the sugar cane, the plants will always grow well.

(Caption on the origin of Rhade)

page 285 #235. Of capturing land.

He who takes over the earth and waters, who calls his own the land of the rich;

he who takes over the forests, the grounds, the places where the rhinoceros and the elephants graze;

he who is afraid of nobody, disobeys (the laws), who goes over the higher mountain, this one is guilty and there is an affair between others (pô lan) and him.

Antomarchi's Notes: Page 285

The Pô Lăn (or more precisely, the clan of the woman pô lăn, by her descendence [illegible], must prove that he is owner of the land since the beginning, by law of original occupant. For this, he recites different geographic areas: mountains, springs, confluents, cliffs, seas…) which are the [illegible] complete genealogical [line] by uterine path of all pô lăn women who follow since the beginning.

These genealogies sometimes contain only [illegible] 12 to 15 generations (cf. legend of the earth translated by D. Antomarchi)

page 286 #236. Of the visitation of properties.

The round basket, the oval basket, the back of the ancestors, one must visit them to see if the ground is getting green, always, if the water runs clear, if the banana trees and the sugar cane grow well.

Every seven years, at the dry season, custom dictates that the (pô lan) go and visit his land and his forests.

That he goes to see the Hole of emergence of which he is the keeper, the forests situated in his domain, the trees "ktong" and "kdjar" of which he is sole owner,

afraid that others try to take earth and waters, the property of the rich.

But nobody would dare take them if there is always someone to watch the Hole, to go visit the land and the forests, to always care for the trees "kong" and "kdjar";

It is for that reason that the land left by the ancestors since a long tome ago, one must always guard it so that the rich cannot take it.

If the aunt dies, the niece must be taught, if the grandmother dies, the grand-daughter must be taught, if a person dies, another must be taught so that the land always stays with its owner, so that nobody can take it away.

page 286

For this all the sparrow hawk's brothers, the spirits of the village, the nephews and nieces must offer the main pot to the owner of the land once every seven years, one a basket of rice, one a basket of paddy, in order that all the sparrow hawk's brothers, the spirits of the village, the nephews and nieces are in good health, the earth grows green, the water runs clear always, the banana trees and the sugar cane grows well, the paddy is not scrawny and gives beautiful grain.

This they know since the ancestors, nobody could have known it before them; it is the custom since always.

Page 287 [Original] Table of Contents
Chapter I

Chapter II

#24 Of disobedience to the chief's orders.

#25 Of disobedience to the chief.

#26 Of disobedience to the chief.

#27 Of respect for the chief and parents.

#28 Of the choice of a chief.

#29 Of those who want to settle the disagreement of others.

#30 Of those who disobey the orders of the chief.

#31 Of the guilty who offer gifts to the chief so that he will agree with them.

#32 Of slandering accusations against the chief to make him look guilty.

#33 Of those who leave their village without informing the chief.

#34 Of those who carry away the inhabitants without telling the chief.

#35 Of those who mistreat the chief because he takes care of the inhabitants and settles their differences.

#36 Of the help that all inhabitants owe their chief.

#37 Of trouble makers.

#38 Of those who spread disorder by talking in the name of the chief.

#39 Of those who incite the inhabitants to not obey the orders of the chief.

#40 Of those who scare the inhabitants with lies.

#41 Of those who preach revolt in the villages in order to cause the inhabitants to abandon their chief.

#42 Of blows and wounds to the chief and assassination of the chief.

#43 Of those who hurt the chief by having accomplices.

#44 Of rebellious ones.

#45 Of trouble-makers of disorders.

#46 Of the traitors who give information to the enemy on the affairs of their village.

#47 Of those who help the enemy fight the village.

#48 Of those who become accomplice of the pirates.

#49 Of traitors who come to terms with the pirates and inform them of the actions of their chief.

#50 Of escape of prisoners.

#51 Of those who do not rush to take to its destination the bracelet entrusted to them by the chief, and who linger on the way.

#52 Of not registering births with the chief.

#53 Of not registering deaths with the chief of the village.

#54 Of those who use the chief's objects or tools without authorization.

#55 Of the inheritance of the goods of the chief (or a person) when his children have left him to live separately.

#56 Of those who scorn the chief's authority by hiding where they come from or where they go.

Chapter III

#57 Of concealment of individuals.

#58 Of the chief who hides some inhabitants (subject to taxes).

#59 Of the chief who hides the problems of the inhabitants.

#60 Of the chief who takes away inhabitants of neighboring villages.

#61 Of the chief who oppresses the inhabitants.

#62 Of the chief of the village who does not take good care of the inhabitants.

#63 Of arbitrary arrests.

#64 Of arresting someone in somebody else's house.

#65 Of the chief who wants to judge an affair which is not in his jurisdiction.

#66 Of the chief who refuses to judge an affair in his jurisdiction.

#67 Of the chief who accepts goods from a culprit to prove him right.

Chapter IV

#68 Of the wanderers who do not want to stay in their villages.

#69 Of wanderers without a permanent home.

#70 Of those who settle in the hut in the field.

#71 Of bad curses [spells].

#72 Of those who being sick transmit their sickness to others.

#73 Of those who spread infectious sickness.

#74 Of non-revelation of infectious diseases.

#75 Of the necessity to confine the lepers by building a hut in the forest.

#76 Of those who accuse without proof someone of suffering a contagious disease.

#77 Of those who, discovering a corpse, do not tell the chief or do not recognize [identify?] the body.

#78 Of those who hide the epizootics and do not inform the chief.

#79 Of those who do not know how to care for their livestock in periods of epizootic.

#80 Of forest fires.

#81 Of those who, not putting out their fire, caused the village to burn.

#82 Of fires in villages.

#83 Of those who force their way into the banned village.

#84 Of those who force their way into a banned village because of epidemic.

#85 Of those who do not treat properly the sick.

#86 Of those who hide or run when called for help or assistance.

#87 Of the obligation for all the inhabitants to help each other for all work.

#88 Of arbitrary arrests in the house of a third party.

#89 Of the lazy ones who do not want to work in the field.

#90 Of wandering women who do not work the field, the house and do not have a known home.

#91 Of those who do not help put our the fires in the villages.

#92 Of arson on houses and rice granaries.

#93 Of burying cold rice in someone else's field.

#94 Of building a small grave on someone else's field.

Chapter V

#95 Of engagements (and breaking off engagements).

#96 Of nonpayment of the dowry.

#97 Of replacing a dead spouse.

#98 Of obligation of always replacing (the dead spouse) by a brother, a sister or a nephew, or if need be by a child of a woman belonging to the same clan.

#98 continued

#99 Of replacing the deceased wife by a too young girl.

#100 Of the old woman who must take a young substitute; she must give him a concubine, afraid that the human race dies down, the house falls in ruins.

#101 Of old woman must give a concubine to her substitute.

#102 Of marriage of an adult man with a too young woman, if the man is unfaithful to his wife, it is not a big deal.

#103 Of the too young husband who does not yet want a woman; his wife can have a lover without it being a big deal.

#104 Of replacing the deceased to have another chief.

#105 Of too young substitute who becomes chief, the chief's son must help him.

#106 Of the woman who, having no children, adopts a girl of her clan; at her death, all her goods go to the child she had adopted.

#107 Of the infertile woman who adopts a girl of sisters or family.

#108 Of not replacing the deceased spouse: the family of the deceased loses her share of the inheritance.

#109 Of the indissolubility of the union.

#110 Of non-consummation of marriage.

#111 Of he who leaves his wife as soon as she has a child and no longer takes care of them.

#112 Of the lazy ones who do not take care of their wives and children, and only wander.

#113 Of obstacles to marriage.

#114 Of adultery.

#115 Of adultery between a man and a woman already married.

#116 Of the widow guilty of adultery when the grave of her husband is not yet deserted.

#117 Of the widow who wants to remarry before the tomb is deserted, if the family of the dead cannot give her a substitute, it can authorize her to take one somewhere else.

#118 Of taking away the husband or wife of somebody else.

#119 Of the woman who seduces the husband of her sister.

#120 Of those who sleep with their slave, that one will be emancipated.

#121 Of the woman who leaves her husband to remarry with his slave.

#122 Of suspicion.

#123 Of slanderous accusations of adultery.

#124 Of one of the spouses who catches in the act of adultery the other without witnesses.

#125 Of slanderous accusations of adultery.

#126 Of accusations of adultery without proof.

#127 Of spouses who leave each other when there is a contract.

#128 Of the one who breaks the contract by leaving his wife to take another.

#129 Of those who get married without telling the chief.

#130 Of he who emigrates to another country and abandon his wife to take a foreign wife.

#131 Of he, who being married, has a child with a young girl.

#132 Of he who is married with a woman and leaves her as soon as she has a child.

#133 Of the young man and the young girl who have relations until they have a child.

#134 Of the husband taken prisoner or slave; his wife does not have to wait for him and can remarry.

#135 Of a woman whose husband has been gone for several years can remarry.

#136 Of he who leaves the village to look for another wife without getting a divorce from the first.

#137 Of those who hit their wives until they are wounded.

#138 Of abortions.

#139 Of slanderous accusations of abortions.

#140 Of the woman who always gives birth to still-born babies; she can have an abortion without problems.

#141 Of the woman who aborts without her husband and her family knowing.

#142 Of the husband must entrust his wife with everything he owns.

Chapter VI

#143 Of the parent's responsibility towards their children.

#144 Of girls who disobey their parents.

#145 Of girls who abandon their parents to go live in another village.

#146 Of children or grand-children who do not take care of their parents or grand-parents; they will not be able to inherit, and the inheritance will go to the woman who took care of them in their old age and whom they have adopted.

#147 Of sons-in-law, children and servants who are impertinent towards their parents or their masters.

#148 Of parents who encourage their children to steal.

#149 Of those who render themselves guilty of fornication in else's home.

#150 Of the head of the family sleeping with his slave; the slave will have to be set free.

#151 Of the young man who fornicates with someone else's slave.

#152 Of rape.

#153 Of rape during sleep.

#154 Of seductions.

#155 Of those who rape pre-pubescent girls who do not yet know the desires of the body.

#156 Of those who seduce children to strip them.

#157 Of incest between related parents.

#158 Of incest between distant relatives.

#159 Of act of fornication with domestic animals.

Chapter VIII

#160 Of voluntary murders.

#161 Of child killings.

#162 Of poisoning by water, alcohol, or food.

#163 Of those who bring death to all the inhabitants by poisoning the spring.

#164 Of murder of someone accused of witchcraft.

#165 Of those who become guilty by listening to bad advice.

#166 Of unintentional murders.

#167 Of those guilty by constraint.

#168 Of blows given without reason.

#169 Of rapes.

#170 Of the master who hits a pregnant servant until she aborts.

#171 Of buying slaves.

#172 Of selling slaves.

#173 Of servants or workers who hurt or kill themselves.

#174 Of accidents caused by indicated traps.

#175 Of accidents caused by non-indicated traps.

#176 Of accidents caused by non-disarmed traps during the day.

#177 Of crimes committed by the insane.

#178 Of crimes and offences committed in a state of intoxication.

#179 Of sons-in-law who strike their parents-in-law until death follows.

#180 Of those who mistreat their mother or father.

Chapter IX

#181 Of the keeping of property.

#182 Of one part of the goods of the deceased husband, must be given back to his mother or his older sister.

#183 Of the single young man who has goods must entrust them to his mother or sisters.

#184 Of the brothers-in-law who squander the goods their sisters-in-law inherited.

#185 Of the impossibility for the husband to give the goods of his wife or daughters to his nieces and nephews.

#186 Of purchases made rashly.

#187 Of those who buy goods from minors.

#188 Of those who refuse and depreciate the merchandise.

#189 Of goods sold too expensively.

#190 Of those who borrow goods and never return them.

#191 Of those who damage the objects they borrow.

#192 Of healers who try to eat the goods of others.

#193 Of healers guilty of swindles and trickeries.

#194 Of those who make a big affair from a small one in order to make a profit.

#195 Of those who pay themselves on the third party's debts owed him. [?]

#196 Of those who inflict unwarranted fines to deprive another.

#197 Of those who enter alone into the home of another.

#198 Of those who enter at night into another's house when everybody sleeps.

#199 Of armed robberies.

#200 Of thefts.

#201 Of servants who rob their masters.

#202 Of those who steal goods that cannot be watched.

#203 Of stealing cereal (grain).

#204 Of the violation of a grave to steal.

#205 Of theft of objects hidden in the ponds.

#206 Of stealing honey on the trees "ktong" and "kdjar".

#207 Of theft of game killed or trapped by another.

#208 Of stealing fish in someone else's nets.

#209 Of stealing domestic animals to eat them.

#210 Of stealing domestic animals.

#211 Of those who, finding a canoe swept by the current, hide it and do not tell the owner.

#212 Of the reward to give to those who, having found a pirogue, tell the owner.

#213 Of the hiding of found objects belonging to someone else.

#214 Of found object given back to their owner.

#215 Of those who receive stolen objects.

#216 Of the breaking of fences to obtain firewood.

#217 Of the enticing away of slaves and servants.

#218 Of those who, having found a jar, are accused by the owner of having stolen it.

Chapter X

#219 Of those who covet the goods of others.

#220 Of bad treatment inflicted upon domestic animals.

#221 Of those who mistreat domestic animals until they are wounded or they die.

#222 Of those who work the animals of others until they are wounded or they die.

#223 Of oxen and buffalo who fight until wounding or killing one another.

#224 Of domestic animals who injure or kill human beings.

#225 Of abandoning animals before the usual time.

#226 Of the devastation of harvests by domestic animals.

#227 Of domestic animals caught in traps set up around a planted field.

#228 Of those who kill the domestic animals who enter their fields or gardens.

Chapter XI

#229 Of keeping the land.

#230 Of the obligation to always keep the land.

#231 Of the rights and duties of the owners of land.

#232 Of the rights of the owners of the ground (Pô Lan).

#233 Of the duty to visit one's land.

#234 Of attacks on the ownership of the land.

#235 Of capturing land.

#236 Of the visitation of properties. Original Text in French and Edé

Original Text in French and Edé

RECUEIL

DES COUTUMES RHADÉES

DU DARLAC

(HDRUÔM HRĂ KLEI DUÊ KLEI BHIĂN ĐUM)

ECOLE FRANCAISE D'EXTREME - ORIENT

COLLECTION DE TEXTES ET DOCUMENTS SUR

L'INDOCHINE

IV

R E C U E I L

DES COUTUMES RHADÉES DU DARLAC

(HDRUÔM HRA KLEI DUÊ KLEI BHIAN DUM)

Recueillies

par L. SABATIER
Administrateur des Services Civils
ancien Résident de France à Banméthuôt

Traduites et annotées

par

D. ANTOMARCHI
Inspecteur de l'Enseignement primaire
des Minorités Ethniques

H A N O I
Imprimerie d'Extrême - Orient

1940

Mnuih mâo klei soh ñu sun ngan
Individu avoir affaire coupable lui offrir biens

kơ Khôa bi khôa lač brei klei găl ñu.
à chef afin chef dire donner affaire juste sienne.

Ñu mniê duah klei, êkei duah kđi, arăn ñu bäng hriê kơ mli mdrông.
Lui femme chercher affaire, homme chercher procès, alors lui venir
trouver à chef puissant.

Kông ñu hriê dal kơ mnut kơ êa, mngan sun, hui khôa dôk he ting kơ tuê,
hluê ting ting buôn, hui khôa hluê tluôn êgar.
Bracelet lui venir offrir à banian tête eau, vaisselle offrir, craindre
chef rester donc côté de étrangers, suivre côté habitants, craindre chef
suivre derrière non-parents.

Hui khôa dôk ting kơ mnu, tu ting mja, sap kđha hui hluê arăng.
Craindre chef rester côté poulet, accepter côté fouine, parole sentence
craindre suivre autrui.

Ñu čiäng khôa lač brei bi tu, blu brei bi kpă ngă brei bi găl.
Lui vouloir chef dire donner afin approuver, parler donner afin droit,
agir donner afin juste.

Ñu amâo mâo jơng, ñu mă jơng pai, ñu amâo mâo ai ñu mă ai êmông, amâo
mâo kbông mă kbông sah mdrông.
Lui ne pas avoir jambes lui prendre pattes lapin, lui ne pas avoir
force lui prendre force tigre, ne pas avoir bouche prendre bouche chef
puissant.

Ñu amâo er êbat bäng kơ đi êman, amâo ar êran bäng kơ đi aseh.
Lui ne pas pouvoir marcher venir pour monter éléphant, ne pas pouvoir
courir venir pour monter cheval.

Ñu hđeh elak bun hin rin tap bäng kơ sah mdrông, bi sah mdrông ba brei
si ba adei bi mnei brei si bi mnei anak, khôa rông brei bi mơak mñai.
Lui enfant faible pauvre dénué seul affamé venir à chef riche, afin
chef riche porter donner comme porter cadet, faire baigner donner comme
baigner enfant, chef protéger donner afin agréable bon.

Anăn ngan ñu brei kơ khôa.
Pour cela biens lui donner à chef.

Kơyâo kčik bi mâo agha, kơyâo êrang bi mâo agha, ami ama ñu hriê
jing kơ khôa.
Arbre kčik tous avoir racines, arbre êrang tous avoir racines, mère
père lui venir faire avec chef.

Djăt êa ñu knang kơ čư bư êa mâo boh tâo kli mâo kđi arăng, ñu knang
hong sah mdrông.
Puiser eau lui appuyer avec montagne, barrer rivière avoir pierres
..., avoir différent autrui lui appuyer avec chef riche.

(Chap. II, no 8)

AUTRES EXEMPLES DE TRADUCTION

Tluah mœ̆a pha msah djiê êman brah mœah knah hlong djiê sah mdrŏng yœ̆ ñu .

Fesses mouillées, cuisses humides, mort éléphant jeune, brisés gongs sonores, mort chef riche à cause lui .

Chap. II, no 22)

Ñu llăng ñu hdeh klŏng ka thâo săng băng ka thâo bit êngit lan hong adiê ka thâo kral .

Lui voirlui enfant, sentier pas encore savoir comprendre, trou pas encore savoir lien, azur terre avec ciel pas encore savoir reconnaître.

Chap. IX, no 7)

Hut-lui plu ariêng mniê toh mŏiêng plu êkei klei boh ñu plu ciăng bŏng ngăn arăng .

Chouette fasciner crabe, femme ôter jupe séduire homme, affaire pensé lui séduire vouloir manger bien autrui .

Chap. IX, no 9)

Anăn ngăn ñu lo kpung dua, mkôa thâo ngăn ălâo êdei ñu lo brei hahn kơh arăng tu .

Alors biens lui encore ajouter deux, rembourser trois, biens devant derrière lui encore donner, ainsi donc autrui accepter .

Chap. IX, no 10)

INDEX
des termes rhadés et des termes conventionnels

ABRÉVIATIONS
employées dans cet ouvrage.

---

ar.	arabe	malad.	maladie
a.s.	au sujet de	marchand.	marchandise
ass.	assassinat	obéiss.	obéissance
č.	čam	p.	pour
circ.	circulation	pers.	personne
compt.	complicité	pouv.	pouvoir
décl.	déclaration	pris.	prisonnier
déf.	défaut	rec.	recel
escl.	esclave	règl.	règlement
escr.	escroquerie	rest.	restitution
év.	évasion	sacr.	sacrifice
f.	fonctions	simul.	simulation
fals.	falsification	subst.	substitution
impr.	imprudence	télégr.	télégraphique
infr.	infraction	tent.	tentative
ins.	insultes	tromp.	tromperie
invol.	involontaire	us.	usurpation
j.	jour	us. de f.	usurpation de fonction
jug.	jugement	vag.	vagabondage
jurispr.	jurisprudence		

DES PEINES

Tout, ... ou .... causé à la .... ou aux biens d'autr
doit être réparé (mkra); son auteur peut en outre être poursuivi (bi kmhal) po
avoir violé les prescriptions de la coutume.

Les peines prévues par la coutume ..... sont :

Io/- Le sacrifice (kpih ou wăt) dont le but .... de calmer les divinités(ya.
que le coupable a irritées. Le sacrifice est dit (wăt) quand il est fait av
un poulet, sans ..... ; il est dit(kpih) quand il est fait avec un porc, un
boeuf ou un buffle, ou tout autre mammifère et qu'on oint les pieds avec ur
mélange d'alcool de riz et de sang de l'animal sacrifié.

Le coupable condamné aux frais d'un sacrifice doit donner l'animal à
sacrifier.

2o/- L'indemnité réparatrice ou amende (kdi). Elle peut être payée en nat
ou en espèces et peut varier d'une piastre (sa song) à ..... piastres(tlâo

Quand l'amende ne pouvait être payée, par suite d'insolvabilité, le coup
..... engageait pour ..... ; il mettait son corps en gage (tuič asei) jusqu'à
que sa famille ait payé l'amende qui l'avait frappé. Par suite d'une inte
rétation abusive de la coutume orale l'engagé pour dettes était réalité e
..... à vie. On estimait que le travail qu'il fournissait suffisait à pei.
..... son entretien et n'était d'aucun rapport pour son maître. Il en était d..
..... de même pour ceux qui ne pouvaient payer les dettes qu'ils avaient ...
..... actées.

3o/- Le remplacement des objets empruntés, perdus ou détériorés.

4o/- Le remboursement du vol. Les biens volés doivent être remboursés au
..... riple de leur valeur (ngăn tle sa kdrěč ba kdi tlâo kdrěč).

5o/- Le paiement du prix du corps (tăm ênua) à la famille de la victime
..... d'homicide ou d'assassinat. La valeur de la personne humaine est éval.
..... un grand gong plat (čhar) d'une coudée et un empan de diamètre pour une
..... ersonne riche, et à un grand gong plat (čhar) d'une coudée et un poing de
..... tre pour une personne pauvre.

6o/- L'esclavage. Le coupable qui ne pouvait payer le prix du corps éta.
..... endu comme esclave (hlun) dans un pays ou à l'étranger (au Cambodge, au l
..... u dans une tribu voisine).

7o/- La peine de mort. Le coupable était ficelé puis mis à mort à coups
..... sabre et de lance, ou pendu à un arbre dans la forêt. Son corps était ens..
.... aux corbeaux et aux vautours, ou aux bêtes féroces.

D. A.

TABLE ALPHABETIQUE

(Les chiffres renvoient aux numéros des textes en français)

INTRODUCTION

Le Coutumier rhadé est un document oral très ancien. Ses origines, comme les des tribus rhadées, se perdent dans la nuit des temps. Quelques textes (No 5 et No 197) font mention de la venue des Rhadés sur le Plateau, probablement au XIIe ou XIIIe siècle.

Les termes archaïques très nombreux confirment l'ancienneté du Coutumier. Il est en réalité un poème. Le juge rhadé récite la coutume en vers. Et la langue rhadée possède une syntaxe et un vocabulaire qui n'ont presque rien de commun avec la langue parlée couramment. En outre l'emploi des formes elliptiques a été poussé jusqu'à ses extrêmes limites. (cf. Exemples de traduction: une longue phrase comprenant trois ou quatre mots essentiels; c'est de ces mots qu'on pourra reconstruire la phrase entière.

Cet emploi abusif de l'ellipse n'a été conçu comme un procédé mnémotechnique, grâce auquel la coutume a pu être transmise de bouche à oreille pendant de longs siècles.

Une autre caractéristique de la langue du Coutumier réside dans l'abondance des métaphores dont beaucoup seraient goûtées de nos meilleurs poètes ("enfant sans expérience ne sait pas encore distinguer le bleu des monts lointains de l'azur du ciel"; une grande maison est "longue comme l'onde sonore du gong", etc..........

Tel qu'il est présenté, cet ouvrage n'est pas à proprement parler un Coutumier. Chaque texte est constitué par plusieurs articles s'appliquant à un cas particulier. Il en résulte qu'un même article se trouve répété dans plusieurs textes différents. Il n'est ainsi pas possible de s'appuyer sur un texte entier pour régler certaines affaires. Il faut puiser dans les différents textes les articles ou paragraphes concernant ces affaires; on obtiendra ainsi des textes nouveaux.

La disposition de l'ouvrage, sa composition et l'absence de table des matières en rendaient difficile la consultation. On trouvera donc dans ce livre une table des matières en rhadé et en français, une table analytique par ordre alphabétique, un index et une liste des observations. Une étude sommaire des peines prévues dans l'ancienne coutume fait suite à cette introduction. La jurisprudence portée à la suite de chaque texte indique les jugements prononcés par le Tribunal de Buon-Ma-Thuot de 1917 à 1938.

Malgré les imperfections qu'on peut relever dans sa présentation matérielle, le "Klei Duê" reste un des plus beaux monuments de la littérature orale rhadée. Nous ne pouvons être reconnaissants à M. SABATIER de l'avoir recueilli et écrit, car, il le leur a souvent dit, "la parole sur le papier vaut mieux que la parole sur les lèvres".

Buon-Ma-Thuot, le 15 Octobre 1939

"...J'étais un homme jeune quand mes pieds ont nouvellement foulé la terre du Darlac, et c'est chez vous que les cheveux blancs ont poussé sur ma tête .

Pendant quatorze fois douze lunes nous avons bu la même eau, mangé le même riz, nous avons été trempés par les mêmes pluies, brûlés par le même soleil, saignés par les mêmes sangsues, affaiblis par la même fièvre."

L. SABATIER.
(Palabre du Serment au Darlac 1926).

I. KLEI [...]

Mnuih knah klong; ktong dut ku, mnuih lu klei.

Nu khăng lang ti êmông, khăng dlông ti yang, khăng wă kang sah mdrong.

Bu gran wang amâo thâo đa, bu gran kga amâo thâo gô, mtô laĉ klei amâo thâo gut.

Asăo êra bi kblăm he ñu trong, mnuih jhong bi hlah, dah blu bi kmhal he ñu.

Ĉim điet ĉhi băng kmong, ĉim prong ĉhi hlăm ei; kđi điet mkă brei điêt, kđi prong mkă brei prong, to dah mâo kđi hong ayong ađei, klei mse soai.

Mâo kđi điet đu ngan song, mâo kđi prong đu ngan ko, tơ mâo kđi ebeh tơ ai, dlai tơ asei, klei ê beh, pu amâo đam klăm amâo dui.

Un mnu rih jih asei, êmô kbao rih jih asei, mnuih mâo kđi klei prong tuĉ asei ñu pô.

Wang boh tăo êka, kga boh tăo ebôr, mtei hĕ ai tiĕñu.

I. DES PEINES

Celui dont la voix résonne comme le son du gong, qui s'agite sans cesse comme le daim à queue courte, qui a beaucoup d'histoires;

celui qui désobéit au tigre, qui se croit plus que les génies, et se montre insolent envers le Chef;

celui qui est comme la manche tordue de la binette ou du coupe-coupe qu'on ne peut pas redresser, celui qui n'écoute pas les conseils qu'on lui donne,

comme le chien gourmand qu'on corrige en lui faisant avaler une aubergine chaude, s'il est mauvais on le punira, s'il se montre insolent et s'il récidive on le condamnera.

On mettra les petits morceaux de viande dans les cornets, et les grands morceaux dans des paniers; de même, pour une petite affaire on infligera une petite amende, pour une affaire grave on infligera une forte amende, toutes les affaires des habitants seront ainsi jugées.

Pour une petite affaire on inflige une amende d'une piastre; pour une grosse affaire on infligera une amende de quatre piastres, pour une affaire très grave excédant le prix du corps il n'est pas possible de fixer le montant de l'amende.

Le porc et le poulet destinés au sacrifice perdent leur corps, le boeuf et le buffle destinés au sacrifice perdent leur corps, de même, celui qui a une affaire très grave perdra son corps (la vie ou la liberté).

La binette et le coupe-coupe usent la pierre lisse ou la pierre rugueuse sur laquelle on les aiguise, les coupables seront punis proportionnellement aux fautes qu'ils auront commises.

Bi kmhal : punir, corriger, infliger une sanction.

Kđi (ĉ.gađi; ar. cađi): procès, différend, affaire, amende, indemnité.

Sah mdrong (Chef riche) expression poétique désignant le Chef, celui qui détient l'autorité, qui commande.

Jih asei, tuĉ asei (perdre le corps) devenir esclave, prisonnier, ou être [...]

JURISPR.-Jug.no 23 du 15 juil. 1919 : Restitution triple.
        Jug.no 55 du 20 sept. 1923 : 3 mois + restitution triple.
        Jug.no 53 du 6 juin 1926 : I an + sacr.kpih+ rest.triple.
        Jug.no 26 du 5 août 1936 : 3 mois + restitution triple .

NOTE .- Cf. Code Hittite de Hrozny :"Si un boeuf,un cheval, un mulet,
un âne quelqu'un vole,son maître le saisit et le prend intact,et outre
celui-ci deux fois il donne." (P.6I).

        "Si des objets quelqu'un trouve et ne rend pas,si son maître
les trouve, trois fois il restitue." (P.95).

JURISPR.—Jug.no 23 du 15 juil. 1919 : Restitution triple.
          Jug.no 55 du 20 sept. 1923 : 3 mois + restitution triple.
          Jug.no 53 du 6 juin 1926 : I an + sacr.kpih+ rest.triple.
          Jug.no 26 du 5 août 1936 : 3 mois + restitution triple .

NOTE .— Cf. Code Hittite de Hrozny : "Si un boeuf,un cheval, un mulet,
un âne quelqu'un vole,son maître le saisit et le prend intact,et outre
celui-ci deux fois il donne." (P.6I).

          "Si des objets quelqu'un trouve et ne rend pas,si son maître
les trouve, trois fois il restitue." (F.95).

2. KLEI NGA HDONG BI MDOR AI MSE.

Tang kŏ krŏă, ma kŏ kĕñ, amĭú răk hĕñ mlâo.

Wang boh tâo ĉkĕ, kga boh tĕ âĉor; bi tŏl ai tiĕ bi mse.

hdong bi djiê soai.

Kĕ amăo mñô.

2. DE CEUX QUI SE FRAPPENT JUSQU'À CE QUE MORT S'EN SUIVE

Ceux qui se frappent à tête comme on frappe les poissons krŏă ou kĕñ (pour les assommer) sans honte ni retenue;

ceux qui comme la binette et le coupe-coupe, et la pierre sur laquelle on les aiguise, s'usent simultanément;

s'ils se frappent mutuellement avec une égale violence,

s'ils succombent tous deux en même temps, pour cela il n'y a pas affaire.

(OVER)

KLEI TLĔ ŜA' KBRĔ, BĂ KĐI TLÂŎ KBRĔ

Ñu duah nao mnê, tlĕ mñêñ, ñu duah wêñ kĭe, kngan ko đĕ ngăn arang;

Ñu duah mâ huang, chuang kmat, mnat mlam ñu duah tlĕ.

Ñu amâo mâo čim bong, ñu amâo mâo mong čhat, ñu kmâo mâo hat drao djup;

Amâo ñu duah ngă ai un knhâo, si amâo knĕ, ñu tlĕ ma mnong nhua arang kđi.

Tơdah arang mâo pan ñu ti knik, mâo kŭk ñu ti ko, dơ dĭng ñu arang mâo sua, čiang bĕ ñu ko êa, hra ko buôn, pô dlang buôn sang.

Mnut ko êa phat brei ênoh, kjoh brei giê kđuĕ brei kđi.

Amâo êra ti kblam he ñu trong, mnuih knong ti Hlah, dah blu bi kmhal he ñu.

Ñu tăm ênua, bă kđi; ngăn ñu To kpung duĕ mnuĕ tlâo, êlâo sa, êdei sa ñu brei.

In arang hun, mnu arang hnuiĕ, čiang bĕ thâo kiĕl drei, êkei thâo pô, êmô kbao thâo mga;

ñu čiu čla bĭ ala hnô, ñu lŏ bi hrŏ ngă mga.

Jug.no 23 du 15 juill. 1919 : Restitution triple.

Jug.no 26 du 30 sept. 1923 : 3 mois + restitution triple.

Jug.no 53 du 6 juin 1926 : I an + sacr. kpih + rest. triple.

Jug.no 26 du 5 août 1930 : 3 mois + restitution triple.

-- Cf. Code Hittite de Hrozny: "Si un boeuf, un cheval, un mulet, un âne qua... un vole, son maître le saisit et le prend intact, et outre celui-ci deux ...s il donne". (P.61).

"Si des objets ... il ne le rend pas, si son maître le ... [P.65].

1. LE MONTANT DU VOL DOIT ÊTRE REMBOURSÉ AU TRIPLE.

Celui qui vole tout ce qu'il trouve, qui allonge la main pour voler le bien d'autrui,

qui vole pendant l'absence du maître, qui marche sans faire de bruit et qui profite de l'obscurité de la nuit pour aller voler;

celui qui n'a pas de viande à manger, d'aliments à découper, de tabac à fumer, et agit comme le porc qui trouve sa nourriture partout, comme le chien qui saisit tout ce qu'il voit; celui celui vole les biens d'autrui sans motif,

Si on arrive à le saisir par les cheveux, à le tenir solidement par la tête, les objets lui appartenant on pourra les lui prendre,

on le conduira devant le banian de la source, le figuier du village, devant celui qui veille sur tous les habitants.

Le banian de la source estimera le montant du vol, jugera à l'aide du bâton, règlera l'affaire définitivement.

Le chef punira le coupable dont on punit le chien voleur en lui faisant avaler une aubergine chaude; s'il récidive il le punira plus sévèrement.

Le coupable devra rembourser le montant du vol et payer une amende, il remboursera le double en sus de la valeur des objets volés, une fois devant, une fois derrière (l'objet volé soit en tout le triple du montant du vol.

Si on a sacrifié un porc ou un poulet pour retrouver l'auteur du vol, celui-ci devra également rembourser valeur des animaux sacrifiés.

si on l'a retenu par... ...par les bras, et qu'on a bien reconnu son visage,

si on l'a tenu comme on dit le boulet, par les patins ou par les ailes, si on a crié pour que d'autres saient,

si on a saisi le turban ou la veste, le sabre ou le coupe-coupe, ou un objet quelconque (appartenant au coupable);

si, nia trace, signe avec le pied (à l'endroit où on l'a pris) on a entaillé la colonne ou le mur témoins, si on a brisé une branche de l'arbuste;

s'il nie on pourra indiquer le lieu (où le coupable a été pris en flagrant délit).

Et s'il y a quatre ou même deux ou trois personnes qui ont vu et entendu,

ainsi on aura une preuve certaine

JURISPR. Jug no. 46 du 2 janvier 1917.
...chage sont que toute accusation soit appuyée de preuves et de témoignages. Les juges autochtones de Banmethuot ont toujours admis ...prin... d'une accusation ne pouvant être prouvée est donc considér... ...fondée et celui qui en est l'objet doit être acquitté.

5. KLEI LO BI KRU KDI HDĂP

Knuê pui leh bhăt,hăt leh djiê,
hung dliê leh tuic.

Kdi leh rai Čam, *Ram* Dam Yuăn.

Knuê pơng tung leh roă,pơng blang
leh roă, ngă kdi leh măc.

Ara anei lê ñu poh kơ gu, ru kơ
lơng.

Knuê ding băng leh kăt,hăt drao
ah kdial.

Kdi leh sir sia,ăngiă kru,thu eh
jiêk.

Hlang krô lo mtah, kpiê djah lo
ih , kdi jih lo adơk.

Êmông pit lo răo,kgăo pit lo ru,
ăp ju jhat lo bi hdơr.

Knuê dih,êman leh kning,čing leh
yul, kdi leh kuôl ka;

Ara anei bơng kê lo mbliu,bơng
... la mbliu,kdi lo hluê sap kbông,
ng buh lo kwa.

Knah hlang,ktong dut ku,mnuih
klei.

... hong bun ngă jhong, blu hong
... čăp.

... kthul ñu,măo kdi arăng kơ

5. DU RENOUVELLEMENT D'UNE
AFFAIRE DÉJÀ RÉGLÉE

Le feu est éteint depuis longtemps,
le tabac (dans la pipe) est consumé,
la forêt a été entièrement traversée.

L'affaire remonte à la disposition
des Chams, à la défaite des Annamites.

Les blessures faites à l'arbre
"tung" et à l'arbre"blang" (pour les
escalader) se sont fermées depuis
longtemps,l'amende a été payée.

Mais aujourd'hui il (le coupable)
met en bas ce qui était en haut,il
met en haut ce qui était en bas.

Cependant le trou(de la flûte)avait
été bien bouché,la pipe avait été
bien bourrée.

L'affaire avait été réglée définitivement, toute empreinte avait été
disparu,l'urine et la fiente avaient
eu le temps de sécher(et de disparaî-
tre).

Mais maintenant la paillote désséc-
chée reverdit, l'alcool qui était fade reprend du goût, l'affaire aqui
était réglée est ressuscitée.

Le tigre qui dormait est réveillé,
l'ours qui sommeilait est dérangé, les
mauvaises paroles sont rappelées.

Et pourtant l'éléphant avait été
bien entravé, les gongs avaient été
bien suspendus, l'affaire avait été
bien jugée.

Maintenant la boulette de riz(dans
la bouche) est retournée(par la langue)
la parole (du juge)est déformée, le
bracelet accepté(par les parties)est
ouvert.

Il(le coupable)est comme le gong
sonore, comme le daim à courte queue,
il a toujours des histoires.

S'il parle avec les pauvres il est
grossier, s'il parle avec les riches
il est insolent.

Celui-là est coupable et il y a affaire entre les autres et lui.

Jug.no 34 du 2 Oct.I918 : I an + 20$00
Jug.no 28 du 30 Mai I923 : 2 an
Jug.no 3I du 3I Mai I923 : I an.
Jug.no 22 du 30 Mars I925 : I mois+ 5$00+ sacr.kpih au Chef
Jug.no 34 du 5 Avril 1926:2 mois+ 4$00+ sacr.kpih au Chef.
Jug.no 52 du 24 Juin I926:I mois+ 5$00.
Cette coutume est également applicable aux différends qui n'ont pas été
...tés devant le Tribunal dans un délai normal.

JURISPR.- Jug.no II du IO juil. I9I8 : 6 mois + 30$00.

Jug.no 82 du 7 nov. I924 : 6 mois à 6 ko + kpih.

Jug.no 44 du I8 juin I925 : 5 ans.

Jug.no 7I du 25 sept. I925 : I mois + 3 ko + kpih.

6. KLEI GAO KLEI BI KUÔL.

Klam sa klei, hrôe sa sap, wir rong anăp mdê.

Ñao ko djuh wơr dja êa, nao ko kma wơr dja wăng kga, ñu mnuih khăng duah ngă, khăng duah rong pla pliê.

Kbông hlăm, kdha bluč, ñu khăng duah kuô mi pliê.

Ñu gao kưng, gao knŏng, gao sap kbông sah mdrong kuôl.

Trong tlê, alê mnêô, ñu khăng duah ndeô mdar.

Aguah čim bhi êkei, hrôe čim bhi miê, kla hlăm thung dliê, ñu lo duah klei mkuăn.

Druk si drao mêah, huah si drang **dang**

Čiet êgao ti orang, hlang êgao Ti hrle, hlê mnông êgao ti pum êjung.

Msei mnêô pral si mêô, mnuih mêô thêo klei lu.

Ñao čiet djo hda, gao pla djo khô ao klei ngă leô mêo kđi.

Anah hlong, kteng đut ku, mnuih lu klei.

Si bang mbah, yah bang kbông, **Kŏng** duh kwa.

Ayan **Khal ñu** mêo klei mtang kŏng.

6. DE LA VIOLATION DES CONTRATS.

Celui qui parle d'une manière la nuit et d'une autre le jour, qui change d'avis dès qu'il a tourné le dos;

celui qui va au bois et oublie d'emporter de l'eau, qui va au champ sans emporter le coupe-coupe et la binette, qui s'engage à faire ceci ou cela et ne le fait pas ou le fait mal;

celui qui a la parole facile et abondante mais parle toujours à tort et à travers;

celui qui passe outre le barrage, qui franchit la clôture, qui désobéit à la parole du Chef, qui ne respecte pas les engagements qu'il a pris;

celui qui est comme l'aubergine qui change d'aspect quand on la pile comme le bambou "alê" (qui de loin semble droit alors qu'il est brisé), celui qui ne tient pas ses promesses;

celui qui le matin comme l'oiseau rouge mâle, le soir comme l'oiseau rouge femelle, qui une fois rentré dans la forêt cherche une nouvelle affaire;

celui dont la voix ressemble au craquement du bambou fendu, au cri du calao;

celui qui est comme l'herbe qui veut s'élever plus haut que les joncs comme la paillote qui veut s'élever plus haut que les bambous, comme les animaux sauvages qui veulent bondir plus haut que la cîme des arbres de la forêt;

celui qui est comme un cheval fort mais dépourvu d'agilité, celui qui est ignorant mais a beaucoup d'histoires;

celui qui désobéit aux signaux des pièges est pris dans ces derniers, celui qui n'obéit pas aux conseils et aux ordres qu'il reçoit sera condamné;

celui qui est pareil au gong sonore au daim à queue courte, qui a toujours des histoires,

celui qui coupe la parole du Chef, qui lui fend la bouche pour l'empêcher de parler, qui ouvre le bracelet qu'il avait accepté;

celui-là est coupable et il y a affaire entre les autres et lui.

7. KLEI BUAL LUI PÔ AMÂO MÂO HUN

7. DES SERVITEURS QUI QUITTENT LEUR MAÎTRE SANS PRÉVENIR.

Mŏng knuê dih ñu hriê akâo dôk dam, klam êa, ñu hriê akâo dôk êra âtung.

Ñu jhong pŏng, ñu rŏng ai ñu mÄ bruă knua khua.

Anei le ñu dôk hruê amâo yong tlam, mlam amâo bô agwah, ñu jik jah êman; ñu dôk amâo yong mâo **trăn** kdrêč.

Ñu tle due wit he ko krei, asei ajân, kbông amâo ñu wah, mbah amâo ñu wuê, amâo ñu puê bi êdah, wah bi thâo, mâo klei ñu čiăng due wit amâo ñu lač hŏng khua.

Anăn klnul ñu.

Celui qui ayant demandé à être employé comme garçon pour porter l'eau celle qui ayant demandée comme jeune fille pour s'occuper du ménage;

celui qui étant de mauvaise souche a accepté de travailler pour son maître,

et qui, maintenant, le jour ne peut pas travailler jusqu'au soir, la nuit ne veut pas rester à la maison jusqu' au matin, qui est vite fatigué de biner ou de défricher, qui est incapable de faire le moindre travail;

qui s'en va en cachette, tout seul sans que sa bouche se soit ouverte, sans rien dire à personne, sans se montrer à personne, sans faire connaître ses intentions, sans informer son maître qu'il voulait s'en aller,

celui-là est coupable.

8. KLEI MNUIH DRU MNUIH SQH   8. DES COMPLICES.

Gơ amâo thâo êbat bằ, amâo hưa mưm, amâo jum klei ñu bi jum brei.	Ceux qui portent celui qui ne peut pas marcher, qui mâchent les aliments à celui qui ne peut pas manger, qui instruit celui qui ne sait rien;
U djam ñu brei, u êei êei ñu udit, arăng amâo bit ñu bi bit brei.	ceux qui donnent des légumes ou du riz à celui qui en manque, qui renseignent celui qui est ignorant;
Aseh ñu thiê, giê hnuăt ñu brei arăng amâo klei ñu bi thâo.	ceux qui donnent le cheval(au coupable) et le fouet pour le frapper qui renseignent celui qui ne sait pas
êbat sa knhuang, čhuang mdrăm, blu hrăm mbit;	ceux qui marchent sur le pas (du coupable), qui adoptent son allure , qui prennent son parti,
Anăn kthul ñu.	Ceux-là sont coupables.

JUGEMENT.6 Jug.no I du 2° janv. 1917 : 3 ans (Piraterie).
    Jug.no I2 du I6 juil.1918 : I2$00 + restitution du vol(Vol).
    Jug.no I6 du I6 juil.1918 : I an (Vol).
    Jug.no 20 du I6 juil.1918 : 20 ans (Piraterie).
    Jug.no 63 du I9 oct. 1926 :3 mois + I00$00 (Assassinat).
    Jug.no° 2 du II juin 1927 : 3 mois (Vol).
    Jug.no° 3 du 3I mai 1929 : I5 j. + 75$00 (Meurtre).
    Jug.no I7 du 20 avr. 1933 : I00$00 (Assassinat).
    Jug.no 22 du 9 juin 1933 : 20$00 (Homicide par impr.).
    Jugent 23 du 2 sept. 1933 : I5 ans et I0 ans (Assassinat).

9. KLEI MNUIH HLUE SAP
KLEI ARANG.

Ñu tu săp giê, hue săp mjâo,
mâo klei arăng ñu mtâo duah hrŏk,
ksŏk hrun, ñu duah dưn tu.

Ñu mjhưt bong amao, ñu mơhao
bong trong, ñu duah gong kbông
hoai.

Arăng amâo thâo êbat ñu ba,
amâo thâo hui ñu mưm, arăng amâo
klei ñu bi jum brei.

Anăn kthul ñu, mâo kdi arăng
kơ ñu.

9. DES COMPLICES

Ceux qui acceptent la décision
du bâton (du sorcier) la parole du
guérisseur, qui s'immiscent dans les
différends d'autrui et comme les
revenants et les sorciers écoutent
tout ce qu'on dit;

ceux qui ont envie de manger les
champignons ou des aubergines, qui
cherchent toujours à ouvrir leur
bouche sans raison;

Ceux qui veulent porter celui
ne peut pas marcher, qui veulent
mâcher les aliments à celui qui ne
peut pas manger, qui veulent instruire
celui qui ignore tout,

Ceux-là sont coupables et il y
a affaire entre autrui et eux.

IO. KLEI MNUIH TỊ KLEI HLỘE SẶP ARÀNG.

Nu tu sặp giê, hlôe sặp mjâo, mâo klei arăng yăl dliê ñu mtâo duah hrơk, ksơk hruñ, ñu duah dưn tu he.

Ñu mjhưt bơng mmao, mhao bơng trong ñu duah gong kbông hơai.

Ĕtiêng tiăp ñu duah bi trei, êsei ắt ñu duah bi mđao, tiê boh arăng blao ñu duah ngă bi jhong.

Amâo thâo êbat ñu ba, amâo thâo huă ñu mum, arăng amâo jum klei ñu bi jum trei.

Alê amâo knur ñu čur hong dhong, alê amâo knur ñu čur hong đao, ñu duah lŏ bi êgao klei yăl dliê; anăn kthul ñu, mâo klei arăng kơ ñu.

IO. DE CEUX QUI SE FONT COMPLICES DES COUPABLES.

Ceux qui acceptent la décision du bâton(du devin), ou celle du guérisseur, qui acceptent tout ce qu'on leur raconte comme les sorciers et les fantômes;

ceux qui ont toujours envie de manger les champignons et des aubergines, qui ne peuvent pas rester san ouvrirla bouche;

ceux qui font se remplir le furoncle qui était crevé, qui réchauffent le riz qui était refroidi, qui excitent les personnes calmes et tranquilles;

Ceux qui portent les personnes qui ne peuvent pas marcher, qui mâchent les aliments à celles qui ne peuvent pas manger, qui créent des histoires à celles qui n'en ont pas

ceux qui taillent avec un sabre ou un couteau le merceau de bambou qui n'est pas pointu, qui créent des histoires là où il n'y en a pas,

ceux-là sont coupables et il y a affaires entre autrui et eux.

II. KLEI MDAP KDI KLEI SOH PRONG AMÂO HUN HONG KHUA.

Hua ñu jăm, mnăm săp, ñu mdap klei.

Ñu huă êsei hlăm adu, ñu boŋ mnu gu bur, dhoŋ ñu ñur he hlăm lăn ñu hmư săp klei arăng wăn waň jŭ jhat amâo ñu wưč bi êdah, wah bi thâo, mâo klei amâo ñu hưn hong khua prong.

Ñu dôk tiŋ tue, amâo ñu hlue tiŋ buôn, ñu tui tluôn êgar.

Ñu huă êsei gu hla, ñu mnăm êa gu êi, kdi ñu luă dhiăr.

Ñu hmư êwa angin ti ktăm, ênai gram ti nnu, ñu hmư săp klei buôn yư ... ... soh prong, mâo klei yhem amâo ñu hưn.

Ñu mta hmô, bô bla, ală mta buh ik, săp ñu thâo, mnâo bit, kbông rắng ha knga ñu hmư, kbông arăng, ... knga ñu săng, ñu dôk dlăng, dôk ... hrăm mcit, ñu amâo wit hriê hưn hong khôa.

Asei ñu ti buôn, tluôn ñu ti êgao, ñu sue dhoŋ đao kơ tač, ñu nač lăng kơ arăng gơ; anăn hgor ktang ñu bi đu, mnuih lu ñu bi bia ... bi blik he buôn saŋ sah mdroŋ. *ñu bi hriă he*

anăn kthul ñu, mâo kdi khup he ... prong.

II. DE CEUX QUI CACHENT UNE AFFAIRE TRÈS GRAVE AU CHEF.

Celui qui donne à manger et à boire (au coupable) en se cachant, qui cache sa faute;

celui qui le nourrit dans sa chambre, qui lui porte des poulets dans la brousse, qui cache ses armes dans la terre, qui entend dire de mauvaises paroles et qui ne fait pas savoir, qui apprend qu'il y a une affaire et n'en informe pas au Chef;

celui qui reste avec les étrangers, qui ne reste pas avec ceux de son village, qui suit des inconnus;

celui qui leur donne à manger sous la feuille, qui leur donne à boire sous le van, se met dans un très mauvais cas.

Celui qui entend le bruit du vent autour du village, le grondement du tonnerre derrière la palissade, qui entend les cris des habitants de l'Est et de l'Ouest, qui sait qu'il y a un grand coupable, qu'il y a une affaire très grave et n'informe pas (le chef)

celui qui rencontre des visages étrangers, qui les a vus de ses propres yeux, qui a reconnu leur voix, leur odeur, qui les a entendu parler et a compris ce qu'ils ont dit, qui les a regardés longtemps, qui a entendu de ses oreilles tout ce qu'ils se sont dit, et qui n'a pas couru en rendre compte au chef;

celui dont le corps est au village, et le derrière en delà de la palissade, celui qui tire le sabre et le couteau hors de leur fourreau, qui convoite les biens d'autrui, qui distend la peau tendre du tam-tam (pour empêcher l'alarme), qui fait que les habitants nombreux se trouvent réduits à quelques-uns, qui affaiblit et ap*pauvre de village du chef riche et puissant,*

celui-là est coupable et il y a affaire très grave entre le chef et lui.

I2. KLEI MČHUR AI.

NU amâo thâo êbat bă, amâo thâo
huă mñm, amâo jum klei ñu bi jum
brei.

U djam ñu brei, u êsei ñu huit,
arăng amâo bit ñu bi hit brei.

Aseh ñu thiê, giê hnuăt ñu brei,
arăng amâo thâo klei ñu bi thâo
brei.

Êbat sa klanang, ñhuang mhrăn,
hlu hmư ebit,

Anăn soh ñu.

I2. DE LA COMPLICITÉ.

Celui qui porte ceux qui ne
peuvent marcher, qui mâche les aliments à ceux qui ne peuvent manger ,
qui instruit ceux qui ne pavent rien;

celui qui offre des légumes ou
du riz à ceux qui en manquent, qui
fait connaître le lieu à ceux qui ne
connaissent pas;

celui qui donne le cheval et le
fouet pour le frapper, qui renseignent
ceux qui ignorent tout;

celui qui marche sur le pas(du
coupable), qui suit dans même allure
qui est toujours du même avis,

celui-là est coupable.

13. KLEI HONG TUE HONG HONG HLUN... ARANG

Ñu mnut ko êa, hra ko buôn, ñu pô diñng buôn sang.

Hong knue oong leh kâ, huä leh kin, leh duah djin hyatleh.

Todah mâo buh djuê nei, klei djuê nän, awak dam mdäp, Sap dam bi hgäm, dam mdäp mnuih t e da mnuih hlun mä arang, tlaih ti hnuh hlong ê- juh due, tlaih ti klong hlong due, da mnuih buô taih, brath khti, sui hruê...

Adê ... aga hu, adê êa mdä... ...ei dôk sa mlam, ...ei ...hruê ...ue juan ...âo ...

Thâo tue hriê ... ...oh dung mdlai, kpei dông...

Thâo agat ...êm ...hlun mä mu- ...ng be.

ÁNg

13. DU RECEL D'ÉTRANGERS D'ESCLAVE OU DE PRISONNIERS

Celui qui est le banian de la source, le figuier du village, celui qui veille sur les habitants,

avant de donner à manger (au coupable) il doit s'attacher, avant de le nourrir il doit le ficeler.

Pour aucune raison il ne doit cacher la cuillère, il ne doit rien celer de ce qu'il voit, il ne doit pas cacher la présence d'étrangers, d'esclaves ou de prisonniers évadés, de ceux qui ont rompu leurs entraves et se sont sauvés, de ceux qui ont brisé leurs liens et se sont enfuis, de ceux qui viennent de villages lointains, qui ont leur rizière (leur foyer) à plusieurs journées et plusieurs nuits de marches

Chacun à ses terres pour son champ sa rivière pour puiser de l'eau.

Le Chef qui autorise des inconnus à rester un jour dans son village, à s'y reposer une nuit, qui reçoit des étrangers et ne les interroge pas

pendant qu'ils viennent visiter le pays, qu'il ... ou pour leur plaisir, pour vendre un tabac ou du sel en paquets, pour échanger des ferments de riz ou du fer,

Pendant que ces étrangers sont *en relation avec les riches du village, et qu'ils viennent pour les salour*

Alors que ce sont des gardiens de porcs, ou des esclaves chargés de surveiller des poules de Kuy ...eux *et qui se sont évadés*

Ñu amâo hriê đak hmôk,dôk
brang, amâo hriê mlang kpin ao kơ
sah mdrong.

Êlâo ñu êsei kơ hma, êa kơ roh,
đoh bung bai kơ bhit.

Ñu djam tle brei,êsei knā,tle
bi huă bong,brei đong dôk hlăm
buôn sang ñu.

Ñu knhuh hlun sah,plah hlun
mdrong,mnuih ayong adei ñu mđăp.

Anăn soh ñu,mâo kđi arăng kơ
ñu prong.

Le chef qui n'enlève pas l'écorce,
qui ne dépouille pas la ramie,qui
n'ouvre pas la veste et la ceinture
(pourmontrer et pour informer);

celui qui nourrit des étragers ou
des prisonniers au champ, qui leur en
donne à boire dans les buissons et
leur offre la corbeille aux provi-
sions dans la brousse;

celui qui leur donne du riz et
des légumes en se cachant,qui leur
permet de rester dans son village,

parce qu'il veut s'empicer de
l'esclave du riche,au serviteur des
autres,

celui-là est coupable et il y a
affaire entre les autres et lui.

WISPR.-Jug.no 22 du 17 mai 1917 : 200$00 (Évasion de pris).
        Jug.no 23 du 14 juil.1918. 3 ans(Prisonnier évadé)
        Jug.no 25 du 12 juil.1918: 3 mois + 5$00 (Ech. d'étrangers).
        Jug.no 37 du 17 sppt.1918: 3 mois + 5$00 (Rec.de Pris. év.).
        Jug.no 38 du 2 oct. 1918: 1 mois +10$00 (-   ).
        Jug.no 42 du 15 juil.1923: 5 ans (Rec. de pris.év.)
        Jug.no 6 du 5 janv. 1925: 1 an rachetable (Rec.de pris.év.).
        Jug.no 86 du 27 nov. 1925: 1 mois + 3 ko et kpih au chef(Vag.)
        Jug.no 44 du 8 juin 1926: 5 ans (Rec.de pris.év.)
        Jug.no 46 du 8 juin 1926: 1 an (Rec. d'étrangers)
        Jug.no 58 du 9 déc. 1926: 1 an + 50$00 (Rec. de pris.év.)
        Jug.no 21 du 9 juin 1933: 20 à 50$00 (Rec. d'esel.).

14. KLEI KŎNG MNUIH MĂO KLEI DUH ÑU MĂO ĂAUH KƠ TLUÔN BUÔN ÊLAN CƠ.

Buh un tu kơ ñu čiêm, buh asâo tu ñu čiêm, buh mnuih tu kơ ñu čiêm rŏng.

Kthul ñu êkei amâo ñu kjiê, mniê kña, mnuih edam êra đi pưk sang ñu ñu êmuh.

Buh aseh arăng tu kơ ñu ka, buh hlun arăng đue tu kơ rŏng pliê.

Kthul ñu djam tle brei, êsai tle kna, brei hua bŏng, brei đong đŏk hlam sang ñu.

Kthul ñu bup-bap tăp braih tlam, anak edam êra bup-bap ñu rŏng ba.

Ñu ttah, kơ ttah, rung kruah ñu lê, hluh aseh mdrŏng amâo ñu kral ñu Pi rŏng ba pliê.

14. DE CEUX QUI REÇOIVENT UN COUPABLE SANS LUI DEMANDER QUI IL EST, D'OÙ IL VIENT, OÙ IL VA.

Ceux qui voyant un porc ou un chien veulent le nourrir, voyant un individu le reçoivent chez eux et le gardent sous leur toit,

ceux-là sont coupables parce qu'ils ne questionnent pas l'homme ou la femme, le jeune homme ou la jeune fille qui montent dans leur maison.

S'ils voient un cheval ou un buffle en liberté ils l'attachent, s'ils voient l'esclave d'autrui ou les prisonniers en fuites ils le reçoivent et les nourrissent sans réfléchir à ce qu'ils font.

Pour cela ils sont coupables parce qu'ils leur donnent des légumes, parce qu'ils leur font cuire du riz en se cachant, parce qu'ils leur permettent de demeurer chez eux;

ils sont coupables parce qu'ils gardent pour leur faire décortiquer le riz le soir, parce qu'ils sont contents le jeune homme ou la jeune fille

parce qu'ils avalent la viande crue ou le poisson crue sans mâcher, parce qu'ils gardent chez eux sans réfléchir l'esclave du riche sans le connaître (savoir).

Pour tout cela ils sont coupables et il y a affaire entre autrui et eux.

I5. KLEI KA BI GA .

Kdi ka bhi aban,kdi ka ân añuê,
mjâo ka gă.

Êlâo ñu dah si gram,êlăm si êmông
si bông ,gŭ si mran.

Mta amâo yong mâô,bô amâo yong tu-
jeh druôm amâo yong tol anăp.

Ñu ĉhi boh mdhur,boh mgu,ñu ĉhi
ĉ dju duam.

Kdi ka phat ênoh,ka kjoh giô,kdi
 djie săp kbông.

Êlâo klei ñu daug,huang ñu ka,êlâo
ñ mdê man.
Ñu tluh kô aseh arăng siam,êman
 mg juk,êman thâo ơriăk hdiêr.

mtê mâo pô mta klei,êkei
ơ mâo pô mta săp,ñu khăp ma klei
ñu.

anăn mg jô,mo buah,soh mdrong
mâo kdi prong.

ẵtu pô kreo,priê ĉe bô,ngăn
.

Celui dont le procès est comme une
couverture ou une natte encore utili-
sable,comme une maladie que le guérisseur n'a pas encore diagnostiquée,

celui qui avant que les juges aient
jugé l'affaire gronde comme le tonnerre,bondit(sur sa proie) comme le tigre
devient fermé comme un cercueil ou une
pirogue(devient exigeant).

Celui dont on ne peut rencontrer le
visage,dont on ne peut distinguer les
traits,qui ne défriche jamais jusqu'au
point fixé(qui n'attend pas que l'affaire soit réglée).

Celui qui considère l'accusé comme
un imbécile,qui le rend idiot comme on
rend quelqu'un malade,

alors qu'on n'a pas encore fixé la
peine,qu'on n'a pas encore mesuré le
bâton,qu'on n'a pas encore fini de pala-
brer,

celui qui avant la décision du juge rend une corde devant l'accusé,l'attache avec une longe,s'empare de ses
chevaux et de ses éléphants,

parce qu'il convoitise le beau
cheval d'autrui,le gros éléphant,l'éléphant qui barrit agréablement;

celui qui agit ainsi sans qu'aucune
femme l'ait conseillé,sans qu'aucun
homme l'ait pensé,qui veut régler une
affaire tout seul,

celui-là sème la discorde,et cela
le donnera pour faute très grave.

Il donnera un porc châtré et une
jarre "bô" à l'inculpé(sa victime)
qui paiera une amende de six "ke"

16. KLEI DUAH ČAP ARANG GŌ HŌAI.

16. DES ARRESTATIONS ILLÉGALES.

Ñu duah tling ka ma čap, dăp bruh ... kơ arăng hōai.

Celui qui cherche à entraver, à arrêter, à ligoter ou à mettre à la c... gue sans motif légal;

Ñu čiăng kơ čing tiɔ ma ɛ̆ran, ñu ... kơ ɛ̆man tiɔ ma pah, ñu čiăng kơ mdrong ñu čap.

celui qui convoitise le gong et poursuit celui qui le porte, celui qui pouravoir l'éléphant ou les biens du riche arrête les gens;

Ñu pah dlăm, ɛ̆lăm ma.

celui qui se jette (sur les passan... pourles dévaliser et les spolier;

Ñu pla drɔo drung bi rung buôn, drɔo drung bi rung sang, arăng dŏk ... ɛ̆đap ñu duah čap tling.

celui qui cultive des plantes vén... neuses pour troubler les villages qui arrête et ligote les habitants vivant paisiblement,

Tơ ñu mâo kdi boh sŏ, yŏ kbei, klei dă, ñu ɛ̆muh kơh mnut kơ ea, hra kơ ..., pô čiăng ndei amuôn buôn sang.

s'il a une vieille histoire (à régler), une histoire vieille comme un tube de tubercule déjà creux, ou'il co... sulte le banian de la source, le figu... du village, celui qui veille sur les noveux et les habitants.

Tơ ñu mâo mt ... mdi akăo, tơ mâo ... ɛ̆muh klua buôn.

S'il a une dette à réclamer qu'il la réclame, s'il a une affaire à régle... qu'il consulte le chef du village.

Si be čiĕt ñu ɛ̆aɔ ti trang, hlang ... mâo, hlô mnông ɛ̆aɔ ti pum ɛ̆jung.

mais s'il est comme l'herbe du ma... rais qui veut s'élever aussi haut que les roseaux, s'il est comme la paillot... qui veut monter plus haut que les bam... bous, s'il est comme les animaux sau... vages qui veulent bondir plus haut qu... les cîmes des arbres;

Sang dlông ñu ɛ̆ut, sang đưt ñu hgao bông, ɛ̆mô kbao ñu mdiĕ.

s'il refuse d'entrer dans la maiso... haute, et enjambe la maison basse, s'il méprise la maison (du chef) où l'on mange souvent du boeuf ou du buffle,

Anăn kdi arăng mâo kơ ñu.

pour cela il y aura affaire entre les autres et lui.

Ar Jugto ... du 19 ... 1925 : 3 ans rachetables.
Ar no 76 du 6 ... 1925 : 1 an restitution de l'amende perçue.

17. KLEI KÛUT MÛEH KƠ ARANG HOAI .

Ñu mûeh kơ anak mli hong, anak
arang hoai.
Blang êlung,êsung hluh,ñu bi
uh gơ hoai.

Êkei êngiê, mniê čih,bih mnông
[guru]

Ñu bi buh bong êmô,bi huô bong
kbao,bi nao êlan bhit pum.

Bi koyao êya,ana pah,duah blu,
duah čhal sah mdrong hoai.

Dok druah, mbah ala,ha blu pliê.

Aseh bong mdiê amâo ñu pao,kbao
bong mdiê amâo wa,mnuih dum nân
amâo hmư.

Čih braih hroh,boh êpang,yang hrue
êkei mniê čih.

Mnông soh pah,druah soh wiêk,
mdrong soh liêk kđi.

Ami lac amâo gô,ama mtô amâo gut,
dja ding kut tơl djiê asei.

Êwi wal pha, êa wal jơng,duah kđi
[...] yang [...],boh kđi ñu duah ma
[pa.]
[...] amâo kđi arang kơ ñu.

[...] rih jih asei ñu, kbao rih jih
asei ñu,duah boh klei jih asei ñu
[ro.]
amâo mâo pô truh dlăng,amâo mâo
[...] djih.

---

17. DES ACCUSATIONS CALOMNIEUSES.

Celui qui calomnie le riche ou
le pauvre sans motif;

celui qui affirme que le tronc
du kapokier est creux,que le mortier est percé,alors qu'il n'en sait
rien;
celui qui accuse l'homme ou la
femme inocents, le bih ou le mnông
inocents,
en racontant qu'il les a vu manger du buffle ou du boeuf,qu'il les
a vu aller par le chemin caché dans
la brousse;
celui qui grimpe sur les arbres
à écorce ou à cannelle pour accuser
mensongèrement le riche sans raison;
celui dont la voix ressemble à
celle du chevreuil,dont la bouche
est comme celle du serpent,celui qui
parle toujours à tort et à travers,
qui raconte que les chevaux et
les buffles ont mangé le riz(dans le
champ)sans les avoir vus,sans que
personne en ait rien su,
alors que le riz n'a pas été
décortiqué,que la courge n'a pas
été cueillie,que le soleil n'a
jamais été touché,
celui-là est comme le tigre ayant
manqué sa proie,comme le chevreuil
n'ayant pu se sauver,comme le riche
ayant perdu un procès.
Ses parents le conseillent mais
il ne les écoute pas,il préfère
jouer la flûte jusqu'à ce qu'il soit
mort.
L'eau et la fumée tourbillonnent
entre ses jambes,les histoires qu'il
a il se les crée lui-même.
Pour cela il y a affaire entre
les autres et lui.
Le porc et le buffle destinés au
sacrifice sont tués, celui qui se
crée des histoires perdra son corps,
Personne ne s'occupera de lui ,
personne ne prendra sa défense.

18. KLEI DUAH MČEH MÀ KƠ ARĂNG HOAI.

Ñu duah mčeh kơ anak mdrong,
duah mčong kơ anak mli, ñu duah bi
duh arăng bong êmô, bi hmô bong
kbao, ñu duah bi nao arăng kơ ĕlan
čut msat.

Soh băng gei, mlei băng kbông,
ñu duah bi awah biu jông kga.

Jik ñu duah bi awah, jah ñu duah
bi awai, ñu duah pai kpồng hnuôr.

Bung ñu duah dai, bai ñu duah
bi hde, ñu duah tle mčhi kơ mnuih
mkuăn.

Anăn mâo kđi arăng kơ ñu.

Le kơ mbloh ñu lač arăng gơ
pồng tung mâo ruă, pồng plang amâo
ruă, nga kđi kơ ñu amâo gỏl.

Arăng dẽ boh jak đei klei jăk
wik.

Le kơ mbloh le ñu lač mluk
amâo mtô, kmlô amâo lač.

Ñu gao kung, gao knông, sap
kbông sah mdrong ñu gao, ăt mâo
kđi arăng kơ ñu mơh.

18. DES ACCUSATIONS CALOMNIEUSES.

Celui qui calomnie le riche ou
le puissant, qui raconte qu'on a
mangé du buffle quand on a mangé du
boeuf, qu'on a été sur le chemin du
cimetière (quand on y a pas été);

celui dont la bouche ment, dont la
parole est coupable, celui qui raconte qu'on est tordu (méchant) comme le
manche de la hache ou du coupe-coupe;

celui qui raconte qu'on a biné
ou défriché, qu'on a ramassé du bois
mort ou des bûches (quand ce n'est
pas vrai);

celui qui jette au loin la hotte
ou la corbeille, qui accuse à tort
des personnes pour leur nuire,

celui-là est coupable et il y
a affaire entre autrui et lui.

S'il prétend ensuite qu'on a
enfoncé des piquets dans le tronc
du cotonnier ou du kapokier sans leur
faire d'entaille, qu'on lui a cherché
une histoire sans raison,

on lui dira que la raison est
pour autrui.

S'il préfère avoir agi par
ignorance, parce qu'on ne l'a pas
conseillé, parce qu'on ne l'a pas
instruit,

il y aura encore affaire avec
lui (et le chef) parce qu'il a passé
outre les signaux d'interdit, parce
qu'il n'a pas obéi au conseil du
chef.

JURISPR.- Jug.no 25 du 28 mai 1923 : 3 mois + 5$00 + kpih (vol).
Jug.no 29 du 31 mai 1923 : I an + 3 ko (pièges).
Jug.no 69 du 28 nov.1923 : 3 ans (inceste).
Jug.no 72 du 17 déc.1923 : 6 mois (esclavage).
Jug.no 55 du 28 juil.1925: 6 mois + I char (meurtre).
Jug.no 4 du 13 juil.1928: 50$00 (meurtre).

Ñu mniê duah klei, êkei drah
kdi.
Ñu mčeh kơ arăng kdi diêt ñu ba
ti diêt,ñu mčeh kơ arăng klei
prong ñu ba kdi prong.

Celui homme ou femme qui aura
accusé mensongèrement autrui à
propos d'une affaire sans gravité
paiera une petite indemnité,s'il a
accusé autrui à propos d'une affaire
très grave il lui paiera une indemnité très forte.

TRESP... Voir au n° 10 page suivante.

19. KLEI LÔ... ;   19. DU MENSONGE

Mlam sa klei, hrue sa sap, wirreng apap mdê.

  Celui qui dit une chose la nuit et une autre le jour, qui agit autrement dès qu'il a tourné le dos;

Knah hlong, ktong đut ku, mnuih lu klei.

  celui qui est (bavard) comme le gong sonore, comme le daim à queue courte, qui a beaucoup d'histoires;

Ñu trong mdêč, amrêč mdar, čar kup đang.

  celui (qui tourne sans cesse) comme les aubergines et le piment (dans le marmite), qui se tient tantôt sur le dos, tantôt sur le ventre;

Ñu nao mue, tle mnêñ, ñu wêñ kiê kngan.

  celui qui va en se cachant, en allongeant la main, comme un voleur,

Anan kdi mâo.

  celui-là est coupable et il y a à faire avec lui.

JURISPR.- Jug. no 12 du 13 fév. 1925. : 3 ans + 30$00 (prime pour tigre).

20. KLEI ANUIH DUAH BLU

Ktak mnut mjing ko ktak hra,êman mjing ko êman knô,pô anei mjing ko nkuan.

Anan khang duah blu brak si drao h,hôah si drang hdang,si člang si h blu.

ko yu bai go,ko ngo bai kpiêl, uôl sa ung sa mô.

ko dlông êdah mtu,ko gu êdah eh dih kun kuê sa ung sa mô.

Puk koa, hma alah,jah druôm amao sng.

Anan êdah khang duah blu pliô, khang duah blu mnam,duah si dum l sleng-

anan ayi mô.

20. DES TROMPERIES.

Celui qui dit que la sève de ba-nian est la sève de figuier,que l'élé-phant mâle est un éléphant femelle,ou celui-ci est un autre;

celui dont la voix est semblab au craquement du bambou qui se bris au cri du calao noir,qui veut que tou soit comme il dit,

qui ne possède qu'une corbeille de marmites à l'Ouest (dans sa maison et une corbeille d'écuelles à l'Est, qui vit seul avec sa femme(et veut faire croire qu'il est riche),

qui a une maison où l'on voit l étoiles en haut, et les excréments porc en bas,qui est obligé de se bâ tir pourcoucher avec sa femme,

parce qu'il est paresseux pour faire la maison,pour faire son champ parce qu'il n'est pas laborieux pour défricher.

celui qui parle à tort et à tr vers,qui raconte n'importe quoi, et suscite ainsi des histoires aux autr

celui-là est coupable et il y affaire entre les autres et lui.

JURISPR.-Jug no 5 du 1 janv. 1917 : 500 (a.s. carte d'impôt).
  Jug.no 19 du 17 mai 1917 : 1 an + 50000 (subst.de pers.).
  Jug.no 43 du 16 juil. 1917 : 500 (fausse déclaration).
  Jug.no 11 du 10 juill.1918 : 6 mois + 30000 (simul.malad.).
  Jug.no 25 du 12 août 1918 : 1 mois + 20000 (subst.pers.).
  Jug.no 56 du 24 sept. 1923 : 6 mois + 10000.
  Jug.no 83 du 7 nov. 1924 : 3 mois + 3000(tromp.sur march.).
  Jug.no 12 du 11 fév. 1925 : 3 ans + 30000(prêm p.tigre).
  Jug.no 19 du 3 avr. 1925 : 6 mois + 10000 + I ko à chef(Impôt).
  Jug.no 5 du 11 janv. 1926 : 6 jours + 2500.
  Jug.no 5 du 1er fév. 1926 : I an (subst.pers.).
  Jug.no 15 du 21 juil. 1927 : 35000(F.décla.a.s. impôt).
  Jug.no 15 du 18 août 1927 : 30000( )
  Jug.no 17 du 9 mai 1937 : 2 mois (faus.cause.d'impôt).

21. KLEI DLAO WAČ,

Ñu kbông druah, mbah ala, ñu
duah ha blu kơ arăng hoai.

Ñu duah dlao wač, kuač kčing
kơ anak mli hong, anak mdrong mang,
ñu duah ktal kang si aroh ñbua.

bruk si drao mčah, huah si
drang hdăng, si čiang si ñu duah ha
blu pliê.

Anŏ ñu blöa, ama liê, kiê kngan
koh, ñu duah dlao loh klên arăng
hoai.

Anăn mğo kđi arăng kơ ñu.

Tơdah ñu dlao wač kuač kčing
kơ bun, ñu kpih brei sa drei un
bŏng.

Tơdah ñu duah dlao wač kơ
sah mdrong, ñu kpih hong un kŏ.

21. DES INJURES.

Celui qui a une bouche comme
celle du chevreuil, ou celle du
serpent, et qui insulte autrui sans
motif;

celui qui crie des injures, qui
griffe et écorche le riche ou le puissant sans raison, qui a toujours des
démangeaisons au menton comme s'il
avait mangé des taros;

celui qui crie comme le culto
noir, ou comme des bambous se brisant
qui parle et insulte (des gens) sans
réfléchir;

celui qui insulte la mère ou
le père (de son antagoniste), qui sou-
haite que les mains soient coupées
qui crie des injures obscènes à autrui sans raison,

celui-là est coupable et il y
a affaire entre autrui et lui.

S'il a injuré une personne pauvre il fera pour elle un sacrifice
avec un porc de un "bŏng".

S'il a injuré une personne riche il fera un sacrifice avec un
porc de un "kŏ".

22. KLEI DLAO WAĆ ARANG.

Ami blôa, ama liê, kiê kngan
koh, lơh liăn ñu dlao.

Ya be klei wăng bơh kneh jơh,
ya be kơi ơh ai tiê ñu ai,ñu
dlao waĆ anăn,ya be kơi jŏng ñu
wai,ai ñu rơh, sĭa mta ñu dlang.

Ñu dlao êbeh tơ ai,diaiơuai,
klei boh ñu bi êbeh.

Tui Ćanh băng êka,kơa băng
ơna,ya be bơna klei ñu ai.

Ñu diah aơ bơn,ñu kpih un song;

Ñu dlao aơi mĭŏng ñu kpih
kbao,

Ñu dlao aơi anăn hbăa,hiam
aơi di mơal.

22.KLEI DLAO WAĆ ARANG,
DES INJURES ET INSULTES.

Celui qui injurie la mère,qui
insulte le père(de son antagoniste)
qui désire que les mains soient
coupées,qui crie des obscénités,

pourquoi crie-t-il ainsi? est-ce
parce que la houe est cassée ou parce
que le sillon est brisé? pour quelle
affaire se fâche-t-il et pourquoi
crie-t-il des insultes ? pourquoi son
coeur est-il mauvais,pourquoi regarde-
t-il ainsi ?

S'il insulte exagérément, au delà
de toute mesure, son cas sera grave.

Si on lui demande où est sa blessure,où est le mal(qui le fait souffrir),si on lui demande pour quelle
raison il se met en colère,il insulte
et injurie.

S'il a injuré la mère d'un pauvre il sacrifiera un porc ou un song;

s'il a injuré la mère d'un riche
il sacrifiera un buffle;

s'il a injuré les parents du roi
ou de la reine,des esclaves ou des
éléphants il donnera.

23. KLEI MNUIH GAO BHIAN.

Leh di êngô , leh doh puôt,
bhian sah mdrong khăng hua blăm,
mnăh thun,khăng bong un kbao.

Tek bi êwi tơ năn,êi bi răp,
gap djuê khăng bi ênum tơ năn soăi.

Jih adei tlaog,yang buôn,jih
amuôn adei, jih mnuih dum nei kơ
dih,bi hrlê ênum tơ năn soăi.

Hlei mâo anak khua mtô tơ năn,
mâo kô dah,tơ anak sah mdrong
čiăng bi hmư bi thao soăi.

Hlei pô ñu jơng amâo hdjul,
hlei amâo khăng,hlei pô ñu amâo
tăng buôt,hlei ñu,mâo kơi sang
tơ ôn kơ ñu .

23.DE LA VIOLATION DES COUTUMES.

Chaque année après la saison
froide,une fois la moisson terminée,
la coutume est que le grand Chef
fête l'année nouvelle en offrant à
boire et à manger,en sacrifiant des
porcs et des buffles.

Pour cela chacun prépare ses hottes
et ses paniers,tous les amis et les
parents se réunissent à cette occasion.

tous les frères éperviers,les
génies des villages,les neveux et
nièces,tous les habitants d'ici et
de là viennent auprès du grand Chef.

Tous ceux qui ont des enfants
et des petits enfants les instrui-
ront,car le grand Chef veut que tous
connaissent cette coutume.

Quant à ceux dont les pieds ne
sont pas légers,dont les talons ne
sont pas durs,ceux qui ne s'empressent pas de venir,ceux-là sont coupables et il y a affaire entre tout
pays et eux .

Cette texte concerne la fête annuelle dite " Fête du Serment"
qui tous depuis le 1er Janvier 1926 au Darlac.Il s'agit donc d'une
nouvelle qu'il faut faire connaître aux habitants et aux Chefs.
Jug. no 15 du 1er sept. 1926 :3 mois(Refus à convocation).

KDRĂĔ II.

CHAPITRE II.

I. KLEI LĂNG SAP KHUA.

24.DE LA DÉSOBÉISSANCE AUX
ORDRES DU CHEF.

Laĕ amâo gô,mtô amâo gŭt,lăng
ti êmông,dlông ti yang,wa kang
mbah .

Celui qu'on instruit et qui n'é-
coute pas,celui qu'on commande et
qui n'obéit pas,celui qui se croit
plus **fort** que le tigre, plus grand
que lesgénies ,qui ouvre insolemment
la bouche;

Laĕ amâo tu,blŭ amâo djo,nga
si kho ngu.

celui qui n'écoute pas ce qu'on
lui dit,qui n'accepte pas les conseils
qu'on lui donne,qui agit comme un
fou et un imbécile;

Duah dôk hlăm kăt alê,dôk
hlăm kăt moê,duah dôk si hlô mrông.

celui qui préfère vivre parmi les
touffes de bambous,dans la brousse,
comme les animaux sauvages,

Amâo êrd si kơiăm trŭng,mtih
hong bi hlah,dah blu ti khhal he
mu.

on le corrigera comme on corrige
le chien gourmand en lui faisant
avaler une aubergine chaude, comme
on corrige les mauvais sujets, comme
on punit ceux qui sont insolents
(envers le chef).

Jurispr.-Jug. no I5 du 2 avril I9I7 :20j00(Infr.à régl.interdissant
        la circulation des éléphants sur lespistes pendant
        la saison des pluies).
    Jug. no I6 du 2 avril I9I7 : 5800 (-   )
    Jug. no 2 du Ier mai I9I8 : 5800 (-   )
    Jur. du 3 octobre 1938   : 1 mois - 5800(Refus d'obéis-
        sance).

2. KLEI AMÂO DUN SAP KHUA.

Khua lač kơ di ñu amâo gŭ,mtô amâo gut,kưt kdja klei amâo dun.

Tơ un rih jih asei ñu,kbao rih jih asei ñu,tơdah ñu duah boh klei jih asei ñu pô.

Tơ dah ami ama ñu mâo ngăn deh gơ ba brei kdi.

Bi tơdah di gơ amâo mâo ngăn, gung hluh tuh bäng asei ñu,hlăo kut trut bäng asei ñu,tơ ñu duah boh klei jao he asei ñu pô.

Hui mniê amâo mă klei,êkei amâo sap,ñu khăng amâo khăp klei khua,hong klei ami ama ñu,ñu khăng mâo gut.

Anăn mâo kdi arang kơ ñu.

25. DE LA DÉSOBÉISSANCE AU CHEF.

Celui qui retient pas les conseils du chef,n'obéit pas à ses ordres, qui n'écoutent pas ceux qui palabrent en chantant,

comme le porc ou le buffle destinés au sacrifice,s'il se crée des histoires il risquera de perdre son corps(sa vie ou sa liberté).

Si ses parents ont des biens ils pourront payer pour lui l'amende (qu'on lui aura infligée);

mais s'ils n'ont pas de biens, (il sera abandonné)comme le mortier percé ou le pilons usé,et si son affaireest très grave il devra donner soncorps(en gage pour payer l'amende ou l'indemnité).

la femme qui refuse d'obéir, l'homme qui n'écoute pas ce qu'on lui dit,ceux qui refusent d'obéir aux ordres du chef,qui ne veulent pas retenir les conseils de leurs parents.

Ceux-là sont coupables et il y a affaire avec ceux.

JURISPR.—Jug. no 2 du 3 janv. 1917: 2$00 + réparation du dommage
causé.

Jug. no 5 du 11 fév. 1917: 5$00(Défaut de carte d'impôt)

Jug. no 6 du 13 mars 1917:20$00(

Jug. no13 du 21 mars 1917:20$00Déf.de carte d'éléphant)

Jug. no14 du 21 mars 1917 :10$00(-

Jug. no 15 du 2 avril 1917:20$00(Infr.à règl.sur la cire.)

Jug. no16 du 2 avril 1917: 5$00(-

Jug. no 26 du 16 juil.1917: 10$00 + rachat arriéré(Défaut
de carte ,désobéissance).

Jug. no 1 du 18 fév. 1918: 1 mois + 20$00 (Non déclaration)
de vente d'éléphant).

Jug. no 4 du 12 mai 1918: 5$00 (

Jug. no 14 du 16 juil 1918:20 $00 (-

Jug. no 21 du 4 août 1918: 10$00 (-

Jug. no 22 du 18 juil.1918: 5$00 (Infr.à un règl.interdisant de faire la champ sur le bord de la route.

Jug. no du 2 mars 1918 :3 mois + paiement du double des
impôts en retard (Défaut de carte).

Jug.no du 2 sept.1918 1 mois + 1$00 (Inexécution des
ordres du Résident).

Jug. du 4 octobre 1918 :15 jours + 10$00(Dé. résumé

3. KLEI GAO KHUA.   26. DE LA DÉSOBÉISSANCE AU CHEF.

Mâo mnut amâo ñu êmuh mnut,
mâo hra amâo ñu êmuh hra,mâo ama
ami amâo ñu êmuh ama ami.

Celui qui ne s'adresse pas au
banian quand il y a le banian, qui
ne consulte pas le figuier quand il
y a le figuier (I); qui ne demande
pas à la mère et au père quand il y
a la mère et le père;

Pui bơng êgao ti troh,êa đoh
êgao knông,săp kbông sah mdrong
ñu êgao.

celui qui se comporte comme l'incendie qui franchit le vallon, comme
l'inondation qui franchit le barrage,
celui qui passe outre la parole du
chef;

Blong ktong băng hdrah,ki dua
nah,ktam jŏng hjan.

celui qui est comme le dois aux
belles cornes brandiquant dans la cla-
clairière(lorsqu'il se sent seul
loin de tout danger);

Ñu dja dai miêô,ñu tiêô dai
gi hdi ñu bi ke.

celui qui tient un chat gris dans
la main et un chat noir dans son
pagne et les excite l'un contre
l'autre;

Êa blung ñu kdăt,êa khăt ñu
kplong,sah mdrong ñu gao.

celui qui enjambe la flaque d'eau
qui saute par-dessus le ruisseau ,
qui méprise l'autorité du chef;

Gao kung, gao knông, săp kbông
ñu gao.

celui qui ne respecte pas le signal de l'interdit ni les ordres du
chef (2);

Aseh ruă rơng,ktong đut ku,
mnuih lu klei.

celui qui remue sans cesse comme
le cheval blessé au dos,comme le
daim à queue courte, celui qui a
toujours des histoires;

Êa lêč bơ hang,yang nga djiê
asei,ñu duah bơh klei tuič asei
ñu pô.

celui qui est comme la rivière
débordant de son lit,comme les mauvais génies causant la mort,celui qui
cherche des histoires à tout le monde perdra son corps (3);

Anăn un rih jih asei,kbao rih
... asei,ñu duah bơh klei jih asei
ñu pô.

comme le porc ou le buffle destinés au sacrifice il perdra son corps.

(1) Le banian et le figuier symbolisent le chef.
(2) Il crée des incidents entre chefs en s'adressant à un autre chef et
non à celui de son village qui est son chef hiérarchique immédiat.
(3)Il perdra son corps:il sera condamné à mort,ou à l'esclavage,ou
aujourd'hui à la prison.
JAISPR.-Jug. no20 du 17 mai 1917: 5500(Non-Déni de vente d'éléphant).
     Jug. no32 du 18 juil.1917: I mois (Jeu clandestin).
     Jug. no 2 du 5 janv.1925:I mois + 5500(Désobéissance).
     Jug. no40 du 30 mai 1925:I mois + 5500(Refus de convocation).
     Jug. no4I du Ier juin1925:I mois +5500(Refus désobéis.)
     Jug. no du 8 août 1928:   I mois +5500(-   ).

4. KLEI AMÂO ÊMUH KHUA HONG AMI AMA.

Mâo mnut amâo êmuh mnut , mâo hra amâo êmuh hra, mâo ama ami amâo êmuh ama ami.

Dhong prong hin ti kseh , hdeh prong ti khua, mâo ama ami amâo êmuh.

Mnut ko êa, hra ko buôn, pô dlâng adei amuôn buôn sang, ñu amâo êmuh .

Nao ko djuh amâo êmuh ama, nao ko êa amâo êmuh ami, čhi mblei amâo êmuh aê aduôn.

Anân amâo klei soh.

27. DU MÉPRIS DU CHEF ET DES PARENTS.

Celui qui ne demande pas au banian quand il y a un banian, qui ne consulte pas le figuier quand il y a un figuier, qui n'informe pas le père et la mère quand il y a le père et la mère;

celui qui est comme un couteau où la lame serait plus épaisse que l'âme, comme un enfant voulant se croire plus grand qu'un adulte, et qui ne demande jamais conseils à ses parents;

celui qui ne consulte jamais le banian, de la source, le figuier du village, l'homme qui veille sur les neveux et les nièces, sur tous les habitants;

celui qui va au bois sans demander au père, qui va à la fontaine sans demander à la mère, qui achète et vend sans consulter les grands parents (les anciens),

celui-là est coupable.

5. KLEI MJING KHUA BUÔN.	28. DU CHOIX DU CHEF.

Kuič pui, hrui mnuih,iêô jih
jaag adei tlang,yang buôn,jih amuôn
adei,jih wit ami na, ama nei,jih
wit aê aduôn arang,jih wit mniê
mlâo, mgâo ti,jih wit mnuih djiê
ami ama lôk bi kbin ty krah buôn.

Qu'on attise les feux et qu'on
rassemble tout le monde, qu'on appell
tous les frères éperviers,les génies
du village,les neveux et les nièces
les mères de ceux-là,les pères de
ceux-ci,les grands-pères et les
grand'mères,les veuves,les gendres
et les belles-filles,ceux dont
les parents sont morts qu'on les
rassemble tous au milieu du village.

Ky gu bi trông, ky dlông bi
dmi,bi git amai,čhai adei,klei
kya bi ôurh.

Qu'on discute en bas,qu'on discute
en haut (discutez là-y-en) que
soeurs discutent avec les frères,
que tout le monde soit consulté.

Tičbě bưng bi kčăp,mup čiang
ky ariš kô êa,hra ko suôn,ky pô
dlang adei amuôn buôn sang.

Qu'on déclare celui qu'on préfère,qu'on choisisse celui qui sera
le banian de la montée,le figuier
qu'il dressera au haut du village,
celui qui veillera aux revenu et
les nières, surtous les habitants,

Bi lač ne ty hin suai,awak
dam bi lo muñ,sap dam lo bi hgăm.

Que tout le monde se prononce,
qu'on ne cache pas la cuillère,que
personne ne cache sa pensée.

A la mort du Chef c'était son gendre,ou son remplaçant auprès de la
Cuve (mnê),ou son beau frère (époux d'une soeur de sa femme)qui lui
succédait. Quand le remplaçant était trop jeune le plus ancien de la
maison devait l'aider dans ses fonctions de Chef.
   Le choix d'un nouveau chef ne devrait donc se faire que lorsqu'il
n'y avait pas de successeur naturel.
   Aujourd'hui le chef de village sont nommé par l'Administration
....

6. KLEI MNUIH DUAH BLU KDI ARANG

29. DE CEUX QUI VEULENT RÉGLER LES DIFFÉRENDS D'AUTRUI

Ñu mjhut bong mmah, ñu mhao bong boñ, băng-kbông ñu ktăl si arôh ebua.

Celui qui a envie de manger des champignons ou des fruits, celui qui a toujours des démangeaisons dans la bouche comme s'il avait mangé des tarcs verts;

Mdê čư mdê bi čong, mdê mdrong mdâ bi buôñ.

celui qui veut pas admettre que chaque montagne a son sommet, que chaque ville a son chef;

Ñu duah bi tu sap giê, ñu duah hlue sap mjâo.

celui qui cherche à faire accepter sa décision comme si c'était la décision du juge ou de la décision du guérisseur;

Yang ñu duah hrok, ksok ñu duah tu, ñu duah blu kdi klei pô mkuan.

celui qui prétend sa parole est la parole des génies, la parole des revenants, qui cherche à juger les différends des autres,

Anan kthul ñu, mâo kdi ko ñu.

celui-là est coupable et il y a affaire avec lui.

Ce texte concerne les cas d'usurpation de fonctions.
JURISPR. Jug.no 29 du 19 oct. 1918 : 8$00 + kpih au chef(Us.de f.)
Jug.no 69 du 28 nov. 1923 : 3 ans (Us.de F.et escroquerie)
Jug.no 16 du 2 sept. 1927 : 6 mois +restitution(Abus de pou
Jug.no 17 du 5 sept. 1927 :20$00 +restitution(Us.de f.)
Jug.no 15 du 18 avr. 1933 : 3 mois (Us. de f.)
Jug.no 25 du 2 sept. 1933 : 2 ans et 5 ans(Us.de f. et comp

7. KLEI GAO SAP KHUA ÑU NAO MGÖ.

30. DE CEUX QUI DÉSOBÉISSENT AUX ORDRES DU CHEF.

Ñu nao mgö,rô mbăl,nao si klei al čön.

Çelui qui agit contre les ordres du Chef,qui s'en va quand on lui dit de rester,qui agit comme s'il était en colère.;

 Čiöt êgao ti trang,hlang êgao ti mbô,hlö mnong êgao ti pum êjung.

celui qui se comporte comme l'herbe qui,veut s'élever plus haut que les roseaux,comme la paillote qui veut monter plus haut que les bambous,comme les animaux sauvages qui veulent bondir plus haut que les cîmes des arbres.

Ñu lăng ti êmông,dlông ti yang ñu khăng wă kang mbah,sap kbông sah mdrong mtô laē ñu amâo gut.

celui qui se croit plus fort que le tigre,plus puissant que les génie. celui qui ouvre isolément la bouche, qui n'obéit pas aux ordres du chef,

Anăn amâo êra bi kblam tr ong, mnuih jhong bi hlôh,dah blu bi kmhal he ñu.

comme le chien voleur qu'on punit en lui faisant happer une aubergine chaudes,comme les mauvais sujets,on le punira.

BIBLIOGR.: Jug.no 6 du 13 janv.1917 : 2$00 + réparation(Infr.à règl.)
Jug.no 15 du 2 avr. 1917 : 20$00 (Infr.à règl.).
Jug.no 16 du 2 avr. 1917 : 5$00 (
Jug.no 25 du 16 juil.1917 : 10 à 25$00 (Refus d'obéiss.).
Jug.no 14 du 13 févr.1925 : I mois + 5$00 (Infr. à règl.).

8. MNUIH MÂO KLEI SOH ÑU SUN NGAN KƠ KHUA BI KHUA LAÊ BREI KLEI GÂL ÑU.

31. DES COUPABLES QUI OFFRENT DES BIENS AU CHEF POUR QU'IL LEURDONNE RAISON.

Ñu mnie duah klei,êkei duah klei,anan ñu bäng hriê kơ mli mdrong. Kông ñu hriê dal kơ mnut kơ êa, ngan sun,hui khua dôk he ting kơ tue,hlue ting buôn,hui khua hlue thien êgar.

Celui qui a une affaire, celle qui a un différend, viennent au chef.Ils remettent le bracelet au benian, offrent des biens au figuier, de crainte qu'il ne se tienne du côté des étrangers ou des inconnus, qu'il ne se range du côté des new parents

Hui khua dôk ting kơ mnu,tu ting mja, sáp kuha hui hlue arăng.

de crainte que le chef soit avec le poulet contre la faine, que sa parole défende la cause des autres;

Ñu čiang khua laê brei bi tu, blu brei bi kpă,nga brei bi gâl.

celui qui veut que le chef dise que son affaire est bonne,que sa cause est juste,qui veut que le che lui soit agréable;

Ñu amâo mâo jong ñu ma jong pai, ñu amâo mâo ai ma ai êmông,amâo mâo kbông ma kbông sah mdrong.

celui qui n'a pas de jambes et demande les jambes du lièvre, celui qui n'a pas de force et demande la force du tigre, celui qui n'a pas de bouche et demande la bouche du chef riche et puissant(pour prendre sa défense);

Ñu amâo ar êbat bäng kơ di êman, amâo ar êran bäng kơ di aseh.

celui qui ne peut marcher et demande à monter sur un éléphant,celui qui ne peut pas courir et demande à monter à cheval;

Ñu hdeh, êläk bun hin, rin tap, bäng kơ sah mdrong.

celui qui se dit faible comme un enfant,pauvre comme un orphelin abandonné,et qui vient trouver le ch

Bi sah mdrong bä brei si ba adei, bi mnei brei si mnei anak,khua rông brei bi moak mñai.

pour que le chef le porte (avec soin)comme on porte le cadat,pour qu'il le baigne comme on baigne un enfant,pour qu'il le protège,que de soit beau et agréable;

Anan ngän ñu brei kơ khua.

celui qui pour cela offre des des biens au chef,

Kơyâo kơik bi mâo agha,kơyâo êrang bi mâo aghe,ami ama ñu hriê njing kơ khua.

parce que comte les arbres il lu faut des racines(pour se soutenir), parce qu'il veut que le chef soit pourlui un père et une mère,

Djao êa ñu knang hong êu,bư êa mâo boh têo kli,mâo kdi arăng ñu knang hong sah mdrong.

parce que quand on revient de la fontaine(et qu'on est fatigué)on s'appuie au talus,quand on construit un barrage on a besoin de pierres plates,quand on a une affaire en cherche l'appui du chef.

Anan mâo kdi arăng kơ ñu.

Celui (qui agit ainsi)est coupable.

9. KLEI KÜUT YAL DLIĚ KLEI LUAR BĬ SOH KHUA.

32. DES ACCUSATIONS CALOMNIEUSES CONTRE LE CHEF POUR LE RENDRE COUPABLE.

Ba si ba adei,mnei si mnei anak,
rông ba ñu moak mñai.

Rông si rông jhung,rông si rông
ñan,kpan mdô,rông ba ñu si rông
ba mô anak pô.

Ñu wăng lu, kgã lu, ñu lo blu
ko ami ama.

Čing hlăm băng ñu suai ko tač,
čhar hlăm băng ñu suai ko tač,ñu
duah naŭ iang mă ko ayong adei hdai.

Ñu alě yur,kpur pu,yu ngo ñu hiu.

Ñu amao mão phi ñu mdi ko tlan,
ñu amao mão phi ñu mdi ko ala,ñu
duah ba săp ko sah mdrong.

Kdeh pông ñu ba, kdeh mra ñu ruah
ñu duah yăl dliě mă hong sah mdrong
klei jăk.

Emong ña kpěč knga,mja mă kpěč
lău,ñu kčut ko arăng amao mão kdi.

Alě mtah ñu bi kro,mô rong ñu
u joh,ñu duah bi soh pah mdrong.

Amu mão kdi ko ñu prong.

Un soh jih asei,kbao soh jih asei,
mu duah soh klei jih asei ñu pô.

Le chef porte(les habitants)
comme on porte le petit frère,il les
baigne comme on baigne un enfant,il
les protège pour que ce soit et agréable;

il les garde comme on garde les
lits,les escaliers,les bancs et les
escabeaux,il s'occupe d'eux comme il
s'occupe de sa femme et de ses enfants.

Celui qui est comme un coupe-coupe
ou une binette tranchants,qui se montre insolent envers sa mère et père

celui qui sort au dehors les gens
čing et čhar enfermés dans les fosses
parce qu'il est malfaisant et jaloux
des biens d'autrui sans raison;

celui,comme le bambou dont le vent
agite toujours la cîme,comme le petit foyer qu'on transporte partout,
qui vagabonde à l'Est ou à l'Ouest;

celui qui n'a pas de fiel va chercher le fiel du python ou du serpent
pour le porter au chef riche et puissant;

celui qui offre le morceau du
filet ou du morceau de l'épaule au
chef pour lui faire accepter comme
vraies(les histoires mensongères il
qu'il raconte).

celui qui agit comme le tigre sa-
saisissant sa proie par le bout de
l'oreille,comme la fouine saisissant
sa proie par le bout du poil,qui accuse les gens(par des insinuations)
sans motif;

celui qui fait dessécher les bambous verts,qui fait se briser les
bambous solides,qui cherche à créer
des histoires au chef riche et puissant,

celui-là est coupable et il y a
affaire très grave avec lui.

Comme le boeuf ou le buffle
destinés au sacrifice,s'il a des
histoires il perdra son corps.

JURISPR.:Jug.no 30 du 31 mai 1923 : 1 an: 10500 + 1 ko et kpih au chef;
Jug.no 51 du 6 nov.1936 :10 jours + kpih au chef.
Jug.no 11 du 2 mars 1937 : 1 an.

II.KLEI KNUIK LUI BUON
AMÃO HƯN HONG KHUA .

33. DE CEUX QUI QUITTENT
LEUR VILLAGE SANS EN INFORMER
LE CHEF.

Nu đue hiu dôk Buôn yu, pu ngo,
bông amão ñu wah hong mnut ko êa,
ra ko Buôn,hong pô dlãng adei
muôn buôn sang.

Celui qui s'en va demeurer dans
le village de l'Ouest,dans le village
de l'Est,sans que sa bouche le fasse
savoir au banian de la source,au figuier du village,à celui qui veille
sur les neveux et nièces,sur tous
les habitants;

Nu gao kung,ñu gao knŏng,ñu
ao sap kbŏng khua buôn.

celui qui passe outre les signaux
d'interdiction,qui désobéit aux
ordres du chef;

Nu dlãng si vẽ,ñu muč si asão,
ñu amão thâo kral djo khua buôn.

celui qui n'a aucune considération
pour le chef,qui le méprise comme un
chien,qui ne reconnaît pas son autorité,

Khua amão tuôm duah du ngã,
ria kăn ñu.

alors que le chef ne lui a jamais
rien fait de mal,qu'il ne l'a jamais
inquiété,

Khua amão tuôm duah čhiah -
đếp sưếp - kdap ñu ôh.

alors que le chef ne lui a jamais
rien reproché,qu'il ne lui a jamais
fait d'injustices,

Anăn kči mâokơ ñu .

celui-là est coupable et il y a
affaire entre le chef et lui.

JURISPR.- Jug.no 12 du 21 mars 1917 : 3 mois.
Jug.no 27 du 27 fév. 1923 : I mois + kbĩC.
Jug.no 20 du 24 avr. 1923 : I mois + kpih au chef.
Jug.no 35 du 25 juin 1923 : 6 mois + 5$00 + kpih au chef.
Jug.no 45 et 46 du 20 Août 1923: I mois + kpih au chef.
Jug.no 55 du 20 sept.1923 : 3 mois + kpih au chef + restitution
de l'objet volé au triple de sa valeur.
Jug.no 73 du 29 sept.1923 : I mois + kpih au chef.
Jug.no 3 du 5 mai 1920 : 2 mois + kpih au chef + rachat
des impôts en retard.
Jug.no 6 du 23 août 1928 : 5$00 + kpih au chef.
Jug. du 6 octobre 1938 : 3 mois.

12. KLEÏ MĐUE HIU MNUIH HLÂL BUÔN AMÂO HUN HONG KHUA .

Êdai amâo ôwa ñu duah ksoh, kuih amâo kdloh ñu duah kẽut, hlô mur hlô rang ñu duah mphẽč, ñu duah ngă mđẽč mdar.

Anăn ñu duah čoh ênông, ñu duah kgông mđue, ñ sue ba mnuih hlăm buôn sang.

Arăng amâo thâo êbat bă, amâo thâo hua mnum, arăng amâo jum ñu bi jum.

Ba blung kđat, êâ khăs kplong; ah mdrong ñu gao .

Anăn kdi mẵc.

34. DE CEUX QUI EMMÈNNENT DES HABITANTS SANS INFORMER LE CHEF .

Celui qui souffle avec le soufflet quand la forge n'a plus d'air (s'éteint), qui fouille dans le trou avec un bâton pour faire sortir la souris, qui surprend/effraie le sanglier ou le cerf qui broute paisiblement;

celui qui saisit avec le bec , qui prend dans sa gueule, qui emporte sur le dos, qui emmène les habitants du village;

celui qui porte ceux qui ne peuvent pas marcher, qui mâche les aliments à ceux qui ne peuvent pas manger, qui instruit ceux qui ne savent pas;

celui qui enjambe la flaque d'eau, qui franchit le ruisseau , qui passe outre les ordres du chef;

celui-là est coupable et il y a affaire entre le chef et lui .

34. KLEI MNUIH BUÔN SANG ČIK ČAM HE KHUA BUÔN KƠYUA ƝU MTÔ LAČ,GHA ƝU BLU KƠI ARANG.

Mnuih ... tơ dahda,êwa tơ ... ok,mnuih khăng duah ngă ... hun.

Mnuih ngă ai dôṅ,hnŏṅ ðut, luk ko asei, khei soh hoṅ djơ ... amâo thâo krâl.

Buh ana mnut ñu koh he ana aut,buh ana hra ñu koh he ana hra, ... ami ama, khua buôn mtô laě ... ñu,ñu lo čik čam he di gơ.

Mnuih wăṅ lu, kgă lu, ñu ... uih amâo lo dui khư gang.

Mnuih hlang ðrên,kmuôn hě̆ ... viê,mnuih amâo dui kriê ...

Luk kơ ñu amâo gô,mtô amâo gưt, ... kdja klei amâo ñu dun.

Asâo êra bi kblăm he ñu trong, ... uih jhoṅ bi hlăh, dah blu bi ... he ñu.

BÊN. Jug.no 1 du 2 janv. 1917 : 5 ans (Rebellion).
Jug.no 2 du 3 janv. 1917 : 3 ans + 24$00 + kpik Rebellion
contre un milicien en service.
Jug.no 15 du 16 févr.1925 : 5 ans + 3 ko et kpik au chef
(Rebellion contre un chef de village et viol).
Jug. du 6 mai 1938 : 1 ans (Insultes et voies de fait envers
un milicien en service. Escroquerie).

35. DE CEUX QUI BRUTALISENT LE CHEF PARCE QUE CELUI-CI S'OCCUPE DES HABITANTS ET RÈGLE LEURS DIFFÉRENDS.

Celui dont la poitrine se gonfle de colère, dont la gorge se serre de dépit, celui qui s'emporte facilement;

celui dont la patience est courte,celui qui n'est plus maître de ses actes,qui ne distingue plus ce qui est bien de ce qui est mal,

celui qui voyant le banian coupe le banian,voyant le figuier coupe le figuier,voyant que le père et la mère ou le chef veulent l'instruire et le conseiller les frappe brutalement ;

celui qui dangereux comme une binette bien tranchante,comme un coupe-coupe bien aiguisé,celui qu'on ne peut plus commander;

celui qui est comme la paillote desséchée,comme le lien (en bambou) trop sec (cassant facilement),celui qui s'emporte facilement,qu'on ne peut plus raisonner;

celui qui ne veut pas écouter ce qu'on lui dit ,qui n'obéit pas aux ordres qu'on lui donne,qui n'accepte pas les décisions (du chef);

Comme le chien gourmand qu'on punit en lui faisant avaler une aubergine chaude,comme le mauvais sujet qu'on corrige,s'il se montre insolent on le punira.

14. KLEI JIH MNUIH BUÔN SĂNG BI DRU HE KHUA BUÔN.

36. DE L'AIDE QUE TOUS LES HABITANTS DOIVENT AU CHEF.

Jih dum adei tlang, yang buôn,
jih dum amiên adei dum nei ko dih,

Todah khua ktôpuk, dru bi
kum cua, ktrohma dru bi kum nga, ktro
bruä puk sang kum dru nga bi leh he.

Hui khua amâo jăk ko, amâo
bo tian, amâo man huä bong.

DJUH DRU BI BA, êa dru bi gui,
Todah hnui puk hma dru bi kum nao
jik hwar.

Ciang puk gri bi mâo pô dra
vei kbang, sang gri bi mâo pô knul,
oh mnuih mchêng ti tul bi dlam brei
ai adei amai đam bi lui.

khua nan êjai hdip ciang bi
enjé to djiê ciang bi lu êsei,
m drông ciang bi êngum.

Lin bi sa knga, ha bi sa săp,
bi khăp sa klei năn soŏi.

Bi hlei pô ñu lăng ti êmông,
jông ti yang, hlei wa kang mbah,
kmil ñu mâo kđi khua ko ñu.

Bo bia mâo kđi điet, bi to-
h mor lä mâo kđi prong.

Tous les frères éperviers, les
génies du village, les neveux et les
nièces, tous ceux d'ici et ceux de là

doivent aider le chef quand
il a de la peine à construire sa
maison, à faire son champ, à réparer
sa demeure,

de crainte que le chef n'aie
mal à la tête, mal au ventre, de
crainte qu'il n'aie pas assez à
manger.

Tous doivent l'aider à porter
le bois de chauffage, à porter l'eau
dans la hotte, à biner et à ratisser
son champ;

Tous doivent réparer sa cabane
(du champ) si elle menace de tomber,
à réparer sa maison et à la consolider si elle penche, tous doivent lui
donner du fil si la jupe de sa femme
est déchirée, jamais ils ne doivent
l'abandonner;

ainsi il aura beaucoup d'alcool
(à offrir) tant qu'il sera en vie, il
aura beaucoup de riz (à offrir) quand
il aura un mort chez lui, et les frères
et les soeurs (habitants) resteront
toujours unis,

car tous l'écouteront d'une seule
oreille quand il parlera, tous parle-
ront d'une seule bouche (quand ils
s'adresseront à lui), tous seront contents d'aider le chef.

Quant à ceux qui voudront se
croire plus fort que le tigre, plus
puissants que les génies, ceux qui
ouvriront leur bouche insolemment,

ceux-là seront coupables et il
y aura affaire entre le chef et eux;

pour une faute légère ils paieron
une petite amende, pour une faute grav
ils paieront une amende plus forte.

Gie dut ñu kéut bằng tlàn,giê
dut ñu kéut bang ala,ñu duăh ba
sap ko sah mdrong.

Ñu amâo mâo čim bằng,ñu amâo
mâo mnŏng chăt,hat drăo djup.

Ñu duah tluiñ ngăn sah,ñu duăh
păah ngăn mdrong,ngăn ayong adei ñu
duăh bi mmla.

Ñu tluiñ ding klap,dap boh ktor
ñu duăh bi wor sah mdrong.

Klam grăn kga djă biu jŏng,ñu
djă klit êmong,duah bi hui buôn sang.

Ding amâo mñê ñu mñê kbŏng,
gŏng amâo mñê mñê kkăo,go amâo mâo
klei ñu bi mâo.

kan pat lu klang,wang dlang lu
lăk buôn sang go dŏk hnŭk ênang
ñu duăh prung.

... drao drung ñu prung
... dja d... drung prung sang, go
... ong ĕdăp,ĕdĕ ñu iăng,yang

Ñu čim mtah, kan mtah,do sah
mdrong ñu duăh bong pliĕ.

... amâo mâo pai,amai amâo
... dhŏng ca amâo mâo pŏ bi

... jih asei,kbao rih jih
... boh klei tuič asei ñu pŏ.

Celui qui introduit le bâton dans
le trou du python,dans le trou du
serpent, celui qui cherche à parler
au nom du chef;

celui qui n'a pas de viande à
manger,pas d'aliments à découper,pas
de tabac à fumer;

et qui cherche à s'emparer des
biens du chef, des biens du riche,des
biens des frères (des habitants);

celui qui fait semblant signaler
l'étui à sel,d'aligner les graines de
maïs,qui cherche à tromper le riche
(pour obtenir ce qu'il désire);

celui qui porte le coupe-coupe sur
l'épaule,qui tient la hache à la
main,qui agite une peau de tigre pour
effrayer les habitants;

celui imite avec la bouche le son
de la flûte que personne ne joue,qui
imite avec les ongles le son de la
guitare,qui suscite des histoires à
ceux qui n'en ont pas;

celui qui comme le poisson "paa"
aux arêtes nombreuses,comme la bine
branlant dans le manche et exigeant
beaucoup de laque pour être fixée,
celui qui sème le désordre dans le
village paisible;

celui porte des plantes vénéneux
à la main pour effrayer les habitants
qui trouble les populations calmes
et paisibles;

celui qui désire la viande et le
poisson frais,qui cherche à manger
les biens des riches;

comme les bananes sauvages que
personne ne ramasse,comme la soeur
aînée que personne ne touche,comme
le couteau usé que personne ne répar

comme le porc et le buffle desti
nés à être sacrifiés (abattus),celui
qui cherche des histoires perdra son
corps.

Jug.no 17 du 9 mai 1917 : 1 an + 20.000 + kpih.
Jug.no du 5 javier 1938 : 3 mois (menaces de mort)
Jug.no du 6 mai 1938 : 1 an (menaces de mort suivies de mort)
Jug.no du 1er juin 1938: 6 mois (Sorcellerie,menaces de mort
suivies de mort)

<table>
<tr><td>

3?. KLEI DUAH BI HÜI APANG
BI AWAH KƠ KHUA.

</td><td>

38. DE CEUX QUI SÈMENT LE
DÉSORDRE EN PARLANT AU NOM DU CHEF.

</td></tr>
<tr><td>

Mnut ñu hiu mnia, kra ñu blei,
kpei đöng ñu chĭ .

</td><td>

Celui qui s'en va échanger du tabac
qui va chercher du sel, qui va vendre
du ferment ou du fer;

</td></tr>
<tr><td>

.... amâo tuôm yua, ña amâo
p.. mtur.

</td><td>

celui qu'on n'a jamais pu employer
à fendre du bois, à puiser de l'eau
celui qui s'en toujours seul, n'import..
ou;

</td></tr>
<tr><td>

ñu hiu mă kơ krei, ñu hiu mă asei
ñ...

</td><td>

celui qui n'a pas de viande à
manger, d'aliments à découper, de taba..
à fumer;

</td></tr>
<tr><td>

ñu amâo čim bông, mmông čhat
kit drao djup.

</td><td>

celui qui fait semblant de figno-
ler l'étui à sel, de ranger les graine..
de ma"is pour tromper les autres;

</td></tr>
<tr><td>

ñu tluiñ đing klap, ñu đăp
toh ktơr, ñu bi wơr arăng gơ̆.

</td><td>

celui qui prétend qu'on lui a
commandé de biner et de défricher,
qui prétend parler au nom du chef;

</td></tr>
<tr><td>

Jik bi awah, jah bi' awai, ñu
..i klei sah mdrong.

</td><td>

celui qui désire le joli tissu
comme un enfant, qui désire le turban
comme un jeune homme, celui qui convoite
les biens d'autrui;

</td></tr>
<tr><td>

Nčeh kơ čhiăm, êdam kơ kun,
ñu duah hnun mă kơ ngăn drăp arăng.

</td><td>

celui qui cherche à embrasser la
touffe de bambous, qui cherche à pren-
dra ce que contient la cuillère, qui
cherche à s'emparer des biens d'autrui;

</td></tr>
<tr><td>

...ŭ ñu duah kuak, awak ñu
nar, ñu ... hnorbnak kơ ngăn arăng.

</td><td>

celui qui dit que le bâton tache-
té est un serpent, que les oreilles
mouchetées sont celles du tigre, que
ses paroles sont celles du chef;

</td></tr>
<tr><td>

Knih brung ala, knga blak êmong,
..ông ñu po ñu lač kbiă mông sah
mdrong.

</td><td>

celui qui veut faire croire qu'il
peut produire l'eau, les pierres, la
pluie;

</td></tr>
<tr><td>

ña mâo nông ñu, boh tâo ble,
.. hiăm hjan mông ñu.

</td><td>

celui, homme ou la femme, qui s'en
va partout cherchant à faire accepter
sa parole (comme s'il était envoyé
par le chef),

</td></tr>
<tr><td>

Ơhei ñu hiu pliê, mniê ñu hiu
.. ñu duah hdăm mă klei.

</td><td>

celui-là est coupable et il y a
affaire entre les autres et lui.

</td></tr>
<tr><td>

Khua mơ̆.kei arăng kơ ñu.

</td><td></td></tr>
</table>

.... Jug.no 80 du 11 octobre 1925 : 5 jours + 30400(Us.de f.).
  Jug.no du 5 janvier 1938 : 3 mois (menaces de mort).

...lques paragraphes de ce texte concernent les affaires de sorcellerie
..r. 9 et 10).

17. KLEI MFAH MNUIH BUÔN SANG
AMÂO BREI GÜI SAP KLEI
KHUA

39. DE CEUX QUI POUSSENT LES
HABITANTS À NE PAS OBÉIR
AUX ORDRES DU CHEF.

Gran wang ñu tăn,kga ênah
lu bi kdloh,ñu bi soh sap kôêng
Sah wurŭng.

Tiêng tiăp ñu lŏ bi trai,
êsei čat ñu lŏ bi mdao,tiê boh
nreng bliao ñu ngă bi jhong.

Gran nâng ñu bi akŏ,gran kga
ñu bi ŗŏng,ñu lông si tiê hong sah
mdrŏng.

Ryorğñu bi êpa,êđa hoh,ěeh
 čŏng ñu bi mdum hong sah mdrŏng.

Anăn ñŏn kđi khua kơ ñu .

Celui qui arrache le manche de
la binette, qui brise le manche du
coupe-coupe,celui qui dit que les
ordres donnés par le chef sont mauvais

celui qui fait que l'abcès
crevé se remplit de nouveau,que le
riz refroidi est réchauffé,que le
coeur paisible des habitants devient
méchant;

celui qui mesure (la longueur)
du manche de son coupe-coupe, qui
compare sa force avec celle du chef;

celui qui mesure les pannes(de
la maison du chef) en brasses, les
tirants en coudées,qui compare le
nombre de jarres et des gongs du chef
au sien,

celui-là est coupable et il y
a affaire entre le chef et lui .

ÊĐÊGA adü mana nŭ ?

18. [illegible] [illegible] ... JIH [illegible] [illegible] ... CAH.

[illegible] ... mâo, êlâo [illegible] ... bih,
[illegible] tuôm dih, [illegible] tuôm [illegible].

Bi ñu mêêh ma mrâo, thâo ma ară,
[illegible] ma klei mdih mbruê.

[illegible] ĉiêt djô hŭa, gao pla djô
kh[illegible], gao klei aê aduôn pô mâo kdi.

[illegible] prong ti keeh, [illegible] prong
ti [illegible], gao ti [illegible] [illegible].

Mâo [illegible] êmuh mnut, [illegible] hra êmuh
ma, [illegible] khua prong êmuh khua prong.

Ñu koh [illegible] khưng gao, koh [illegible]
khăng dlông, [illegible] kbông khăng mnhưr.

Ñu [illegible] [illegible] bi êdah, [illegible] ñu wah
[illegible] phêo, [illegible] lêô lŏ hŏng khua.

Hla [illegible] ñu [illegible], hla [illegible] ñu săp,
ñu [illegible] klei hŏng [illegible] ayŏng.

Ñu dja dai miêô, [illegible] dai gi, kdi
[illegible] ma mrâo.

Ĉiêt ñu gao ti trang, [illegible] gao
[illegible], [illegible] gao ti [illegible] êjung.

Anăn mâo kdi prong.

40. DE CEUX QUI EFFRAIENT LES HABITANTS PAR DES MENSONGES.

Celui qui raconte d'autrefois il n'y avait rien, qu'on ne voyait rien, qu'on n'obéissait pas, qu'on ne se soumettait à personne;

que tout cela a été inventé depuis peu, depuis maintenant seulement, que lui seul connaît les choses d'autrefois;

celui qui passe outre les signeaux indiquant des pièges s'y trouve pris, celui qui viole la coutume des ancêtres se crée des histoires.

Celui qui est comme une lame de couteau qui veut être plus grosse que le manche, comme un enfant qui se croit plus grand qu'un adulte et désobéit à ses parents;

celui qui ne consulte pas le banian quand il ya le banian, qui ne demande pas au figuier quand il y a un figuier, qui ne consulte pas le grand chef quand il y a un grand che[f];

celui qui coupe les bambous au dela de la longueur fixée, qui passe outre les ordres du chef;

celui qui n'informe pas (le chef pour qu'il sache, qui ne montre pas pour faire voir, qui ne dit jamais rien;

celui qui cache ce qu'il sait sous une feuille, qui ne fait rien connaître aux frères;

celui qui tient un chat gris dans sa main et un chat noir dans son pagne (et les excite l'un contre l'autre), celui qui cherche toujours de nouvelles histoires;

celui qui est comme les herbes voulant s'élever plus haut que les joncs, comme la paillote voulant monter plus haut que les roseaux, comme les animaux voulant bondir plu[s] haut que les cimes des arbres,

celui-là est coupable et il y a affaire très grave avec lui.

[illegible] Jug. no 25 du [illegible] juil. 1917 : 5 ans (Troubler la tranquilité publique).
[illegible] du [illegible] nov. 1919 : 10 jours & 3 ko et kpih.
Jug. [illegible] du 12 nov. 1925 : -
[illegible] 1938 : 3 mois.

IO bis.KLEI ÑUIH DUAH KŎI AP,
KEI SAP KO PHUNG MNUIH DUÔN
SANG ARĂNG AKUAN,ÇIĂNG BI PHUNG
BI CU LUI HE KHUA DI GO :

Êran măng ñu duah tah,kga ênah
ñu duah bi kdlch,ñu duah bi sŏh naŏ
hriê mnuih buôn sang arăng.

Kdeh pông ñu duah ba,kdeh pha
ñu duah runh,ñu duah mă klei jak
mi ai arăng.

Ŏbung jut,knut hbei,klei bŏh
ñu duah mdi.

Giê aŏê kaur ñu čur hŏng dhŏng,
iê muôê tmur ñu čur hŏng daŏ,tiê
bŏh arăng blaŏ ñu ngă bi jhong,
t... klei arăng dôk jak ñu duah ngă
... mat.

...ăng amâ thâê êbat ñu ba,
... mô thaŏ huă ñu naŭ,arăng
... ñu duah bi jum brei.

... lei,êkei lu nu,abŭ
... ñu duah mat kma.

... ñu duah kŏut băng tlăn,
... duah kŏut băng ala, ñu
... ŏu dhat ko mnuih buôn
...

... ñu duah bi trei,êsei
... ,tiê bŏh arăng blaŏ
... jhong.

... sŏh ñu mâo klei arăng ko
ñu .

...Jug.no 25 du IŌ juillet 1917:5 ans(Excitation à la révolte).
Jug.no 48 du 5 nov. 1936: 3 mois à IO.co (Exc.à la révol.).
Jug.no II du 2 mars 1937: I an (-).
Jug... du 25 février 1937: 5 ans(Rebelliton et exeit.rév.)

Celui qui cherche à arracher le
manche de la binette,ou le manche du
coupe-coupe,celui qui cherche à créer
des histoires,aux habitants dans les
villages voisins;

celui qui vá offrir un morceau
de filet ou un morceau de cuisse,
celui qui cherche à exciter les habitants en leur disant que sa cause
est bonne;

celui qui pique comme la pointe
de rhizôme de bambou,comme le bâton
à creuser pour chercher des tubercu
celui dont les propos ne visent qu'à
exciter les populations;

celui qui taille avec un cou...
ou un sabre le bâton qui n'est pas
pointu,qui rend mauvais le coeur des
habitants qui était bon,qui excite
des histoires aux frères qui vivent
paisiblement;

celui qui porte ceux qui ne peuvent pas marcher,qui mâche les alim...
à ceux qui ne peuvent pas manger,ce
crée des histoires à ceux qui n'en
ont pas;

celui qui a toujours des histoires, celle qui a beaucoup de dettes,
ceux qui comme les poissons et les
grenouilles ont beaucoup de tanières
pourse réfugier;

celui qui introduit un bâton d...
le trou du python pour l'en déloger,
qui introduit une baguette dans le
trou du serpent pour l'en faire sort...
celui qui cherche à répendre la mauvaise parole dansles villages;

celui qui fait que l'abcès cre...
se remplit de nouveau,que le riz ...
refroidi est réchauffé,que les coeurs
paisibles deviennent mauvais,que les
chefs tranquilles deviennent inquiet...
celui-là est coupable et il y
a affeire entre les autres et lui.

42. DES COUPS ET BLESSURES AU CHEF ET DE L'ASSASSINAT DU CHEF.

Ñu êmah ko kơyâo kpă, kgă bong,
ñu tluh ko anuih pral jong kagan.

Arăn kông ñu duah duăt, kwat
ñu duah tling, ñu duah bi mjăng bing
kna.

Ñu duah čhai hlăm kô troh, hlăm
btoh ôc, anuih dua điâo ñu bi kru,
ngă ko ag.

Ñe ñu mdrœn, kăm ñu mdru, ơjơ
pral ñu bi guh ko gô.

Ñu tluh ko êman gơ ti sdring,
ling gơ ti ktal, anôn dhong ñu gao,
mao ñu sut, ñu bi êmut ko sah mdrong
ñu duah êam biêng, thiêng amao he gô.

Kơyâ mhơ bi êmat ñu khăt he
mtih, jăng jing jing ñu duah koh
điê ôc.

Ñu ..u... ko arăng anâo mâo boh,
ñu ... čhah koh mâo ... kđi, ñu nač
... ...l mdrong hdăt.

... ku arăng mâo ko ñu prong.

... jih asei, kbao rih jih asei
... ... klei tuič asei ñu pô.

... pa arăng tuč bi mâo, anuih
... bi jih, ... juê ôngsố, amai
... ñu, duah dl ñu ngă ései gu hla
... roh, ... dl ñu doh bung
...

arăng čap ... di ñu jih.

Celui qui convoitise l'arbre bien
droit, ou le coupe-coupe tranchant, qui
est jaloux de l'homme laborieux (et
riche),

et pour cela fait l'échange du
bracelet (avec les autres) pour avoir
des amis (des complices);

celui qui va s'entendre en haut
du vallon, au fond du ravin, avec deux
ou trois individus pour qu'ils l'aident à nuire au chef;

celui qui s'entendre avec d'autres
pour se procurer du poison, pour réunir
plusieurs lances afin de tuer le chef;

celui qui convoite l'éléphant du
chef attaché devant la maison, les gongs
suspendus à la barre, et qui pour cela
astique son sabre, aiguise son couteau,
parce qu'il est jaloux du chef et
qu'il a l'intention de le frapper ou
de l'assommer;

celui qui coupe la cime de la
plante qui bourgeonne, qui frappe celui
qui a été fait chef pour le tuer;

celui qui cherche à nuire aux gens
sans raison, à les frapper sans motif
parce qu'il est jaloux des riches (de
ses semblables),

celui-là est coupable et il y a
affaire très grave contre lui.

le Porc et le buffle destinés au
sacrifice perdent leur corps, celui
qui se crée des affaires (comme celle-
ci) perdra son corps.

S'il a trois ou quatre complices
on les poursuivra, ainsi que ses parents
ou ses sœurs s'ils lui ont donné à
manger et à boire en cachette, s'ils
lui ont porté des hottes et des paniers
pour cela on les arrêtera tous.

Bul. Ad.-Jug. no.15 du 16 février 1925 : 5 ans + 3 ko + kpih.
     Jug no.40 du 27 août 1923   : 6 mois + 2 ko + pih.

20.KLEI BI HGUM DRU NGA JU JHAT KO KHUA.

43. DE CEUX QUI FONT DU MAL AU CHEF PAR COMPLICITÉ .

Êsei băng hma, êa hlăm roh di ñu doh bung bai ko tač.

Ceux qui portent du riz au champ (pour les pirates);ceux qui leur portent de l'eau dans les buissons,qui leur donnent des paniers hors du village;

Asei ti buôn, tluôn ti êngao, sue dhong deo ko tač,di ñu dru nac iang ko sah mdrong.

ceux dont le corps est au village mais dont les pieds sont à l'extérieur,ceux qui tirent le couteau ou le sabre hors(du fourreau)pour aider les ennemis du chef;

Di ñu koh kông êpa,dua braih êi,mli sah mdrong di ñu bi hgum.

ceux qui coupent des douzaines de bracelets,qui portent des pleins paniers de riz(aux ennemis),qui s'entendent(avec ces derniers) pour faire du mal au chef;

Di ñu bi čhai hlăm ko troh, ktrê hmih êa,mmih pa êma,dua tlăo di ñu iêô bi ênum .

ceux qui vont conspirer au haut du vallon,sur les berges de la rivière,ceux qui se réunissent à quatre ou cinq,à deux ou trois;

Êman di ñu bi tling,čing yuôl di ñu bi yuêl ka,di ñu bi mta klei, brei sap,di ñu khăp kbông mbah.

ceux qui entravent l'éléphant qui suspendent les gongs,qui scellent le contrat,qui donnent leur parole, qui se font les complices(des ennemis)

Skei di ñu bi brei giê,amiê x bi u sap,di ñu bi khăp sa klei năn soai.

ceux qui touchent le bâton, celles qui approuvent les paroles(des ennemis),ceux qui sont d'accord(avec eux),de crainte que le lendemain ou un autre jour l'eau ne soit versée, le tas de bois ne soit démoli,la faute de tous ne soit rejetée sur un se

hui ko aguah êdei, hrue mkuan êa duah bi tuh,djuh mkăn,hui duah hlăm klei ko sa čô.

Di ñu nao bi ra-ru,kgu rê, dê mbuh bi ênai sa năn.

ceux qui s'en vont en groupe, qui se lèvent tous ensemble(le matin qui tendent ou défendent(la corde de leurs arbalètes)en même temps;

di ñu sa mdrau,sai di di ñu pôk di ñu dun bi guh.

ceux qui aident (les ennemis) à espionner,qui (les) aident en leur prêtant leurs lances ou leurs épieux;

alê amâo hluh di ñu ciăng čǎo,
êrao amâo hluh di ñu čiăng ir,kpa
kpa di ñu čiăng dhir băng,di ñu
čiăng nač iăng ko' sah mdrong hdai.

Todah mniê arăng kral drei,to
čkei arăng kral pô,êmô kbao arăng
kral mgăt,mnuih pă arăng tui bi mâo
mnuih tlâo arăng tui bi jih,wit juê
ǎngai, amai adei di ñu arăng čăp
jih moh,todah di ñu ktrâo hluê mdiă
ktiă hluê ǎngin, todah di ñu dru
čin ai hrăm mbit.

Un rih jih asei, kbao rih jih
asei,duah beh klei tuič asei di ñu.

ceux qui veulent percer les
bambous qui ne le sont pas,qui veulent
creuser des tanières aux tortues et
aux varans qui n'en ont pas,ceux qui
veulent nuire au chef sans raison;

si de la femme on connaît le
corps,si de l'homme on connaît le
visage,comme on peut connaître le
propriétaire des boeufs ou des buffles
en voyant leur gardien,s'ils sont
quatre on les poursuivra on les
arrêtera,s'ils sont trois on les pour
suivra et on les ficelera,on arrêtera
également leurs frères et leurs soeurs
s'ils se sont comportés comme la sau
terelle recherchant la chaleur du
soleil,comme la perruche recherchant
le souffle du vent,s'ils ont aidé les
coupables,s'ils se sont faits leurs
complices;

comme le porc ou le buffle destinés à être sacrifiés (aux divinités)
ceux qui se rendent coupables(de tels
crimes)perdront leur corps.

- JUG.no 62 du 25 août 1925 : 5 ans(Enlèvement du chef).
- Prison perpétuelle(-).

X21. KLEI MNUIH AMÂO ĐAŎ.

Bung amâo đua, jia amâo tŭh,
amâo duh brua aê aduôn.

Braih amâo dan, êlan amâo tă,
amâo ngă brua aê aduôn.

Ai đơng, hnơng đut, hlut kơ
asei, hlei pô hriê ñu koh, hlei pô
hriê ñu tlơ.

Ngă lăng hlang drêñ, knuêñ hêč
jêč ai tiê.

Leh nguôm kơ trei, ke hjei
kơ tlơh.

Hlei pô bă kniêng, čiêng rông,
kgông eh moiêk, djam brei, êsei
čiêm.

Arăng mă niêm, kriêm but kơ
pô anăn.

Pưk uê, hjiê tal, mal găp, pưk
prăng, adrăng điô, mnuih kho mgu
ñu mjiê.

Hao mduh ñu blah, mlah ñu koh,
coh kăn thâo găl kăn thâo.

Jih mnuih joh đaŏ, laŏ gô kơ
di ñu.

Tơ dah si dưm, (bia anei mrâo)
dưm ti kơyâo gô, čar hlô mnong arăng
mdih ñu anăn.

44. DES INSOUMIS.

Ceux qui ne portent pas la
corbeille(sur la tête), qui ne ver-
sent pas l'impôt, qui n'exécutent pas
les travaux prescrits par les ancêtres ;

ceux qui ne donnent pas le riz,
qui n'entretiennent pas les chemins
qui ne font pas les travaux ordonné
par les ancêtres;

ceux qui sont insolents, emportés
téméraires, qui frappent avec le sabre
ceux qui les approchent et les per-
cent avec la lance;

ceux qui semblables aux brins
de paillote, aux liens de bambou dé-
sechés (se cassant facilement), s'em-
portent facilement;

ceux qui lèchent la rosée jusqu'à en être rassasiés, qui mordent
le fer jusqu'à ce qu'il se brise;

ceux qui s'occupent d'eux en
leur apportant du bétel du riz et
des légumes,

ceux-là seront poursuivis.

Ceux qui cache dans les cabanes
dans les greniers, dans les abris
provisoires, couchant sur la paille
cherchant à tuer le passant inoffen-
sif;

ceux qui frappent quand on va
chez eux, qui tuent quand on va les
voir, qui ne savent pas ce qui est
bien et ce qui est mal;

ceux qui obligent tout le monde
à se coucher devant eux, à leur obé

autrefois on les pendait à un
arbre et jetait leur corps en pâtu
aux bêtes fauves.

Amâo brei hua êsei siam, bong
djam jäk ôh.

On ne leur donnait plus de bon
riz et de bons légumes à manger;

Chi he kơ êmô lao, kơ kbao mdhur
ngän kur yuăn .

on les échangeait contre les
bœufs aux Laotiens, contre des buffles
aux Mdhurs, contre des biens aux
Cambodgiens ou aux Viêtnamiens;

Chi kơ tue, mblei-hong Mdhur,
čr kơ ngän Bih Mnông.

on les vendait aux étrangers ,
on les échangeait aux Mdhurs, on les
vendait comme esclaves aux bihs et
aux Mnôngs.

wäng boh tâo êkä, kga boh tâo
čtor, mtol he ai tiê.

La pierre rugueuse est usée par
la binette qu'elle aiguise, le coupe-
coupe est usé par la pierre lisse
qui l'affûte, les insoumis sont punis
sévèrement par ceux qu'ils ont mal-
traités .

Jug.no 9 du 20 mars 1917: paiement des impôts en retard.
Jug.no 28 du 16 juil.1917: I mois + 10$00 + paiement des im-
    pôts en retard.
Jug.no 30 du 16 juil.1917: I mois + 20$00.
Jug.no 31 du 16 juil.1917: 2 mois + 10$00 + paiement des
    impôts en retard.
Jug.no 9 du II juil.1918: 6 mois + paiement des impôts
    en retard.
Jug.no 10 du II juil.1918: 8 mois.

22. KLEI DUAH MDHUA BUÔN SANG ARANG.

Tluôn mơêa, pha msah, djiê êman brah, mčah knah hlong, djiê sah mdrong yua ñu.

Êman yang mơya ñu duah hơua kơyâo klông, êman yang mơya ñu duah hơua kơyâo kpang, ñu duah hơua sang sah mdrong.

Ñu mă tiê êmông, lông tiê kgâo, ñu lông tiê kâo lư hong abâl, ñu kral djam bât hra kba hong phi, mdi lang ai sah mdrong, thâo jhong thâo ktang be.

Ti ñu dôk ti rai kmrong, ti ñu ong ti rai hdrah, ti dôk ti mčah uôn sang yua ñu.

Čiang kơ čing tiơ êran, čiang . . . jơh, čiang kơ sah mdrong . . . . ye arăng.

Ti dôk ti joh kpong, ti ñu ng ti joh arha, ti ñu dôk ti djiê . . buôn.

Ñu duah koh msuăt, ñu duah wăt . .iê, ñu duah mdjiê mčа mčum.

Anăn ung jô, mô buah, sah . ong dru âl sơai kơ ñu anăn.

. .ăn kthul ñu mâo kdi arăng ñu prong.

45. DES FAUTEURS DE DÉSORDRES.

Ceux qui font les cuisses sont mouillées, que les fesses sont humides que les gongs sont brisés, que les éléphants sont morts, que le chef est tué;

ceux qui s'appuient contre l'arbre "klông" ou l'arbre "kpang" comme l'éléphant du dieu crocodille ceux qui cherchent à s'installer dans la maison du riche;

ceux qui évaluent la force du tigre, qui évaluent la force de l'ours qui essaient si les griffes sont acérées ou émoussées, qui goûtent le potage poursavoir s'il est fade ou assaisonné ou piquant, ceux qui agacent le chef pour savoir s'il est faible ou énergique;

ceux qui détruisent la forêt là où ils s'installent, qui détruisent la brousse là où se fixent, qui sèment le désordre là où ils habitent;

ceux qui poursuivent celui qui porte un gong pour s'en emparer, qui poursuivent l'éléphant pour s'en saisir, ceux qui pour être riches font du mal à tout le monde;

ceux qui abattent les troncs là où ils s'installent, qui coupent les racines là où ils se fixent, qui font mourir le chef là où ils demeurent;

ceux qui frappent avec le sabre, qui fouettent avec le rotin, qui font mourir sans raison,

provoquant la colère des époux, la haine des épouses, le courroux des chefs,

ceux-là sont coupables et il y a affaire très grave entre les autres et eux.

JISPR.- Jug.no 56 du 28 juil. 1925 : Prison perpétuelle.
Jug.no 62 du 26 août 1925 ;
Jug.no 86 du 2 déc. 1925 : 10 ans.
Jug.no 95 du 8 déc. 1925 : Peine de mort.
Jug.no 41 du 7 juin 1926 : 10 ans.

23. KLEI ANUIH LHIAR DUAH YAL DLIÊ,DUAH HƯN KLEI ÑU HMƯ HLÃM BUÔN PÔ HONG ROH.

46. DES TRAÎTRES QUI RENSEIGNENT LES ENNEMIS SUR LES AFFAIRES DE LEUR VILLAGE.

Giê đụt ñu duah kčut băng tlãm,giê đụt ñu duah kčut băng ala, ñu duah ba hiu sap hlãm buôn sang pô kơ tač êngao.

Celui qui introduit le bâton dans le trou du python, ou dans le trou du serpent, qui va répéter au dehors les paroles qu'il a entendues dans le village;

Ñu duah dja čing mong,yong čing ana,ñu duah ba sap kbông kơ buôn yu,pu ngo,ñu duah ngã si khê ngu.

celui qui porte un petit gong à la main,un grand gong à bout de bras,qui porte les paroles du chef dans les villages de l'Ouest ou de l'Est,qui agit comme un fou et un imbécile;

Ñu mjhưt bong mao,ñu mhao bong boh,bang kbông ñu ktal si aroh êbua.

celui qui a envie de champignon qui désire manger des fruits,qui a dés démangeaisons dans la bouche comme s'il avait mangé des taros vert

Ñu hmư amâo thâo dôk hmư,ñu thâo amâo dôk sa thêo,mâo klei ñu duah hưn hong arăng êgar.

celui qui a entendu,qui sait et fait semblant de ne rien connaître, celui qui cherche à informer les étrangers de ce qui se passe dans son village;

Ñu hmư sap arăng bia,ñu duah bi ksua kơ đlông,ñu hmư kbông arăng ñu bi ksua kơ lu,ñu buh kru arăng điêt ñu lač prong,ñu hmư sap arăng yăl dliê ñu ba hiu hưn.

celui qui a entendu quelques paroles et cherche à déformer et à les grossir,celui qui a vu une empreinte (de pieds)et dit qu'il y en avait un grand nombre,celui qui écoute parler le chef et s'en va répéter ses parol (aux ennemis);

Ñu huă amâo thâo kđăm,mnăm amâo thâo kriê,ñu duah yăl dliê tlô klei hră buôn(sang) êlan.

celui qui mange et ne sait pas arrêter,qui boit et ne sait pas se modérer,celui qui va raconter dans la brousse ce qu'il a entendu dans son village,

anăn kthul ñu mâo kđi khua kơ ñu.

celui-là est coupable et il y a affaire entre le chef et lui.

JURISPR.- Jug.no 21 du 17 mai 1937 : 1 mois à 100$00(Commerce avec insoumis).

24. KEI MNUIH BUÔN DRU NGÃ NGA BLAH BUÔN ÑU PÔ.

Ñu amão dôk ting kơ mnu, ñu tu ting kơ mja, săp kơha ñu hlue arăng.

Asei ñu ti buôn, tluên ñu ti êngao, ñu sue dhong đao kơ tao, ñu naõ iang kơ mnuih buôn sang đum nan.

Ñu ma klo ñu dlăm hruh hông, kbông ñu ti nei băng gei ñu čhi tu, kbông ti nei băng gei čhi tong, ñu bông angin, ñu dru min ai mbit hông arăng.

Ñu mniê lu klei, êkei lu săp, ñu duah khăp duah tu kdi arăng.

Ñu wăng lu blư kơ ami, kga lu blư kơ ama, ñu anak êdam êra lo blư kơ khua, kơ buôn sang ñu pô.

Ñu mniê lu klei, êkei lu nư, amâo ajik lu băng ñu duah mŭt kma.

Ñu êbat sa knhuang, čhuang mdram, ñu tui êbat hram mbit hông arăng kru sa nan.

Anăn kthul ñu mâo kdi arăng kơ ñu prong.

47. DE CEUX QUI AIDENT LES ENNEMIS À COMBATTRE LEUR VILLAGE.

Celui qui ne reste pas du côté du poulet, qui adopte le parti de la fouine, qui obéit à la parole des autres;

celui qui a son corps dans le village et son derrière à l'extérieur qui tire le couteau et le sabre hors (du fourreau), qui hait les habitants de son village;

celui qui jette la pierre dans le guepier, qui a sa bouche dans le village et accepte la parole des ennemis, qui a ses lèvres ici et sa langue là-bas, qui se nourrit d'air et se fait complice des ennemis;

celle qui a beaucoup d'affaires celui qui a toujours des histoires, se range toujours du côté des étrangers;

celui qui est tranchant comme une binette ou un couppe-coupe et se montre insolent envers sa mère ou sa père, celui, jeune homme ou une jeune fille, qui est insolent avec le chef, avec les habitants de son village;

celui homme ou femme, qui a toujours des histoires, ou des dettes; celui qui est comme les poissons ou les grenouilles qui ont beaucoup de tenieres pour se cacher;

celui qui marche du même pas (les pirates), qui avance à la même allure, qui suit les autres en marchant sur leurs traces,

celui-là est coupable et il y a affaire très grave entre les autres et lui.

JURISPR.- Jug.no 1 du 2 janv. 1917 : 3ans.
Jug.no 20 du 16 juill.1918 :20 ans
Jug.no 50 du 25 juil.1925 : Prison perpétuelle.

25. KLEI MNUIH BA ÊLAN KƠ ROH
HRIÊ ĚLAH NGA BUÔN
~ÑU KÔ.

Arăng amâo thâo êbat ñu bă,
arăng amâo thâo hua ñu mum, arăng
amâo jum klei ñu bi jum brei, arăng
amâo thâo bit ñu git brei.

Lliê ñu ba, êa ñu tât, arăng
jak ñu hriê mmat mlam ñu brie bi bit,
Jak ñu čhoi leh hlam kơ trah, ktuê
hroh êa, anăn ñu ba bi bit brei êlan.
Êman leh jak ñu tling, čing yuôl, jăk
leh ñu bi kuôl kâ hong arăng.

Anôk mnư ktang, bang jang kjăp,
prap leh mdih mbrue leh ñu buh.

Anôk mnư rang, bang jang ring,
anôk bang čing čeh, knong aseh êman
ñu naê bi bit.

Anôk mnư ktang, bang jang prong,
...sang seh udrong dôk, ñu naê
...ê brei.

...na ñu dru kbong, krong ñu dru
buh, mnuih êtuh êbâo, ñu hlu duah bi
bit.

Ayua năn mnuih sa tuh arăng
...mnuih sa bâo arăng mdjiê, mdiê
...ik hriê arăng čuh, hnuh klong arăng
brei, klei arăng kâ, mna hlun arăng
ajing.

Ênuar kô jih arăng sua, êman
...na arăng čung, čeh klung hliêng
arăng gui, arăng hrui ma jăh jang
...ang kat.

Tudah mniê arăng thâo drei,
...ei arăng thâo pô, êmô kbao arăng
hrui ngăt, dao prong arăng brei,
...uong kư, atao grư ak arăng čiêm he
ñu.

48. DE CEUX QUI SE FONT
COMPLICES DES PIRATES.

Celui qui porte ceux qui ne
savent pas marcher, qui mâche les
aliments à ceux qui ne peuvent pas
manger, qui intruit ceux qui ne connaissent pas;

celui qui les guide dans la fo...
qui leur indique les gués, qui les
dirige dans l'obscurité de la nuit;

celui qui s'entend avec eux
près de la source, qui les conduit
tout le long de la rivière, qui leur
indique le chemin (du village);

celui qui avec eux entrave
l'éléphant, suspend le gong, scelle le
pacte d'amitié;

celui qui connaît bien la
résistance de la palissade, de la
grande porte, les points faibles de
l'enceinte, qui fait connaître le po...
faible de la palissade ou de la port...
les fossés où sont cachées les jarr...
et les gongs, les pieux auxquels sont
attachés les chevaux et les éléphant...

qui indique (aux pirates) les
points solides de la palissade ou d...
la grande porte, les maisons riches,

qui aide à arracher les lancett...
(protégeant le village), qui guide...
cent ou mille individus,

et qui est cause que cent ou
mille personnes sont tuées ou emmené...
(en esclavage), que les maisons et le...
greniers sont incendiés, que les can-
ques ou les entraves sont passées
aux habitants, que ceux-ci deviennent
esclaves ou prisonniers,

que les éléphants mâles et les
éléphants femelles sont enlevés, que
les jarres grandes et petites sont
emportées, que tous les habitants son...
emmenés,

si de la femme on connaît le cor...
si de l'homme on connaît la personne...
si des boeufs et des buffles on connaît le gardien,

avec le grand sabre on le décapitera, avec le couteau tranchant on
l'égorgera, et on jettera son corps
en pâture aux vautours et aux corbeaux.

26. KLEI MNUIH LHIAK NGA GAP HONG KOH,NAO HUN KLEI KHUA ÑU PÔ .

Ñu tle nao je aguah,krah mnit, êkutpit dih.

Khua ñu tle nao ktleh,hdeh ñu tle nao bi hač,ñu tle nao lač,yal dliê hong arăng,khua ñu amra hriê lah hlăm sang,wang hlăm buôn.

Khua leh koh kông êpa, ua braih êi,mli mdrong leh khua bi kbin.

" Êkei di ih bi kriê,mniê biat,di ih bi êmiat răng mă,đam đuah hiu mniê sa drei,êkei sa čô .

" Di ih bi prăp mă mnư bi ktang, wang jang bi kjap,di ih kăp bi kriê răng mă."

Anăn êmô arăng puh he ko êngao, kbao arăng puh he ko dliê,mâo anak êkei mniê arăng puh he hlăm čư mtâo.

... čuk hrah,êbah mnông,kông ...... šok piêô jih arăng mdăp, ... ra ênao, jih arăng mdăp,

...ăn todah mniê arăng thâo asei, êkei arăng thâo pô, êmô kbao arăng kral mgat,

Dao prong arăng brei he ko ñu, hong lư,mtao grư ak arăng čiêm he ..,dliê mâo koyao gô,čar hlô mnong ...ăng nao ..dih he ñu.

... kuhul ñu hiu,mgu êbat.

...n rih jih asei ñu,kbao rih jih ...i ñu,ñu đuah toh klei tuič asei ...

49. DES TRAÎTRES QUI PACTISENT AVEC LES PIRATES ET LES RENSEIGNENT SUR LES ACTES DE LEUR CHEF.

Celui qui s'en va à l'aurore (vers les pirates)en se cachant,ou au milieu de la nuit,pendant que tout le monde dort;

celui qui va prévenir(les pirates à l'insu du chef et des habitants, qui va les trouver en se cachant pour leurfaire connaître que son chef ira les combattre dans leur village,

ou'il(son chef)a déjà distribué une brasse de bracelets à ses alliés, ou'il leur a fait porter du riz,qu'il a déjà convoqué d'autres chefs riches et puissants,(qu'il a dit à tout le monde):

"Vous les hommes veillerez bien, vous femmes ferez bien attention,tou vous serez très prudents,personne ne sortira(du village)seul,

"Vous renforcerez la palissade, vous consoliderez la grande porte, vous serez prudents et attentifs."

Celui qui fait que les ennemis prévenus chassent leurs boeufs hors du village,poussent leurs buffles dans la forêt,envoient leurs femmes et leurs enfants dans la montagne,

qu'ilscachent leurs jarres de grande valeur,leurs bijoux et leurs vaisselle enfermés dans les boîtes tous leurs objets et tous leurs biens

si de la femme on connaît le corps si de l'homme(coupable)on connaît la personne,si des boeufs et des buffles on connaît le gardien;

avec le grand sabre on le décapitera,avec le couteau tranchant on l'égorgera,et on jettera son corps en pâture aux vautours et aux corbeaux ou bien on l'emmenera dans la grande forêt,on le pendra à un arbre,et on l'abandonnera aux bêtes sauvages,

cela parceque'il ne sait pas où il faut aller et où il ne faut pas aller.

Comme le porc ou le buffle destinés à être sacrifiés,celui qui se rend coupable(de trahison)perdra son corps.

27 . KLEI ANA DUĚ .

Kong khuê ñu laĉ dôk klong,
dong klă,ñu laĉ mă bruñ khua jak.

Anei le ñu blu mlam sa klei,
hrue sa săp;wir rong anăp ñu lo
duah klei mkuañ.

Tlaih tơ hnuh ñu êluh duě,
tlaih tơ klong ñu hlong duě.

Ñu ñǔ phun alê,kdê phun moô,
săp khua atô laĉ ñu lui he mtluôn.

Alê ñu lo yur, kpur pǒ, yú
ngǒ ñu lǒ hiu.

Biêt ĉǔ duah ĉǔ bi dlông,
biêt krông duah krông bi prong.

Ñu sǐ băng mbah,yah băng
ong,kông buh kva.

Ñu duě he hngăp,dap he ñat,
... Côk êlat êyang,amâo ĉiăng
... khua.

Blu mlam sa klei, blu hrue sa
săp,wir rong anăp ñu lo duah klei
mkuañ.

anăn kdi moô.

50. DES EVASIONS DE PRISONNIERS.

Celui qui avait promis de rester tranquille,de ne pas bouger,de
bien travailler,pour le chef,

et qui pense une chose la nuit
et une autre le jour,qui agit tout
autrement dès qu'il a le dos tourné;

celui qui abandonne ses entraves pour se sauver,qui quitte sa
cangue pour s'enfuir;

celui qui se cache dans la
forêt de bambous,qui se cache dans
la foêt de roseaux,qui méprise les
ordres du chef;

celui qui se rend libre comme
la cime des bambous agitée par le vent
comme le foyer portatif,(qui n'est
pas fixé au plancher),celui qui s'en
va à l'Ouest ou à l'Est;

celui qui étant(caché) surune
petite montagne en cherche une plus
haute,étant sur un petit fleuve en
cherche un plus grand;

celui qui fend la bouche (du
chef),qui coupe les lèvres,qui ouvre
(quitte)le bracelet qu'il avait accepté; .

celui qui se sauve pour toujours,qui se cache sans faire aucun
bruit,qui se tient tranquille mais
refuse de travailler encore pour le chef;

celui qui pense une chose le
jour et une autre chose la nuit,qui
agit autrement dès qu'il a le dos
tourné,

celui-là est coupable et il y
a affaire entre le chef et lui .

Jug.no 22 du 17 mei 1917 : 2 ans.
Jug.no 15 du 16 juil.1918: 5 ans + 15 ans(Ev.et tent.d'ass.).
Jug.no 23 du 14 juil.1918: 5 ans (Ev.et vol.).
Jug.no 37 du 17 sept.1918: 3 ans.
Jug.no 38 du 2 oct. 1918: 3 ans.
Jug.no 39 du 17 sept.1918: 4 ans.
Jug.no 43 du 11 nov. 1918: 1 an.
Jug.no 44 du 28 oct. 1918: 2 ans.
Jug.no 37 du 13 juil.1923: 1 an + 20$00.
Jug.no 4 du 5 janv.1925: 1 an.
Jug.no 27 du 3 avril1925: 3 mois + 10$00.
Jug.no 68 du 28 nov. 1925: 2 ans.
Jug.no 68 du 9 déc. 1926: 20 ans.
... ine de prison s'ajoute à celle déjà prononcée,et le temps déjà
...

28.KLEI KHUA ŇOIT KŎNG TI
ŇMUIH BUÔN SANG ŇAO KLEI
JĔČ,ŇU AMÂO BA BREI BI DJAL
KÔNG HE HLĂM ÊLAN.

51.DE CEUX QUI NE S'EMPRESSENT
PAS DE PORTER À LA DESTINA-
TION LE BRACELET QUE LE CHEF
LEUR A CONFIE,ET QUI S'AT-
TARDENT EN CHEMIN.

Di hruŏ,trunmdar,thar yua,
ñu ba kŏng krah,ka amrĕč čiăng bi
ŏng,kpiĕt hdung čiăng bi djal.

Celui qui(a reçu l'ordre du
chef)de monter ou de descendre,qui
a été chargé de porter le bracelet,
celui à qui on a (remis le bâton su-
lequel on a)attaché un piment et un
morceau de charbon afin qu'il aille
vite.

Anei le ñu êdu ko,kro ŏian,
ñu êdu êran êbat; anŭ ñu bi kŏng,
ŏng ñu bi kram,ñu ba truh tơl je
iguah,krah mlam,tlam mnit,hlăk bit
hiŏ.

celui qui malgré cela a la tête
pensante,le ventre lourd,qui va san
se presser,qui retarde la transmission du bracelet ou du collier,qui
n'arrive ainsi qu'un matin,ou au
milieu de la nuit,ou le soir tard
quand tout le monde dort,

Aňăn mse si ñu ngơ luič he h
lăm dliê,liê hlăm êa,mse si tha
he kơ muôr hdam,ñu bi dam dih he
hlăm krah êlan klŏng,kŏng krah ñu
ba kơ sah mdrong amâo yong truh tơl

celui-là agit comme s'il avai
perdu(le bracelt)dans la brousse ou
dans la rivière,comme s'il l'avait
jeté aux fourmis ou aux termites,
comme s'il était resté couché au
milieu du sentier,et le bracelet
qu'il portait au chef puissant ne
peut pas lui parvenir(au moment voul)

Aňăn kthul ñu, mâo kdi khua
kơ ñu.

Celui-là est coupable et il y
a affaire entre le chef et lui.

29. KLEI KHIÊNG ANAK AMÂO HUN HONG KHUA BUÔN .

29. DE LA NON-DÉCLARATION DES NAISSANCES AU CHEF .

Da rơng, kơ̆g krah, êdah tian prŏč.

Quand les reins(de la femme) se creusent,quand le corps se penche en arrière,que le ventre sort en avant,

Truh yăn kiu bi mnga,moŏ bi mnga,ana klŏng kpang truh yăn luh hla,mniê ba tian tlơh năng mlan kkiêng.

et que vient la saison où les manguiers fleurissent, où les arbres perdent leurs feuilles, où la femme enceinte doit accoucher;

Ba anak êkei siam kiê̆, ba anak mniê siam kngan,tian prŏč leh jăk truh.

quand le garçon ou la fille viennent au monde avec de jolies mains,quand l'accouchement a été aisé

kgu aguah,êdah yang hrue, tơdah dơ hmuič, dơ duh,dơ ênuh dơ brei,klei đih pui arŏk,ñu duh min, čhin mkra he bi jăk dŏk dơng bơng hua.

le matin, au lever du soleil, ce qu'on a promis, (aux génies) on le donnera afin que la parturiente se rétablisse,qu'elle se remette rapidement,afin que tout soit bien;

kgu tinăn sa čŏ êkei, sa drei mniê,nao dak he hmŏk,dŏk brang, nao blang kpin ao hong mnut kơ êa, kra kơ buôn,hong pŏ dlăng adei tlang yơ̆ buôn, pŏ dlăng amuôn adei bi ....

après cela un homme ou une femme ira enlever l'écorce,dépouiller la ramie,ouvrir la veste et le pagne devant le banian de la source,devant le figuier du village,devant celui qui veille les frères éperviers,les génies du village,devant celui qui veille sur les neveux et nièces afin qu'il sache.

klei pŏ ñu hla ktu jăm,hla .... bap,klei pŏ mdap klei kkiêng ...k,amâo ñu nao hun hong khua,kthulcơu.... mâo klei khua kơ ñu.

Celui qui cachera(la naissance sous une feuille,qui dissimulera l'acc ....ment,qui n'ira pas informer le le che....

....ui-là sera coupable et il y aura afi....ire entre le chef et lui

30.KLEI DJIÊ ANUIH,GAP DJUÊ ÑU AMÂO NAO HUN HONG KHUA BUÔN.

Anuih djiu ênuam,duăm êngĭ, ti pui arôk,buê iêô,mjâo tu,hu kbuĕ

Anuih djiu amâo ruam,duăm amâo suaih,amâo tlaih ti añuê abăn.

Anăn phat hong un amâo hlao, mdrôohong kbao amâo grăng,yang čiăng kơ asei tơl djiê.

Anuih bru mdiê,djiê asei,bru mdiê djiê rŏk,ksŏk mtâo ma ba asei.

Găp djuê ñu sa čô êkei, sa drei mniê, amâo nao huñ hong mnut kơ êa, hra kơ buôn,hong pô dlăng adei amuôn buôn sang.

Djiê anuih khua hui mâo nư alăm asei,klei hlăm pô,da hui duah ling êmô mtâo,kbao mdrŏng,da ngăn song be êgar.

Djiê anak ĭ hrah,anak grah krua,djiê anak hlăm pha mtih,amâo ñu nao dak hmôk,dôk brang,amâo dlang kpin ao hong-khua.

Djiê hđeh hui amâo thâo čôk hia, djiê anuih khua hui mâo klei blu jal,ñu amâo nao hum.

Anăn kthul ñu,mâo kdi khua kơ ñu,ñu ba kdi ngăn kơ un song kpih.

53.DE LA NON-DÉCLARATION DES DÉCÈS AU CHEF DE VILLAGE.

Quand une personne es malade ou fiévreuse,quand elle se tient toujours près du feu,on appelle le guérisseur ou la guérisseuse pour la soigner.

Si le malade ne guérit pas,s'il ne recouvre pas la santé,s'il ne quitte plus la natte et la couverture

si on sacrifie des porcs et des buffles sans obtenir sa guérison , si la volonté des génies est que son corps meure,

si le malade meurt et devient semblable au grain de riz pourri dans la terre,aux herbes flétries qui se décomposent,si son corps est emporté par les démons et les fantômes,

et qu'il n'y ait pas un homme ou une femme de sa famille qui aille en informer le banian de la source, le figuier du village,celui qui veille sur les neveux et les nièces et les habitants,

parce qu'on craint que le mort n'ait laissé des dettes à payer,des affaires à régler,qu'il n'ait emprunté des boeufs au roi,des buffles au riche,des biens ou de l'argent des voisins;

si le mort est un nouveau-né,ou un enfant ayant succombé à une maladie infantile,ou un enfant qu'on tient encore sur les genoux, et qu'on ne va pas enlever l'écorce,dépuailler la hanie,ouvrir la veste et le pagne devant le chef,

si le mort est un enfant et qu'on craint de ne pouvoir le pleurer comme il faut(en prévenant le chef),si le mort est un adulte et que par crainte des affaire qu'il laisse en contestation on ne va pas informer (le chef de son décès),

pour cela on est coupable et il y a affaire avec le chef,on paiera à ce dernier une amende de un kơ et on lui sacrifiera un porc de un song.

3I. KLEI ƆNUIH TLE ꞂA YUA DO NGAN KHUA.

Wăng ti ktai ñu pai jik,kga
ꞇi ktai ñu pai koh,do arăng pioh
ȇmȇt ñu tle yua.

Hril ñu mă wak,ktiƀ ñu mă
wak,êman knhăk ñu mă aguê,ñu tle
ꞏꞏꞏꞏꞏ yua do ꞇah mdrong.

Biȇr amâo ñu kaŏng,ŏng amâo
ꞏu kña,do khua mdrong amâo ñu akâo,
ꞏâo ñu ȇmuh.

ñu pui ꞏꞏꞏ pha, ȇa wăl jŏng,
ꞏꞏꞏꞏꞏ ꞏꞏ ꞏꞏꞏ ꞏꞏꞏꞏg yang hrue.

ꞏnăn kthul ñu,ꞏꞏꞏ kꞏꞏ khua kƣ
ñu.

54. DE CEUX QUI UTILISENT LES OBJETS OU OUTILS DU CHEF SANS AUTORISATION.

Celui qui prend la binette
pendue à la tringle pour biner, le
coupe-coupe pour couper,celui qui
utilise sans autorisation les objets
que les autres gardent soigneusement,

celui qui se sert de perruches
et de péroquets pour en capturer
d'autres à la glu,qui emploie l'éléphant chasseur(d'autrui)pour en capturer d'autres au lasso,qui prend
sans autorisation les objets du riche pour s'en servir;

celui qui ne demande pas pour
couper le palmier,pour utiliser le
morceau de fer,celui qui prend les
objets du chef riche sans les lui
demander;

celui qui est comme la chaleur
du foyer réchauffant les cuisses(de
celui accroupi devant le feu),comme
l'eau de la rivière tourbillonnant
autour des jambes,celui qui se crée
des histoires en plein midi(inutilement),

celui-là est coupable et il y
a affaire entre le chef et lui .

32. KLEI DUI DUN NGAN DRAP KHUA ÑU, KƠYUA PHUNG ANAK ANEH ÑU BUI HE LEH, ÑU DUE DÔK SANG MDÊ.

Anak ñu pô, čô ñu phun, di ñu ktơr kmun pô pla, ami ama pô pu, pô ba, dleh kue eh, dleh mbeh pui, dleh pit gui mlam.

Tơl leh bo êmong, prong prin, di ñu pưk di ñu tlah, ênah mdê, djam bal djam blê di ñu bong hjan.

Di ñu mta tim buh kơ di gơ ami ama, kđuh tim člăng, di ñu amâo lo čiăng khăp kơ ami ama pô.

Anăn buh anak Bih di gơ rông, buh anak Anông di gơ čiăng, buh anak Kriêng kơyông di gơ duiñ ciêm ba mjing kơ anak pô, čô phun, bi mâo brei pô čơh brua, ngă brei hma, pla brei kmun ktơr.

Hui dju amâo mâo pô kia, di gơ rua amâo pô dlăng,

hui amâo mâo pô gui brei djuh, duh brei êa, amâo mâo pô knă, brei êsei djam, amâo mâo pô mñam brei kpin ao kơ di gơ; di gơ duah mjing mă anak hiêng, anak hông, anak liê kông mngan.

---

55. DE LA SUCCESSION DES BIENS DU CHEF (OU D'UNE PERSONNE) QUAND SES ENFANTS L'ONT ABANDONNÉ POUR ALLER HABITER SÉPARÉMENT.

Les enfants, les petits enfants sont comme le maïs, comme les concombres que l'on cultive soi-même ; les parents les ont créés, les ont portés, ont peiné pour les tenir propres, pourqu'ils n'aient pas droit ont passé de mauvaises nuits.

Si, devenus grands et forts, ils (les enfants) quittent la maison, s'ils s'en vont cultiver un autre champ, s'ils mangent séparément la viande et les légumes;

s'ils ne connaissent plus leurs parents, s'ils ne veulent plus les voir, s'ils ne témoignent plus d'affection envers leurs parents;

si les parents adoptent un enfant Bih ou Anông, un enfant Kriêng ou Kơyông (I), l'élèvent et le nourrissent, en font leur véritable enfant pour avoir quelqu'un qui travaille pour eux, qui fasse le champ, cultive le maïs, les concombres et les légumes,

craignant de n'avoir personne pour les veiller et les soigner quand ils seront vieux ou malades;

craignant de n'avoir personne pour aller chercher du bois, pour puiser de l'eau, pour cuire le riz et les légumes, pour tisser des pagnes et des couvertures, des jupes et des vestes, ils adoptent un enfant de guêpe ou de frelon, un enfant qui ne possède rien, ni bracelet ni vaisselle,

---

(I) Bih, Anông, Kriêng, Kơyông : tribus du Darlac.

Tơdah ruă ko, bo tiăn,ruă
kngan jơng,phung anak gơ anăn
dlăng ba.

Tơ di gơ bru mdiê,djiê asei,
phung anak aneh ñu pô kăn lo trah
dlăng,ơmăng djo kơ ami ama di ñu,
di ñu dlăm lui hi,hbi lui tla,dju
amâo di ñu dru kia,rua amâo di ñu
dru kriê,mâo kpiê êsei amâo di ñu
lo dru mdrao,djiê di ñu amâo dru
čap kmăp dơr,

anăn dơ ngăn êbeh, čeh êhuê,
êbeh ti buê mjâo,amâo lo mâo kơ
phung anak ñu pô,bha kơ phung anak aneh
dlk ... jok sang semi djăp mta,
ra enao.

afin qu'ils ont mal à la tête
ou au ventre,s'ils ont les bras et
les jambes fatigués,leurs enfants
adoptifs les soignent et les aident.

Et si plus tard,quand ils seront
pourris comme le grain de paddy,quand
ils seront morts,leurs propres enfants ne viennent pas les voir et
les assister,s'ils les abandonnent
et les oublient,si pendant leur maladie ils ne sont pas venus pour les
veiller et les aider,s'ils ne leurs o
ont pas offert de l'alcool quand ils
en avaient pourles soigner,si après
leur mort ils ne sont venus aider
à les rouler (dans une natte),s'ils
ne sont pas venus leur rendre les
derniers devoirs,

alors, tous les biens qui resteront après avoirpayé le guérisseur
ou la guérisseuse,reviendront, non
à leurs propres enfants,mais à leurs
enfants adotifs demeurés avec eux ,
tout ce qu'ils possèdent leur reviendra en totalité.

33. KLEI MNUIH MUIĚ LEH ANAN ÑU MDAP KLEI DUE HIU HONG KHUA.	56. DE CEUX QUI MÉPRISENT L'AUTORITÉ DU CHEF EN LUI CACHANT D'OÙ ILS VIENNENT ET OÙ ILS VONT.

kbông ñu mdap, sap ñu bi hgăm,
ñu blu ăm ư hong sah mdrong.

Celui qui cache sa parole, qui
cèle ce qu'il faut dire, qui ne fait
pas tout connaître au chef;

Ñu dlăng ti ko mse si kpong,
dlăng ti jong mse si koyâo, ñu amâo
thâo kral sah mdrong.

celui qui considère sa tête
(du chef) comme une souche, ses
pieds comme une bûche, celui qui ne
connaît pas le (pouvoir du) chef;

Ñu dlăng si uiĕ, muiĕ si asâo
ñu amâo thâo kral djo sah mdrong.

celui qui le considère avec
mépris, qui le traite comme un chien
qui ne veut reconnaître l'autorité
du chef;

Ñu tuôm hong khua ti krah
ôan dong, ktong prong, ti krah êlen
dong adei êrô, khua tlăng kña, ha
uh ñu, ñu amâo dak knôk, dôk brang,
ñu mlang kpin ao hong khua.

celui qui rencontre le chef au
milieu de la grande route, au pied
d'un arbre, sur le chemin fréquenté
par les habitants et qui, quand le
chef l'intérroge ou le questionne,
n'enlève pas l'écorce, ne dépouille
pas la ramie, n'ouvre sa veste et
son pagne,

ăr kthul ñu, mâo kdi khua

celui-là est coupable et il y
a affaire entre le chef et lui.

KDRÔC III.   CHAPITRE III.

I. KLEI MDAP MNUIH.   57. DE LA DISSIMULATION
                                              D'INDIVIDUS.

Awak ñu mdap, sap ñu hgam,   Celui(chef)qui cache la cuillère,
ñu bi kngăm mnuih.   qui tait la parole(qu'il faut dire),
                                      qui dissimule des individus(coupable),

snong knuê čuh koh kdang,   alors qu'on doit brûler(jusqu'à
hlang koh mngač,lač koh bi thâo.   ce que la terre)se crapelle,qu'on
                                      doit fendre(le bois jusqu'à ce qu'on
                                      voit)clairement(à l'intérieur),qu'on
                                      doit parler pour faire connaître;

Tơ mniê amâo mă klei, êkei   si une femme ou un homme refusent
âo mă sap,amâo khăp ư klei ñu.   d'obéir(au chef),s'ils n'exécutent
                                      pas ses ordres,

Ñu hriê dak hmôk koh,dôk   il(le chef) doit venir écorcer
klang,mlang pkin ao koh.   le bois,dépouiller la ramie,ouvrir
                                      la veste et le pagne (devant le
                                      grand chef).

Jak lêh čao knong;pong kliang,   Les piquets et les clous ont été
ïng asêh êsan kă.   bien enfoncés,les chevaux et les
                                      éléphants ont été bien attachés(des
                                      instructions ont été données);

Giê lêh gang,hlang lêh kuôl,   la barre a été assujettie,la
mưe, miê êtieng,kdiêng knhâo   paillote nouée, le rotin solidement
kăp asan jak lêh ñu mă.   attaché,et les a pris la baguette
                                      en bambou, le doigt ou le bout de
                                      l'ongle(qu'on lui a tendu,il a promis
                                      de bien exécuter les ordres).

ñăn yao kdi srang.   Pour cela il est coupable.

2. KLEI KHUA MDĂP BUÔN SANG.

58. DU CHEF QUI DISSIMULE DES HABITANTS

(Assujettis à l'Impôt).

hnut kơ êa,hra kơ buôn,ñu pô
dlăng adei amuôn buôn sang,

Le banian de la source,le fi
guier du village,celui qui veille
sur les habitants,

mơng knuê ñu laǎ amâo lŏ mâo
dôk sa čŏ êkei, sa drei mniê.

s'il a dit qu'il ne restait
plus un seul homme ou une seule fe
me (à déclarer),

Ară anei le, lo mâo he mnuih
dôk hlăm kmrơng,dơng hlăm dliê,dôk
sa mniê sa êkei.

alors qu'aujourd'hui on en
trouve encore vivant dans la forêt
ou dans les cabanes(aux champs) ,
vivant seuls,hommes et femmes;

kbông ñu mdăp, sap ñu bi hgăm,

s'il a caché sa parole,s'il
a tu ce qu'il devait dire,

ñu soh kbông luar,čhuar kbông
blu,čhu bong wêč êhung.

il est coupable parce qu'il a
menti,parce qu'il n'a pas dit ce
qu'il fallait dire,parce qu'il a
voulu tromper.

anăn ñu dăp mne,ñu tle mnêñ,
ñu wêñ kiê kngan.

En dissimulant ainsi(des habi
tants) il a volé(le fisc ?);

čiang kơ čing ñu êran,čiang
kơ êman pah,prăp sah mdrong ñu
tle.

(il a agi)comme celui qui co r
pour voler le gong(à celui qui le
transporte),pour s'emparer de l'é
phant et de l'argent du riche.

anăn ngăn ñu kpung dua,mkua
tlâŏ,ngăn êlăo êdei ñu brei.

Pour cela il remboursera le
double en sus,soit en tout le tripl
une fois devant et une fois derri
(le montant du détournement)il dou
ra.

Leh kơ kbloh le,ñu lo laǎ
pong tung amâŏ,pong amâŏ ruă,nga
kdi kơ ñu amâŏ djo.

Après cela il ne pourra pas
dire qu'on a entaillé l'arbre sans
lui faire de blessure,qu'on lui a
infligé une amende sans raison;

Ară anei ñu laǎ pong tung leh
ruă,pong blang leh ruă,ngă kdi kơ
ñu leh gal.

il sera forcé de reconnaître
que l'entaille faite à l'arbre l'a
blessé,que la peine qu'on lui a
infligée est raisonnable.

JURISPR.-Jug.no 9 du 20 mars I9I7;no I0 du 20 juil.I9I8,no 8 du 30 m
I9I9,no 25 du17 juil. I9I9,no 26 du 30 mai I923,no 50 d
30 août I923, : 2 à 4 mois de prison + I à 5000 d'amend
Jug.no 4 du 30 mars I9I9 : 5000 .no 9 du 30 mars I9I9:20j.
Jug.no II et I2 du 4 mars I923,no I8 du 23 fév.no 72 du 29
no 77 su 5 oct,I925,no 9 du 2 juil.I927,Jug.du 2 mars I938: 5 à 3000
L'amende infligée est parfois proportionnelle au nombre de person
lesquelles dissimulées.Le chef peut être également tenu pour respons
de la liquidation des impôts dus par ceux qu'il n'a pas inscrits au r
du village.

3. KLEI KHUA BUÔN MDAP KDI ADEI AMUÔN BUÔN SANG .

59. DU CHEF QUI DISSIMULE LES AFFAIRES DES HABITANTS.

Ih wăk-wai,pai jong, mâo kdi ayong adei hlăm buôn ñu mdap.

Celui qui,l'araignée ourdissant sa toile,comme le lièvre s'enfuyant, dissimule tous les différends entre les habitants;

Kbông ñu mdap,săp ñu bi hgăm, ñu čiăng duah lăm·dap he kdi ărăng gơ .

celui qui cache sa parole,qui tai ce qu'il faut dire,qui ne fait pas connaître les affaires des habitants parce qu'il ne veut pas les régler;

Ñu amâo hriê čuh bi kđang, ablang bi mngač,ñu amâo hriê lač bi thâo .

celui qui ne vient pas brûler pour qu'on voie la terre,qui ne vient pas informer pour faire connaître (au grand chef);

anăn kthul ñu,mâo kdi khua kơ ñu .

celui-là est coupable et il y a affaire entre le grand chef et lui.

JORIEPR.- Jug.no 32 du 17 sept. 1918 : 5000.
        Jug.no 2u 2 août 1938 : 10000.

4. KLEI KƠ KHUA BUÔN PLAH
   MNUIH BUÔN ARĂNG.

60. DU CHEF QUI ENLÈVE DES
    HABITANTS AUX VILLAGES VOISINS.

Ñu mă buôn sah, ñu plah buôn
mdrong, buôn ayong adei ñu mmiă.

Celui qui enlève les habi-
tants du village **riche**, du village
prospère, pour les installer dans
son village à lui;

Ñu amâo wưč bi êdah, ñu amâo
wah bi thâo, mâo mnuih kma dôk hlăm
buôn ñu amâo hưn.

celui qui n'écarte pas(les
herbes) pourfaire voir, qui n'informe pas pourqu'on sache, qui ne
fait connaître quand des personnes
(d'un autre village)viennent s'installer dans son village à lui,

Anăn mâo kđi arăng kơ ñu.

celui-là est coupable et il
y a affaire avec lui.

5. KLEI KHUA NGA SOH KƠ ANƯIH BUÔN SANG .	6I. DU CHEF QUI OPPRIME LES HABITANTS.
Ñu mnut kơ êa,hra kơ buôn, ñu pô dlăng adei amuôn buôn sang.	Celui qui est le banian de la source,le figuier du village, qui veille sur tous les habitants,
Ñu làm lap, ap gư, ktư jua adei tlang.	s'il ne protège pas bien les habitants et les opprime,s'il écrase les petits frères éperviers;
Ñu mniê lu klei, êkei lu săp, wir rong anăp mcê.	s'il agit comme l'homme ou la femme ayant beaucoup d'histoires, si dès qu'il tourne le dos il agit différemment;
Ñu trong mcê ,amrêč mdar, čar kup dang mcê.	s'il tourne en tous sens comme les aubergines et les piments(dans la marmite),s'il coupe tantôt en long tantôt en travers;
Mdeh pông ba,mra ruah,ñu duah mâ săp jăk.	si de ceux qui lui apportent des filets ou des épaules(de boeuf) il accepte les raisons,
anăn mâo kdi arăng.	celui-là est coupable et il y a affaire avec lui .

JURISPR.- Jug.no 69 du 28 nov. 1923 ? 3 mois + I0$00(Escroquerie).
Jug.no 35 du I5 mai 1925 : I an(dont I0 rachetables à 20$00 par mois). § Amendes illégales).
Jug.no 76 du 5 oct. 1925 : I an + restitution des sommes illégalement perçues.
Jug.no 43 du 7 juin 1926 : I00$00 + 40 ko + révocation(Concussion).
Jug.no 5 du 4 mai 1927 : I mois + 50$00+ restitution des sommes illégalement perçues.
Jug.no I du I0 juil. 1928 : I00$00 (Exactions).
Jug.du 2 août 1938 :3 mois + 20$00 + révocation + restitution des sommes illégalement perçues.

6. KLEI KHUA BUÔN AMẢO JAK RÔNG
ADEI ALUÔN BUÔN SANG.

62. DU CHEF DE VILLAGE QUI NE
S'OCCUPE PAS BIEN DES
HABITANTS.

DƯK plei krô ñu tuh êa, tơdah
gơ mđa ñu kti khắt, đhê gơ čăt hriê
kơ dlông ñu pah he kơ gu.

Quand le pied de potiron est sec
il faut l'arroser, quand il s'étend
trop il faut couper le bourgeon
terminal, quand il monte trop il faut
le ramener vers le sol.

Ñu amâo jak bá kniêng, čiăng
rông, ñu amâo jak kgông ch mđiăk.

Si(le chef) n'offre pas l'écorce
(à chiquer), s'il ne protège pas bien
les habitants), s'il ne s'occupe pas
bien (d'eux);

Ñu ba amâo djo si ba adei,
ñu bi mnei amâo djo si bi mnei
anăk, ñu rông ba amâo mđăk mñai.

S'il ne(les) porte pas comme on
porte le petit frère, s'il ne les
baigne pas comme on baigne les enfants, s'il ne veille pas bien sur
eux;

Ñu amâo jak ke kông, amâo jak
rông buôn sang, ñu rông amâo ênang
ôđp.

s'il ne mord pas bien le bracelet
et ne s'occupe pas bien bien des
habitants afin qu'ils vivent dans
la tranquillité;

Tơdah čoh ñu ke, tơ le ñu
tơng, jơng kngan ñu đuah kruit.

s'il mord ceux qui se rendent
coupables et dévore ceux qui tombent,
s'il leur brise les bras et les
jambes(au lieu de les aider);

Kông un amâo truh kreo, rông
kbao amâo truh knô, mâo kpiê čeh tuk
čeh bô amâo yong mnăm.

si (à cause de lui) le porc qu'on
élève ne grossit pas, si le buffle
ne devient pas un beau mâle, si on
ne peut jamais boire l'alcool des
jarres tuk et bô(parce qu'on ne vit
pas tranquille),

Tông prong ñu knua, êđa prong
ñu in, mnuih rin tạp ñu đuah đu ngă
gơ.

i parce qu'il assomme avec la parue
ou avec la solive, parce qu'il opprime les pauvres et les malheureux;

Ñu ami jhat yua, ama jhat rông,
mâo kông mngan hlăm sơk piê amâo
ôk.

parce qu'il est une mère ou un
père élevant mal ses enfants, parce
que(à cause de lui)il ne reste plus
rien au fond des hottes(armoires).

Ami ai ami mja, ama ai ama
êmông, ñu rông jing jai, ñu kčat
jing jai.

I est mère comme une mère-fourmi,
père comme un père-tigre, au lieu
protéger (les habitants) il leur donne des coups de griffes.

Dôk hlăm êa amâo êdăp, dôk
hlăm rưăp amâo ênang, dôk hlăm
kuang êmeh êman amâo thâo mdao.

(A cause de lui) ceux qui se
baignent ne peuvent trouver de fraî-
cheur, ceux qui vivent dans les marais ne peuvent trouver la tranquillité, ceux qui se réfugient entre les
pattes des rhinocéros ou des éléphants ne se sentent pas réchauffés,

Soh jơng hgao, kdao juă, soh
êjai huă mnăm ñu čiăng ko kđi.

ceux qui font un faux pas il
les opprime, ceux qui commettent la
moindre faute en buvant ou mangeant
il leur inflige une amende.

Soh blu ñu tu knga, soh ha ñu
tu săp, găp djuê ñu amâo lo răk
djo.

Si quelqu'un parle mal il tend
l'oreille, si une autre se trompe
il sévit, ceux de son clan même ne
sont pas épargnés.

Kmanoaok ñu khua huôn.

Pourcela le chef est coupable.

JURISPR.- Jug.no58 du 20 août 1925 : I mois + 5400 (Non-application
de la loi sur le mariage).
Jug.no I02 du 30 déc.1925: 5400 (Non-application de la loi
sur le mariage).
Jug.no 29 du 7 août 1936 : 3 mois.

7. KLEI DUAH ČAP TLING ARANG HOAI .	63. DES ARRESTATIONS ARBITRAIRES.

7. KLEI DUAH ČAP TLING
   ARANG HOAI .

63. DES ARRESTATIONS
   ARBITRAIRES.

Ñu duah tling ka,ma čap,dap hnuh kleng kơ arăng hoai.

Si(le chef) cherche à entraver, à arrêter les gens, à leur passer à la cangue ou le collier de force sans motif;

Ñu čiang kơ čing tio ma êran, ñu čiang kơ êman tio ma pah, ñu čiang kơ sah mơrong ñu duah čap tling arăng.

s'il poursuit pour avoir le gong ou l'éléphant,si pour s'enrichir il arrête les personnes;

Ñu pah dlam,êlam mơ.

s'il se jette sur elles et les arrête(pour les dépouiller);

Ñu plaơ draơ drung bi rung buôn,plaơ draơ drung bi rung sang arăng,arăng dôk ênang êđăp ñu duah čăp tling.

s'il cultive des plantes venéneuses pour effrayer les habitants, il trouble ceux qui vivent paisiblement ,

Tơ ñu mâo kđi boh sô,yô hbei, klei đưi đa ñu êmuh kơh mnut ko êa, hrư kơ buôn pô dlơng acei amuôn buôn sang.

ceux qui,lorsqu'ils ont une affaire vieille comme un tubercule creux,une affaire remontant à autrefois,vont toujours trouver le banier de la source,le figuier du village, qui veille sur les habitants,

Tơ ñu mâo nơ wuh,nuh akâo, tơ mâo klei ñu êmuh kơh khua buôn.

ceux qui ayant une créance à recouvrer la réclament (selon les usages), ceux qui ayant un différend à régler consultent habituellement le chef;

anei si be čiet êgao ti trang, hlang êgao ti mbô,hlô mnong ñu êgao ti pum čjung.

s'il se comporte comme l'herbe de marais qui veut s'élever plus haut que les roseaux,comme la paillote voulant monter plus haut que les bambous,comme les animaux sauvages voulant bondir plus haut que la c... des arbres;

Sang ciêng suê ñu mut,sang đut ñu hgao,sang bơng êmô kbao ñu mưč .

s'il refuse de passer sous la grande maison,(du grand chef)préférant enjamber(opprimer) la petite maison (du pauvre),s'il méprise la maison où l'on mange souvent du boeuf ou du buffle(l'autorité du grand c...

anăn mâo kđi arang kơ ñu.

pour cela il est coupable et il y a affaire avec lui.

JURISPR.- Jug.no 5 du 4 mai 1927 : I mois + 50,00 + restitution des amendes illégalement perçues.
Jug.no 8 du 22 fév.1933: 50,00 + restitution.
Jug.no I6 du I9 av.1933: 5 ans + révocation + restitution.

6! KLEI ČAP MNUIH HLA. PÔE S SANG ARANG .

Ñu duah čap arāng mang, wang sang hong,ñu duah čap anak sah mdrong avong adei hdai.

Ñu duah trua si knam,dlam si wah,ñu duah pah si tlang aja.

Klam dê dlông,yông prong,ñu duah čap mnuih bäng sang sah mdrong, bäng sang ayong adei,anân mâ kdi arăng kơ ñu.

Sang dlông ñu mut,sang đut ñu hgao,sang bong êmô kbao ñu mnô.

Ñu dlăng kơ arăng si mlâmatô si asâo,ñu amaô thâo kral djô mnuih kmun.

Mlei grăm, klêu yang, mlei sang pŭk arăng.

Tơ ñu čap hlăm sang sah mdrong, ñu ba kdi ngăn sa kơ,leh anân kbao kpih rô sang.

Tơ dah hlăm pŭk sang bun bin rin tep,ñu ba kdi ngăn tlâo kơ leh anân un dua song kpih.

64. DES ARRESTATIONS DE PERSONNE DANS LA DEMEURE D'AUTRUI.

Celui qui arrête les gens sans motif,qui s'introduit dans la maison sans raison pour arrêter le riche ou le pauvre arbitrairement;

celui qui prend comme avec une nasse ou un hameçon,bondissant sur sa proie comme un épervier ou une fouine;

celui qui profane les pannes et les pitrants en arrêtant les personnes (coupables)dans la demeure du riche ou dans celle du pauvre,

celui-là est coupable et il y a affaire entre lui et autrui(le maître de la maison),(parce que)

il méprise la maison longue (du riche),il enjambe la maison courte (du pauvre),la maison où l'on mange souvent du boeuf ou du buffle il ne respecte pas.

Il regarde les gens avec mépris, il les considère comme des chiens, il ne respecte pas les personnes.

Il arrête le tonnerre et les divinités ,et profane la demeure d'autrui.

S'il arrête une personne quand celle-ci se trouve dans une maison riche il paiera une amende de un kơ et fera le sacrifice d'un buffle au maître de la maison.

S'il arrête une personne quand elle se trouve dans une maison pauvre il paiera une amende de trois kơ et fera le sacrifice d'un porc de deux song(au maître de la maison).

79. KLEI KHUA PHAT HE KDI HJAN, KDI ÑU AMAO DUI PHAT.

Kdi diăn sa ñŏk, pui arôk sa êpa, hong tlê bon la, ñu tle phat he kdi ko krei, asei hjăn, kdi arăng prong, kna ka djăp, asăp ka tuôm.

Ala bai êlâo ñu duah ôut he khua, jong ñu hyuă hong knug, ñu duah bling kđum he.

Kdi asei ka tok arăng bi êwi, bi ka răp, asăp djuê arăng ka ênum.

Kdi ñu phat he ênoh, kjoh he giê, ñu duah mijiê he kdi ko krei, asei hjăn ñu.

Anăn kthul ñu măo kdi khua prong kơ ñu.

65. DU CHEF QUI VEUT JUGER UNE AFFAIRE QUI N'EST PAS DE SA COMPÉTENCE.

(Une affaire importance comme) une chandelle une coudée ou un x cierge d'une brasse, il veut la juger tout seul, de tout son coeur et de toute sa rate, en se cachant, sans réunir ses adjoints ni sa famille.

Les défenses écartées (de l'éléphant il veut les rapprocher avec une bague de rotin, les pattes (de devant) il veut les entraver, il veut lui attacher les quatre pattes.

Il ne réunit pas les habitants, il ne répare pas le van détérioré, les deux parties il ne les entend pas.

Il fixe le montant de l'amende il rompt le bâton du juge, il règle l'affaire tout seul, sans consulter personne.

Pour cela il est coupable et il y a affaire entre le grand chef et lui.

JURISPr.e
Jug.no 76 du 5 oct. 1925 : I an : restitution des amendes illégalement perçues (Abus d'autorité).
Jug.no 5 du 4 mai 1927 : I mois + 50\$00 + restitution.

10. KLEI KHUA HNGAH AMÂO PHAT KDI, KLEI ĐU ĐUI PHAT.

Ñu mnut ko êa, hra ko buôn,
ñu pô dlăng adei amuôn buôn sang.

Nâo kdi mta djuê nei, klei
ijuê nan, ñu amâo phat ênoh, amâo
ñu kjêh giê, amâo ñu bi mdjiê brei
kdi.

Adei amuôn, buôn sang bi mâo
kdi tong mlo, kdi ko giết, mâo kdi
driết druôt amâo ñu phat brei.

Ya be wăng buh, knah joh,
ya be kdi bi soh nao hriê hong
mnuih buôn sang.

Lip khư griô amâo ñu kdah,
knguôr khư griô amâo ñu kdah, ñu
jing sah mdrong amâo ñu lač brei
kdi kơ adei tlang yang buôn.

Kda gri amâo ñu dra brei hong
kbang, sang gri amâo ñu bi knul,
mdiêng bi tul, amâo ñu djip kčing
brei.

Anan kthul ñu, rai mnuih
buôn sang ñu.

Un xi bi đai amâo suai brei
bruh, mnu kčeh amâo ñu ktuh brei
btat, mâo klei ju jhat hlam buôn
sang amâo ñu lač brei klei.

66. DU CHEF QUI REFUSE DE JUGER UNE AFFAIRE DE SA COMPÉTENCE.

Si le banian de la source, le
figuier du village, celui qui veille
sur les neveux, les frères et les
habitants;

si, quand il y a affaire pour
ceci ou pour cela, il ne fixe pas le
montant de l'amende, s'il ne prend pas
le bâton du juge (justice), s'il
n'éteint pas le différend;

Si, quand les habitants ont entre
eux un indifférend insignifiant, comme
renflement de gourde ou un col de
bouteille, un différend très léger,
il refuse de le régler;

(à cause de cela) les haches sont
toujours ébréchées, les briquets sont
brisés, il y a toujours des histoires
entre habitants.

(Cela parce que) les vans abîmés
ne sont pas réparés, les cribles ne
sont pas raccommodés, parce que celui
qui est devenu chef ne règle pas les
différends des petits éperviers,
des génies du village,

parce que la cabane qui penche
dangereusement il ne l'étaie pas,
parce que la maison qui menace de
tomber il ne la consolide pas avec
des supports, parce qu'il ne raccommo-
de pas la jupe déchirée.

Pour cela il est coupable car
il extermine tous les habitants.

A la truie qui va mettre bas
il ne prépare pas la litière, à la
poule qui va pondre il n'arrange pas
un nid, aux habitants divisés par
toutes sortes de différends il ne
rend pas la justice.

JURISPR.— Jug. no 32 du 17 sept. 1918 : 5400 d'amende.

II. KLEI KHUA JA KČAL IČ SUR, DI RU LAČ KLEI GAL KO GO.	67. DU CHEF QUI ACCEPTE DES BIENS D'UN COUPABLE POUR LUI DONNER RAISON.

Ñu lač ñu hmư bheč mta arieng, tlao kơ arăng mkăn. Arăng mmuiñ êjai jah, mmah êjai tlao, mnuih mñê duah klei, êkei duah kđi, mli mdrong duah sap.

(le chef) prétend voir et entendre, comme les crabes et les escargots, les gens ... parler;

alors qu'ils chantent (pour le blâmer) en défrichant, qu'ils mangent en riant (en critiquant) de ceux, hommes ou femmes, qui ont des histoires ou du chef qui est injuste;

Arăng mling mñê bhang, mlang mñê tlam, klei êdam êra arăng ...

alors que les habitants sont comme les oiseaux mling et mlang chantant le soir pendant la saison sèche, que jeunes hommes et jeunes filles ne font que chanter (récriminer contre le chef);

alors qu'on a entendu le murmure du vent hors du village, le grondement du tonnerre de l'autre côté de la palissade,

alors qu'on entend des gens réparent leurs houes et leurs coupe-coupe, parler entre eux du différend qu'il faudra régler.

S'il est certain que l'homme ou la femme (accusés) sont coupables et, comme le tigre et le rhinocéros craignent les pièges, craignent d'être punis et lui offrent des biens (pour avoir raison); si malgré leur culpabilité il admet qu'
... revenant de la fontaine on a besoin de s'appuyer contre le talus, (pour se reposer), que pour construire un barrage sur une rivière on a besoin de pierres plates, que ... faut soutenir celui qui donne le plus;

koyêo dơ boh tih ñu kna, kơyân
dơ pha knang, tơ arâng di puk sang
lui mơai ñu; kbông ñu dap, săp ñu
tăng, lui mơai ñu; pô dê, boh tih
tlaih lo djo êa, pha tlaih djo kñit,
ko pô bhit tlaih lo djo ksi, kdi
arâng kơ gơ tlaih mâo, ñu lač brei
kdi gal gơ khă bi brei ngăn kơ ñu
dơnei.

kdi arâng djơ, ñu lač soh.

Anăn kthul ñu.

S'il soutient l'arbre gros
comme la cuisse ou le molet, s'il
ne punit pas celui qui s'est introduit dans la demeure d'autrui,
s'il ne dit pas ce qu'il faut dire,
s'il répare la houe (du coupable),
s'il ne dit pas qui a tort et qui
a raison, si le coupable n'est pas
inquiété,

que ses jambes se mouilleront
encore, que ses cuisses seront encore
frottées de gingembre, que ses cheveux seront encore peignés quand
il s'emmêleront;

si le chef renonce à régler
le différend et trouve normale la
conduite du coupable parce que ce
dernier lui a donné des biens;

s'il donne tort à celui qui
a raison,

pour cela il est coupable.

Reg. 20 du 6 juin 1933 : 400$00 d'amende.

KDRĚČ IV.

I. KLEI MNUIH RUNG Ň ŇÔ DÔK
HLAN BUÔN SANG PÔ.

Mnuih rah rừng lu bưng huĕ,
mnuih rah rang lu kang duah kbăk,
amâc jak dŏk buôn anei ñu đuĕ dôk
kơ buôn mkuăn.

Ñu ngă ĕrum êngăo tlơ tluôn,
asei ñu ti buôn,tluôn ti êngăo,suĕ
dhong đao tha lŭi kơ tač.

Ňjai ñu hdip mse si kbao dliê,
djiê mse si kbao yang,tơ leh ñu
jing čim tlang amâo mâo pô lơ suh
hơi.

Hbơng lui he băng msat,ktat
băng trơh,joh jơng kngan đun mơh,
amâc mâo pô lơ pap hơi.

Ñu băng gơi bai si krang,
Chang si ŭip,amâo mâo pô lơ đui
djip kăing

Mơ khư grio amâo mâo pô lơ
đui klei,nguôr khư grio amâo mâo
...đui kđah,tar đơ sah mdrong,
jih duĕ ayong adei,amâo mâo pô lơ
đui mtô tač.

Tơ ñu kĕč duah duih,mnuih
duah klei,tơ ôkei mniê duah kdi,
mâo pô lơ trơh đlang,ơmang
jih,hlong hbơng lui hi,hbi lui tha,
lui êa kpuh đưng he.

Mơ un rih jih asei, kbao
jih asei,ñu duah boh klei jih
asei ñu pô.

68. DES VAGABONDS QUI NE VEULENT
PAS RESTER DANS LEUR
VILLAGE.

Celui qui vagabonde mange toutes
les calebasses, accroche son menton
partout, quand il ne se plaît plus
dans un village il s'en va dans
un autre.

Il agit comme on pique aux fesses avec une aiguille, son corps est
dans le village mais son derrière
est à l'extérieur, il tire le sabre
ou le couteau du fourreau et ne les
rentre plus.

Quand il est vivant il est comme
le buffle sauvage(on peut le rencontrer); quand il meurt il est comme
le buffle du génie(que personne ne
voit); quand il sera devenu épervier
(après la mort)il n'y aura personne
pour le regretter.

On le jettera dans une fossé ou
au fond d'un ravin, ses membres se
briseront et personne ne le pleure-
ra;

parce qu'il a la bouche large
comme l'ouverture d'une nasse,comme
un grand van,et que personne ne peut
le corriger;

parce que personne ne peut réparer le van,personne ne peut réparer le crible,ni le chef puissant,
ni les frères,ni les habitants,
personne ne peut lui donner des
conseils.

S'il est comme le moustique qui
cherche à piquer,comme l'homme ou
la femme qui se créent des histoires
personne ne s'occupera de lui,per-
sonne ne prendra sa défense; on
l'abandonnera à son sort et il sera
emporté par le courant du fleuve.

Comme le porc ou le buffle destinés au sacrifice, il a des histoires
il perdra son corps.

JUOER.—Jug.no 2 du 3 janv. 1917: six ko d'amende (30:00).
        Jug.no 8 du 27 fév.et no 60 du 15 oct.1923,no 81 du 31 oct.1924,
        ...no 3 du 5 janv. et 49 du 15 juil.19.. : I an de prison.
        Jug.no 3 du 5 mai 1927 : 2 mois + rachat impôts en retard+ kpih
        ...au chef.
        Jug.no du 4 oct. 1938 : I mois +: 5:00...
        Jug.no du 4 oct. 1938 : 6 mois + 10:00.

2. KLEI KƠ MNUIH HIU DƠK HŨNG AMÂO MÂO BUÔN SANG.	69. DES VAGABONDS QUI N'ONT PAS DE DOMICILE FIXE.

● Mnuih dhong đa,kga ku, mnuih lu klei,.

Celui qui est comme un couteau tordu,comme un coupe-coupe usé, et qui a toujours des histoires;

Mnuih aseh kmuê,kbao kmuê, mnuih amâo mâo djuê ana, ama ami.

celui qui est comme un cheval ou un buffle abandonné,qui ne sait plus à quelle famille il appartient,qui n'a plus ni père, ni mère;

Mluk amâo mâo pô mtô,kmlô amâo pô lač.

celui qui est comme l'ignorant que personne n'instruit,comme le muet à qui personne ne dit rien;

Ñu duah due hiu jơng mngơ, ko myu ,si kru hlang.

celui qui s'en va les jambes à l'Est et la tête à l'Ouest comme le boeuf sauvage dans les savannes

Ñu amâo mâo čin bơng,mnong čhat het drao djup,amâo dôk hnong,dơng klit,ñu duah ngă klei ju jhat hra buôn ôlan.

celui qui n'ayant ni viande à manger,ni aliments à couper,ni ta- bac à fumer,ne sait pas se tenir tr tranquille et cherche de mauvaises histoires dans tous les villages où il passe;

Ñu duah djơ hluăt ênga,ba hluăt duah si hui mnuih buôn yu,pu c,ñu duah ngă si kho mgu.

celui qui tient une chenille velue ou une grosse chenille verte dans la main pour effrayer les habitants des villages de l'Est ou de l'Ouest,et qui agit toujours comme un fou ou un idiot,

amâo mâo hči arăng kơ ñu.

celui-là est coupable et il y a affaire avec lui.

Un rih jih asei, kbao rih jih ,ñu duah dôk klei jih asei ñu

comme le proc ou le buffle des- tinés à être sacrifiés,s'il cher- che des histoires il perdra son corps.

_____ Jug.no4 du 28 janv. et 12 du 21 mars 1917,jug.nos 24 du 15 mai 47 du 27 août 1923,jug.nos 5 du 5 janv. 29 du 8 avr. et 42 du 1er juin, nos 47 du 13 juil.57 du 1er août et 18 du 23 févr. 1925 ,jug.no 4 du 5 mai et 9 du 2 juil.1927 : 1 à 6 mois de prison + 5900 d'amende + paiement des impôts en retard.
Jug.du 2 mars 1938 :3 mois + paiement du double des impôts en retard.

3. KLEI ᴀNUIH DŌK HLAᴀ
PŪK HᴀA.

aru kơ hᴀa, bra kơ mdiê, ᴀᴀiê
hluôy duah dŏk hlam kăt alâ, kuê
hlam kăt mdô, duah dŏk si ᴀlô mᴀᴊng.

ᴀᴀơ rang, băng jang ring ñu
dᴊăng, băng čing čeh, car aseh êman
ñu čua.

ᴀu tluôn ti mdô, bôᵗti mbah
băng, ñu duah êmang kơ ču mtâo.

ᴀsei ti buôn, tluôn ti êngao,
ᴀᴜa dhong dao kơ tač, ñu duah nač
ᴀᴀᴇ kơ sah ᴀdrong.

ᴀu dŏk băng trăp, ñu dăp băng
ᴀᴊiê, ñu dŏk sa mniê sa êkei.

ᴀᴜan mâo kdi kơ ñu.

70. DE CEUX QUI FIXENT DANS
LA CABANE DU CHAMP.

Ceux qui parpillent dans les
champs, au milieu des touffes de
paddy, qui demeurent n'importe où,
dans les touffes de bambous mâles
ou femelles, comme des animaux
sauvages;

ceux qui laissent la palissade
ou la grande porte(de leur village)
en ruine, qui regardent dans les fosses à gongs et à jarres, dans les
prés où il y a des chevaux et les
éléphants;

Ceux dont le derrière est sur
un escarbeau et le village tourné
vers la porte parce qu'ils songent
à fuir vers la montagne haute;

ceux dont le corps est dans
le village et le derrière à l'extérieur, et qui sortent le sabre ou
le couteau du fourreau parce qu'ils
sont jaloux du riche;

ceux qui vivent dans les marais
qui se cachent dans les cabanes
abandonnées, qui vivent seuls,

Ceux-là sont coupables et il
y a affaire avec eux.

JᴜᴀᴀᴀTᴀ.- Jug.no 27 du 30 mai 1923 : I mois.
    Jug.no 53 du I7 sept.1923: I mois + I0$00 + kpih au chef.
    Jug.no 86 du 2 déc. 1924 I0 jours: 2ᴀ00 + kpih au chef.
    Jug.nos 32 du I4 avr. et 63 du Ier sept.I925 : I mois + 500.
        + kpih au chef.
    Jug.no I9 du 2I avr. 1933 : 3 mois
    JugFno 28 du 14 nov. 1933 : I mois.
    Jug.no du 3 octobre 1938 : I5 jours + I0$00.
    Jug. du 4 octobre 1938 : 3 mois + I0$00.

4. KLEI KWAK .

    Ñu du ban duê, añuê ti, sok drai, cai, bô, go hưng, bưng bah, ñu dja čeh abu, êlu mngan, un ñu du, mnu ñu kkung krah buôn.

    Braih amâo ñu hiu moyor, ktơr amâo ñu hiu mđup, atâo kjang, yang kwak; tơ ruahe mnuih hlam buôn, tio nao sa čô êkei, sa drei mniê lač kơ ñu, brei ñu hriêdlâng mnuih dju bia, rua ktang, yang adiê ñl kơyua klei anân, gie ktrâo, mjâo lač, kwak sđai, kơyua ñu gan ti pin êa, tơ hma tač, tơ anôk dliê khâng sač yao.

    Tơ mnuih dju bia, rua ktang, dju bia rua êdu ñu dlang, tơ liê un mnu brei ñu buh ala ñu.

    Tơ dah mnuih dju ruam, duam suaih tlaih ti añuê abân, đum liê mnơng arăng ñu lo bi hnô brei đui nân.

    Bi tơdah mnuih dju amâo ruam, duam amâo suaih amâo tlaih ti añuê abân, tơ djiê ñu tâm brei ênua, djiê kơyua atâo kjang, yang kwak, ñu du abân duê, añuê ti, kthul braih amâo hiu moyor, ktơr amâo mđup.

    Djiê atâo kjang, yang kwak, kăk gưn yua anân.

    anân sơh ñu.

71. DES MAUVAIS SORTS.

    Celui qui quitte le village en emportant les nattes et les couvertures, les hottes et les corbeilles, les marmites et les écuelles, les jarres et la vaisselle, les porcs et les poulets;

    Si à cause de cela une personne tombe malade dans le village, en enverra un homme ou une femme le prévenir afin qu'il vienne voir celui qui est malade un peu ou beaucoup car c'est à cause de lui que les génies se sont irrités, le guérisseur l'a dit en mesurant le bâton, c'est parce qu'il a passé devant la fontaine, devant le champ, devant les lieux où on va souvent pêcher.

    Si pour la personne malade un peu ou beaucoup, on a sacrifié des porcs ou des poulets, on les lui montrera pour qu'il voie de ses propres yeux.

    Si le malade guérit, s'il peut quitter la natte et la couverture, tout ce qu'on a dépensé pour le soigner, il devra le rembourser.

    Mais si le malade ne guérit pas, s'il ne peut plus quitter la natte et la couverture, s'il meurt il paiera le prix du corps, car il est mort parce que les morts et les génies se sont irrités, parce qu'il est parti en emportant ses nattes et ses couvertures, sans offrir un peu de riz ou de mais (en passant devant chaque maison);

    en agissant comme il a fait, les morts se sont vengés, les génies se sont irrités, et c'est à cause de ça la que le malade est mort.

    Pour cela il est coupable.

5. KLEI YUa RUK DUAH DUAH DI
KƠ SANG PÔ MKUAN .

72 . DE CEUX QUI ÉTANT MALADES
COMMUNIQUENT LEUR MALADIE À
D'AUTRES.

Thun mơyang, bhang mđia,
adu adiê ngã jhat.

Dans les années funestes,quand
il fait très chaud,que les génies du
ciel répand le mal,

Ñu yang biê, adiê nga,rua
duam.

si le malade que les divinités
ont frappé,que le ciel a rendu malade,

Ñu amâo thâo kơu kơyăm,amâo
thâo kăm guam.

ne sait pas rester chez lui
comme lorsqu'on fait le deuil,s'il
ne sait pas se tenir tranquille;

Êman yang mơya ñu duah hơua
kơyâo kčik,êman yang mơya ñu
duah hơua kơyâo kpang,ñu duah
hơua buôn sang sah mđrong.

si comme l'éléphant du Génie-
Crocodile il cherche à se frotter
contre l'arbre kčik ou contre l'arbre
kpang,s'il cherche à se frotter aux
habitants riches et saints,

Djiê mnuih suh,êbuh mnuih
kuang,djiê wang lu,kga lu,djiê
mnuih thâo kpư kñhal.

causant ainsi la mort de personnes jeunes et robustes,riches ou
pauvres, de personnes bien bâties
(pouvant encore travailler)comme des
houes ou des coupescoupe bien tranchants,de personnes agiles et solides

amâo kđi arăng kơ ñu .

pour cela il y a affaire entre
autrui et lui .

JURISPR.- JUG.no 79 du 30 oct.1924 : 6 mois + 3 ko + kpih(Contamination
et adultère).
JUG.nô I9 du 25 févr1925: I an.

6. KLEI DUAH BI DJO RUIH LA KƆ ARĂNG.

73. DE CEUX QUI PROPAGENT DES MALADIES CONTAGIEUSES.

Ling ñu duah tak, lak ñu duah mniă, ñu duah ba hiu kɔ buôn yu, pu ngɔ, ñu duah bi djo kɔ anak sah mdrong.

Ǒut ñu duah ba, la ñu duah mdi, êa phi bal ñu duah bi trah mnêi anak arăng.

Gɔ tơl amâo yong bi anek mniê amâo yong thiê anak êkei, amâo yong brei djuê kman tian êtuh, djuê kman tian êbâo, kơyua klei ǒut la ñu duah mdi anăn.

Djuê amâo bi knăt, hăt amâo lar, djuê arăng amâo yong lar êngum ơyua ñu.

. . . . Gô . . . bi knăt ñu duah kti . . . rŏng gŏ, anak sah mdrong amra . . . anak, ñu duah bi tuič he

. . . . anăn kthul ñu, mâo kdi arăng . . . kơ ñu.

Celui qui communique les plaies et les dartres, qui les propage dans les villages de l'Est ou de l'Ouest, qui contamine les habitants riches;

celui qui transmet la variole ou donne le pian obligeant ainsi les autres à se soigner avec des médecines âcres ou amères;

celui qui fait que les femmes ne pourront plus donner d'enfants, plus de filles ni de garçons, qu'elles ne pourront avoir une famille nombreuse comme les germes du mal, nombreuse comme si elles avaient cent ou mille ventres, parce qu'il leur aura donné la variole ou le pian;

celui qui fait que la famille ne se multipliera pas, que le tabac ne bourgeonnera pas, que la race ne proliférera pas;

celui qui des bambous alê ou moô bourgeonnant coupe la cime, qui des habitants riches pouvant avoir de nombreux enfants éteint la race,

celui-là est coupable et il y a affaire entre autrui et lui très grave.

_____ Jug.no19 du 25 févr. 1925 : I an.
Jug.no20 du 5 févr. 1926 : I an + 4500 +:3 ko ÷ kpih
(Époux adultère ayant contaminé sa femme).

7. KLEI AMÂO HUN MÂO MNUIH RUA DUAM DUI DJO KƠ ARANG .

Thun hang,bhang mdiê,lu khang
rua asei mlei,da djo čut,djo la,
da êka jŏng kngan,trah amâc thâo
hlao, mdrao amâo thâo grăng.

Da pit hlong rua, leh hua hlong
djiê,da êkei.Lu khang
mtuk hnak, hmak blan,da rua tian ô
eh,hlong djiê êxiê he,klei rua duam
dui djŏ kơ mnuih briêng hrač,tač
êngao.

Sa čô êkei,sa drei mniê,kbông
amâo nao wah hŏng mnut kơ êa,hra
kơ buôn,pô dlăng adei amuôn buôn
sang.

Tu tlăn tung duah mjua,ala êa
mŭng,mnuih buôn sang suaih asei
mlei ñu nač.

Djăp mta ra ênao,mâo klei ju
jhat,bi nao hun kơh hŏng khua.

Anei le ñu mdăp kbông,dlŏng
êgei,mâo klei anei anăn hlăm buôn
ñu amâo hun.

mŭn kthul ñu,mâo kđi arăng
kơ ñu,

74. DE LA NON-DÉCLARATION DES MALADIES CONTAGIEUSES.

A la saison sèche,quand il
fait très chaud,beaucoup de personnes sont malades;certaines ont la
variole,d'autre le pian,d'autres
ont mal aux jambes;malgré tous les
soins qu'on leur donne on ne peut
les guérir.

Des personnes tombent malades
en dormant,d'autres meurent
après avoir mangé,des hommes e
ues femmes.Il y en a beaucoup
qui sont enrhumées,qui toussen
qui ont mal au ventre,qui vo-
missent ou ont la diarrhée,pui
elles meurent.
Toutes ces maladies peuvent se pro-
pager à l'extérieur et atteindre le
habitants d'autres villages.
Si personne,ni homme ni fem
me ne va en informer le banian de l
source,le figuier du village,celui
qui veille sur les neveux et les
nièces,sur tous les habitants,

c'est comme si on cherchait
à introduire un python ou un serper
d'eau dans la maison,comme si on
était jaloux de voir les habitants
en bonne santé.

Pour toutes les affaires,
surtout por celles qui sont mauvai
il faut toujours aller informer le
chef;

si on cèle ce qu'il faut di
si on a les dents trop longues,si
dans le village il y a une affaire
qu'elle longue et qu'on ne va en informer le chef;

Pour cela on est coupable et
aura affaire avec le chef.

La présence d'un python dans la maison est considérée comme
profanatoire,comme un avertissement des divinités;aussi la
maison est-elle toujours abandonnée.

8. KLEI MNUIH DJO PHUNG BREI NGA PUK TRUNG HLAM BHIT DLIÊ KO ÑU DÔK.

Mnuih djo čut,djo phung la, dăm duah ba ko buôn sang ôh.

Hui phung ñu duah ba,čut la duah di ko arăng.

Kčyua nan asĭ msa,găp djuê ñu bi ngă brei puk hlăm dliê,hjiê hlăm kmrong,brei ñu dơng dôk hjăn ñu.

Di ñu bi ngă he brei trung hlăm dliê,hjiê hlăm bhit,dăm brei ñu wĭt ko buôn,puk arăng dăm brei ñu duah kan,ea dăm brei ñu mnăm mñei ti ko,hui djo mnuih buôn sang dum nôn ko dih.

Hui phung ba,čut la duah di ko mnuih mkuăn,arăng djă ti amĭ ..asa bĭ,kthul di ñu amâo thâo ..dliê anak čô di ñu,yang biê .. .., mâo klei ruăduam hlăm ..dliê.

Anăn mâo klei arăng ko di ñu.

75. DE LA NÉCESSITÉ D'ISOLER LES LÉPREUX EN LEUR CONS-TRUISANT UNE CABANE DANS LA FORÊT.

Celui qui est atteint de variole,de lèpre ou de pian,il ne faut pas le garder dans le village;

de crainte qu'il ne transmette la lèpre,la variole ou le pian,aux autres habitants.

Pour éviter cela,ses parents ou sa famille lui construiront une cabane dans la forêt,un abri dans la brousse,et il devra y habiter seul.

Il lui prépareront une maisonnette dans la forêt,un abri dans la brousse,et on lui interdira de revenir au village,de pénétrer dans la maison,de boire à la même source que les habitants,de se baigner dans la même rivière,de crainte qu'il ne transmette(sa maladie)à tous les habitants d'ici et de là.

De crainte qu'il ne donne la variole,la lèpre ou le pian,à d'autres,on s'en prendra à la mère qui l'a enfanté,au père qui l'a élevé s'ils ne savent pas s'occuper de lui,s'ils ne savent pas garder l'enfant que les génies ont frappé,que le ciel a maudit en faisant souffrir son corps;

pour cela il y aura affaire entre les autres et eux(les parents).

9. KLEI DUAH MČEH KƠ ARANG
BI HRO KO BUÔN SANG ARANG
LAČ DJO ČUT.

Ñu mčeh kbông diông êgei,
klei boh ñu mčeh.

Alê ñu bi hmao, drao ñu bi
hmô,ñu duah tô tăn kơ arăng hŏai.

Asei arăng jăk ñu duah koak
he hrue, asei arăng jăk ñu duah ôi
koak he klei,ñu duah brei he boh
ju jhat kơ arăng.

Ñu duah **duch** čhi boh mdhur
ngu,klei dju duam kơ arăng.

Êlang êlung, êsung hluh,ñu
duah bi buh ha mnuih buôn sang
arăng djo čut la.

Ñu duah mčeh kơ anak mli
hong,ñu duah mčeh kơ anak mdrong
mang,.

Anăn hăc kđi arăng kơ ñu.

76. DE CEUX QUI ACCUSENT SANS
PREUVE UNE PERSONNE D'ÊTRE
ATTEINTE D'UNE MALADIE
CONTAGIEUSE.

Celui qui calomnie avec la
bouche,qui a les dents longues,qui
invente des histoires;

celui qui raccourcit les bambous aïeou mô s'élevant très haut,
qui agit de même avec autrui,sans
raison;

celui qui met une liane au co
personnes bien portantes,qui leur
passe une corde,dans le but le leur
susciter de mauvaises histoires;

celui qui cherche ainsi à
créer des histoires de Môhur,des
histoires d'idiot,en accusant in-
justement les autres d'être malades

celui qui prétend que le kapokier est creux que le mortier est
percé,qu'il a vu des habitants at-
teints de variole ou de pian;

celui qui calomnie ainsi des
personnes honorables,des personnes
riches sans preuve,

celui-là est coupable et il
y a affaire entre les autres et lui.

NOTA.- Jugement 65 du 12 nov. 1923 : 10 jours + 3 ko + kpih au chef
(Individu ayant répandu de fausses nouvelles au sujet d'une
épidémie de variole).
.... au Nord de M'DRAK et dans la vallée du
.... en Pun-yên.

10. KLEI BUH MNUIH DJIÊ AMÂO
HUN,THÂO DAH AMÂO NAO BLANG
BI TUL GA KƠ ASEI.

Hua ñu jơm, mnăm ñu săp, ñu
mdăp, ñu mdiêng.

Tơ ñu buh mnuih duah đih krah
klông,dlông êlan,da kpiê ruă,čuă
êba,da lu thun hang,bhang mdiă,adu
adiê ngă jhat.

Da hui asah drăm krah êlan,
êman juă krah klông,da hui êmông
ma hlăm bhit pum.

Athul ñu amâo nao dlăng tol
ală,nao bi ga tul kơ asei,klei djiê
aru amâo ñu nao kral.

Ñu buh mnuih êlâo ñu êluh đue.

mnăn mse si ñu giê mnung tle
tiê... iê mniêng ñu tle brei,mse si
klei ñu tle mdjiê hlăm bhit pum.

mse si ñu tle kă hong kuôt,
ñu tle ruôt hong klei,mse si ñu tle
brei mta kju đao.

Anăn mâo klei kơ ñu.

---

77. DE CEUX QUI DÉCOUVRANT
UN CADAVRE N'EN INFORMENT
PAS(LE CHEF? CE NE RECON-
NAISSENT PAS LE CORPS.

Celui qui cache ce qu'il
mange,ce qu'il boit,celui qui cache
tout,

s'il voit une personne allon-
gée au milieu de la route,ou en travers du sentier,soit parce qu'elle
est ivre,soit parce qu'elle est
morte par suite d'une épidémie,pen-
dant les grandes chaleurs,quand le
ciel répand le mal,

il doit craindre que les
chevaux ne l'écrasent,que les éléphants ne piétinent son corps,que
le tigre ne l'emporte dans la brousse.

S'il ne va pas voir de près,
s'il ne va pas reconnaître le corps
s'il ne va pas voir si la mort a
déjà fait son oeuvre,il est coupable.

S'il voit une personne(al-
longée) devant lui et qu'il se
sauve,

c'est comme s'il l'avait
assommée lui-même avec un gourdin
ou avec un bâton,comme s'il l'avait
assassinée dans la brousse en se
cachant,

c'est comme s'il l'avait trans-
percée avec une lance,comme s'il
l'avait étranglée avec une corde,
comme s'il l'avait frappée à coups
de sabre.

Pour cela il y a affaire avec
lui.

II. KLEI MNUIH ĂDĂP ÊMÔ KBAO
RUA DJIĔ AMÂO NAO HƯN
HỌNG KHUA

Thun hang hhang mdiê, Aê Diê
mtrun êa rua duam djiĕ êmô kbao.

Êmô ku kdao, kbao kwâ jŏng,
amâo dui bơng rơk mnăm êa.

Khua, mnăm leh hiu mtă, hua
leh hiu mtăn, jăh mnuih dum nan kơ
dih leh hiu hƯn leh sơai.

Ñu brei hua kăm, mnăm biăt,
ñu brei bi êmiăt mă mdê bi buôn.

Ñu gang, bang jang păng,
khua brei dăng ka, bi ngă rup kơ
êmô kbao ti êngao, ktăm buôn.

Ñu mnut čăt kơ êa, hra čăt
kơ buôn, ñu pô dlăng adei amuôn
ti sang,

khua lač kơ ñu amâo ñu gô,
ghă amâo ñu gưt.

Ñu lăng ti êmông, ñu dlông ti
yang, ñu wă kang sah mdrong.

Ñu kuič pui, hrui mnuih,
adei amuôn buôn sang amâo ñu iêo hƯn,

ñu amâo wač bi êdah, wah bi
thâo amâo klei rua êmô kbao amâo ñu
hƯn hơng khua (sah mdrong).

Anăn klhul ñu, mâo kđi kơ
ñu prong.

78. DE CEUX QUI DISSIMULENT
LES EPIZOOTIES ET N'EN
INFORMENT PAS LE CHEF.

Pendant les années funestres,
à la saison chaude, le Maître du Ciel
répand sur la terre les eaux qui font
mourir les bœufs et les buffles;

Les bœufs aux jarrets faibles,
les buffles aux pattes molles ne
peuvent plus manger ni boire.

Après avoir bu et mangé (à la
fête annuelle), le chef a donné des
conseils, tous les habitants d'ici
et de labas il les a instruits;

il a prescrit (ou'en cas d'épi-
zootie) les animaux doivent être
nourris et abreuvés sous la maison,
il a dit que chaque village devait
prendre des mesures de protection,

en renforçant la palissade, en
barrant la grande porte et les che-
d'accès, en suspendant les cranes
de bœufs et de buffles à l'extérieur
du village.

Celui qui est le banian qui
pousse à la source, le figuier qui
croît en haut du village, celui qui
veille sur les frères et les neveux
sur tous les habitants;

et qui n'écoute pas les con-
donnés par le chef, qui n'obéit pas
à ses ordres;

celui qui désobéit au tigre,
qui se croit plus puissant que les
dieux, qui passe outre la parole du
chef;

celui qui n'entretient pas le
feu, qui ne réunit pas les habitant
pour les instruire;

celui qui n'écarte pas les
herbes pour faire voir, qui, lorsqu'
y a des buffles et des bœufs malades, n'en informe pas le grand chef

celui-là est coupable et il
y a affaire très grave avec lui.

Jug.no 47 du 24 juin 1923: I mois + 10$00; au chef de village:
8 jours + 10$00.

Jug.no 51 du ler sept.1923: I an au chef de village qui n'a p
informé les autorités supérieures.

12. KLEI THUN RUA DJIE EMÔ KBAO AMÂO THÂO KIA KRIÊ MDÊ BI BUÔN.

12. DE CEUX QUI NE SAVENT PAS S'OCCUPER DE LEUR BÉTAIL EN PÉRIODE D'ÉPIZOOTIE.

Thun moyang bhang mdia, Aê Du Aê Diê ngă jhat.

Thun moyang, bhang mtrun, thun heng, bhang msih, jih adei amuôn buôn sang, hră êgar tar lăn, hră êgar tar buôn êlan,.

mdê buôn mdê bi gang, mdê sang mdê bi gông, mdê knông mdê bi jut, dam duah bi brei êmô kbao luă mut kma.

mdê anak mdê bi mtô, mdê čô mdê êmô kbao mdê bi kiă kriê mă.

klei pô ñu lăng ti êmông, bi yang, hlei pô ñu wa kang m ñu, tha êmô kbao duah mut êmô kbao buôn arăng mkuan, duah djie êmô kbao arăng, kthul ñu, kui arăng mâo kơ ñu.

Un rih jih asei, mnu rih jih asei, ñu duah boh klei jih asei ñu pô.

Pendant les années funestres, quand il fait très chaud, le Maître du Ciel répandie mal.

Pendant les années funestres, à la saison sèche, quand il fait très chaud, les maladies se répande surtous les habitants, dans tous le villages, dans toutes lesrégions , dans tous les pays, par tous les chemins.

Les villages doivent se protég les signaux kung et knông seront placés sur tous les chemins d'accè et on interdira aux boeufs et aux buffles (de l'extérieur) de pénét (dans le village).

De cela tous les enfants et petits enfants(tous les habitants seront instruits,tous les boeufs buffles doivent être surveillés (isolés).

Celui qui désobéit au tigre, parce qu'il se croit plus puissan que les génies, celui qui passe ou tre la parole(du chef) en continu à laisser en liberté ses buffles et ses boeufs,en les laissant all dans les troupeaux d'autrui, si le boeufs et les buffles d'autrui me rent il sera coupable et il y aur affaire avec lui.

Comme le porc ou le poulet de tinés au sacrifice, s'il se crée ainsi des histoires il perdra son corps.

JURISPR.—Jug.nos 33 et 34 du 25 juin 1923 : I mois + 10$00 ; au chef qui n'a pas rendu compte : 5 jours + 10$00.
Jug.no 46 du 27 août 1923 : 6 mois + 15 ko pour 20 buffles morts.
Jug.no63 du 25 oct. 3 mois(circulation de bestiaux malades.

13 . KLEI ČUH PUI DLIÊ.

80. DES INCENDIES DE FORÊTS.

Êkei khăng duah čuh pui pliê,
niê khăng duah čuh pui mčum, da
nang duah čuh si bum kngal.

Ceux hommes ou femmes qui
allument du feu sans réfléchir, sans
faire attention, comme les aveugles
et les sourds;

Êkei khăng duah čuh pui pliê,
niê duah čuh pui amâo djo, da khăng
nuah čuh si kho ngu.

ceux hommes ou femmes qui mettent le feu n'importe où, sans prendre de précaution, comme des fous et
des imbéciles;

Alê bi knat di ñu khat he
prong gơ, mơô bi knat di ñu khat he
prong, tơ yang gơ brei sah mđrong,
ơng gơ di ñu čăp he, kngan gơ di
ñ tling he.

ceux qui coupent à la cime des
bambous alê et mơô qui bourgeonnent,
qui arrêtent en les retenant par les
pieds ou les mains les génies qui
donnent la richesse;

Alê jih krô, mơô jih rai, anôk
ti nja dôk jih pui bơng sươt.

ceux qui font que les bambous
alê et mơô sont détruits, que les gîtes
des lièvres et civettes sont brûlés,

anăn amô kdi arăng prong.

ceux-là seront une affaire très
graves avec autrui (avec la société).

...dê anak mdê bi mtô mă, mdê
... mô bi lač anăn .

Chacun doit instruire ses enfants et ses petits enfants,

...hui nao kơ djuh amâo thâo
...da amâo thâo nao ênue.

de crainte que s'ils vont à la
fontaine ou au bois ils ne savent
pas aller,

...duah čuh he pui arôk.

de crainte qu'ils n'allument
du feu avec la torche,

...nao kơ luma brua amâo thâo

de crainte que s'ils vont travailler au champ ils ne sachent aller,

...djă pui kluič duah tuič he
...djă pui kluič duah tuič he
...du duah buiê he pui hiăm bhit

que s'ils portent un tison (torche) il ne mettent le feu aux buissons
ou à la brousse en le jetant dans les
broussailles,

...ñu anăn trơng, bơng he
...klang leh anăn djăp

et qu'ainsi le feu ne prenne et
ne dévore la forêt, les buissons, les
roseaux, la paillote et tout ce qui
pousse et vit (dans la forêt);

Da hlong bong ho puk sang
arăng.

Da puk arăng ngă hlăm dliê,
djiê arăng hlăm hma, da ka yong
kdier pring.

Anăn tơ mniê arăng thâo drei,
go êkei arăng thâo pô mâo kđi, arang
dơ prong.

Tơdah amâo ngăn arăng du tơl
êngiă asei pô.

de crainte que le feu dévore
les maisons et les villages, les
abris dans la forêt, les cabanes dans
les champs si les alentours n'ont pas
encore été nettoyés.

Si l'homme ou la femme (coupable)
on reconnaît la personne, il y aura
affaire très grave avec eux.

S'ils ont des biens (pour payer
les indemnités), on les condamnera
(au maximum), jusqu'à perte de leur
corps.

Jug... Jug.no 13 du 2o mars 1923, no 52 du 2 sept.et no 85 du 2 déc.
1924, no I du 5 janv.no 43 du 8 juin et no 46 du 22 juin
1925 : 3 mois de prison et 10400 d'amende.
Jug.no 20 du 2I mars 1925 : I mois + 10400 (Incendie invol.)
Jug.no 30 du 8 avril 1925 : 3 mois + 10400 + Koih au Pôlan.
Jug.no 39 du 23 mai 1925 : I mois + 10400; au coupable de
négligence : 5400.
Jug.no 67 du 23 sept. 1925 : 5400 (L'inculpée est une femme
vieille et sans famille).
Jug.no 9 du 4 mai 1936 : 3 mois + 10400.
Jug.no 13 du 9 juin, no 20 du 9 juillet, no 24 du 5 août 1936 :
I mois + 5400 (Incendie involontaire) (Chef négligent).
Jug.no 43 du 7 sept. 1937: 20400 (L'auteur de l'incendie est
fonctionnaire).

14. KLEI AMÂO TRUIH MBJIÊ HE PUI,PUI BÔNG HE BUÔN SANG.

81. DE CEUX QUI N'ÉTEIGNANT PAS LEURFEU CAUSENT L'INCENDIE DU VILLAGE.

Prong pit ñu kdăm,prong ñăm ñu pit,pui kiuič amâo ñu yong, ui prong amâo ñu truih,pui duah ang he do mnuih jih buôn sang.

Celui qui s'endort d'un profond sommeil,parce qu'il est fatigué,ou parce qu'il a trop bu,sans éteindre le feu,sans retirer les tisons,peut causer un incendie qui dévore les maisons et les biens.

Knue bŏng leh ki, hua leh kin ñ din hoyat.

Avant de boire et de manger, (le jourde la fête annuelle)tout le monde a été prévu,tout le monde a été instruit (par le chef) la même chose a été dite et répétée plusieurs fois.

Kthul ñu krué mtak amâo mă dró,ênô kbao amâo mă klei,ekei mniê amâo tu sap.

Il est donc coupable celui qui est comme la roued ou l'égreneuse fonctionnant mal,comme le boeuf ou le buffle refusant la longe, comme l'homme ou la femme n'acceptant pas les conseils (du chef);

Lač amâo ñu tu blu amâo djo, u ngă si khŏ ngu,ruô anak amâo mč,mâo čô amâo ču lač, ñu ngă klei nač lăng,

car il n'écoute pas cnecdon lui parle,il ne suit pas les conseils qu'on lui donne,il agit comme un fou et un imbécile,ses enfants et ses petits enfants il ne les instruit pas,il agit comme s'il voulait nuire aux autres.

Anăn amâo kai arăng ko ñu.

Pour cela il ya affaire entre les autres et lui.

Cf Code Hittite de Brozny : Chi un homme libre une maison incendie,la maison il rebâtit', mais ce qui dans la maison au dedans soit homme soit boeuf,soit mouton,il ne rebâtit pas (p.77).

15. KLEI PUI BONG BUÔN SANG

Pui hlia êa mŭng, pui hliá
a hrip, lip knguôr jih.

Kmeh sang kơng păk, kmeh sang
ang hjiê, mdiê buič brơng ărăng jih.

Go klai, bai hbăo, boh tăo sah,
leh ria djam jih.

Jhŭng kpan, čhan mŏ, hgơr sô
võng jih.

Čen tăk hrah, čeh êbah mnŏng,
... ărăng băng sok piêô,

Sơ drai, hai-bô, kdô kuung,
... diêt prong jih.

ao ju, ao hrah, ao mah, ao
Kdran... ... ... mdrong
K dal

... dlông, vông taih, traih
... jih.

... pui ... leh, kmê dih bơng
... lu, ... leh kla, din hơyơt kơ
... ... tlang, vơ g buôn amuôn.

... luk leh mtô, kmlo leh lač,
... ktah hut, kpul agei, klei mtô
... kbah.

... ... , gao ... , gao khŏng
... ... mtô ... gưt,
... ... dưm.

... ... dlông, dlông ti
... ... , klei khŏng ...

62. DES INCENDIES DE VILLAGES.

Le feu a tout dévoré, l'eau a
tous emporté, les grands vents (la surface de la terre sont anéantis.

Les cloisons des maisons, les
piliers des greniers, le riz des
granges, tout est anéanti.

Les marmites à teintures, les
paniers de cendres salées, les pierres
à aiguiser, les pots à légumes, tout
a été détruit.

Les lits de camps et les grands
bancs, les escabeaux de bois escaliers
les tam-tams, gongs aux dessins,
tout a été anéanti.

Les grandes jarres à ragu, les
belles jarres mnŏng, les bijoux et
la vaisselle enfermés dans les
grandes huttes,

les jolies hottes jaraï, les
paniers à couvercles, les sacs et les
musettes, les grans et les petits
paquets, tout cela est détruit.

Les vestes noires et rouges, les
vestes brodées d'or ou brochées, les
objets précieux, les biens inesti-
mables, toutes les richesses, tout a
été anéanti.

Les longues solives, les grandes
pannes, le riz et le paddy tout a été
brûlé.

Par crainte de cela, avant de
boire et manger (à fête annuelle) les
neveux ont été prévenus, les habitants ont été instruits, tous ont été
conseillés.

L'ignorant a été instruit, le
muet a été enseigné (par geste). La
bouche (du chef) n'est pas restée
fermée, ses lèvres ne sont pas restées
immobiles, il n'a pas manqué d'instruire et de conseiller sans cesse.

Si on passe outre les signaux de
pièges, si on n'écoute pas la parole
du chef, si on ne suit pas les conseils
qu'il a donné, si on désobéit à celui
qui instruit, si on ne retient rien
des coutumes qu'on a chantées;

Si on (désobéit) au vieux, si on
veut se croire plus puissant que les
génies, si on n'écoute pas la bouche
qui instruit,

16. KLEI KĂM JHAT THUN BHANG ARĂNG HŎ ĔE.

Kuič pui hrui mnuih,kuič pui
ă adei amuôn, buôn sang.

Thun yan,mlan năng,klei khăng
thun bhang,ciăng bi jak jih sang
ng jih buôn, jih amuôn adei.

Kung leh duah gông,knŏng čut,
ăô brei tue yuăn duah mut kma
lam buôn sang ciăng bi ĕdăp ĕnang.

Djăp ĕlan klei leh duah dăng,
juăng kbăk,ĕruĕ leh duah pram,ĕjam
ĕ,hlei tue duah mut mur mgŏ,mă do
u djă ti asei,kơng kga,djă pioh he
ng tlch năng knăm kăm gung,knăm
khŏ,knăm hơng ĕmô kbao,tlâ
ne mlam.

Ĕrip ruh,ĕguh sue,mơng
klŏng,do ñu wit he tơnăn.

Ĕ klei ñu kčhul nao mgŏ,rô
ăô thăô krăl anôk djo hong
kĕi,tơ kơn diĕt ñu ba kdi
prong ñu be kdi prong.

83. DE CEUX QUI FORCENT L'ENTRÉE D'UN VILLAGE INTERDIT.

Qu'on attise les feux et qu'on
rassemble tous les neveux et nièces,
tous les habitants(pour écouter ceci:
    A certaines époques,dans les
années funestes,quand il fait très
chaud(et qu'il y a des épidémies),
on interdit le village afin que les
habitants se portent bien,afin qu'ils
soient rassurés.
    On place les signaux kung et
knông(surles chemins d'accès)pour
empêcher les étrangers de pénétrer
dans le village et de troubler la
tranquillité des habitants.
    Sur tous les chemins on tend des
cordes aux quelles on suspend des
cercles en rotin,ou bien on entasse
des branchages épineux.Si un étranger
force ces barrages on confisquera
tout ce qu'il porte sur lui,on saisira de sa personne et on le retiendra
au village pendant toute la durée
de l'interdit,qu'il sagisse d'interdit pour les pièges ou d'interdit
pourla consommation de viande de
bœuf ou de buffle,sans que cette durée puisse excéder trois jours et
trois nuits.
    Dès qu'on aura retiré les brancha-
ges épineux,les barrages en rotin,
dès que les chemins seront ouverts,
on lui rendra sa liberté et ses biens.
    Mais ppur avoir éte ignorant,pour
avoir forcé(l'entrée)sans réfléchir,
sans se demander si ce qu'il faisait
était permis ou défendu,pour cela
il paiera une amende;pourun interdit
peut important il paiera une petite
amende,pour un interdit plus important il paiera une amende plus forte.

27.KLEI KAN JHAT THUN BHANG, HUA DUam,ARANG KÔ KAA HE KƠ BUÔN.

Thun ksang,bhang mdiã,adu diengã jhat.

Kơu kơyam,kăm guam,čiăng mun bi ênang,bhang ti jăk,kăm jih dôi amuôn buôn sang.

kung gŭng,knŏng ĕăt,ñu duah mŭt kam hlăm buôn sang anăn kthul.

Tơdah yang biê,adiê ngã lo klei ruĕ duam,mơai ñu.

Tơ un djiê ñu lo bi kgu,tơ amu djiê ñu lo tla,tơ luiĕ kpiê ba ba ñu lo čio.

Tơdah anuih dju amâo ruam, amâo suaih,amâo tlaih ti añuê dôi ñu.

djiê ênua kơ ñu,tơdah ti la ñu.

84. DE CEUX QUI FORCENT L'ENTRÉE D'UN VILLAGE INTERDIT POUR CAUSE D'ÉPIDÉMIE

Quand l'année est funeste,que la saison mêâhe est horride,que le ciel répand le mal;

quand tout le monde est en deuil (à cause d'une épidémie),pour que l'année soit bonne(relativement),que la saison soit meilleure,tous les habitants demandent que le village soit interdit.

Celui qui pénètre dans le village quand les signaux d'interdiction sont placés sur les chemins d'accès celui-là est coupable.

Si les génies se fâchent, si le ciel s'irrite,s'ils répandent de nouveau la maladie de la mort,il en sera tenu pour responsable.

Les porcs et les poulets sacrifiés et les jarres offertes (aux divinités) il devra les rembourser.

Si les malades ne guérissent pas, s'ils ne peuvent pas quitter la natte et la couverture,c'est lui qui en aura toute la responsabilité.

Si la mort survient il devra payer le prix du corps,s'il n'y a que blessures(séquelles)il paiera une indemnité.

TS.KLEI AMÂO DJAL MDRAO MNUIH
RUA ČIANG DJIĚ.

Dju amâo ñu kia, rua amâo ñu
kriĕ,mâo,kpiĕ êsei amâo ñu bi mjrao.

Buĕ amâo ñu iêô,mjao amâo ñu
ia,amâo ñu bi kum hœu kbuiŏ.

Amâo ñu trah mao,trao gun,mâo
un mnu amâo ñu ŏuh,amâo ñu duh min
rei kơ mnuih rua duam.

Mnuih dŏk dju beng aban,hlak
ĕman hlam mhuě,mnuih điăng ĕhuĕ
leh sup bjŏ.

Mâo ĕmô amâo ñu ŏuh,mâo kbao
amâo ñu ŏuh,amâo ñu duh kơ atâo
yang.

Ĕa amâo ñu brei, êsei amâo ñu
knă,amâo ñu mtrut brei kơ huă bong.

Ñu amut kơ êa, hra kơ buôn,ñu
pô mât amuôn buôn sang,

Mluk amâo ñu mtô,kalô dah,ñu
amâo je sa mlam,giăm sa hruĕ,adei
krung,yang buôn amuôn adei amâo ñu
trah dlang, ĕmang djơ.

Ñu dŏk he hngăp,ñu dăp he ñat,
ñu dŏk he êiăt eyăng.

Dju amâo ñu kia, rua amâo ñu
gr̆ng,mnuih buôn sang amâo ñu iêô
mthuŏ.

Mnan kthul ñu mâo kdi khuă kơ
ñu.

85.DE CEUX QUI NE SOIGNENT PAS
CONVENABLE ENT LES MALADES.

Ceux qui ne s'occupent pas des
malades,qui ne les veillent pas,qui
ayant du riz et de l'alcool ne les
soignent pas;

ceux qui n'appellent pas l'ac-
concheuse ou la guérisseuse(à temps)
qui ne songent pas à faire soigner
(le maldĕè);

ceux qui ne lui donnent pas les
soins nécessaires,qui ne le tiennent
pas propres qui, ayant des porcs et
des poulets,oublient de les sacrifii
(aux divinités pour obtenir sa guérison),

et font que le maldĕè reste
longtemps sur la natte,sans la décou-
verture,jusqu'à être faible et n'avo
même plus la force de parler;

ceux qui ayant des boeufs et des
buffles ne les abattent pas pour les
offrir aux âmes des morts;

ceux qui ne donnent pas d'eau
(au malade quand il a soif),qui ne
lui font pas cuire du riz,qui ne le
forcent pas à se nourrir,

si le banian de la source,le
figuier du village,celui qui veille
sur les habitants,

n'instruit pas l'ignorant,s'il
n'enseigne pas le muet,s'il ne va pas
voir(le malade) une fois de jour,une
fois de nuit,s'il ne s'occupe jamais
des frères éperviers,les génies du
village,des neveux et des nièces,

s'il reste toujours chez lui,
bien tranquille,comme s'il se cachait;

s'il ne va pas voir ceux qui
sont malades,s'il ne s'intéresse pas
à eux et ne demande pas de leurs
nouvelles aux habitants qui passent
devant sa maison,

pour cela il est coupable et il
y a affaire avec lui.

I9.KLEI MDAP HE ASEI THÂO
DAH TLE DUE HIU HE TODAH
ARANG IĜO RUNG DRU DONG.

Mniê amâo mă klei,êkei amâo
mă săp, amâo khăp u klei arăng.

Ñu lăng ti êmông,dlông ti
yang,ñu wă kang mbah, săp sah mdrong
mtô lač amâo gŭt.

Ñu amâo blu se knga,ha se
săp,amâo ñu khăp klei sa ai hăn.

Ječ roh êmeh amâo ñu mjan,
ječ roh êman amâo ñu mjok,ječ klei
ksok mtăo im amâo ñu dru cang ênuh,
amâo ñu dru duh mgei,ječ klei djiê
bru amâo ñu dru dor.

Ñu dôk he hngăp,ñu due dap
he ñat,ñu hlong dôk êiat êyang.

amâo roh êmeh amâo ñu dru bi
mdjeh ,ječ êmông amâo ñu dru dong,ječ
klei sah mdrong,klei ayong adei
amâo ñu nao dru.

anan kthul ñu mâo kdi khua
kơ ñu

86. DE CEUX QUI SE CACHENT OU
SE SAUVENT QUAND ON APPELLE
AU SECOURS OU À L'AIDE .

Ceux,hommes ou femmes qui n'é
coutent pas les conseils qu'on leu
donne, qui désobéissent aux ordres
du chef;

ceux qui se croient plus forts
que le tigre,plus puissants que le
génies,qui se montrent insolents
avec le chef,et passent outre les
conseils qu'il leur donne;

ceux qui n'écoutent pas d'une
grande oreille,qui ne parlent pas d
d'une même bouche,qui n'ont pas le
même coeur(que tous les habitants
et le chef),

ceux qui n'accourent pas quand
on appelle au secours pour chasser
les pirates ou les éléphants,qui ne
vont pas assister les familles vic-
times des sorciers et des fantômes
qui n'aident pas à ensevelir les
morts;

ceux qui restent toujours chez
eux,qui se tiennent cois comme s'il
se cachaient,sans se soucier de ri

ceux qui n'aident pas à chass
les rhinocéros et les éléphants,à
tuer le tigre quand on appelle au
secours,qui n'aident pas le chef ou
les habitants quand il ya un trava
important à faire,

ceux-là sont coupables et il y
a affaire entre le chef et eux.

20. KLEI JIH MNUIH BUÔN SANG
BI DRU HE DJAP BRUA-KLEI
HDANG GAP DI ÑU.

Ktrạ djuh dru ba,ktrọ êa dru
gui,ñnui puk sang dru bi kum ngã ,
ruã kơ asei bi dlăng.

Hdip bi lu kpê, djiê bi lu
dơr,wơr bit klei bi dru mtô.

Blu bi sa knga,ha bi sa săp,
bi khăp u sa klei nan soai.

Jih buăl hlăm sang,yang buôn,
jih amuôn adei dum nei kơ dih,bi
dru soai.

Hlei mniê amâo mă klei,êkei
amâo tu săp,hlei pô ñu amâo khăp u
klei anei kơhul ñu,amâo kơi khua
kơn kơ ñu ñu ngã yang kơ khua buôn
n sang kpih.

87. DE L'OBLIGATION POUR POUR
TOUS LES HABITANTS DE S'EN-
TR'AIDER POUR TOUS LES TRA-
VAUX.

Le lourd fagot de bois il faut
aider à le porter,ainsi que la lour-
de charge d'eau; il faut aider à
terminer la maison en construction,
ceux qui sont malades il faut aller
les voir.

Quand un vivant(donne une fête
il faut aller nombreux boire de son
alcool,quand quelqu'un meurt il faut
aller tous à son enterrement,quand
une personne a oublié ce qu'on lui
avait appris il faut l'aider à s'instruire de nouveau.

Il faut tous écouter d'une
même oreille,parler comme s'il n'y
avait qu'une seule bouche,vouloir
tous d'un même coeur,

tous, serviteurs et habitants,
neveux et nièces,tous ceux d'ici et
delà doivent toujours s'entr'aider.

Ceux ou celles qui n'acceptent
pas les conseils,ou refusent ces
paroles,ceux qui n'aiment pas en
tenir compte,ceux-là seront coupables
et il y aura affaire entre le chef et
eux,ils sacrifieront un porc de un
song pour le chef.

21. KLEI ČAP MNUIH HLĂM PŬK SANG ARĂNG,

Ñu duah čap arăng mang,wang sang hong,ñu duah čap anak sah mdrong,anak ayong adei hdai,

Ñu duah truă si kñăm,dlam si wah,ñu duah pah si tlang mja:

Klăm dê dlông,yông prong, ñu duah čap mnuih băng sang sah mdrong,sang ayong adei,anăn măo kdi arăng ko̐ ñu.

88. DES ARRESTATIONS ARBI-TRAIRES DANS LA MAISON D'UN TIERS.

Ceux qui arrêtent une personne sans ordres,qui pénètrent dans la maison d'autrui sans autorisation pour se saisir du riche ou du simple habitant;

ceux qui capturent comme avec une nasse ou un hameçon,qui saisissent comme l'épervier ou la fouine;

ceux qui convoitent la grande solive ou la longue panne et qui pour cela arrêtent une personne quand elle se trouve dans la maison du riche ou dans la maison de l'habitant,

ceux-là sont coupables et il y a affaire avec eux.

23. KLEI MNIÊ DUE HIU RƯNG, ALAH
AMÂO NGA BRUA HMA, KPAIH MRAI,
LEH ANAN AMÂO MÂO BUÔN SANG
DÔK SA ANÔK.

Mniê kêč amâo mâo djué, ruê amâo
ô ana, ñu mnuih amâo mâo ama ami.

Ruh ruah mse si mnu duah ktat,
hat buôn anei ñu due nao dôk ko
uôn adih, jhat sang anei ñu due nao
ôk sang mkuan.

Rah rung, mnuih lu bưng hua,
ljam sang anei, esei sang adih, ti
ñu nao ti ñu dih, ti ñu dôk ti pit.

Ñu amâo dôk hnong, dong kla,
mâo ñu ngă brua hma, amâo ñu gui
tjuh, amâo ñu duh êa, amâo ñu nao ko
ma pưk.

Ñu amâo ma kpaih, čaih mrai,
mâo ñu dai êsung hlâo, amâo ñu dôk
o jăk.

Ñu duah due hiu jong mngo, ko
yu, mse si kru hlăm hlang.

klei ñu amâo ñu gô, mtô ñu
o thao tjo, ñu nga si mnuih kho
u.

Hŏng ñu bai si krang, bung gei
ang si lip, mniê amâo dui lo djip
ing.

Anan asâo êra bi kblăm he trong,
uih jhong bi hlah, dah blu bi kmhal
ñu .

90. DES FEMMES VAGABONDES QUI NE
TRAVAILLENT NI AU CHAMP, NI À
LA MAISON, ET N'ONT PAS DE DO-
MICILE CONNU.

Celle qui est comme une mouche
ou un moustique sans famille, comme
un enfant sans père ni mère;

celle qui est comme la poule
cherchant (un nid pour pondre), qui ne
se plaisant pas dans ce village s'en
va dans cet autre, qui trouvant cette
maison mauvaise s'en va dans une autre;

celle qui comme les vagabonds a
beaucoup d'écuelles, qui mangent les
légumes dans une maison et le riz
dans une autre, qui se couche et s'endort où elle se trouve;

celle qui ne sait pas se tenir
tranquille, qui ne se conduit pas bien,
qui ne travaille pas au champ, ne va
pas au bois, ni à la fontaine, ni à la
cabane, du champ (pour le garder);

celle qui ne prépare pas le co-
ton, ni le fil, qui ne manie jamais le
pilon et le mortier, et se conduit
toujours mal;

celle qui s'en va les jambes à
l'Est et la tête à l'Ouest, (qui erre)
comme le boeuf sauvage dans les sa-
vanes;

celle qui n'écoute pas les conseils qu'on lui donne, qui n'obéit pas
à ceux qui commandent, agissant toujours comme les fous et les idiots;

celle dont la couche est large
comme l'ouverture d'une nasse ou d'un
van, et qui est incorrigible,

comme le chien gourmand qu'on
corrige avec une aubergine chaude,,
comme l'homme mauvais qu'on punit,
celle qui se conduit mal sera puni
de même.

Jug. no 49 du 15 juillet 1925 : 5 ans (Vagabondage, paresse et
défaut de papiers).

24. KLEI AMÃO NAO DRU RUNG
BUH PUI BONG BUÔN SANG.

Roh êmeh bi dru nao mjan,
roh êman dru nao mjŏk, roh ksŏk al
um bi dru nao čang ênuh, duh mgei,
klei rung rãng dru bi hmư.

Anei le ñu dŏk he hngăp, dap
mat, ñu dŏk he ô-iăt êyâng, buh pui
bong buôn sang, pus hjiê amâo ñu
nao drú dong, dru rung brei.

ñu ngă mse si ñu dŏk ting tue,
amâo ñu hlue ting buôn, mse si ñu
tui tluôn ôgar.

Ječ amâo ñu xoh, todah buh roh
amâo ñu dru nao mnah, ječ klei
aguah plam amâo ñu dru nao mbit.

amân kchul ñu nao kđi khua
co ñu .

91. DE CEUX QUI N'AIDENT PAS
À ÉTEINDRE LES INCENDIES
DE VILLAGES.

y a

Quand/il/des rhinocéres et des
éléphants(dans le champ)il faut aider
à les chasser, quand les sorciers et
les fantômes donnent la maladie ou
la mort il faut aller assister(les
familles atteintes)quand il y a un
malheur il faut toujours s'entr'aider

Celui qui reste tranquillement
chez lui, qui se tient coi comme s'il
se cachait, celui qui voit le feu
dévorer les maisons et les greniers
ne va pas aider à combattre l'incendie;

celui qui agit comme s'il n'é-
tait pas du village, comme s'il était
étranger, et reste indifférent(devant
le sinistre);

celui qui ne s'empresse pas de
combattre les pirates à coups de sabre ou de lance, qui n'aide jamais
(les autres)quand il y a quelque
chose d'urgent à faire le matin ou
le soir;

celui-là est coupable et il y
a affaire entre le chef et lui.

TRIBA.- Jur no 5 du II janvier 1926 . 3900.

25. KLEI MNUIH DUAH ČUH BUÔN SANG, PŬK HJIÊ ARĂNG.

92. DES INCENDIES VOLONTAIRES DE MAISONS OU DE GRENIERS.

Êiê arăng duah iang, yăng duah nač, ñu dja pui kluič ñu duah tuič hlung, ñu dja pui kluič ñu duah tuič sang sah mdrong, sang ayŏng adei klei amâo thâo.

Celui qui est jaloux du voisin, malfaisant comme les génies et cherche à mettre le feu à la paillote pour détruire la maison du riche, la maison des frères, sans qu'on sache pourquoi,

Tơdah mniê arăng thâo drei, tơdah êkei thâo pô, ệmô khao arăng thâo kral mgăe, tơdah arăng mâo dja ñu ti knŭk, mâo kčik ti pal, mâo kral he bô mta ñu, klei arăng dang, juăng kă, umă hlun arăng mjing.

si de la femme (coupable) on reconnaît le corps, si de l'homme reconnaît la personne, si des boeufs et des buffles on reconnaît le gardien, si on peut le saisir par les cheveux ou par le bras, si on le reconnaît à son visage, on l'attachera avec une corde, on le garrottera, et on le gardera comme esclave ou prisonnier.

Tơdah êkei arăng koh mdjiê, bi tơdah mniê arăng či he ñu kơ ệmô mtao, khao mdrong, kơ ngăn ayong adei.

Si c'est un homme on le coupera la tête, si c'est une femme on la vendra contre des boeufs au roi, contre des buffles au riche, ou contre des biens aux frères, aux habitants),

Đăm un lo thâo, đăm asâo lo mñg, đăm bung go lo mčah

cela pour que le porc ne sache plus, pour que le chien perde ses habitudes, pour que les bois et les marmites ne soient plus brisés, (pour que les coupables ne puissent plus récidiver).

Chron.—Jug. no 6 du 11 février 1917 : 10 ans (Insoumission, coups et blessures, vol, incendie de maison).
Jug. no 27 du 6 août 1926 : 10 jours (Menaces d'incendier).
Jug. no 2 du 11 janvier 1937 : 6 mois + 5 kơ × kpŭh (incendie d'un grenier, coups et blessures).

26. KLEI PLA ÊSEI AT HLAM HMA ARANG.

93. DE L'ENFOUISSEMENT DE RIZ FROID DANS LE CHAMP D'AUTRUI.

Hlah lăn ala,êa djuh arăng
hui kuê amâo lo hriê,mdiê amâo lo
jing,hui ksing koông,lăn Amâo čăt
mdiê,dliê amâo čăt kuê,djuê amâo
jing sah mdrong;tơdah anak mnuih
schŏn klei arăng bi mlei.

Celui(qui enfouit du riz froid)
profane la terre,les eaux et les bois
d'autrui,et à cause de cela le riz
ne pousse plus,le millet ne vient
plus,la forêt ne se constitue plus,
le clan ne peut plus prospérer,la
race s'éteint,tout cela par ce que
quelqu'un a commis un péché très grave.

Hui lăn amâo mda,êa amâo mrâo,
pla mtei kbâo amâo čăt jing,mdiê
kuê hui ksing koông,amâo lo dlŏng
amâo lo bi asăr.

A cause de cela la terre ne
reverdira plus,l'eau ne jaillira plus
(des sources),les bananiers et la
canne à sucre qu'on plante ne pous-
seront plus,le riz et le millet ne
donneront plus d'épis ni de grains,
ils ne monteront plus(comme avant).

Tơ mniê thâo droi,êkei thâo pô
ênâ kbâo thâo kral mgăt,tơ arăng
kral he pô pla êsei at hlam anăn,
tơ arăng mă djă he ñu ti sơk,ênơk
ti pŭl,kral he bô mta ñu nik tam,
arăng ba ñu kơ mnut kơ êa,hra kơ
buôn,kơ pô dlăng adei amuôn buôn
sang.

Si on reconnaît le coupable,comme
on peut reconnaître le propriétaire
de boeufs ou de buffles en voyant le
gardien,si on connaît celui qui a
enfoui du riz froid dans le champ,
qu'on le saisisse par la hotte,qu'on
le retienne par le bras,qu'on regarde
bien son visage,et qu'on le conduise
au banian de la source,au figuier du
du village,à celui qui veille sur les
neveux et les frères,sur tous les
habitants.

Mnut kơ êa phat brei ênoh,kjơn
brei ktơ,mdjiê brei kdi.

Le banian de la source examinera
l'affaire,la jugera et tâchera de la
régler définitivement.

Si tơ mniê amâo mă klei,êkei
amâo mă săp,amâo ñu khăp ư klei
khua ñu,khua ñu hriê tăt ñu kơ khua
kring.

Mais si l'homme ou la femme n'accepte pas sa décision,le banian de la
source les conduira au chef de secteur.

Khua kring tăt brei kơ sang
phat kdi,phung anei lo tlăng kña,ha
amuh thơ ñu.

Le chef de secteur les conduira
devant le tribunal qui les interroge
de nouveau.

Si tơ ñu pô anăn čhu he kiê,
djiê he kngan ñu êkei duah pla pliă
mniê duah pla adum,ñu duah ngă si
mnuih tuei kngan,kthul ñu,atâo ñu
lang kơ arăng.

S'il(le coupable) reconnaît sa
faute,s'il avoue son crime,s'il reconnaît qu'il a mal agi,qu'il a agi à la
légère comme le sourd ou l'aveugle,
il sera déclaré coupable parce qu'il
a été malfaisant comme les esprits
des morts,

Anăn kdi arăng mêa kơ ñu.

et il y aura affaire entre autres
(le propriétaire du champ et le propriétaire du sol) et lui.

Un dua song kpih pô hma.

Il donnera un porc de deux songs
au propriétaire du champ,

Un sa kơ pui lăn.

et un porc de un ko(au propriétaire
du sol)pour purifier la terre.

27. KLEI NGA MSAT HLĂM HMA ARĂNG.

94. DE LA CONSTRUCTION D'UN PETIT TOMBEAU DANS LE CHAMP D'AUTRUI.

Hlah lăn-ala êa ndjuh arăng, hui kuê amâo lo hriê, mdiê amâo lo jĭng, hui ksing kơŏng, lăn amâo čăt mdiê, dliê amâo čăt kuê, djuê amâo mdrong, sơnăn klei arăng bi mlei.

Tơdah ñu kue kbut, kbut msat wat gơng kut plao hlăm pưk hma arăng, ñu hlăp ngao, tlao êbeh, ñu mčeh mă klei hjăn ñu.

Ñu tăm brei ênua, ba brei kđi, čiăng khin amâo lo brei, mlei amâo lo tu, ju jhat bi hlao, kuê bi jăk lo hriê, mdiê bi jăk lo brei, asei mlei bi suaih mngač.

Anăn mâo kđi.

Ñu tuh brei lăn hong kbao kô.

Un kô kpih brei pô hma .

Celui qui profane la terre, les eaux et les bois d'autrui et fait qu'ainsi le millet ne vient plus, le riz ne pousse plus, qu'ils ne donnent plus d'épis ni de grains, que la terre ne produit plus rien, que la forêt ne se reconstitue plus, que le clan ne peut plus prospérer parce qu'il a commis un péché très grave;

s'il a édifié un petit tombeau dans le champ d'autrui, s'il a fait le tumulus et planté les poteaux funéraires, en faisant cela il plaisante avec excès, il s'amuse sans mesure, il se crée des histoires très graves.

Il devra rembourser la valeur de la récolte, payer une indemnité (au propriétaire du champ et au propriétaire du sol), pour annahiler l'effet du péché, pour effacer le mal qu'il a fait, afin que le millet et le riz poussent encore bien, que les personnes soient en bonne santé.

Pour cela il y a affaire.

Pour purifier la terre il donnera un buffle blanc au propriétaire du sol,

et au propriétaire du champ il donnera un proc blanc pour le sacrifice.

JURISPR.- Jug. du 8 mars 1938 : 2 ans de prison.
   Jug.du 5 septe 1938 : I ans : kpih avec un buffle blanc
      et un gros porc (pour avoir planté les poteaux funéraires
         dans le champs d'autrui.).

KDRĚČ V.

CHAPITRE V.

I. KLEI ALIH KÔNG BI DÔK UNG MÔ .

95. DES FIANCAILLES ET (DE LA RUPTURE DES FIANCAILLES).

Hbu hbiê, mniê êkei, klei boh
di ñu bi khăp mă.

S'ils se désirent, s'ils s'aim
la jeune fille et le jeune homme, si
c'est leur unique préoccupation,

Anăn di ñu iêô bi kbin adam
edei, amiêt khua, awa mduôn, ding ti
kbông, kông ti kngan, êlan blu yăl
di ñu iêô.

qu'ils réunissent les frères e
soeurs, les oncles et tantes, ou'ils
présentent leurs témoins le pipeau
à la bouche, le bracelet au poignet.

Añu bi lông, kông bi lih,
kông adih kơ anei, kông anei kơ dih,
kông êkei kơ mniê, kông mniê kơ êkei.

Les colliers et les bracelets
seront échangés, le bracelet de ce
ci sera donné à celle-là, le brac
let de celle-là à celui-ci, le br
celet de la femme à l'homme et le
bracelet de l'homme à la femme.

Ênô kbao amâo mâo pô ngô klei,
êmâo amâo mâo pô ngô sap, di
ñu bi khăp mă di ñu dua, kơyua nan
lăh kông tơn ti amnê ti ñu bi mă
tu hjăn di ñu mơh, amâo mâo pô smup
mơyơr ti kiê kngan di ñu ôh.

On ne passera pas la corde a
coup, de force, comme aux boeufs
aux buffles, on ne les obligera pa
s'unir; s'ils s'aiment et se désir
les bracelets seront posés sur une
natte, ils les prendront tout seul
librement, personne ne les leur pré
sentera, personne ne les leur mett
dans la main.

Ngu aguah, êdah yang hruê le,
ñu êbei mlam ñu blu sơ klei, hruê
ñu blu sơ ddp, wir rong anăp ñu lo
duah klei mkuăn, ñu amâo lo jing dôk
ôh sơ mniê anăn.

Mais si le lendemain matin, a
lever du soleil l'homme ayant parl
d'une manière la nuit, parle d'un
autre manière le jour, si dès qu'i
a tourné le dos il agit différen
s'il ne devient pas l'époux de la
femme qu'il a choisi,

Anăn *hěn gơ mniê, ñu ba bœi
kui kô gơ ngan kô.* un kông kpih.

enregistrant ainsi il la laiss
il devra lui payer une amende de
ko et lui sacrifier un porc le un

2. KLEI AMÃO BREI NGAN PNU.

Jak buăn dơng,krơng pioh pnu
ana agha dơng.

Êgao kning kčah,knah mguăn,
klei buăn tra ñu gao.ñu kã ktai dai
ayun,thun bhang ñu bi krŭi.Mlan
klun thun mdê,tê tiêt lo mñê mkuăn.

Boh suai mhtp,boh sup mtlŭh,
buh ala mta.ñu brei hong kla,ba
hong alah,ñu mtah čiang kơ mtâo
anak.

Čim ñu mñah,kan ñu mñah,sah
mdrong ale,ênô kbao ñu kpe wiên.

Ñu blu mlam sa klei,hrue sa
sap,wir rơng anăp mdê.

Anăn kaie ñu bi atut,mnut ñu
krañ ka.Tơ be kdi tiê êka,la bleh,
ênô kbao pleh wiên;ya be kdi ding
trông,kơng hra.Tơ ñu mão kdi ñu lač
be,ơ gun krông kđông êa,sap kčha
ñu.

Tơ dah mão kdi boh sô,yô hbei,
klei dum dơ,tăm brei ênua,ba brei
kdi.

Ñu buah mñê mñah,bi kčah
mñê brei ala.Kơl kã ñu gao.

96. DU NON-PAIEMENT DE LA DOT.

Ce qui a été promis il faut
donner,la dot fixée il faut la payer
(à la famille de l'époux),

au jour fixé dans le contrat,
sans faire attendre,sans toujours
remettre à plus tard.

Mais si on est comme la tringle
à couvertures(qui se balance),si on
tergiverse,si on remet d'année en
année,si on laisse passer les mois
et les années et qu'on attend chaque
fois que les cigales chantent;

si on montre les mangues et les
letchis qu'on ne les donne pas,si
on ne donne pas volontiers ce qu'on
a promis et qu'on donne néanmoins
un gendre;

si on présente la viande et le
poisson avec regrets,si on promet
au chef de payer et que chaque fois
on change des taches du pelage des
boeufs et des buffles (promis);

si parle d'une manière le jour
et d'une autre la nuit,si on agit
autrement dès qu'on a tourné le dos;

si on est comme l'arbre knia
(Irvingia oliveria) au tronc noueux,
comme l'arbre mnut au tronc tortueux

si (la famille de l'épouse)a été
blessée au coeur,si les marques des
boeufs et des buffles ont été changé
si on a refusé de boire(à la jarre)
et qu'on rejeté le bracelet;

s'il y a une affaire à régler
qu'on le dise,si la rivière déborde
ou est à sec,si de mauvaises paroles
ont été prononcées qu'on le fasse
savoir.

S'il s'agit d'une vieille affaire
datant d'autrefois on la réglera.

Mais si on ne donne pas ce qu'on
a promis,si on ne paie pas au jour
fixé,si on viole le contrat après
avoir accepté;

kong năn yoh ai thun dôk gang,
bhang dôk guốn,.Pluh bit hma,ema
bit ksơr lah mãa leh.Nga ñu blei
ging deh amão ar,nga blei ēman deh
amão dui,bơk anei ñu blei mnga
ngăti djă chun moin.

si on fait attendre des mois et
des années,le temps de faire dix
champs nouveaux,de cultiver cinq
champs anciens;

si on agit comme ceux qui achè-
tent des gongs et des éléphants sans
pouvoir les payer,si on achète la
fleur parfumée et qu'on la garde
pour son plaisir;

Ñu brei mlan anei,hrue arã,
ēnăn kơh hmei tu,nga anak hmei
amão jăk ơoh brua,amão jăk nga hma,
amáoh lơi sang ama,êla kơ sang ami
amão mao.

cette nuit même,ce jour même il
faut payer (ladot),puisque ce n'est
pas parce que le gendre travaille
mal le champ ou le jardin(de ses
beaux-parents),ce n'est pas parce
qu'il reste dans la maison de son
père le matin,dans la maison de sa
mère le soir(que la dot n'est pas
payée).

Tơ ñu amão brei mlam anei,
yang anak hmei, hmei sua wit kơ
hmei.

S'il (les beaux-parents)ne paie
pas cette nuit même,l'époux reviendra dans sa famille;

amãi kthul ñu.

et à cause de cela les beaux-
parents seront coupables.

3. KLEI DJIÊ ĔKEI LƠ ČUÊ BREI NUÊ.

Joh adrung lo hrua,ti tria lo
hrô,djiê pô enei lo čuê hong pô
mkuăn.

Blut djuê hlang,djang knôk,
blut djuê bi dôk bi rong mong đum.

Hma kpuh,djuh mñêng,hŏiêng
hŏui ko mjeh kir aê,plei kir wa
mjeh hdrô bla mong hdăp mong đum.

êda

Bhian mong/ti dlông,yông ti
gu,mông yu kma ngo,mauih bhian čuê
nuê bhiăn brei mong ênuk aê aduôn
đum.

Amâo djo lo bi mŏuh mn mñâo,
thŏô mraju...hrô êlao aê,ka thăo
...đuôn.

hui kpur kdang,sang kruh,hui
ôguh wit kăue,hui kpur kdang,sang
tlăp,nặp blu ênguôt.

A...n bhiăn tloh lo bi hrô,ênuk
kbuê,bhian lo bi tă mdum.

hui bru ko hma,bru ko mdiê,hui
bliê bluôt,hui kmôt ho si êa hiem
ko mâo,hui amâo lo mâo čô anăk.

...nên klei bhian khăng lo ei
čuê.

97. DU REMPLACEMENT DE L'ÉPOUX DÉCÉDÉ.

Quand les travers se brisent
on les remplace,quand le plancher est
cassé on le répare,lorsque quelqu'un
meurt,on le remplace par un autre.

Cela pour conserver la semence
de la paillote,la grappe de "knôk",
pour conserver la semence(de la race
transmise depuis autrefois.

Il faut la conserver comme on
conserve le vieux champ,comme on conserve la vieille bûche,la semence de
ancêtres,des oncles,des tantes; il
faut la conserver précieusement comme on conserve la semence de riz hâ-
tif et de riz tardif.

C'est la coutume de poser les
chevrons sur les pannes,dans tout le
pays,de l'Est à l'Ouest;c'est la co-
tume de renouer,de donner un rempla-
çant(au conjoint décédé),cela depuis
avant,depuis les ancêtres d'autrefois.

Cela on l'a pas inventé récem-
ment,on ne peut pas l'avoir fu avant
les ancêtres.

De crainte que le foyer ne se
désagrège,que la maison ne tombe en
ruine,que la palissade ne se disperse
de crainte que la parole ne dise la
désespérance;

la coutume répare ce qui est cassé,consolide ce qui est faible;

de crainte que la famille ne se
disperse dans les champs comme les
touffes de riz,de crainte qu'elle ne
soit anéantie,que la race ne tarisse
comme l'eau dans la montagne aride,
de crainte qu'il n'y ait plus d'enfants et de petits enfants;

pour cela,la coutume dit toujours
de renouer,de toujours remplacer
(l'époux décédé).

... klei lije "bi čuê brei nuê"(renouer en donnant un rempla...
...rt de l'un des époux de la famille du défunt le remplace cette...
... marie e lie,non seulement comme,a la femme,mais le plus de liberté...
...ô de la femme.Une fois qu'il a été scellé plus rien ne doit pouvoir...
...ider les liens,même par mort.

...soi du remplacement compense donc le mariage et en brisure le...
...mnités de violation entraîne la ...agrégation du foyer,brise de...
... et sème la division dans les familles

4. KLEI BHIĂN ČUÊ, BIA DAH ANAK ANEH AMUÔN ADEI KOUT THUNG AMÂO MÂO, DUAH AKÂO ANAK AMAI ADEI HLĂM SA DJUÊ.

Joh adrung bhiăn lo bi hrua, joh tria bhiăn lo hrô, djiê pô anei lo čuê hong pô mkuăn.

Tloh lo čuê, êhuê lo kbuă, bhiăn arăng khăng lo mă mdum mong tum.

Djiê amiêt lo čuê hong amuôn, djiê aduôn lo čuê hong čô, djiê pô anei lo bi mgang hong pô mkuăn.

ñu duah ta trăp pla mnang, ta trang pla kbâo, ñu amâo mâo anak kout thung ñu pô, ñu duan mă anak anei, ñu duah pei anak adei, amâo mâo hlăm buôn anei ñu nao duah hlăm buôn mkuăn, kha bi sa djuê năn.

→ anak adei ñu duah blei, anak adei ñu duah pah, amâo joh adrung amâo duah min.

ñu kpa klang, sang tlâo, tap blu ênguôt.

djrŭ duah bi rông, čiông bhiăn djiê hong tum, ka thâo hlao gŭ amâo čiău aduôn.

duah ñu atah hlô ôn, čô hô mlir mdah ñu duôc gui hlao, mhul ñu.

98. DE L'OBLIGATION DE TOUJOURS REMPLACER(LE CONJOINT DÉCÉDÉ) PAR UN FRÈRE, UNE SOEUR OU UN NEVEU, OU À DÉFAUT PAR UN ENFANT ISSU D'UNE FEMME APPARTENANT AU MÊME CLAN.

Quand les solives sont faibles, il faut les consolider, quand le plancher est mauvais état il faut le remplacer, quand celui-ci meurt il faut le remplacer par celui-là.

Ce qui est cassé il faut le réparer, ce qui est faible il faut le consolider, c'est une coutume très ancienne de toujours remplacer.

Quand l'oncle meurt le neveu le remplace, quand la grandmère meurt la petite-fille la remplace, quand celui-ci meurt on le remplace par un autre afin qu'il y ait toujours quelqu'un(pour perpétuer la famille le clan).

On nettoie le bas-fond pourri planter des aréquiers, on coupe les roseaux pour y planter de la canne à sucre, si on n'a pas d'enfant, même tout petit dans sa famille(pour remplacer le mort), on en cherchera un dans celle de ses soeurs, s'il y en a pas dans ce village on le cherchera dans un autre, il suffit qu'il appartienne au même clan(que le disparu qu'il faut remplacer).

L'enfant de la soeur aînée on le paiera, celui de la soeur cadette on l'achètera, celui d'un (parent)riche on l'échangera contre des biens;

de crainte que le foyer ne se désagrège, que la maison ne tombe en ruines, de crainte que les bouches ne disent la désespérance:

la coutume dit de conserver toujours la famille et toujours sa maison, et la détruire, si cela ne se fait pas les gens médisent les apostrophent.

tout en bas vers en semble celui qui est joint et qui est le plus sombre, celui qui est le ...

Todah ting kơ êkei amâo ču
brei nuê,ênuah duah diêt kơ amuôn
adei ñu.

Si c'est la famille de l'homme
(décédé)qui ne veut pas donner de
remplacant,une petite part seule-
ment de la succession(ênuah duah)
reviendra aux nièces (aux héritières
du mort.

Todah ting kơ mniê amâo čuê
brei nuê,amuôn adei ting kơ êkei
mâ mnai kpin ao prong,lui kơ anak
aneh diêt.

Si c'est la famille de la fem
(décédée)qui refuse de donner une
remplacante (au veuf),une grande pa
acquis en commun (mnhai kpin ao)
reviendra aux nièces(appartenant a
clan) du veuf,et les enfants issus
de son mariage(avec la défunte) n
ront qu'une petite part.

Jug.no 25 du 2 avril 1925 :Le chef du clan du défunt a été
condamné à la prison jusqu'à ce qu'une remplacante ait été
au veuf.
Note du Résident: J'attire l'attention de M.le Résident Supérieur
sur cet important jugement et sur la loi fort intéressante qui mot
la condamnation du nommé Y-Dju. Elle assure la continuité de la
et de l'accroissement du patrimoine familial. Sa non-observation
et sa violation depuis vingt cinq ans environ a été une des princi-
pales causes de la déchéance sociale des tribus malayo-polynésie
du Darlac;les grandes familles ont été considérablement amoindries
ou ont disparu,et les richesses ont été dilapidées.
Y-Dju n'est resté que vingt-quatre heures en prison;la rempla-
cante qui était inexistante a été trouvé dans le minimum de temps
possible.
Jug.no 21 du février 1926 :restitution des biens ênuah duah
usurpés sous prétexte qu'on qu'on n'avait pas trouvé de remplacant.

5. KLEI ČUĒ MÑIÊ ĐIÊT HÔNG ÊKEI PRÔNG.

99. DU REMPLACEMENT DE L'ÉPOUSE DÉCÉDÉE PAR UNE FILLE TROP JEUNE.

Joh adrung lo hruā, joh tria lo dluih, luič mnuih lo čuē.

Quand les traverses ou le plancher sont en mauvais état il faut les changer, quand une personne meurt il faut toujours la remplacer;

Tloh lo čuē, êhuê lo kbuā, lo mtă mdum hông čō.

Ce qui est cassé il faut le réparer, ce qui est faible il faut le consolider, toujours il faut remplacer par les petits enfants (le disparu),

Kpur amâo brei kdang, sang amâo brei tlăp, săp blu amâo brei ênguôt.

(cela) pour que le foyer ne se désagrège pas, pour que la maison ne tombe pas en ruine, pour que la parole qu'on dit ne soit pas désespérance,

Čiang kơ mnuih čoh bruā, ngă hmā, pla kmun ktơr si aguah.

pour avoir encore quelqu'un qui travaille la terre, qui fasse le champ qui cultive la main, et le concombre comme au matin.

Bia dah čō hmoi hlăk đih hlăm mun, mun hlăm ăbăn, blak đbăn hông mi ama čdi.

Si la petite-fille (donnée comme remplaçante) n'est encore qu'une enfant se couchant sur un matelas, se roulant dans la couverture, ne pouvant pas encore séparer de ses parents;

Nei gơ hdeh điêt ih čung ba, ih mnuih khua ih đôk guôn.

si elle est trop petite il faut la protéger, et l'homme adulte (à qui elle est donnée) doit savoir attendre,

Hdeh amâo blum ih mjum hông kông, hdeh amâo hlum ih mjum hông čăn.

si elle est craintive il faut la rassurer en lui offrant des bracelets, si elle est timide il faut l'enhardir en lui donnant des colliers.

TODaH IH jŏng ti êlan, mngan ti dliê; tŏdăh ih tle piu hiu mniê dum moh, kdi amâo mâo; bia dah kha ih bi jăk ŏoh bruă, ngă hma, pla kmun ktŏr, kha bi jăk ih ... roh, koh bur, ur ktia hril, jăk ke kŏng, rŏng cŏ, ke kŏng rŏng anak, rŏng bi mnak mñai, mâo djuê aseh mjeh kbao, kia bi jăk, mâr un ti gu, mnu ti diŏng, mâo kŏng mngan hlam sŏk picŏ pioh êmiêt bi jăk.

ʼi ih le, hui ih amâo ar ... ang, čang ...r, buh mnga kŏi băng hdrah, mnga ...l ...ng kwan, buh mniê mkwăn ih ... r...thul ih do čo ngăn ...ă... ... ...muê sdai, kdi ih ba he ...o... ...t mlun, trun mtah, sa ...a... ... t... čhang amâo mâo.

Et si (l'homme) a les pieds sur le sentier et les mains dans les buissons, s'il fornique avec une femme, cela ne fait rien, il n'y aura pas affaire; mais il ne doit pas oublier de bien travailler la terre, de faire le champ, de cultiver le maïs et les concombres;

il doit bien nettoyer les abords (du champ), arracher les mauvaises herbes, crier aux perruches et aux perroquets (pour les chasser du champ)

il doit bien conserver le bracelet (du mariage) et s'occuper de la petite fille (remplaçante) pour que ce soit beau et agréable;

il doit bien garder les chevaux et les buffles (de la jeune fille remplaçante), les porcs sous (la maison), les poulets sur (l'avancée), les bijoux et la vaisselle dans les hottes, il doit les conserver.

Mais s'il ne sait pas attendre, il voit la fleur jaune dans les buissons ou la fleur rouge dans les fougères, s'il voit une autre femme et qu'il la désire (comme épouse), il sera coupable, et tous ses biens resteront à la remplaçante, il lui paiera en outre une amende et il partira (de la maison de ses beaux-parents) tout nu, sans rien emporter, même pas une chique de bétel.

6. KLEI ČUĒ NUĒ ŠDAK KO VNIĒ
MDUÔN,VNIĒ ANĀN DŪI BREI
HJUNG KO NUĒ KƠYUA DAH ÑU
KDUÔN AMÂO LO BĀ ANAK HUI
TUIČ DJUĒ,HUI KAI PŪK SANG.

Šun yông lo hrua,êun êda lo
krua,ñu mduôn amâo lo rbrua ngā
djam, pam êsei,amâo lo thâo buh
ma êsei djam,anăn ñu lo mkrua brei
čô ñu pô hjung kơ nuê.

Hui tuič djuē, êhuê anak;ñu
ho hriê kơ khua,mta mmăt;hăt draê
riê kơ êiô .

Ñu amâo lo bā anak,čiăng kpur
kdang,sang kruh,êguh war dăm

...ui tuič ñu lo čuê,hui
...anak,ñu lo ma mdum brei
...ñu,čiăng bi jăk čoh brua,
...,čiăng bi jăk ke kông,rông
...,...čô bi anak,rông anak bi
...bi dam lăo dih;čiăng djuê bi
...,čăt mdar bi lar êngum.

...ei brei hjung.

IOO. DE LA FEMME ÂGÉE QUI
PREND UN JEUNE
REMPLACANT;ELLE DOIT
LUI DONNER UNE CONCU-
BINE DE CRAINTE QUE LA
RACE NE S'ÉTEIGNE,QUE
LA MAISON NE TOMBE EN
RUINE.

Quand les pannes ou les tirants
sont faibles il faut les consolider,
quand la femme est vieille,qu'elle
ne peut plus faire la cuisine,qu'elle
ne voit plus pour cuire le riz(qu'elle
ne peut plus avoir d'enfants),elle
doit consolider(le foyer)en donnant
sa propre petite-fille,en donnant
une concubine au remplacant(de son
époux décédé).

Cela de crainte que la semence
ne soit perdue,de crainte qu'il n y
ait plus d'enfants,car la tête vieil-
lit,la feuille de tabac se flétrie.

Si elle ne peut plus porter d'
enfants,et si elle ne veut pas que
le foyer se désagrège,que la maison
ne tombe pas en ruine,que les pieux
de la clôture soient arrachés;

pour que la race ne s'éteigne
elle renouera encore,pour que la
souche ne s'affaiblisse elle la con-
solidera,elle se fera remplacer par
sa petite-fille,car elle veut que le
champ soit bien travaillé,que la
famille soit bien protégée,bien soi-
gnée,bien nourrie,que ce soit beau
et bien comme tout le temps elle veut
que la race se perpétue,qu'elle bourgeonne comme l'arbre"mdar",qu'elle
se multiplie toujours.

Dans ce cas-là il faut donner une
concubine.

7. KLEI KÔ ADUÔN ÑU BREI
HÊ HJUÊNG KO NUÊ ANĂN
ČIANG BI DI ÑU MÂO ANAK
ANĔH BAA BREI LUIŎ DJUÊ.

IOI. LA FEMME ÂGÉE DOIT
DONNER UNE CONCUBINE
A SON REMPLACANT POUR
AVOIR DES ENFANTS .

Kô ñu ko khue, mta kjhuh, luh
buk biêk hriê ko mluôn, ñu amâo dui
lo knā êsei, brei djam, ñu amâo lo
thâo buh mñam kpin ao ko ung ñu nuê

Quand la tête de l'épouse vieil-
lit, que son visage se ride, que ses
cheveux blanchissent et tombent, que
sa lèvre devient pendante, qu'elle ne
peut plus cuire le riz, faire la soupe, qu'elle ne voit plus pour tisser
des ceintures et des vestes à son
jeune remplècant;

Anăn ê-un·yông ñu lo hrua, ê-un
êda ñu lo krua, ñu duah mă kô ñu,
ñu mdum brei hjuêng ko ung ñu nuê.

quand la panne est pourrie il
faut la remplacer, quand le tirant
est faible il faut le consolider ,
quand la femme est vieille elle doit
donner (choisir) une de ses petite-
fille et la proposer comme concubine
au remplacant de son époux.

Ung ñu nuê·asei hlăk gơ, mtâ
sugơê·hlăk hiu·sơ̆ yao, anuih hlăk
nao ngă puk hma čiang bi mâo pô tui
djă brei êa, ba êsi, bi mâo pô mñam
kpin ao ko gơ...

Car le remplacant est jeune et
vigoureux, il a encore le visage frai
il est encore alerte, il est solide
et peut encore travailler au champ,
il veut quelqu'un qui le suite pour
porter l'eau, pour lui porter le riz,
il veut quelqu'un pour lui tisser
la ceinture et la veste (il veut une
jeune femme).

Čiang bi mâo djuê kman, čiang
...bâo, čiang bi mâo hdeh êlek bi kum,
sơi čiôh hê guê, hui čhuê hê kdiek,
...sơi ko khum lêh, mao mnut , het
sơo lêh ê-iê, ñu mnô did lo mâo
...ak ôh.

Il veut une famille nombreuse
comme le genre du mil, une famille
de mille ventres, il veut avoir des
enfants comme avant, de crainte que
la digue ne se rompe, que le sentier
ne soit plus visible, car sa femme
est vieille, ses yeux ne voient plus
son visage est flétri comme la fe...
feuille de tabac, elle ne peut plus
avoir d'enfants.

Tojah čhiăn mjê sơnăn anăn,
čiah čhuôn êkei sơnăn neh, ala ...
mñăn mơ·o knga, klei kô mrng h...ip,
ko aja lo duah mkoh mă amâo, thâo
mră snei, klei čhiăn mong dum.

Quand la femme ou l'homme sont
vieux, on fait ainsi; c'est la coutume depuis toujours depuis les ancêtres; cela on l'a pas inventé depuis
peu, depuis aujourd'hui, c'est la coutume depuis autrefois.

Klei pô ñu gao klei klei.

Klei hui gao ...

8. KLEI DÔK UNG PRONG MÔ ĐIÊT,
TODAH UNG TLE PIU AMÂO MÂO
KĐI ÔH.

102. MARIAGE D'UN HOMME ADULTE
AVEC UNE FEMME TROP JEUNE;
SI L'HOMME TROMPE SA FEM-
ME IL N'Y A PAS AFFAIRE.

Êra kdre,êra kdriêng,ka bi
tiêng ksâo,ka thâo kơ êkei hrue.

Si la femme est encore une
petite fille aux seins pas encore
formés,ne sachant pas encore désirer
l'homme;

Ksâo hlăk ktang,kuang hlăk
knia,ka thâo nga êra êdam.

si elle a encore les seins dur,
le yoni étroit,si elle ne sait pas
encore faire la jeune fille;

Ko ka ktrei,êgei ka uă,brua
knuă ka thâ.

si ses cheveux ne sont pas
coupés,ses dents pas encore sciées,
si elle ne sait pas encore rien faire

Hđeh hlăk klei lăn,pan êñan,
hlăk kuan ami ama.

si c'est encore une enfant
jouant par terre,si elle est encore
obligée de se cramponner pour grim-
per l'escalier,si elle ne peut pas
encore se séparer de ses parents,

Hlăk dih bĕng hnum,hlăk pĕm
hlăm abăn,hlăk đhăn hong ami ama.

si elle couche encore sur le
matelas,si elle s'enroule encore dans
la couverture,si elle recherche encore son père et sa mère;

Anăn čiăng kơ ñu hđeh čung ba
ue ông tu,gơ,ka thâo mă djam,pam
ei,ka thâo brei hăt êhăng,ka thâo
ong kơ ung kjar.

son époux devra attendre qu'elle grandisse,car elle ne sait pas
encore préparer la soupe,cuire le riz
elle ne sait pas encore offrir le
le tabac et le bétel,elle ne sait pas
encore désirer le mari.

Tơ ñu jơng ti êlan,kngan ti
iô,tơ ñu tle piu hiu mniê dum
moh,kđi amâo mâo ôh.

Si son mari a les jambes sur
la route et les mains dans la forêt,
s'il a des relations avec une autre
femme (mariée ou non)il n'a pas
affaire contre lui.

Jug.ma ôn du 8 déc.1942: il n'y a affaire.

9. KLEI UNG DIÊT ÑU KA THÀO
ČIANG KƠ ANIÊ,AĜ ÑU DUI
MÀO PIU AMÀO MÀU KBI ÒH.

103. DU MARI TROP JEUNE QUI NE
SAIT PAS ENCORE VOULOIR
LA FEMME; SA FEMME PEUT
AVOIR UN AMANT SANS QU'IL
Y AIT AFFAIRE.

Tuič lo čuě, êhuê lo kbua,
khian lo mã mdum.

Ce qui a disparu il faut le remplacer,ce qui est faible il faut le
renforcer; c'est la coutume de toujours remplacer.

Joh adrung lo bi hrua,joh tria
lo bi hrô,tơ djiê pô anei l o čuě
hong pô mkuăn,čiāng kơ adei tui
tluôn,amuôn ti anăp,kha bi găp djuê
ayang,hdeh mong kŏut kŏiêng dum-
mŏh.

Si les traverses sont brisées,
il faut les remplacer,si le parquet
est cassé il faut le réparer,si celui-
ci meurt il faut le remplacer par
celui-là,si l'on veut des ... qui
suivent devant ... derrière il faut
toujours prendre le (remplacant)dans
la famille du mort,même si c'est un
petit garçon haut jusqu'au genou ou
la hanche.

Hui kpur ... ,sang tlap,săp
... ênguôt.

Cela de crainte que le foyer ne
désagrège,que la maison ne tombe en
ruine,que la parole ne dise la tristesse.

... ka ... tă roh dum, ka
... koh ..., ka ... ur ktia hril
... mluk kum dru ti mtô,kmlê dah,
... kơ krua hma dru bi lač.

Si (le remplacant) ne sait pas encore nettoyer les ... du champ,
s'il ne sait pas encore couper les
touffes d'herbes,s'il ne sait pas encore crier aux perroquets ... ...
perruches,cela ne fait rien,s'il est
ignorant on l'instruira,s'il est
muet on l'expliquera par gestes,s'il
est paresseux pour travailler au
champ on lui apprendra à être laborieux.

Ñu aniê mnuih lan ênkian,êman
... ani,ñu aniê lah ... uăng,ñu
... krua klei ... .

Elle,la femme,elle sait déjà son
affaire,elle est comme l'éléphant
dressé,elle est déjà mère,elle peut
surveiller tous les travaux.

... ñu ... hiu,piu tle,dliê
... ñu ... dum koh,kha bi jăk
... brei djan,kơ bi jăk ñu
... brei kin ... kơ ... nuê gơ.

Si elle rencontre un homme ...
qu'elle attire dans la forêt pour
s'amuser,elle peut le faire sans
qu'il y ait faute,mais il faut qu'elle
prépare bien le riz et les ... ...,
qu'elle tisse bien la ceinture et la
veste pour son remplacant.

kha ñu mta dăm ktro,ko dăm êgah,
kha ñu dăm alah blu tlao hong nuê,
... amâo mâo kơyua nuê adôk diêt.

Il ne faut pas que ses yeux soient
lourds,(triste)que sa côte soit fa-
tiguée,il ne faut pas qu'elle déteste
parler de rire avec son remplacant.
Il n'y a pas affaire parce que le
remplacant est encore petit.

10. KLEI DJIĔ MDRONG LO ČUĔ BREI JING KHUA BUÔN.

Jŏh adrung hrua, joh tria hrô, djiĕ pô buôn lo bi git juĕ êngai amai adei, brei mnuih lo čuĕ, nuĕ brei brei ñu dôk ti knul, gul ko čŏng, brei ñu đong rong čing char, brei ñu duah thar yua adei amuôn, buôn sang si ayang đam.

Brei ñu dôk ti knul, gul ti ko, brei ñu lo dôk mông mô anak ayang.

Hui kpur kdang, sang tlap, sap blu ênguôt.

Hui adei tlang, yang buôn, amuôn adei bru ko hma, bra ko mđiê, hui đliê hluôt he.

Hlă dah hma kruh mtei kbâo, hma hrô mtei čik mtei ñra; kdrap ko pu, pnu yong, rong be lo bi brei, bi knô lih ama, un ana lih ami, bi tuk čoh bruh, ngă hma, pla kmun ktor.

104. DU REMPLACEMENT DU DÉCÉDÉ POUR AVOIR UN AUTRE CHEF.

Quand les traverses sont faibles il faut les renforcer, quand le paquet est cassé il faut le réparer, quand le chef du village meurt il faut convoquer les bananiers sauvages, les sœurs, pour renouer, pour donner un remplaçant, pour mettre quelqu'un sur le lit du chef, pour tenir le couvercle de la hotte à objets, pour avoir quelqu'un qui garde les plats et les gongs renflés, pour avoir quelqu'un qui commande aux habitants, comme faisait le mort.

Il faut donner quelqu'un pour rester sur le lit du chef, pour être assis sur son escabeau, pour garder la femme et les enfants du mort.

Cela de crainte que le foyer ne se désagrège, que la maison ne tombe en ruine, que la parole ne dise la tristesse.

De crainte que les frères éperviers, les génies du village, les frères et les neveux ne soient dispersés dans les champs, disséminés parmi les riz, de crainte qu'ils ne se dispersent un peu partout.

Dans le vieux champ on plante des bananiers, dans le nouveau champ on plante des ananas; au remplaçant on donnera une dot si petite soit-elle, on sacrifiera un porc pour le père (du remplaçant), une truie pour la mère, cela pour que le remplaçant travaille bien la terre, pour qu'il cultive bien le champ, pour qu'il plante le concombre et le maïs.

Les éléphants on les enchaînera de nouveau, les gongs on les reprendra, la conversation de mariage on la renouvellera.

II. KLEI NUÊ ÊKEI JING KHUA BUÔN ADÔK ĐIÊT ARĂNG BREI ANAK ÊKEI DUI DRU ÑU.

Ñu amâo thâo êbat dru bă, amâo huă mumf ñu amâo jum klei dru bi jum brei.

Ñu amâo thâo đi čư dru ktung, amâo thâo trun dhung dru doh, ñu amâo thâo beh klei dru bi lač, dru bi ntô brei.

Hđeh du bla, êra đeñ du, jua dru ka hmao arăng.

Ñu ka tul kơih, ñu ka jih dar, ñu ka anga thâo.

Ñu ndeh dru bi hriăm, êdam ntô, brah knô ana dru bi mjuăt.

Dru brei ñu ting rong, đong ting anăp, sap blu dru bi ntô lač.

Anăn anak êkei dui dru dlăng bruă buôn sang hơng ñu, ñu hlông ka thâo klông, hơng ka chôo bơng, ñu dlông arih nơw adơng ka dei thâo.

107. DU TROP JEUNE REMPLAÇANT QUI DEVIENT CHEF, LE FILS DU CHEF DOIT L'AIDER.

Celui qui ne peut marcher on le porte, celui qui ne peut pas manger on lui mâche les aliments, celui qui ne connaît pas les affaires on l'instruit.

Celui qui ne peut pas escalader la montagne on l'aide en le tirant, celui qui ne sait pas descendre la pente on l'aide en le retenant, celui qui ne sait rien on l'instruira pour qu'il sache.

Si (le remplaçant) est encore un tout jeune enfant, s'il est comme une petite fille, si l'empreinte de son pied n'égale pas encore celle des grandes personnes,

s'il n'a pas encore voyagé, s'il n'a pas encore été partout, s'il n'a encore rien vu ni rien entendu;

si ce n'est qu'un enfant il faut l'instruire, si ce n'est qu'un jeune homme il faut le conseiller, s'il est comme le petit éléphant mâle ou femelle il faut le dresser.

Il faut l'aider par derrière et par devant, il faut lui apprendre à parler et à discuter.

Pourcela le fils du chef l'aide à s'occuper des affaires du village, car il est comme le taon qui ne connaît pas encore son chemin, comme la guêpe qui ne connaît pas encore son nid, il ne sait pas encore veiller sur les habitants du village.

12. KLEI MNIÊ AMÂO MÂO ANAK MĂ MJING ANAK MNIÊ KƠ ANAK ARĂNG HLĂM SA DJUÊ, DƠ NGĂN DRAP ÑU MÂO BĔA KƠ ANAK ÑU MJING ANĂN SÔAI.

Ñu mniê plao amâo bă anak.

Anak mniê mdiê mjeh, hdeh mơng kŏut kơiêng amâo mâo, ñu duah ma he anak anai, pai anak adei, amâo mâo anak anei ñu ma anak mkuan hlăm sa djuê năn.

Amâo mâo pô gui djuh, duh êa, amâo mâo pô ngă hma brua kơ ñu.

Hui ruă hlăm ko, bo hlăm tian, amâo jak măn hua bong, amâo mâo pô kuiê brei pui, gui brei êa, tuk êsĕi brei djam, mñam brei kơiêng ao kơ ñu.

Hui dju amâo mâo pô kia, ruă amâo mâo pô kriê, djiê amâo mâo pô pĭt brei ala, kơ brei jông, hui kuê amâo mâo bŏng, bŏng amâo mâo pô ngă hui amâo mâo pô hơyua čăp brei.

Hui mâo ĕmô kbao amâo mâo pô čuh, amâo mâo pô duh dơrbrei ñu.

Anăn dơ dŏ ngăn ñu mâo lĕ kơ anak ku mjing anăn, djăp mta ra kơiêng ñu mâo bĕa anei.

106. DE LA FEMME QUI N'AYANT PAS D'ENFANTS ADOPTE UNE FILLE DE SON CLAN; À SA MORT TOUS SES BIENS REVIENDRONT À L'ENFANT QU'ELLE A ADOPTÉE.

Celle qui est stérile et ne peut pas avoir d'enfants, pas de fille (pour conserver) la semence du paddy, pas d'enfant qui lui arrive au genou ou à la ceinture, cherche à adopter l'enfant d'une soeur aînée ou celui d'une soeur cadette; si elle n'en trouve pas chez celles-ci elle ira chez d'autres, chez des familles de même clan qu'elle.

Cela parce qu'elle n'a personne pour aller chercher du bois ou puiser de l'eau, pour faire le champ et travailler pour elle;

parce qu'elle craint que si elle a mal au ventre ou à la tête, si n'a plus d'appétit, il n'y ait personne pour lui faire du feu, transporter l'eau, lui cuire le riz et les légumes, lui tisser des jupes et des vestes;

parce qu'elle craint, si elle tombe malade, de n'avoir personne pour la garder et la soigner, si elle meurt, de n'avoir personne lui fermer les yeux et lui attacher les pieds, pour lui élever les poteaux funéraires et lui fabriquer un cercueil; parce qu'elle craint de n'avoir personne pour l'envelopper (dans une natte ou une couverture);

parce qu'elle craint de n'avoir personne pour abattre les boeufs et les buffles qu'elle possède, personne pour creuser sa tombe et l'ensevelir.

Pour cela tous les biens qu'elle possède elle les laissera à l'enfant qu'elle aura ainsi adoptée et à qui reviendra tout l'héritage.

Bi tơdah anak ñu mjing anăn
amâo jak čoh brua ngă hma,kơ ñu,
dju amâo kiă,rua amâo kriê,amâo
jak duh min chăn mkra kơ ñu,tơ
puk tŏah,ênah mdê,djam blê bal
anak ñu bơng hjăn,tơdah djiê ñu
amâo anak ñu čăp,kmăp amâo dơr,kut
amâo čŏng,bơng amâo mâo pô ngă,
rua duam amâo ñu mdrao,dơ ngăn
drăp ami ama ñu mâo,amâo ñu dưi
dưn ôh,ñu wit mlun,trunmtăh sa
dah pok amâo mâo ôh kơ ñu, ñu trun
que hđai.

bi tơdah ñu dru ñuh biă ñu
dưn ngăn.

Mais si l'enfant adoptive ne
travaillepas bien pourelle (sa mère
adoptive),si elle ne fait pas bien
le champ ,si quand(sa mère) est malade elle ne s'occupe pas d'elle et
ne la soigne pas,si elle ne fait pas
bien les sacrifices rituels,si elle
abandonne le champ et la cabane,si
elle mange ailleurs les légumes dou
et acides,si quand sa mère adoptive
meurt elle ne l'enveloppe pas et
n'ensevelit pas bien sa dépouille,
si elle ne lui élève pas les poteaux
funéraires et ne lui fait pas fabriquer un beau cercueil,qu'elle ne lui
a pas donné les soins néanmoins quer
elle était malade,

elle ne pourra hériter de tous
les biens que possèdent ses parents
adoptifs,qu'elle s'en ira toute nu,
sans rien amporter, elle n'aura pas
droit même pas une pièce de ses
parents, elle devra quitter la maison sans rien.

Mais si elle s'est occupé un
peu de sa mère adoptive,si elle l'a
aidée un peu, elle pourra hériter
une petite part.

I3. MNIÊ PLAO MÃ ANAK MNIÊ, JUÊ ÊNGAI MJING ANAK ÑU:

Ñu yang amâo brei bã anak mniê,
amâo thiê anak êkei,yang amâo brei
anak kơ ñu.

Ñu duah mã anak amai,pai anak
adei,amâo mâo tơnei ñu duah mã tơ-
dih,mjing kơ anak pô ðô phun.

Hui amâo jăk kơ amâo bơ asei,
amâo jăk kơ amâo bơ tian,hui amâo
bi man hua bơng,hui êsei amâo mâo
pô be,êa amâo mâo pô gui,pui amâo
pô răm,hui amâo mâo pô bïu hrăm
mbït.

Čiăng bi mâo pô kia brei jơng,
krông brei kngan,čiăng bi mse si
anak kõin mơng tian prŏč pô.

Hui amâo mâo pô knă êsei,amâo
... ei jơm,hui amâo mâo pô mñam
... ao.

... bi mâo brei pô kpit ală,
... brei jơng,tơdah djiê ñu čăp,kmap
... kut ñu čông brei,bơng ngã
... yua čăp brei.

... anân duh ... til hruh tlang,prang
... ai,dum do ngăn aê aduôn dum
... kre diêt,dum ngăn
... go hưng,bưng hua čeh yang
... ơng gui,kung hrue,kbiê ênin,djăp
... ra ênăc,bha ñu sơai.

IQ7. DE LA FEMME STÉRILE QUI ADOPTE UNE FILLE DE SOEURS OU DE PARENTÉS.

Celle à qui les divinités ne
donnent ni filles ni garcons,celle
qui ne peut pas avoir d'enfants,

peut prendre l'enfant de sa soeur
aînée ou de sa soeur cadette,si elle
n'en trouve ici elle n'aura qu'à
aller en chercher ailleurs,et l'enfant qu'elle adoptera deviendra son
propre enfant,comme s'il était de
sa couche .

Cela parce qu'ellecraint qu'ayant
mal à la Tête ou au ventre,etant
souffrante et ne pouvant plus se
nourrir,il n'y ait personne pour lu
préparer le riz,pour lui porter de
l'eau et lui faire du feu,personne
à qui adresser la parole ;

parce qu'elle veut quelqu'un
pour guider ses pas,pour la souteni
par le bras,parce qu'elle veut un
enfant qui soit pour elle comme
l'enfant sorti de son ventre;

parce qu'elle craint de n'avoir
personne pour lui cuire le riz,pour
lui préparer les légumes,pour lui
tisser les jupes et les vestes;

parce qu'elle veut quelqu'un
qui lui ferme les yeux(à sa mort),
qui lui attache les pieds,qui ense-
velisse sa dépouille,lui élve des
poteaux funéraires et lui fabrique
une bière,quelqu'un qui l'enveloppe
(dans un suaire).

Pour cela,tous les bols en forme
de nid d'épervier,les cuvettes en f
forme de nid de vautour,tous les
biensque lui ont laissés les ancêtres reviendront à(sa fille adoptive),les petites soucoupes,les petits
bols en cuivre,tous les menus objets
les marmites fêlées,les écuelles
pour manger le riz,les jarres dans
les fosses,les chaudrons venant du
pays Hrôe,les marmites venant du
pays Ênin,tous les biens qu'il y a
dans la maison reviendront à sa fill
adoptive(à sa mort);

Anăn čiăng mjing kơ ñu anak
miê mdiê mjeh,čiăng kơ ñu hdeh
ông kơut kơiêng,hui tuic̆ djuê ,
hui ŋa.

pour cela elle adopte une fille,
pour conserver la semence du riz,
pour avoir une enfant qui lui arrive
au genou ou à la taille,parce qu'
elle craint que sa famille,ne dis-
paraisse,que sa race ne s'éteigne.

I4. KLEI DJIÊ ÊKEI AMÂO ČUÊ REI, ÊNUAH DUAH LUIČ, WIT KNONG WANG KGA.

Tar dê kơ dlông, Yông kơ gu, tar yu kma ngê.

Djiê mnuih bhiăn čuê, nuê brei klei bhiăn ma mdum.

Si anei le, djiê mnuih amâo ñu čuê, nuê amâo ñu brei, adei amuôn ñu amâo ñu čuê.

Joh adrung amâo ñu lo hrua, joh tria amâo ñu lo hrô, djiê pô anei amâo ñu lo čuê hong mnuih mkuăn.

Ya be klei wăng beh, kneh joh, soh nao hriê.

Ngă un rih gơ amâo čăm, nga bao rih gơ amâo koh, nga soh klei deh êlan gơ amâo kpih mdrao deh.

Thâo dah dju gơ amâo jăk kiă, nga amâo jăk krie, mâo kpiê êsei gơ mâo mdrao deh.

Thâo dah gơ mâo êmô kbao gơ mih, amâo gơ koh mdrao be.

Thâo dah msat kđang, bông blang khru, thâo dah gơ amâo jăk kơu kơyăm, kam guam be, anăn mnuih amâo ñu čuê, nuê amâo ñu brei kơ gơ.

Ñu amâo hơui kơ hma kpuh, kơ ñih mơhiêng, amâo ñu hơiêng hơui brei kơ gơ.

I08. DU NON-REMPLACEMENT DE L'ÉPOUX DÉCÉDÉ; LA FAMILLE DU DÉFUNT PERD SA PART D'HÉRITAGE.

Partout on place les tirants su les pannes, partout de l'Ouest à l'Est quand une personne meurt la coutume dit de la remplacer, de donner un remplaçant, c'est la coutume de toujours remplacer ce qui a disparu, de toujou combler les vides.

Mais si au lieu de cela, on ne remplace pas la personne décédée, si on ne donne pas de remplaçant, si on ne veut pas renouer avec les neveux du défunt;

si on ne répare pas les solives brisées, si on ne refait pas le plancher abîmé, si on ne remplace pas par un autre celui qui est mort;

si on ne répare pas la binette ébréchée, si on remplace pas le silex brisé, si on va et vient inutilement,

alors que les porcs ont été abattus, que les buffles ont été sacrifié (pour les funérailles du défunt), alors que les fautes des enfants ont été absoutes par un sacrifice,

alors que le malade a été bien soigné, qu'il avait été bien surveillé, qu'il n'avait manqué ni d'alcool ni de riz,

alors qu'on n'a été avare ni de boeufs ni de buffles, qu'on a sacrifié ce qu'il fallait pour soigner le malade,

alors que le (tumulus du) tombeau ne s'est point crevassé, que le cercueil ne s'est point soulevé, que la veuve a fait convenablement le deuil, qu' elle a respecté tous les interdits,

pourquoi donc n'y a-t-il personne pour renouer, pourquoi ne donne-t-on pas de remplaçant à la veuve ?

Mais si on (la famille du mort) n'a aucune pitié pour le champ abandonné (la veuve), pour la vieille souche, si on n'a aucune pitié pour le veuve,

Anăn kir duah ênuah hrui kơ
lu amâo mâo.

La famille du mort ne pourra pas
prétendre à sa part d'héritage.

Wĭt mă knŏng wăng diêt,kga
liêt, hna kniêt đing tiông,klit
jua leh anăn dhŏng kri dum năn yŏh.

Elle aura seulement droit à une
petite binette,à un petit coupe-coupe,
à une arbalète ordinaire avec un
arquois,à une seule sandale,à un
petit couteau à tailler et ce sera
tout.

Pkhan 27 du 6 févr.1926 : restitution de la part dits
"ênuah-duah".

15. KLEI AMÂO DUĬ BI LUI UNG MÔ.

Hbu hbiê, mniê êkei, klei bôh di ñu čiăng bi khăp u mă hdăng găp di ñu.

Añu di ñu bi lông, kông bi liñ, kông adih kơ anei, kông êkei kơ mniê, kông mniê kơ êkei, kơ krei asei hjan di ñu.

Aseh amâo mâ pô mgô trao, kbao klei, êkei mniê amâo mâo pô mgô kông añu.

Ôman di ñu brei mnut kơ êa bi tling, čing yuôl, brei ăt kuôl ka bhiăt kpung ung mô.

Lui kơ êdei, aguah ngă čim ơhi êkei, hrue čim bhi mniê, kma hlam čhang diiê lui lo duah klei mkuăn.

Lui čim lo kdăt, s'mặt lo kdăt, ala ư d'a lo duah klei mkuăn.

Pơk mô tơl djiê, gai kpiê tơl h, tông knah tơl arăng mă ti ṇan.

Ụi blu hlam sa klei, hrue ... ... pơ wang lu lo duah klei

109. DE L'INDISSOLUBILITÉ DE L'UNION.

Ils s'aiment, ils se désirent, l'homme et la femme, ils ont accepté de vivre ensemble.

Ils ont échangé le collier de perle, ils ont échangé le bracelet celui-ci à celui-là, le bracelet de la femme à l'homme, le bracelet de l'homme à la femme, ils l'ont échangé tout seul, librement.

Le cheval on ne l'oblige à porter le collier, le buffle à accepter la corde, l'homme et la femme personne ne les a obligés à accepter le bracelet et le collier.

Ils ont demandé au chef de l'entraver l'éléphant, de suspendre les gongs, de sembler le contrat, (maintenant) ils sont comme l'arc et le fût de l'arbalète, ils sont mari et femme.

De crainte que plus tard ils ne fassent comme l'oiseau mâle le matin, comme l'oiseau femelle le soir qu'en rentrant dans le bois ils ne cherchent une affaire.

De crainte qu'en frappant (le bâton) ne bondisse, qu'en cinglant (le fouet) ne rebondisse, de crainte qu'en chantant l'homme ne cherche une affaire différente.

Il faut rester avec sa femme jusqu'à la mort, il faut boire l'alcool jusqu'à ce qu'il soit insipide, il faut frapper le gong (sans arrêt) jusqu'à ce qu'un autre prenne le mailloche.

De crainte que la nuit l'homme ne parle d'une façon et le jour d'une autre, qu'en tournant le dos il pense autrement.

anei le đei mtă mtăn băn
kuai êya,aguah pla čơl êla buič
he .

On l'a bien conseillé de crainte
qu'il nefouille pas le sol pour
chercher le gingembre,ou'il n'arrache le soir ce qu'il a planté le
matin.

amâo djo drung drang,yang biê
adiê nga,amâo djo klei ruă duam ,
dih ñu čiăng bi lui troh dong êlong
thu ,amâo gu kăt.

Ce ne sont pasles tempêtes,ou
le Génie du Ciel,ce n'est pas la
maladie oui les séparent,ils veulent
se quitter,tout à coup ,sans motif.

Di ñu gao kung,gao knông,săp
kông sah mdrong di ñu gao.

Ils passent outre le signal
"Kung" et le signal "knông",ils
passent outre la parole du chef
(oui les avait instruits).

Pui bong êgao troh,êa doh mlai
knông,săp kông sah mdrong bi
kuôl di ñu gao.

Comme l'incendie oui franchit
le précipice,comme la crue oui franchit le barrage,ils passent outre
la conversation et la parole du chef

Tơdah nmiê duah klei,êkei duah k
di,pơa êra bi kblăm he ñu trong,
nah jhong bi hlah,dah blu bi
mñil he ñu,bi kjar ăt jak čung si
ênih,ung rua hi jak due nao kơ
hma.

S'ils cherchent à créer des
histoires ils seront punis,comme
est puni le chien gourmand avec
l'aubergine (chaude),comme est puni
celui oui est insolent avec le chef,
car toujours le mari doit suivre la
femme,toujours il doit l'accompagner
au champ.

anei le,mta soh,boh blăt,
angañ amâo maô .

S'ils agissent ainsi,il n'y a
pas affaire très grave.

ñu si băng mbah,yah băng
, kông buh kơ.

Di ñu gao čiăt djo hda,gao
djo krong,gao săp kông sah
mdrong kuôl,maô kđi khua kơ di ñu.

Mais ils ont la bouche sciée
largement,si le bracelet qui était
scellé est ouvert,s'ils passent outre
le signal "tiêt" et sont blessés par
des fléchettes,s'ils passent outre
le signal"pla" et sont blessés par
des lancettes,s'ils passent outre
la parole du chef et la conversation
du mariage,alors il y aura affaire
entre le chef et eux.

Jug.no 34 du 35 juin 1926 : divorce accordé.
Jug.no 6 du 13 juin 1929 : 15 kơ + kpih à l'époux abandonné.

I6. KLEI DÔK UNG MÔ BI LIH LEH KÔNG AMÂO LO-JING BI DÔK.

Êkei bi kjiê, mniê tra, anak êdam êra êmuh.

Aseh amâo mgô trao, kbao klei, êkei mniê amâo bi mgô săp kbông. ôh.

Leh kbloh hui mlam di ih blu sa klei, hruê di ih blu sa săp, wir rông anăp di ih lo blu klei mdê.

... anei lah leh ih u hdjŭng, ...ung kla, ih mô kông krah arăng, ... kơ kbloh le ih jik lo alah, ... êmuh, mruh hruê mlam mkutn ih ... lo ciang dôk.

... anei ơñu arăng bi lông, kông bi ... kông ih kơ arăng, kông arăng ... ih .

Ihu ana, agha dŏng, ... hông kpiê ... arăng brei.
... aura arăng pu, pau yong, ... ra arăng brei soai.
... lông brei dăm ti gu, añu ... ti tila, anei ama arăng hriêêmun ... ih ciang moh kơ mô kông ... añuê ih mă tu, hmei ... blu, hmei amâo brei ôh ti ... ih, hui kơ kbloh dih ih ... pô êlan mgô ih.

... êkei ih amâo lo jing d ... arăng, kbul ih mô kdi

IIᵒ. DE LA NON-CONSOMMATION DU MARIAGE.

L'homme et la femme, le jeune homme et la jeune fille ont été consultés.

On oblige le cheval à porter le bât, le buffle à accepter la corde au museau, mais on n'oblige pas l'homme et la femme à se marier, de crainte qu'ils ne parlent d'une façon la nuit, et d'une autre le jour, decrainte qu'après avoir tourné le dos ils n'agissent autrement.

Aujourd'hui ils consentent librement, l'un accepte le bracelet de l'autre, sans songer que plus tard ils pourront être paresseux pour biner, fatigué pour défricher, sans penser qu'un autre jour ou un autre mois ils ne voudront plus vivre ensemble.

Maintenant ils ont changé le collier, ils ont changé le bracelet, le bracelet de l'homme à la femme et le bracelet de la femme à l'homme.

La dot a été donnée, le porc mangé l'alcool bu.

Les biens ont été donnés, la dot, l'argent tout cela on l'a donné.

Le bracelet a posé par terre, le collier sur le parquet, les parents et les témoins étaient présents "si vous voulez la femme prenez-le librement, le bracelet posé par terre, nous sommes vos témoins, nous ne vous obligerons pas à prendre de crainte que plus tard vous ne nous reprochiez de vous avoir contraint de l'accepter.

"Mais si vous l'acceptez librement et qu'ensuite vous refusez de demeurer ensemble, alors vous serez coupables et il y aura affaire entre les autres(famille de la femme ou de l'époux) et vous.

... Méthode litolite : "Si un homme la fille ne prenne pas encore ... , ... le prix d'achat de la femme qu'il avait donné il ...

17. KLEI ANUIH DŎK KƠ TOL
MÂU ANAK ÑU DUE HIU, AMÂO
ÑU RÔNG BA KƠ ANAK .

Puk blia, hma blung, ung nah ñei
plei nah dih.

Ñu djam sang anei, êsei sang
adih, ñu wit kơ krai, ñu lai kơ tluôn,
ñu wit kơ amuôn adei ñu.

Puk amâo ñu čua, hma amâo ñu
nga, brun klei amâo ñu čhin, amâo
min kơ ku ktông, amâo ñu rông ba
kơ anak ñu.

anâo krhul ñu.

III. DE CELUI QUI ABANDONNE
SA FEMME DÈS QU'ELLE A UN
ENFANT ET NE S'OCCUPE
PLUS D'EUX.

Celui qui n'a plus de maison,
ni de champ, qui se tient d'un côté,
et laisse sa femme de l'autre;

celui qui mange les légumes
d'une maison et le riz dans une
autre, qui rentre chez lui, qui revien
en arrière, qui retourne dans sa famille;

celui qui ne construit pas la
cabane, qui ne fait pas le champ, qui
pense même pas à poser des pièges,
qui ne s'occupe pas de sa femme et
de ses enfants,

celui-là est coupable.

18. KLEI ALAH AMÂO NGÂ PŬK HMA KƠ MÔ ANAK, KMANG DUAH HIU DÔK RUNG.

Mnuih pŭk kba, hma alah, jah druôm amâo kriäng.

Pŭk amâo čua, hma amâo ngä, bruä knuä amâo duh min.

Djam sang enei, êsei sang adih, ti ñu nao ti dih, ti ñu nao ti däm.

Ti hua ti ñu duah däm, ti mnăm ti ñu duah dih, ti ñu nao ti jih thun mlan.

Kah rung amâo mâo bưng hua, rah rung amâo mâo sang dôk, mnuih amâo mâo anôk dih pit.

Mđung si Y-Tria, ra si Y-Run, mnuih amâo mâo phun êduk.

Ñu rông mô amâo mơak, rông anak amâo si... ñu kmang duah ngä êdam hŏng mniê mkuăn.

Ñu pit amâo thâo mdih, dih amâo thâo kgu, ami ama ñu blu kăn ñu thâo..., mnuih amâo lo dui thâo mkhu...

Ñu amâo lo thâo min kơ tien..., knga ñu amâo thâo lo kpu ngei klei črit čhin, hin tap.

... kthul ñu, amâo kdi arăng ñu.

112. DES PARESSEUX QUI NE S'OCCUPENT PAS DE LEUR FEM-NE ET DE LEURS ENFANTS ET NE FONT QUE VAGABANDER.

Celui qui est paresseux pour construire la cabane, pour faire le champ, pour abattre les arbres et débricher;

celui qui ne construit pas la cabane, qui ne fait pas le champ, qui pense jamais à travailler;

celui qui mange les légumes dans cette maison et le riz dans cette autre, qui se couche où il va, qui passe la nuit où il se trouve ;

celui qui passe la nuit où il mange, qui se couche où il boit, qui passe des mois et des années partout où il va;

celui qui vagabonde et n'a pas de calebasse pour manger, qui vagabonde et n'a pas de maison demeurer, qui n'a rien pourqu coucher;

celui qui vagabonde comme Y-Tria qui est gourmand comme Y-Run, qui est comme celui qui n'a ni pied, ni tête;

celui qui ne s'occupe pas de sa femme ni de ses enfants, qui ne cherche qu'à faire le jeune homme avec les autres femmes;

celui qui s'endort et ne se réveille plus, qui se couche et ne se lève plus, qui n'écoute pas ses parents qui le conseillent, que personne ne peut plus corriger;

celui qui ne pense pas à la famine, dont les oreilles ne retiennent rien, qui ne cherche pas à sortir de la pauvreté et de la misère,

celui-là est coupable et il y a affaire entre les autres et lui.

19. KLEI BI MTAH UNG MÔ.

113. DES EMPÊCHEMENTS AU MARIAGE.

Tơ joh adrung ñu lo bi hrua,
joh tria dkuih ,tơ djiê mnuih ñu
sue,êhuê ñu lo kbua ñu lo mtă mdum
rei.

Si les traverses sont cassées
on les répare,si le parquet est cassé
on le répare,si quelqu'un meurt on
renoue,ce qui est faible on le consolide,il faut toujours remplacer.

Anăn ñu hung klang,hang klit,
ñu mđhit tiơn tiê ,hui kpur kđang,
sang tlăp,saăp blu ênguôt,hui amâo
pô ba kniêng,ciêng rông mô anak ayang,
ayang.

Elle(la veuve)désire les os(un
remplaçant),elle préfère la viande,
elle veut de tout son ventre et de
tout son coeur,de crainte que le foyer ne se désgrège,que la maison ne
tombe ne ruine,que la parole ne dise
la tristesse,de crainte de n'avoir
personne à porter surla hanche ,de
crainte qu'il n'y ait personne pour
s'occuper des enfants de la veuve,
des enfants du mort.

anăn tăoh ñu čiê,êhuê ñu kbua
dam bi brei,adei ma kơng,bi mâo pô
rông hđeh ôlak,rông ngăn drăp si
đăp dum, bi pưk dam duah kblang,
ang kruh,bi êguh wơr dam ksue.

Pour cela le lien rompu il faut
renouer,ce qui est sur le point de
casser il faut le consolider, les
beaux-frères doivent donner le(remplaçant)et accepter le bracelet pour
avoir quelqu'un qui garde les enfan,
qui garde les biens comme avant,
pour que la cabane ne tombe pas,
pour que la clôture ne soit pas
arrachée.

i pô pla,amĕ pô ba,ñu
uah čim ơhi êkei,hrue
ơ,kna hlăm dliê ñu lo
uah klei mkuan.

La mère(conçoit(l'enfant),le pè..
le porte,cependant ils(les beaux-
frères) font comme l'oiseau mâle
le matin,comme l'oiseau femelle le
soir,quand ils rentrent dans la forêt ils agissent autrement.

guơh ñu pla,êla ñu buič,mlam
ñu brei,hrue ñu sua,êla ñu sue.

Le matin ils plantent,le soir
ils arrachent ;la nuit ils donnent
(le remplaçant),le matin ils le
reprennent.

ñu klei,hrue sa săp,
dô.

La nuit ils parlent d'une façon
le jour ils parlent d'une autre dès
qu'ils tournent le dos ils agissent
différemment.

trong duah mdĕč,aurĕč mdar
r kup dang.

Ils tournent sans cesse comme
l'aubergine et lepiment(dans la marmite),ils coupent tout de l'intérieur
à l'extérieur(dans le mauvais sens).

ñu kač kniă,kia kdrang,kbông
pah dut,kut kdja ñu lo
klei mrêo.

Ils dessinent de belles figures
(font de belles promesses),mais les
paroles sacrées ils les nient,ils
cherchent de nouvelles histoires en
chantant.

kŏng knue awak ñu mdăp, săp
ñu bi hgăm, lo ara anei lĕ ñu lo
wơr bit wit ma kpin, wơrbit wit ma
ao, ñu gao sah mdreng, săp ayong
adei ñu gao, ding ti khŏng, kŏng ti
khgan, êlan pô blu, pô kuôl ñu gao
soai.

Anăn uñô kdi arăng kơ ñu.

Avant ils ... cachaient la cuillère, ils cachaient la parole, aujour
d'hui ils oublient de prendre la ...
ceinture, de prendre la veste, (ils
ne réfléchissent pas), ils passent
outre la parole du chef, ... outre
la parole des frères, ils passent
outre le bracelet au poignet, le
témoin, le pipeau à la bouche, ils
passent outre tout cela.

Pour cela il y a affaire entre
les autres(veuve, témoin, chef) et
eux (les beaux-frères).

20 . KLEI TLE PIU .   114. DE L'ADULTÈRE.

Lam ñu ñu,ɓiu ñu kma,ñu duah
hœa mô sah mdrong,mô ayong adei
ñu tle.

Ñu nga sang pong,ñu dong
ane,tle čhai klei.

Êman ñu tle tling,čing ñu
tle yuôl,kuôl kă, klei ñu bi mta
mtăn leh.

Ñu prong gruh,knhuh ai,ñu
mlei čư mtâo,ñu bi mâo mô sah
mdrong.

Ñu plah čiang kơ bha,sua
čiang kơ duĭ,

Asen ñu sua,mla ñu plah,mô
sah mdrong ñu mmiă.

ñu koh ku êman,ñu čăm mngan
ji ñu duah hœa mô sah mdrong.

ɓman mâo kdi arang kơ ñu.

Celui qui entre dans les appar-
tements,qui pénètre dans la chambre,
qui frôle la femme du riche,la femme du frère,qui la prend en se cach-
chant;

celui qui cherche un coin pro-
pice,qui attire la femme pour lui
parler à voix basse;

celui qui entrave l'éléphant
ou suspend les gongs en se cachant,
qui fait une conversation secrète,
qui s'entend avec la femme d'autrui

celui qui se croit puissant,
qui se croit fort et audacieux,qui
franchit la montagne escarpée,qui
cherche à posséder la femme du rich

celui qui veut que la femme de
autres soit à lui,qui veut qu'elle
tombe en son pouvoir;

celui qui s'empare de la corne
de rhinocéros,de la défense d'éléphant,qui s'empare de la femme du
riche;

celui qui coupe la queue del'
éléphant,qui brise le bol à impôt,qui
touche la femme du riche,

celui-là est coupable et il y
a affaire entre les autres et lui

PUNITION.-Jug.no 46 et 47 des 4 et 5 oct.1936 : 5500 + 6 ko + kpih au
            conjoint trompé.
         Jug.no 52 du 7 nov. 1936 : 5500 + 6 ko + kpih.
         Jug.nos 9 et 10 du 2 mars : 1937 : 5500 + 6 ko + kpih.
         Jug.no 20 du 5 mai 1937 : 5500 + 6 ko + kpih.
         Jug. du 5 août 1938 : 6 ko + kpih un ko.
         Jug. du 4 oct. 1938 : 5500 .
         Cf. Code Hittite :"Si un homme une femme dans les monts saisit,
c'est un crime de l'homme et il meurt.mais si dans la maison il la saisit,de même la femme a péché; la femme meurt.Si l(homme (mari) de la
femme les trouve il les peut tuer;de punition pour lui il n'y a pas"
    (9).

21. KLEI BI TLE PIU HONG MNIÊ LEH KÂU UNG, LEH ANAN ÊKEI LEH KÂU KÔ BOH.

kdi amâo lo blu lu, hiu taih,
êmeh êman ti kdrun soai.

Kdi amâo lo blu khăng tăng kraih,

kdi amâo lo dleh yaih pui arôk.

kdi bơng amâo lo dleh kdah,
mmah klañ, kdi amâo lo ngăñ blu.

Êbuh leh mniê, djiê leh êkei,
chiăm ao, dao kgă, ngăn lă liê leh
lĕh mă leh.

Êkei leh giê, mniê tĭe, êmeh
êman leh păn leh ti ku, piu leh mă
lĕh hlăm anih añuê.

Kô ksua, knga kuih, di ñu mniê
duah klei êkei duah kdi.

a čô leh mâo kuiêt, sa čô leh
mâo ung kjar mơh, tu mdê tok mdê bi
liêô, mdê piêô mdê bi gui, tu lui
mdê ung mdê bi đu ma, mdê mô mdê
bi đu mê.

Di ñu ngă gơ ti anăp abăn song,
ti rong djuh ktu, piu tle, ung dôk,
piu tle mô dôk mơh.

Anăn ami mtô amâo sah, ama dah
amâo gut, dja ding wŭt tơl djiê asei
rô.

Anăn soh di ñu .

115. DE L'ADULTÈRE ENTRE HOMME ET FEMME DÉJÀ MARIÉS.

Il est unitile de parler beaucoup, d'aller plus loin parce que le
rhinocéros et l'éléphant ils se sont
désaltérés au même endroit.

Il est inutile de parler fort,
de discuter à haute voix;

car l'affaire est claire, la bro-
se est répandue.

Pour manger on n'a pas besoin
de broyer, pourmâcher on n'a pas besoin de memuer, la langue, pour régle
cette affaire on n'a pas besoin de
crier très fort.

La femme et l'homme ont avoué
le turban, la veste, le sabre, le coupe-coupe, toutes sortes d'objets on
les a saisis (comme preuve).

On est sûr qu'ils sont allés
se cacher dans la forêt.

L'homme a accepté la décision
du bâton du juge (a avoué), la femme
avoué l'adultère, l'éléphant et le
rhinocéros ont été saisis par la
queue, de même on les a surpris sur
les lieux, sur le fait.

Leur tête est comme celle d
porc-épic, leurs oreilles comme cel
de la souris (ils ignorants), ils on
cherché le mal, la faute,

celui-ci a déjà une femme,
celle-là a déjà un mari, chacun sa
hutte et sa corbeille.

Celle qui a trompé son mari
paiera une amende à son mari, celui
qui a trompé sa femme paiera une
de à sa femme.

Car ils se sont cachés en
une couverture devant et un fagot
dans le dos, celle-ci a un mari et
l'a trompé, celui-là a une femme et
il l'a trompée.

Leursparents leur ont donné
des conseils mais ils ne les ont p
écoutés, ils aiment jouer de la flû
jusqu'à leurmort.

Pour cela ils sont coupable

22. KLEI MNIÊ TLE HIU, MSAT UNG ÑU KA LUI.

II6. DE LA VEUVE COUPABLE D'ADULTÈRE QUAND LA TOM-BE DE SON MARI N'EST PAS ENCORE ABANDONNÉE.

Msat hlăk kue, ktue hlăk mbuĕn hlăk dôk hovôn atâo yang.

La tombe n'est pas encore couverte le tumulus n'est pas encore achevé, on s'occupe encore de l'âme du mort,

Msat kđang he, bồng blang kbru, kơyua ñu amâo jăk kơu kơyăm kăm guam.

et le tombeau s'ouvre et le cercueil se soulève, parce que la veuve ne fait pas bien le deuil,

Ñu buk amâo jăk rang, kang amâo kpung, ñu amâo jăk kăm kơ ung kjar ñu bru mđiê djiê esei.

parce qu'elle ne laisse pas tomber ses cheveux en désordre, parce qu'elle ne pose pas le menton dans sa main, parce qu'elle ne fait pas bien le deuil pour son mari défunt, pourri comme le grain de paddy.

Ñu ktu dua, êbla tlâo, piu êtuh êbâo ñu tle.

Elle se couche avec tout le monde avec deux ou trois, avec cent ou mille amants.

Hat sa anung ñu tlah đung dua, hra sa anung ñu tlah đung mtlâo, piu êtuh êbâo ñu čiang.

Le paquet de tabac elle le partage en deux (une part au mort, une part à son amant), le paquet de sel elle le partage en trois, en cent, en mille parties, car elle veut deux, trois, cent, mille amants.

Ñu êkei bi hiu, piu tle, dliê se hgĕ h, ñu bi nao.

Elle séduit les hommes, elle couche avec les maris, elle les emmène dans la forêt,

Msat dôk kue, ktue dôk dja, brah hong tâo yong ka bi leh, ko mtei hđi ka pla, mnu ada ka mphiơr, ka wĕt, ka lui msat ôđng.

quand le tombeau est à peine couvert, quand le tumulus est encore entretenu, quand on n'a pas encore fini de s'occuper du mort, quand le banal et la patate n'ont pas encore été plantés (sur le tumulus), quand le poussin n'a pas encore été lâché (dans le fossé), quand le mort n'est pas encore oublié, quand le tombeau n'est pas encore abandonné.

anăn soh ñu, mâo kđi găp djuê yang ung ñu kơ ñu.

Pour cela elle est coupable et il y a affaire entre la famille du mort et elle (la veuve infidèle).

msat oun ñu ngă brei yang hong yơng, leh anăn ngăn tlâo ko an brei ênua ba brei kđi.

Si la famille du mort est pauvre elle lui sacrifiera un porc de deux piastres et lui paiera une amende de douze piastres.

msat mdrong ñu tuh hong kbao, anăn ngăn năm ko ñu brei.

Si la famille du mort est riche elle lui fera le sacrifice d'un buffle et lui paiera une amende de vingt piastres.

23. KLEI ꞨNIÊ DJIÊ UNG ꞨU LO DÔK UNG MꞨÂO, ꞨSAT UNG ꞨU DÔK DJA, HiÄ DAH GAP DJUÊ AYANG UNG ꞨU BREI ꞨU DÔK UNG AKUAN DI ꞨU AꞨÂO MÂO ꞨNUIH ꞨUÊ BREI.

II7. DE LA VEUVE QUI SE REMARIE AVANT L'ABANDON DU TOMBEAU, SI LA FAMILE DU DÉFUNT NE PEUT LUI DONNER DE REMPLACANT ELLE PEUT L'AUTORISER À PRENDRE UN AILLEURS.

Bru mdiê,djiê asei,klei tuič, adei tui tluôn,amâo/ lo mâo,amuôn ti anăp amâo lo mâo.

Le riz est pourri,le corps est en putréfaction,tout est bien fini, de petit frère(du mort)il n'y en a pas,de neveu(fils de la soeur du du mort)il n'y en a pas(pour remplacer le mort).

Leh bi git leh hong amai, bi čhai leh hong adei,klei boh leh bi ꞙmuh.

Les soeursaînées (du mort)ont été consultées,les soeurscadettes ont été entendues,l'affaire du remplacement a été envisagée et résolue

ꞨNuih čuê,nuê brei,klei lo bă mduh amâo lo mâo.

Pour remplacer le mort,pourdonner unremplacant à la veuve il ne reste personne,(et la famille du mort dit à la veuve) :

Tu ih dê,todah buh kmun luh, ktơr luh,todah buh êkei buôn yu, pu ngo,ih bi mdjo mgăl,ih bi dôk mă.

"si le concombre et le maïs peuvent se reproduire tout seuls(l'homme ne le peut),si vous voyez l'homme du village de l'Ouest ou de l'Est et qu'il vous plaise,vous pouvez vous marier.

Hui kpur ih kdang,hui sang tlăp hui sap blu ênguôt.

"Cela de crainte que votre foyer ne se désagrège,que votre maison ne tombe en ruine,que la parole ne dise la désespérance,

Hui amâo mâo pô ta brei roh, koh brei bur,hui amâo mâo pô ur brei ktia hril.

" de crainte que vous n'ayez personne pour nettoyer les abords du champ,pour couper les touffes envahissantes,pour crier aux perruches et aux perroquets(qui viennent manger le riz);

Hui anak ih hia,hma mrok,sơk piêč tap,hui knap bung bai.

"de crainte votre enfant ne pleure que votre champ ne soit envahi par les herbes,que vous n'ayez plus de hottes,ni de paniers,ni de corbeille

Hui amâo mâo pô čiêm un,mtrun mnu,hui amâo mâo pô blu hong buôn sang.

"de crainte que vous n'ayez personne pour nourrir vos porcs,pour s'occuper de vos poules,de crainte que vous n'ayez personne pour parler aux habitants;

hui ôman amâo mâo pô êyun,
hlun amâo mâo pô yua, čeh tuk čeh
he amâo mâo pô jia, tu ih duah ma
ung dlăng ti ih khăp.

Hmei amâo khiĕ jŏng, krŏng
kbông, hmei amâo ⅄ mhŏng tim brei ôh.

Hmei amâo čiang kơ boh, čeh
kơ kơ i ôh, khă bi un ih mbu he msat,
m⸳⸳⸳a ngă yang, sang atâo atiêt nao
bi mnăm he, čiang bi thâo hong yang,
bi klang hong atâo, yang bi thâo,
atâo bi hmư.

Kđi amâo mâo ôh, kông bi buh
he.

"de crainte que vous n'ayez personne pour s'occuper de vos éléphant
pour commander à vos esclaves, pour
faire l'alcool dans les jarres, vous
pouvez chercher vous-même le mari
que vous désirez.

"Nous ne nous opposerons point
par la force, point par la parole,
nous ne vous empêcherons point de
choisir un mari.

"Nous ne vous chercherons point
d'affaire, nous ne demanderons pas de
réparation, mais vous ferez le sacrifice du porc sur le tombeau, le sacrifice du poulet sur la tombe du mort
vous boirez l'alcool pendant le sacrifice, pour que les génies sachent
pour que l'âme du mort sache.

"Ainsi il n'y aura pas affaire
et nous échangerons le bracelet qui
scellera notre accord."

24. KLEI PLAH UNG MÔ ARANG.

118. DE L'ENLÈVEMENT DE L'ÉPOUX OU DE L'ÉPOUSE D'AUTRUI.

Prong ghuh,mruh ai,mlai ču mtâo,.

Celui qui se croit et redoutabl et escalade la montagne escarpée;

msan sua,mla plah,ung mô sah mdrong,ayong adei ñu mmia.

celui qui s'empare de la corne de rhincérrs ou de l'ivoire de l'él phant,qui enlève la femme du riche ou du frère;

Ami mô amâo sah, ama dah amâo gur,kur klja klei amâo dun.

celui qui ne tient pas compte des conseils de sa mère et de son père,qui n'écoute pas quand on di cute des affaires en chantant;

Grän wäng ñu bi mkä,grän kgä ñu bi mmšng,ñu bi lông ai tiê;yông ñu bi êpa,eda hoh,čeh čing ñu bi mdum.

celui qui mesure le manche de la binette ou le manche de coupe-coupe,qui compare sa force(à celle du mari);

celui qui mesure la longueur de panne en brasse,celle du tirant en coudées,qui compte les jarres et l gongs,

Anänmâo kdi äräng kơ ñu prong.

celui-là est coupable et il y a affaire très graves entre eux et lui.

Tơ bun ngân näm ko,un ko kpih; bi tơ mdrong soh ngän sa boh čhar sa hoh sa kpät,kbao kpih.

Pourun (mari) pautre il pai une indemnité de six ko et un por de un ko pour le sacrifice;si le mari est riche il lui paiera une indemnité égale à la valeur d'un gong čhar une coudée et un empan de diamètre,et un buffle pour le sacrifice.

ñu suh kơ mnga tông-môŋ, ñu dlong kơ moyap,ñu hung khap kơ pô mkuän.

Et si(la femme enlevée)préf la fleur tông-môŋ,si elle préfè le panache multicolore,si elle pr fère son ravisseur(à son époux),

Đơ ngăn čhiên ba, kre điêt,
ngăn điêt duôt, sơk drai, hai bô,
kđô kđung, anung điêt prong, čeh
yang bang gri, djuê aseh mjeh êmô kbao
un ti gu, mnu ti dlông, kông mngăn
bha sđai.

tous les biens, les tasses, les
petits bols en cuivre, tous les menus
objets, les hottes jarai, les corbeil
les, les sacs, les musettes, les pl
petits paquets, les jarres grandes
et petites, les chevaux, les boeufs
et les buffles, les porcs sous la
maison, les poules sur l'avancée,
les bracelets et les colliers, la
vaisselle, tout cela restera à celui
qui porte l'arbalète et le carquois
(au mari).

Pơk knua, hma mkă, hra dơng găn.

On évaluera les maisons, on
mesurera les champs en longueur et
en largeur.

Tơ čim điêt kmong, tơ čim
prong knut, hlô mut hlô rang ki.

On enveloppera les petits morceaux de viande dans un cornet, on
enfilera les gros sur une broche, et
on comptera le nombre de têtes de
cerfs et de sangliers(tués par le
mari délaissé).

Tơ hlô điêt kđi điêt, tơ hlô
prong kđi prong, tơ sah mdrong arăng
'lang.

S'il a tué peu de gibier l'indemnité sera petite, s'il a tué beau
coup elle sera grande(cela s'il est
pauvre); s'il est riche on appréciera

ULBER.- Jug.no 40 du 4 sept.1936 : 10$00 + 12 ko + kpih.
Jug.no 21 du 4 août 1936 : 5$00 + 6 ko + kpih.
Jug.no 55 du 7 oct. 1937 : 5$00 + 6 ko + kpih.
Jug. du 4 octobre 1938 : 5$00 .

25. KLEI ANIÊ SA AMI BI PLAH UNG ADEI AMAI

Nu mnia mrai hrah, plah mrai čam,
plah go djam esei, ung adei amai hưi
ah.

Ung adei, plei amai, ñu plah čiang
y bha, ñu sun čiang ko đui, lui koh bih
ung, arang êgar schan.

Nga hdih amâo thêo ko ñu, nga hnei
âo thêo, mse si asêo lheh lhêo kdul.

Ñu se rông hriê, sa kiê khia, amai ba
tian nik, anan amâo đui đu, mlei; tu
ung brei ñu đôk hram mbit, bia dah ñu
jing hjung leh anan bi kpih he jih ñu
thêo anan hong un, yang bi thêo; atâo
bi tmu, bi jak čoh bruă, nga hma, bi jak
plah kmun ktơr, kuê bi hriê, mdiê bi jing
tam duah koing koông.

Bi hkrê ung ñu, ung ñu tam brei
sua, be brei kdi ko mô ñu.

25. DE LA FEMME QUI SÉDUIT L'ÉPOUX DE SA SOEUR.

Celle qui s'empare du fil rouge
ou du fil noir, de la marmite à légu...
ou de la marmite à riz, du mari de la
soeur aînée ou de la soeur cadette;

celle qui s'empare du mari de la
soeur aînée ou de la soeur cadette
pour le faire sien, qui agit comme
elle était étrangère (au clan), si
la soeur aînée qui commet cette fa...
elle se couvre de honte et d'oppro...
aux yeux de tout le monde.

Car on ne sait comment la puni...
on ne sait que faire, parce qu'el...
est comme le chien qui ne peut qu...
les talons de son maître.

Parce qu'elle est issue du mê...
dos, de la même souche, de la même...
qui les a portées dans son ventre...
ne peut pas lui infliger d'amende...
ce que c'est mal, c'est profanatoi...
le mari restera avec les deux soe...
mais qu'elle ne sera seulement co...
bine ; puis sacrifiera un porc po...
tous les trois, on l'offrira aux g...
et aux morts pour qu'ils sachent;
pour qu'ils puissent encore trava...
leur champ, cultiver le maïs et le...
combre, pour que le millet vienne...
pour que le riz pousse bien et d...
et donne de beaux épis.

Quant au mari, il paiera une a...
de à sa femme (pour l'avoir trom...

26. KLEI ÊKEI TÔ SANG BI TLE HONG HLUN, ANĂN ÑU BI ÊNGIÊ HE.

Ñu phung mlêo, phung gi dôk tơ ko čŏng, trun tơ lăn ñu bŏng he mnong un asăo.

Ñu êkei hiu, piu tle, dliê se sier bi nao hong agăt ea, mnuih pla lo, hong mnuih khăng ne gơ bŏng ñu hlam sang.

Gơ mniê amâo blum ñu hjum gơ hong hăt, gơ amâo blum ñu ajum hong kniêrg ênăng, gơ amâo jhong čiang kơ ñu, ñu ngô gơ hong kông ñu; anăn gơ čiang he êdi kơ ñu; bi tŏah gơ amâo čiang ôh kơ ñu, gơ anei dôk hui kơ mta dhong kơ êngao, đao kơ kseh, gơ hdehêluk hui ah kơ ñu khua pô blei.

Agu tonăn le, mô ñu buh ñu êkei kjoh hla, mniê dus hmŏk, dôk hlam bhit pum sa mniê sa êkei. mô ñu mâo păn ti kniă, kčik ti ko, de čhiam ao mô ñu mta ba hun hong adam adei.

Bbuh mniê, djiê êkei, klei blu amâo lo lu, mniê piu hlun ñu anăn, lir dliê, kruôp dliê; mniê tơ yač, gơ mngač asei mlei gơ, gơ wit kơ juê anyai kơ amei adei gơ.

Si kdrec ñu de, ñu tăm ênua, ba ư kơ mô ñu; tŏdah bun un đua song kpih mô ñu, ngăn thăo ko ba kdi; bi tŏdah mdrong kbao kpih mô ñu, ngăn năm kơ ñu brei.

---

120. DE CEUX QUI COUCHENT AVEC LEUR ESCLAVE, CELLE-CI SERA AFFRANCHIE.

Le chat gris, le chat noir, qui se tient habituellement sur le couvercle de la hotte, descend à terre pour manger la nourriture des cochons et des chiens.

Lui, l'homme, il s'en va dans le bois avec son esclave porteuse, avec celle qui travaille son champ, qui fait la cuisine chez lui.

Si elle n'est pas contente, il la console avec du tabac, avec de l'écorce et du bétel; si elle lui résiste, il la tente avec le collier, sinon elle lui cède; en ne lui cédant pas, elle craint que le couteau ne soit tiré hors (du fourreau), que le sabre sorte tout seul, elle craint celui qui l'a achetée (elle ne peut se refuser).

Après cela si la femme voit son époux écraser les feuilles mortes, si elle voit l'esclave avec de l'écorce sur la tête, si elle les voit dans le fourré, l'esclave et l'homme elle les saisira par le toupet, par la tête, elle saisira le turban et veste et elle les montrera à ses beaux-frères.

Si elle avoue, si l'homme avoue on n'aura pas besoin de discuter longtemps, et l'esclave maîtresse de l'homme sera libre comme le grillon ou la sauterelle dans les buissons, comme le riz qui est dehors, son corps sera libre et elle retournera chez ses soeurs dans sa famille.

Quant au mari il paiera une amende à sa femme; s'il est pauvre il lui sacrifiera un porc de un song et lui paiera une amende trois ko; s'il est riche il lui sacrifiera un buffle et lui paiera une amende de six ko.

27. KIEI MNIÊ ANAK ÔG MDRONG DÔK UNG HLUN HLĂM SANG .

Ung ami ama čiăng tlăng kña, ha êmuh ênuh leh adam adei, ungleh oi djo, mô leh bi jing, čing čhar leh kbăk, lăk čai leh bi gam, adam adei dum năn leh jih tuôm soai, êrah êmô leh bi čaĂ, êrah kbao leh bi kpih, mnu ana agha dong, un leh bong, kpiê leh mnăm, ami rai amai ring ring, ami jing k'kiêng leh bi kpih wăt leh soai.

ñu le dôkung hrue ka bo tlam, tlam ka bo aguah, ñu lo duah mă ung luăn, ñu lo suh kơ mnga tông-mông, ñu lo dlông kơ mnga moyăp, ñu lo hăp dôk mă ung hlun ami ama ñu hlăm sang, anăn ñu lui he ung ñu roh dong, êlông thu; ñu čiăng lui he ung ñu amâo mâo gŭ kat, ñu tăm brei rua, ñu ba brei kđi kơ gơ, anăn gơ êmô kbao wit kơ ana, un mnu wit kơ ana, anuih wit kơ ama ami.

ñu dê bung djuh kơ yu, ñu lo pu ngo, êasl ko kơ gah ñu lo mă ba kơ ôk, ñu dôk he ung hlun hlăm sang.

Ami ama ñu lač kơ ñu amâo ñu ô, mtô amâo djo, ñu nga si kho mgu,.

ñu bei si krang, ñu si lip, ñu mnuih amâo lo dưi bi djŏng.

121. DE LA FEMME QUI ABANDONNE SON MARI POUR SE REMARIER AVEC SON ESCLAVE.

Ses parents lui ont cherché un mari, ses frères ont eu du mal à le lui trouver, le mari a consenti, la femme l'a accepté, les gongs ont été suspendus, la laque et la résine ont été collée à l'arbre, tous les frères ont été prévenus, avec le sang de buffle et de boeuf ils ont été oints, la dot a été payée (aux parents du mari), le porc a été mangé, l'alcool bu; les tantes maternelles, les cousines, sa propre mère ont participé aux sacrifices.

Elle n'est même pas resté avec son mari jusqu'au soir, même pas jusqu'au matin, et elle cherche déjà un autre mari; elle préfère la fleur blanche, la fleur multicolore, elle préfère l'esclave de ses parents qui est à la maison; pour cela elle abandonne son mari dans le vallon, dans le ravin, elle abandonne sans motif.

Elle lui paiera une amende, et comme le petit du boeuf ou du buffle qui revient vers sa mère, comme le petit du porc ou du poulet qui revient vers sa mère, le mari retournera chez ses parents.

Elle prend la hotte à l'Ouest et la place à l'Est, elle prend le coussin dans la salle commune et le porte dans sa chambre, elle prend l'esclave qui est dans la maison et elle en fait son mari.

Ses parents lui donnent des conseils et elle ne les suit pas, ils l'instruisent et elle ne les écoute pas, elle agit comme les fous et les imbéciles.

Elle a la bouche large comme l'ouverture de la nasse, large comme le grand van rond, c'est une fille qu'on ne peut plus corriger.

Ung ñu anăn nga puk kba, ngă
hma alah,jik jăh amăo kriăng, ñu
čiăng bong ma do nwăn hdăp măo êluih.

Trei hua ñu dôk dăm,trei anăm
ñu pit dih,ñu čhin duah nga bi jih
bi rai ngăn drăp kmha ñu.

Amâo amâo čjam ñu duah blei
hong ngăn,amâo măo êsei ñu duah
djir hong ngăn,ko ênir puk hma
amăo ñu mih,êmô kbao, čing char,
čeh yăng,tu djăp mta ra ênao do
ngăn arăng hdăp,ñu duah chi bong
he jih.

Anăn kthul di ñu dua, mniê
hong êkei hlun.

Son nouveau mari est paresseux
pour construire la cabane,paresseux
pour travailler le champ,paresseux
pour biner et défricher,il mange
les biens de ses beaux-parents qu'il
a eu sans peine.

Lorsqu'il est rassasié il se
couche,lorsqu'il a bien bu il s'endort,il ne cherche qu'à manger les
biens de ses beaux-parents.

S'il manque de légumes ou de
riz,il en achète avec les biens de
sa femme,mais il ne pense jamais au
travail du champ;les boeufs et les
buffles, les gongs plats et les
gongs renflés,les jarres, tous les
biens,tout l'héritage de ses beaux-parents,il vend tout,il mange tout.

Pour cela ils sont coupables
tous les deux.

28. KLEI TRIH .

Ñu duah hmăt arăng hong brăm,
čam hong knih, ñu duah trih dah
arăng hŏai.

Êkei ñu duah blu pliê, mniê
duah blu mŏum, ñu duah blu si bum
kngăl, ñu duah al čŏñ kơ arăng hŏai.

Ñu duah trih dah, trăh yao, ñu
duah dlao wač kơ anak mli hong, kơ
anak mdrong hŏai.

Arăng êkei êngiê, mniê čih, bih
mnŏng suar.

Todah sit êkei hiu, pĭu tle
dliê se siêr nao, ya ñu amâo mă ti sơk,
čhŏk ti păl, kral bô mta, todah asei
đue le dhong, asei đue le čhiăm.

Ñu hmăt ênai angin ti ktăm, ênai
ti mnu, ñu duah tu mă săp klei
yăl dliê hlăm êlan djuh êa.

Da lu êkei duah djă giê, mniê
djă arôk, da duah jhŏk mdlao mnhuă,
lu arăng duah mtah plao.

Kthul ñu, mtâo ñu ruăt hrôk,
sơk krum, êlâo ñu duah dum tu he
sơ klei arăng.

Arăng amâo kđi arăng kơ ñu.

Todah ñu duah trih anak bun,
kpih brei un song; todah ñu duah
trih anak sah mdrong, ñu kpih hong
ko.

122. DE LA SUSPICION.

Celui qui frappe avec la flèche,
qui frappe avec le balai, qui suspecte
les autres sans motif;

l'homme qui parle à tort et à
travers, la femme qui parle sans savoir
ce qu'elle dit, ceux qui parlent comme
l'aveugle (qui n'a rien vu), comme le
sourd (qui n'a rien entendu), qui se
fâchent sans motif;

ceux qui suspectent tout le monde, qui jettent l'épervier dans l'eau
trouble, qui insultent l'enfant du
riche (enfant du chef) sans raison (qui
suspectent)

l'homme ou la femme innocent
comme le Bih ou le Mnông.

s'ils sont sûrs que l'homme est
allé faire l'amour dans le bois,
pourquoi ne l'ont-ils pas saisi par
la hotte, pourquoi ne l'ont-ils pas
saisi solidement par le bras afin de
reconnaître son visage; s'il a laissé
tomber son couteau ou son turban,
pourquoi ne les ont-ils pas ramassés?

mais ils entendent le vent gronder
aux alentours du village, ils entendent
gronder le tonnerre derrière la palissade, et ils croient à tout ce qu'on
raconte sur la route du bois ou de la
fontaine.

Ceux qui tiennent le bâton à la
main et cherchent à frapper à droite
et à gauche, qui cherchent à glisser
la mauvaise parole,

ceux-là sont coupable; ils sont
comme le sorcier qui accepte tout ce
qu'on lui dit, comme les démons qui
exaucent toutes les malédictions; ils
ont tort de croire tout ce qu'on leur
raconte.

Pour cela il y a affaire entre
les autres et eux.

S'ils ont suspecté une personne
pauvre ils feront le sacrifice d'un
porc de 1500; ils ont suspecté une
personne riche ils feront le sacrifice
d'un porc de 4500.

29. KLEI TRIH AMÂO DÂO NA.

Ñu duah kmất hong bram, ồăm hong ..,ñu duah trih dah,trih yao hoai.

.. ñu êkei duah blu pliê,,mniê duah mừm,ñu duah blu si bun kngăl.

Tơdah êkei duah blu,piu tlê dliê mờr duah bi nao,mông êkei ñu mâo mã klê,mniê mã bi kngen,êmeh êman mâo ..u,piu tle mông mâo mã bằng enih ..

Ñu ami duah blua,ama koh,loh liên o ñu duah dlao wač,kuač kông kơ ng hoai.

Athul ñu krum amâo ñu duah dlăng. Bng iệp,ñu amâo duah tliêp mật nlam...

Nga si êmô kbac deh,ñu păh ti rong ... hlăm buđč brong iệp,tơdah si đing ... ek deh,ñu blah dlăng lăng khiêng .. ....

Anei arăng čih braih hroh,čih boh ng yang hrue,êkei mniê čih bih mnông r.

Êkei ñu bi ăngiê he brei,mniê bi .,bih mững ñu bi suar he brei.

.. ñu trih buh un song,tơ ñu trih ..ng un kơ ñu kpih.

123. DES ACCUSATIONS CALOMNIEUSES D'ADULTÈRE.

Ceux qui frappent avec la flèche, qui frappent avec le balai, qui sont ... loux sans raison.

L'homme jaloux qui parle sans rien savoir,la femme jalouse qui parle sans réfléchir,ceux qui parlent comme des aveugles et des sourds,

s'ils voient un homme et une femme dans le bois,qu'ils les saisissent par la main,comme on saisit par la queue l'éléphant ou le rhinocéros qui veut se sauver,qu'ils les prennent sur le lieu,sur le fait.

Ceux qui sont jaloux et insultent le père ou la mère sans motif,qui injurient les gens grossièrement et les accusent sans raison,

ceux-là sont coupables parce qu'ils n'ont pas cherché à voir par-dessous la maison,par-dessus le toit,à travers la cloison,parce qu'ils n'ont pas gui- té,parce qu'ils n'ont pas épié,le so.. la nuit,sans que nul ne soit douté.

Parce qu'ils agissent comme avec les boeufs et les buffles,qu'on frappe sur le dos(pourvoir s'ils sont deux méchants).

Le paddy dans le grenier,il faut regarder pourvoir s'il y en a,le riz en bache..,il faut le fendre pour voir s'il y a des insectes à l'intérieur,.. coupables il faut les surprendre sur le fait.) S'ils accusent ceux qui sont innocents comme le riz blanc,innocent comme le fruit"êpang",comme le rayon soleil;s'ils accusent l'homme et la femme innocents comme le Bih et le Mnông étrangers,

l'homme on le laissera en liberté, la femme on la relâchera,le Bih ou le Mnông on les innocentera.

S'ils ont accusé par jalousie un pauvre ils lui feront le sacrifice d'un porc de 1800,s'ils ont accusé un riche ils lui feront le sacrifice d'un porc de 4800.

30. KLEI ÊÂO MÃ UNG HÔ BI TLE PIU ÊÂO MÃ HJAN.

Ñu duah mã krei asei hjan,
mnuih mkuăn amâo buh amâo thâo .

Bing amâo ñu ba, kna amâo ñu
jak, mnuih pă êmă dua tlâo amâo ñu
iêô laĉ, iêô hưư .

Ñu duah hnut arăng hong bram,
ñu duah ĉăm hong knah, ñu duah trih
duh arăng hdôi.

Ñu duah truc si knăm, ñu dlăm
si wah, ñu duah pah mã arăng si tiang
mja.

adeh êpông ñu duah ba, kdeh
ra, ñu duah ruah, ñu duah nă săp klei
ñu yŭ dliê hong sah mdrong.

Ñu mã arăng amâo mâo tuh, ñu
mã arăng amâo klei, ñu duah mã adei ayong
oai

Ñu tluh ko kơyâo kpă, ñu tluh
ko kga kông, ñu tluh ko mnuih jong
ajan ktal.

arăng amâo mâo kđi .

I24. DE L'UN DES ÉPOUX QUI SURPREND L'AUTRE EN FLAGRANT DÉLIT D'ADULTÈRE SANS TÉMOINS.

Si on a surpris (les coupables)
tout seul, alors que personne n'a rien
vu, rien entendu;

si on n'a pas emmené de camara-
de, si on n'a pas appelé d'ami, si on
n'a pas prévenu deux, trois, quatre ou
cinq personnes;

si on cherche à fouetter (l'amant)
avec la flèche, si on cherche à le
frapper avec le balai, si on est jaloux sans motif, sans pouvoir faire
la preuve;

si on a pris les coupables comme
dans une nasse, si on les a pris comme une ligne, si on a mis la main sur
eux, si on les a surpris comme l'épervier et la faine surprennent leur
proie;

si on offre le filet ou l'épaule (de boeuf) au chef pour chercher
à la corrompre et avoir gain de cause;

si on a surpris les coupables
sans preuve, sans témoin, si on
accuse les frères sans raison,

parce qu'on désire l'arbre droit
le corps-coupe tranchant, l'homme agile
et fort, (on veut obtenir réparation)

Il n'y a pas affaire (d'adultère).

31. KLEI MNUIH DUAH ČHAL UNG
MÔ ARANG TLE HU ŇU DUAH
KA HE ARANG HOAI.

Ňu duah mă soh, koh mjâo, ñu duah
ka arăng amâo mâo kđi.

Puk arăng jăk ñu duah rah he
hlang, sang arăng jăk ñu duah rah he
kuê, añuê abăn arăng jăk ñu duah đoh
he tlăn ala.

Ňu duah mă anak mli Hong, anak
mdrong hoai.

Amâo mâo pô đi hrun, trun mđar,
duah êman amâo mâo pô mdar go lăn.

Ñu mjhưt bơng mmao, ñu mơhao bơng
rong, ñu gong kbông soh.

Kha dah ñu mă arăng êkei hlăm
niê, aniê hlăm bhit, ñu păn koh ti
k, čhôk ti păl, ñu kral he koh bô
ka ai nik tam.

 Gleh mniê due ñu mă he čhiăm
go, tơ êkei due ñu mă dao kga,
amdi go lă liê ñu mă, snăn koh sit
k.

dng amâo lo dleh kđah, mmah klañ
he lo ngăñ blu.

ah ñu mă hjăn do mniê amâo
ai, ñu mă hjăn do êkei amâo mâo kđi.

---

125. DES ACCUSATIONS
CALOMNIEUSES D'ADULTÈRE.

Celui qui cherche à rendre coupables les innocents, qui dérange le guérisseur, qui accuse les autres sans
preuve;

celui qui arrache de la paillote
de la cabane, des autres, qui est belle
qui introduit des caléotes dans les
maisons tranquilles, qui traîne les
serpents sur la natte et la couverture des gens paisibles.

Celui qui calomnie des gens tranquilles, les gens riches sans raison.

Celui qui n'a personne pour monter dans sa maison et le conseiller,
personne pour descendre de sa maison
et l'instruire, personne pour piétiner
sa rizière avec l'éléphant ou le rhinocéros.

Celui qui a toujours envie de
champignons, d'aubergines, qui a toujours envie de faire du mal.

S'il prend les autres sur le fait,
l'homme dans le fourré, la femme dans
buisson, qu'il les saisisse par la
hotte, qu'il les saisisse fortement
par le bras, qu'il reconnaisse leur
visage sans se tromper.

Si la femme se sauve, qu'il saisi
se son écharpe ou sa veste, si l'homme se sauve, qu'il saisisse son sabr
ou son coupe-coupe, ou d'autres objet
quelconques, ainsi qu'il y aura certi
tude.

Et pour manger il ne sera nécessaire de mastiquer, pour avaler il ne
sera pas nécessaire de mâcher, si on
a la preuve, on n'aura pas à discuter
beaucoup.

Si on n'a saisi que des objets
appartenant à la femme ou à l'homme
seul, il n'aura pas affaire, (les preu
sans insuffisantes).

Todah ñu ma do jih dua nah,
wit do mniê ,wit do êkei,leh anăn
ñu dôk ti ktong lêô lač,dôk ti hrač
lêô dah,hong sah mdrong hiư huñ.

Mais si on a saisi des objets
des deux côtés,des objets de la femme et des objets de l'homme,on se
tiendra sur l'arbre à ruches ou sur
l'arbre à résine,on avertira tout le
monde,puis on ira informer le chef.

Anuih sa bi thao,anuih tlâo bi
tuh,anuih êtun,êbâo bi hmư,snăn
mâo kdi yơh.

Et si on a informé une personne,
si on a prevenu trois personnes, si
cent, mille personnes ont entendu,
ainsi on aura la preuve certaine et
il y aura affaire.

Anei ñu êmông soh pah,druah
soh wiêk,mdrong soh liêk kdi.

Sinon,comme le tigre on aura donné un coup de patte dans le vide,
comme le chevreuil on aura donné un
coup de boutoir dans le vide,et le
chef ne pourra pas juger (faute de
preuves).

JURITA..Jug.no 6 du 10 févr.1923 : I an + I ko + kpih.
Jug du 6 juillet 1938 : 2 kpih avec 2 jarres d'alcool.

32. KLEI ČHAL TLE PIU TU KLEI ARANG YAL DLIĚ A.ĂO MĂO KA.

ñu čhal anak mli hong,anak mdrong hmei.

Todah sit êkei dliě hiu,piu tle,dliě se sier bi nao,čhiăm ao dao kgă,do ngan la liě amăo ñu ma.

Tơ anei gơ duc ñu sue mă ding hat,anei duc ñu mă ao mă čhiăm.

Êkei ñu ma ti kiě,mniê ti kngan, mă dôk dih hlăm anôk,dôk hlăm anuê siam,amuih dua riêng nan bi buh bi thăo anei,snăn koh gơ sit êdi.

Tơ hlăm dliê êkei kjoh hla, mniê dua hnôk,di ñu duah dôk hlăm di ñu.

dôk hlăm kmrông,đang hlăm dliê gơ amniê sa êkei.

Buh ajik dôk bi tle,aro bi ba, mng măo ma ti kiê kngan,snăn koh gơ sit.

Êkei ñu ma čhiăm,mniê ñu mă kpung,dliêng ba kơ mnut ko êa,hra buôn,pô dlăng adei amuôn buôn sang.

Êkei êlăo ñu duah tu he săp giê sap mjâo,măo klei arăng yăl dliê hong ñu,ñu mtăo ruăt hrôk, kơ kmrun,ñu duah dun tu he klei anăn,

snăn kthul ñu ,măo kdi arăng hong ñu.

I26. DES ACCUSATIONS D'ADUL- TÈRE SANS PREUVES.

Celui qui accuse les personnes innocentes sans raison,qui accuse les riches sans motif,

s'il est sûr que l'homme et la femme sont allés dans le bois pour s'aimer,ou'ils sont allés dans les buissons pour se cacher,pourouoi n'a- t-il pas saisi le turban,la veste,le sabre,le coupe-coupe ou d'autres ob- jets leur appartenant?

S'ils se sont sauvés que n'a-t-il saisi la pipe,la veste ou l'écharpe?

Que n'a-t-il saisi l'homme et la femme par la main,que ne s'est-il souvenu de l'endroit où ils se sont couchés,du lieu où ils ont déroulé la natte et la couverture,que n'a-t- il fait et toucher à tout ceux qui se trouvaient près de là,ainsi il aurait eu des preuves certaines.

Si l'homme avait froissé des feu- illes par terre,si la femme avait des brindilles dans les cheveux,cela au- rait prouvé ou'ils étaient allés dans la forêt,ou'ils s'étaient couchés dans les buissons,dans les fourrés, et on aurait été sûr que l'homme ou la femme s'étaient unis.

Si on voit les grenouilles ac- couplées,les crapauds accouplés,si on prend les coupables sur le fait, si on les saisi par la main,on est sûr(de leurculpabilité).

De l'homme on saisira le turban, de la femme on saisira la jupe,et on les présentera au banian de la bource au figuier du village,à celui qui veille sur les neveux et les frères, surles habitants du village.

Mais si au lieu de cela il accep- te la désision du bâton,la parole du sorcier,les histoires que les gens racontent,si comme les sorciers et les démons il croit à tout ce qu'on lui dit,

pour cela il est coupable,et il y a affaire entre les autres et lui.

33. KLEI LUI UNG MÔ HƠAI LEH
BI KUÔL LEH.

Ung bi mô,mô bi mjing,čing
char leh bi yuôl,ung mô leh bi kuôl
ka leh.

Nu lui amâo mâo boh,ñu soh
amâo mâo klei ung mô adei ayong ñu
lui hơai.

Dơ êman bi kning,čing yuôl,
dơ klei kuôl ka,phun bi mô kniet
kpung,ung mô ñu tau hê brei ênua,
ba brei kdi dơ năn.

Nu êmuh ding ti kbông,kông ti
hngan,ñu êmuh êlan pô blu pô kuôl.

Jak êman leh tling,čing leh
yuôl,leh jak bi kuôl ka leh,nu ba
o kdi dơ bi kuôl anăn.

Kông tuh bi mtloh tơnăn,kông
soh kleh,aseh êman mô čar bi dưng,
ñu bi lông tơnăn,kông bi lih,kông
adih kơ nei,kông êkei wit kơ mniê
kông mniê wit kơ êkei,kdi amâo lo
bi mâo ôh,tơ êkei čiang dôk mô dôk,
tơ mniê čiang dôk ung dôk.

127. DES ÉPOUX QUI SE QUITTENT
QUAND IL Y A
CONTRAT.

Si le mari et la femme sont déjà
unis,si les gongs plats et les gongs
renflés ont déjà suspendus,si le contrat de mariage est déjà scellé.

S'ils se quittent sans raison,
s'ils commettent la faute sans qu'il
y ait affaire,si le mari de la soeur
et la femme du frère se quittent sans
motif;

si les éléphants sont déjà entra-
vés,si les gongs sont déjà suspendus,
si le contrat les a unis comme l'arc
au fût de l'arbalète,le mari à la
femme,(si l'un quitte l'autre),il
devra rembourser(la dot) il devra
réparer.

A ceux qui ont tenu le pipeau
dans la bouche,à ceux qui ont accepté le bracelet de garantie,à ceux qui
ont porté les paroles et qui ont ar-
rangé l'union,(aux témoins)il faut
demander les clauses du contrat.

Si l'éléphant a été bien entravé
si les gongs ont été bien suspendus,
si la conversation a été bien scellée
il faudra rembourser selon ce qui a
été convenu.

Si le bracelet qui était fermé a
ouvert,si le bracelet était soudé
brisé,si les chevaux et les éléphants
s'en vont dans les pâturages diffé-
si les colliers avaient été échang-
le bracelet de l'homme sera rendu
la femme et le bracelet de la femme
à l'homme,et ainsi il n'aura plus
affaire;le mari pourra chercher une
femme et la femme pourra chercher
un autre mari.

JURISPR.- Jug. no 46 du 20 août 1923: I mois + indemnité prévue au con-
trat + kpih.
Jug.no 54 du 25 juin 1926 : 5$00 $:divorce accordé.
Jug.nos 21 et 25 des 4 et 5 août 1926 :5400+ 6 ko + kpih.
Jug. du 4 juillet 1938 : I0 ko + kpih un ko.

34. KLEI ƀŏ... MƠH LŬ MƠ DƠ NAO DƠ... M... KRƐM.

125. DE CELUI QUI ROMPT LE CONTRAT ABANDONNANT SA FEM-ME POUR EN PRENDRE UNE AUTRE.

Đi ti êk, rŏk ti ƀah, duah ung kjar, ... mâo pô tah rơh, kuh ƀtiêng, amâo mâ... ƀ ciêng rông.

Elle monte dans la chambre, trav... se la salle commune, cherche son mari (époux), car elle n'a personne pour a... toyer les abords du champ, pour coup... les bambous, elle n'a plus personne pour l'aider.

Anăn tio nao adăm adei thăng kña, ênuh.

Alors elle envoie ses frères demander au mari (pourquoi il est p... ti).

Ñu u hdjơng, drơng kla, ñu ma leh ... ng krah, sap kƀong mbah leh ñu u.

Il avait pourtant été concenta... il avait accepté le bracelet, sa bo... avait dit oui.

Koyua năn êsei ƀung, mnu čuh, ênuh ... ăm adei nao tlung ma, ba tu kơ sang.

Les frères et les oncles (de la femme) avaient porté le riz et le p... let (à la famille du mari), ils s'ét... donné la peine d'aller le chercher... de le conduire à la maison.

Un djiê, kpiê kkang, buôn sang iêô...

Le porc avait été tué, l'alcool préparé, tout le village avait été vité.

Jơng bi mia, êa kpih, bi lih miêl ha ... ƀiêt kpung, ung mô di ñu.

Les pieds avaient été oints, le... pieds du mari et ceux de la femme ... les avait unis comme l'arc et le... de l'arbalète.

Un knô lih ama, un ana lih ami, pnu ... ... dông, un bong kpiê mnăm, jih wit ... ... i, amai adei, ami rai, amai ring, ... jing kkiêng, amiêt sa, awa sa drei, ... yơng bi ênum tơnăn.

Un porc avait été sacrifié po... le beau-père, une truie pour la be... mère, la dot avait été payée, le po... mangé et l'alcool bu par toute la ... mille, les soeurs, les tantes, les o... les frères tous réunis pour cela.

... kơng sapăn, abăn ba, mtil kpung êa ... ... leh drei.

On avait donné huit bracelets ... couverture, une ceinture, un bol en cuivre, pour rembourser la peine ... la mère avait eue à élever (l'hom...

Anăn ôman bi knăng, čing yuôl, bi ... ... ka, hui tŏng čing sah, tông knah ... ..., hui tlăp sla dlăng ñu lui.

Ainsi l'éléphant avait été bi... entravé, les gongs biens suspendus... contrat bien scellé, de crainte qu'... ne se lassât de frapper les gongs, ... se regarder.

in pong,kpiê pong, ngăn gŏng ko
n leh brei.

Anei le mlam ñu blu sa klei,hrue
săp,wir rong anăp ñu lo duah klei
hn.

Ñu lo tluh ko mnga kñi bang hdrah,
ta hrah bang kwăn,buh mniê mkuăn ñu
čiăng.

Ñu lui he mô ñu tam-la,tla tăm-
ng,ñu lo duah dŏng he buôn sang mkuăn.

Ñu gao kung,ñu gao knŏng, săp kbŏng
h mdrong kuôl ñu gao,ñu si bang mbah,
b bang kbŏng,kŏng leh buh ñu lo wă.

Anăn kthuh ñu, măo kdi arăng ko ñu.

Le sacrifice du cochon et de l'al
nool avait été offert aux parents,le
témoins avaient été rétribués.

Mais maintenant,il(l'époux) parl
d'une manière le jour et d'une autr
la nuit,il tourne le dos et agit autrement.

Il désire la fleur jaune dans la b
la fleur rouge dans les buissons,il
voit une autre femme et il la désir

Il abandonne sa femme parce qu'il
est lassé,il abandonne parce qu'il
l'aime plus et il s'en va demeurer
dans un autre village.

Il passe outre les signaux des p
ges "kung" et "knŏng",il passe outr
la parole du chef,il viole le contr
il fend la bouche de ceux qui le cо
seillent;le bracelet qu'il a achepo
est ouvert.

Pour cela il est coupable et il
affaire entre les autres et lui.

Jug. no 19 du 21 avril 1923 : I an + 5,00 + I ko à la femme + ko
au Pô-lăn (2è union incestueuse).
Jug.no 24 du 1er avril 1925 : 5 ans.
Jug.no 65 du 11 sept. 1925 :15 jours + 5,00.
Jug.no 40 du 4 sept. 1936 :10,00 + 12 ko + kpih.
Jug.no 27 du 9 juin 1937 : 6 mois + 5,00 + 16 ko.
Jug. du 6 octobre 1938: 10,00 +12 ko + kpih.

35. KLEI DŎK MÔ ANAK AMÂO HƯN HONG KHUA BUÔN .

129. DE CEUX QUI SE MARIENT SANS RENDRE COMPTE AU CHEF.

Ñu dŏk mô anak ko krei, asei hjăn, hong mnuih dum năn amâo ñu hưn.

Ceux qui se marient tout seul sans rien dire, sans prévenir personne,

Hnut ko êa, hra ko buôn pô dlăng adei amiên buôn sang amâo ñu hưn.

sans informer le banian de la source, le figuier du village, celui qui veille sur les frères et les neveux, sur tous les habitants;

Ung rô, mô rô, ñu bi dŏk ko tuôt amât hjăn.

ceux, mari et femme, qui vivent ensemble (maritalement), qui se sont mariés sans rien dire à personne,

Êman amâo tuôm tling, čưng amâo tuôm yuôl, amâo tuôm bi kuôl kă.

sans que l'éléphant ait été entravé, les gongs suspendus, le contrat scellé;

Ñu amâo tuôm wah knăl, yal bi thâo, amâo ñu tuôm hưn klei ñu dŏk ung mô.

ceux qui ne disent rien pour qu'on sache, qui ne font pas savoir qu'ils se sont mariés;

Sang dlông ñu mut, sang đut ñu hgao, sang bong êmô kbao ñu mưč.

ceux qui passent la maison haute, qui enjambe la maison basse, qui méprisent la maison (du chef) où l'on mange le boeuf et le buffle;

Êa hlung ñu kdăt, êa khăt ñu kplung, săn mdrong ñu gao.

ceux qui sautent par-dessus la flaque d'eau, qui enjambe le torrent, qui passent outre les ordres du chef,

Anăn amâo kđi arăng ko ñu.

(ceux-là sont coupables) et il y a affaire entre le chef et eux.

JURISPR.-Jug, no 32 du 21 mai 1923 : 2 ko au chef.

Jug.no 21 du 25 mars 1925: 10 jours + 5000 + kpih au chef.

Jug.no 70 du 25 sept. 1925: 3 ans à l'homme et,1an à la femme.

36. KLEI ÊKEI ...O LEH ...O ÑU
ĐAO ĐÔK ÔU ÊA AKUAH ÑU LUI
HE ...O ÑU LEH AÑAN ÑU ĐÔK
MNIÊ TUE .

...nuih đue hiu jơng mngo, kŏ 'mơ'-
y', jơng mngo ko mngăn, mnuih đue hiu
hra lăn ala.

...lô ñu, ñu lui he ti geh, brah sa
ping, amâo ñu lo hming hdri djo kơ
gơ.

Ñu ciuh kơ mnga kŭi hlăm hdrah,
mnga hrah hlăm lăn, ñu ruh mniê mkuăn
ñu đôk he.

Mlon đeh khao arang ktuê ti kru,
...ng đue hiu nô tui đuah.

...ñu ngă si ko ksua, knga ruih,
...ñu ...ih lu klei.

...ñu đuah đôk he klong, đơng kla,
...ñu puk hma hlăm buôn, hlăm čar
...mkuăn.

Ñu bơng boh bir amâo ñu mblang,
ñu bơng boh mnang amâo ñu ƀle, ñu
... kčuôn sang arang amâo ñu hun
bơng ... buôn.

Ñu bơng kmun amâo ñu hun hơng
...mei, bơng mksei amâo ñu hun hơng
adei, ...amâo boh klei amâo ñu hun hơng
...ala.

...amâo kthul ñu mâo kdi arang
... ñu prong.

Ñu rih jih asei, kbao rih jih
asei, ñu đuah boh klei jih asei ñu
...ih.

130. DE CEUX QUI ÉMIGRENT
DANS UN AUTRE PAYS ET ABANDON-
NE LEUR FEMME POUR PRENDRE
UNE FEMME ÉTRANGÈRE.

Celui qui s'en va les jambes
à l'Est, la tête à l'Ouest, les jambes
au Nord, la tête au Sud, qui s'en va
n'importe où;

celui qui abandonne sa femme
dans la salle commune, qui la laisse
dans un coin, sans penser à elle, sans
aucun regret;

celui qui désire la fleur jaune
dans le bosquet, la fleur rouge dans
le champ, qui voyant une autre femme
veut demeurer avec elle;

celui qui est pareil au cheval
et au buffle qui brisent leur lien
et qu'on suit à la trace, qu'il s'en
va ferme le suivra et le cherchera.

Celui qui agit comme s'il avait
une tête de hérisson, des oreilles de
souris, qui a beaucoup d'histoires;

celui qui s'installe ailleurs,
pour toujours, qui construit sa cabane et fait son champ dans un autre
pays, dans le pays des étrangers;

celui qui mange le fruit de ...
réguier sans l'ouvrir, qui mange la
noix d'arec sans rien rejeter, qui
s'en va dans le pays des étrangers
sans prévenir le chef de son village

celui qui mange le concombre
rien dire à sa soeur, qui mange la
pastèque sans rien dire à son frère,
qui a une affaire et ne dit rien à
ses parents,

celui-là est coupable et il y a
affaire très grave entre les autres
et lui.

Le porc et le buffle destinés
à être sacrifiés perdent leur corps;
celui qui cherche des histoires risquera aussi son corps (sa vie ou sa
liberté).

37. KLEI ÊKEI MÂO MÔ ÑU BI BA HE ANAK KƠ MNIÊ ÊRA.

Ñu dê leh mâo kniêt kpung ung ñô.

Gơ dê kga ôniêng, ksiêng hna, êra êtung ka mâo ung kjar.

Ñu tluh kơ gơ mse si tluh boh mơza, mse si tluh kơ djam mmih, ñu kơ gơ mong mdih mbrue.

Kha dah ñu tluh kơ gơ tle kơh bi lmang, čiang bi măn, tơl ble mlan kong tuh ñu bi mtloh he kơh, kông koh kleh, aseh êman mdê čar bi dong.

mei le ñu bi tle hong gơ tơl bei hlăm băng mtrun, tơl hơei kur ru ul ju he kuôp ksäo, tơl êa rong, kong sh tơl êdah tian prôč.

gua anan abăn ba kơ buê, añuê l, ri ksal ñu brei.

Gơ ba he anak ko krei, asei ñu, anan ñu tăm brei ênua, ba brei ñi kơ gơ, ngăn ko leh ana un kpiê ih.

131. DE CELUI QUI, ÉTANT MARIÉ, A UN ENFANT AVEC UNE JEUNE FILLE.

L'homme a déjà l'arc et le fût, il est déjà marié.

Elle (la jeune fille) est comme le coupe-coupe sans manche, comme l'arbalète sans corde, elle est célibataire, elle n'a pas encore de mari.

Il la désire comme on désire le fruit vert, les légumes sucrés, il la désire depuis hier, depuis avant-hier.

S'il la désire il peut avoir des relations avec elle, mais il faut qu'il soit prudent, il faut qu'à la nouvelle lune le bracelet soit ouvert, il faut l'ôter et le rendre, il faut que le cheval et l'éléphant s'en aillent dans des pâturages différents.

Mais s'il reste avec elle jusqu'à ce que le tubercule donne des rejets, que la patate crève la surface du sol, jusqu'à ce que le bout des seins brunisse, que les reins se creusent, que le ventre ressorte,

pour cela il devra donner la couverture pour l'accoucheuse, la natte pour le nouveau-né, le couteau à tailler lame en bambou (pour couper le cordon).

Et à la jeune fille qui sera seule pour porter son enfant il devra payer un secours, il lui donnera des biens pour une valeur de un "ko" et lui fera le sacrifice d'un porc et d'une jarre d'alcool.

38. KREI DÔK MÔ AMÂO BI KUÔL, DÔK TOL MÂO LEH ANAK ÑU LUI.

132. DE CEUX QUI VIVENT MARITALEMENT AVEC UNE FEMME ET L'ABANDONNENT DES QU'ELLE A UN ENFANT.

Ung rô, mô rêk, dôk ko krei asei mjan,.

Ceux qui se sont mariés tout seul sans témoins, sans contrat;

Buh un čiăng bong kčeh, buh čeh čiăng mnăm kpiê, buh mniê čiăng dôk.

ceux qui voyant un cochon ont envie de manger de la viande, voyant une jarre ont envie de boire de l'alcool, ceux qui se rencontrent ont envie de vivre ensemble,

Ñman amâo tuôm tling, čing amâo tuôm yuôl, amâo tuôm bi kuôl ka.

et ne songent jamais à entraver l'éléphant, à suspendre les gongs, à sceller le contrat (de mariage);

Ñu dôk tol hbei hlăm băng mtrun, hbei kur ru, tol ñu kuôp ksâo, tol mâo anak ñu ba leh.

celui qui reste avec une femme jusqu'à ce que le tubercule donne des rejets, que la patate engendre le sol, jusqu'à ce que le bois dur se noircisse, jusqu'à ce qu'un enfant nienne,

Ñu lo lui he go trôh dong, dong thu, ñu lui amâo mâo gu kat.

et qui l'abandonne ensuite dans le ravin escarpé, dans le vallon raide, qui l'abandonne sans raison,

Amuê dih aseh amâo mâo pô mgô ko, kbao klei, êkei mniê amâo mâo mgô kông añu.

alors que personne n'a obligé le cheval à porter la longe de l'éléphant, le buffle à porter la corde au cou, personne ne l'a obligé (l'homme) à échanger le collier ou le bracelet (avec la femme);

amâo djo ung ami ama čiăng kña, krah, amâo djo ung tuôm ênuh adam ai.

celui qui n'a jamais demandé à ses parents ou à ses frères d'aller informer les parents de la jeune fille,

Ara anei ñu tim he ko go sa nuh, alah sa hrue, ñu êkei tim lo k mniê.

et qui ensuite ne veut plus de sa femme, qui ni le matin ni le soir ne la désire plus, qui est lassé de sa femme et ne veut plus vivre avec elle,

anăn kctul ñu mâo kdi drăng ko ñu ba kdi ko mô bi mâo ngăn go čiel ce anak mse si ung rô leh bi dô dlah.

celui-là est coupable, il paiera une amende à sa femme pour qu'elle puisse élever son enfant, comme s'il y avait rupture de contrat.

Juris.— Jug. no 36 du 26 juin 1923 : 1 mois.
    Jug. no 39 du 13 juil. 1923 : 6 ko et kpih à la femme.
    Jug. no 22 du 9 févr. 1926 : les biens acquis en commun restent
        à la femme qui abandonne son mari, si elle a un enfant de lui.
    Jug. no 28 du 4 mars 1926 : 1 mois + 3 ko.

39. ALEI MNIŜ PLUE HONG ÊKEI PLUE BI TLE PIU TOL MÂO MPAK.

amâo djo mŏeh mã mŭâo, amâo djo
thâo mã mrã, tar êda ko dlông, ŏyông
ko gu, tar yu bra ngo, ahei plue, mniŝ
hemi, bhian bi tle piu mong dim.

Bia dah tle nã bi hming, ŏiang
an bi man, tle nlan kŏng nuh bi kcloh
he.

Tle ko ktam bi ngăm hong nai,
tle tô ktam bi ngăm hong nma, auak
ŏdam êra teh anăh êkei plue, mniŝ
nang tntăn bi tle piu ncuh, hŭm păk
bi găl ô-e, hma bi găl ông, kning mtei
bhao bi găl dah.

ahei le ñu tle amâo bi hming,
ñu diang amâo bi man, tle nlan kŏng
nuh nmâ ñu bi mnloh he; kŏng koh
nuh ñu bi kleh, aseh êman amâo ñu
nemâo mtŏ ear bi dong.

ñu bi tle tol dă rong kong bruh,
tol đeah blan mrŭ, tol bhei blang
mran, bhei burru, tol ju kuŏp ksâo,
bŏ aeo enak nuon.

amăn kthul ñu êkei, tođah ñu
hlur dok ha piu ñu ango, kdl amâo
ah.

ai todah ñu amâo blang dŏk he
ah, piu ñu amăn, ñu brei bi ala he
tŏn ko buŏ, amŭŏ ko ĭ, đang pieh ĭ Y
tewh, abăn ê-un, kpin kăit jhit kbut
ah gih jang ngŏn sa ko lăh amăn un
ani ñu koh he brei mniŝ anăn.

133. DE JEUNE HOMME ET DE LA JEUNE FILLE QUI ENTRE - TIENNENT DES RELATIONS JUSQU'À CE QU'IL Y AIT UN ENFANT.

Ce n'est pas une chose nouvelle,
cela ne date pas d'aujourd'hui, mais
partout les vivants se posent sur la
pander, oue partout, de l'Ouest à l'Est,
depuis toujours, les jeunes gens et
jeunes filles se cherchent.

Mais en cela il faut être prudent,
il ne faut pas s'engager et quand la
nouvelle lune se montre il faut s'ar-
rer.

Si on s'attaque aux choses im-
médiates du village il faut se garder
du père et de la mère de celle avec laquelle on est une jeune homme ou jeunes filles jeunes et fiançailles gardi-
ras se recherchent, il faut veiller à
ce que la maison soit à sa place, à
ce que le camp soit bien délimité,
à ce que les bananiers et la roseau
craie soient bien alignés, (il faut
éviter l'inceste).

Mais ils s'accouplent sans que
s'ils plaisent sans mesure, si quand
nouvelle lune se montre, ils ne rom-
pas le bracelet (qu'ils ont échangé)
s'ils ne s'en vont pas chacun de son
côté comme les chevaux et les éléphants;

s'ils se fréquentent jusqu'à
les reins (de la femme) se creusent, à
le ventre se montre, jusqu'à ce que
le manioc donne des rejets, que le tubercule crève le sol, jusqu'à ce que
le bout des reins blanchisse, jusqu'à
qu'il y ait un enfant;

pour cela l'homme est coupable
s'il renonce sa maîtresse il n'y a
affaire.

Mais s'il n'épouse pas sa maî-
sse, il devra lui donner de quoi ache-
ter une couverture pour l'accouché,
une natte pour le nouveau-né, un couteau pour tailler une ... un bambou
(pour couper le cordon ombilical),
une couverture double (tripée), une
une ceinture (pagne) roulée, tout ce
qui est nécessaire pour coudre le

tout cela ayant une valeur de un
" ko " ,et il lui donnera également un porc de un " song " pour
le sacrifice.